MW01232109

BASIC AND CONTEMPORARY ISSUES IN ENTREPRENEURSHIP

PROF. O. A. OGUNBAMERU (Ed.)

Warren Publishing, Inc.

Published by Warren Publishing, Inc.
Huntersville, NC
www.warrenpublishing.net

ISBN: 978-0-9894814-4-1

Library of Congress Control Number: 2013949301

CONTENTS

List of Contributors

Adedoyin, J. O. (PhD) Department of Political Science, University of Ilorin, Ilorin, Nigeria.

Adegbite, S. A. (PhD) Institute for Entrepreneurship and Development Studies, Obafemi Awolowo University, Ile-Ife, Nigeria.

Adeigbe, Y. K. Department of Entrepreneurial and Management Science Programme, Lead City University, Ibadan, Nigeria.

Adekeye, D. S. (PhD), Department of Sociology, University of Ilorin, Ilorin, Nigeria.

Adekunle, A. R. (PhD) General Manager (Sales), Xerox Nigeria, Limited, Lagos, Nigeria.

Aderemi, H. O. Department of Management and Accounting, Obafemi Awolowo University, Ile-Ife, Nigeria.

Adesunkunmi, S. O. Department of Management and Accounting, Obafemi Awolowo University, Ile-Ife, Nigeria.

Adisa, A. L. (PhD) Department of Sociology and Anthropology, Obafemi Awolowo University, Ile-Ife, Nigeria.

Agunbiade, O. M. Doctoral student, Department of Sociology, University of Witwatersrand, Johannesburg, S. A.

Ajiboye, O. F. Graduate of Sociology and Anthropology, Obafemi Awolowo University Ile-Ife, Nigeria.

Akanmu, O. E. Department of Sociology and Anthropology, Obafemi Awolowo University, Ile-Ife, Nigeria.

Akinbami, C. A. O. (PhD) Institute for Entrepreneurship and Development Studies, Obafemi Awolowo University, Ile-Ife, Nigeria.

Akinola, G. O. Department of Management and Accounting, Obafemi Awolowo University, Ile-Ife, Nigeria.

Ayeni, O. O. Department of Public Administration, Obafemi Awolowo University, Ile-Ife, Nigeria.

Egbuwalo, M. O. (PhD) Department of Economics, Bowen University, Iwo, Nigeria.

Fayomi, G. (PhD) Institute for Entrepreneurship and Development Studies, Obafemi Awolowo University, Ile-Ife, Nigeria.

Ikuteyijo, L. (PhD) Department of Sociology and Anthropology, Obafemi Awolowo University, Ile-Ife, Nigeria.

Jegede, C. T. (PhD) Institute for Entrepreneurship and Development Studies, Obafemi Awolowo University, Ile-Ife, Nigeria.

Kehinde, O. O. National Centre for Technology Management, Obafemi Awolowo University, Ile-Ife, Nigeria.

Kolawole, T. O. Department of Sociology, Federal University, Oye-Ekiti, Nigeria.

Longe, K. (PhD) Department of Sociology, Ekiti State University, Ado-Ekiti, Nigeria.

Makinde, T. J. (PhD) Department of Public Administration, Obafemi Awolowo University, Ile-Ife, Nigeria.

Ologunde, O. A. (PhD) Department of Management and Accounting, Obafemi Awolowo University, Ile-Ife, Nigeria.

Oluwale, B. A. (PhD) African Institute for Science, Policy and Innovation, Obafemi Awolowo University, Ile-Ife, Nigeria.

Opatola, M. O. (PhD) Institute for Entrepreneurship and Development Studies, Obafemi Awolowo University, Ile-Ife, Nigeria.

Osezua, O. C. (PhD) Department of Sociology and Anthropology, Obafemi Awolowo University, Ile-Ife, Nigeria.

Owoeye, O. I. Doctoral student, Department of Anthropology and Archeology, University of Pretoria, Pretoria, S. A.

Owolabi, F. Department of Sociology, Ibrahim Badamosi Babangida University, Minna, Nigeria.

Titilayo, A. (PhD) Department of Demography and Social Statistics, Obafemi Awolowo University, Ile-Ife, Nigeria.

Zaggi, H. Y. Stellenbosch University, Stellenbosch, S. A.

Acknowledgements

I sincerely appreciate all the contributors for their prompt response to the call for chapters.

Messrs. Kola Taiwo and Timmy Ademakinwa deserve special gratitude for their computer processing of the work.

I cannot but appreciate my wife, who has always been a pillar of support. I use this opportunity to wish you a happy retirement life.

Forethought

THE ARRIVAL OF A BOOK THAT MAKES A DIFFERENCE

There are books and there are books on entrepreneurship, but *Basic and Contemporary Issues in Entrepreneurship* marks the arrival of a standard and timely book put together by an assemblage of competent scholars in the field of entrepreneurship. The scholars are drawn from different fields: sociology, anthropology, management, accounting, psychology, demography and statistics, technology and political science.

The book focuses majorly on both basic issues and contemporary issues in the field of entrepreneurship. The thirty-chapter book addresses issues relating to conceptual classification of terms, the history of entrepreneurship, theories of entrepreneurship, business statistics, competencies of entrepreneurs, constraints of entrepreneurs, leadership, entrepreneurial process, attitudes and finance. Other issues covered in the book include: preparation and presentation of a business plan, entrepreneurship education, entrepreneurial skills, gender and entrepreneurship, globalization and entrepreneurship, and entrepreneurship in reducing poverty, crime and unemployment.

The book is written in simple English, thereby making it reader-friendly. It is a must book for students at all levels, lecturers, non-governmental organizations, government at all levels and consultants.

Chapter 1

ESSENTIAL ISSUES IN ENTREPRENEURSHIP

Adisa, A. L.

Introduction

This chapter presents the following:

(i) The history of entrepreneurship and conceptual clarifications;
(ii) Issues involved in successful running of entrepreneurship.

(i) The History of Entrepreneurship and Conceptual Clarifications

In tracing the history of entrepreneurship, reference will always be made to a number of scholars, such as Richard Cantillon and Jean-Baptiste Say. The concept, entrepreneur, is itself a derivative of the French verb *entreprendre*, which means "to undertake" (*Webster's New Explorer Encyclopedic Dictionary* 2006). However, entrepreneurship has been viewed differently by scholars at different times. For instance, Morris (1998) presented seven perspectives on the nature of entrepreneurship as follows: Entrepreneurship entails the creation of (i) wealth, (ii) enterprise, (iii) innovation, (iv) change, (v) employment, (vi) value, and (vii) growth. In the contemporary times, more related concepts now evolved to avoid scholars' disagreements and myths in definitions of entrepreneurship based on members involved (**solopreneurship, copreneurship**), scope, nature of business and activities involved (**technopreneurship, intrapreneurship**). Before the concepts are discussed, the works of Cantillon and Say will be briefly perused.

Contributions of Richard Cantillon

Richard Cantillon was an Irish man but was given a Spanish name, and, after the death of Louis XIV, he arrived in Paris with a group of speculators who invested in various ventures and became quite wealthy. His connections to Ireland, Spain and France made his associates to always describe him as a cosmopolitan. Cantillon's essay entitled "Essay on the Nature of Commerce" was originally written in English and published in England between 1730 and 1734. The essay, or a portion of it, was subsequently translated by the author himself for use by a French friend and published in 1755 in French and titled "Essai sur la Nature du Commerce en General."

In his essay, Cantillon wrote that land is the source of all wealth; and he recognized three types of economic actors, namely:

(i) landowners, who are financially independent;
(ii) entrepreneurs, who engage in market exchanges at their own risk in order to make a profit; and,
(iii) hired people, who avoid active decision-making in order to secure contractual guaranties of stable income.

Cantillon's entrepreneurs did not initiate change, nor were they innovators. Instead, Cantillon used a risk theory of profit as a means to identify entrepreneurship. For example, he wrote that the role of his entrepreneur was to transact purchases at certain prices and sales at uncertain ones. According to Cantillon, wholesalers buy (from carriers) at a certain price and sell (to retailers) at an uncertain price. Retailers buy (from wholesalers) at a certain price and sell (to consumers) at an uncertain price. Farmers, carriers, wholesalers, and retailers are all entrepreneurs (Cantillon 1755).

Social standing was not a characteristic of Cantillon's notion of entrepreneurship. In fact, he identified beggars and robbers as entrepreneurs, provided they earned uncertain income. In sum, any person who in any transaction faces an undeterminable income, revenue, profit or loss, is an entrepreneur in Cantillon's sense. Barreto (1989) described Cantillon's contribution toward the development of a theory of entrepreneur as follows:

Cantillon's entrepreneur is a crucial part of the market system, buying at a fixed price and selling at an uncertain one. The willingness to do this allows exchange to take place. Furthermore, the responsiveness to profit opportunities drives the market toward equilibrium. Cantillon's distribution theory focuses entirely on the type of income earned. Receipt of an uncertain income is the identifying feature of the entrepreneur. By the middle of the eighteenth century, Richard Cantillon had presented the first theory of entrepreneurship—casting the entrepreneur as a speculator in an uncertain environment.

Contributions of Jean-Baptiste Say

Jean-Baptiste Say was a journalist, a cotton manufacturer, and a pioneer in the mechanization of the French textile industry. Say (1821) highlighted the required features of an entrepreneur as follows:

(i)   An entrepreneur must already be rich or have the ability to borrow capital based on connections.

(ii)   Entrepreneurs must be solvent, intelligent, prudent, and honest, and be "regular" in their work habits.

(iii)   Say also indicated that the entrepreneur must possess moral qualities, judgement, perseverance, and knowledge of the world.

Say made a tripartite division of the functions to be found in any process of production: effort, knowledge, and the "applications" of the entrepreneur. Knowledge of how to do something was considered a necessary but not a sufficient condition for production. The really important step was the application of this knowledge to a specific end. For this purpose an entrepreneur was needed. It was the entrepreneur, in Say's view, who would give value to every other factor of production.

Another issue of interest in Say's work was the determination of an entrepreneur's income, which as submitted is a function of financial resources, connections, personal qualities and sheer luck. Say noted that the entrepreneur obtains income in the following manner:

The entrepreneur hires the factors of production (knowledge, labour, capital, and natural agents) and remunerates them for their efforts (wages, interest, and rents) from the sale of the product. The residual is the entrepreneur's return, in equilibrium, exactly equal to the entrepreneur's wage determined by the forces of supply and demand.

Other General Views about Entrepreneurship

Many people associate entrepreneurship with the start-up of business, but this is a very narrow view. Entrepreneurship can occur in organisations of all sizes and types. Seeking and capitalizing on opportunity, taking risk beyond what is secure, and having the tenacity to push an innovative idea through to reality represent the essence of what entrepreneurs do. Entrepreneurs make change happen as a function of vision, hard work, and passion.

Entrepreneurship has both attitudinal and behavioural dimensions; it is both a way of thinking and acting. As a way of thinking, the entrepreneur focuses on opportunities, demonstrates healthy dissatisfaction with existing ways, has a sense of optimism, places emphasis on the future and how things can be, and embraces change. As expressed earlier, a number of concepts which evolved as a result of aptly describing entrepreneurial activities in different dimensions are discussed as follows:

Copreneurship

Copreneurship entails an arrangement where couples join forces in the professional and personal areas; it is as old as the concept of family itself. Historically, the husband-and-wife team represents a very traditional economic unit. However, in the last decades, couples who are running a business venture together are called copreneurs and may, to some extent, be regarded as a new phenomenon, not in the least due to the entry of women into the workforce. Among the Yoruba people of southwestern Nigeria, it was rare to find a couple managing the same business; the husband would either take to farming and/or hunting while the woman would occupy herself with trading or artisanry.

The fact still remains that adequate scholarly attention is yet to be given the interface between work and love, as manifested by these couples. Nonetheless, a substantial subset of business partnerships are founded and grown by copreneurial couples, especially in societies which are not patriarchal but liberal to women and where divorce rate is low. Patriarchy and high divorce rate will singly or collectively discourage venturing into copreneurship. Estimates indicate that approximately a third of family businesses in the US are run in a copreneurial fashion.

At the heart of the family businesses and copreneurs lies the question: How will emotional and kinship ties among business owners and managers affect the business and its leadership? Another key issue highlighted by the copreneurial phenomenon represents the particular challenges involved in business partnership, particularly where leadership is shared. Under what circumstances are two heads better than one? Copreneurs are uniquely positioned to address these issues since they capture the essence of family business in a concentrated form.

Although there are many ways to define copreneurship, the definition used here assumes that the business partners are: (i) married, (ii) work together in the business, and (iii) jointly make decisions regarding the most important aspects of the running the business.

The consideration of benefits derivable from the coming together as husband and wife is done as follows:

Emotional Drain or Emotional Support

Sharing your work and personal space as a couple may be both a blessing and a curse. On the upside, the spouse knows exactly what the other faces at work and is able to understand and empathize without lengthy background stories needing to be rehearsed. The downside is that if the business is going through a rough patch, both partners are deeply immersed and may be less able to detach and remain positive to the other person, partly since they are unable to draw energy from a separate daily source, normally provided by unshared workplace.

Work-Love Boundaries

Copreneurs are required to derive satisfaction from both work and work needs of the same person, the potential distress they face in the grey zone between home and work is greater than that of dual carrier couples. As a consequence of the multiple roles and needs in the copreneurial relationship, these couples develop special strategies to cope with its inherent complexity, for example, by explicitly agreeing that the bedroom is off-limits when it comes to business issues. Couples who have their business activity from home, and thus a lack of physical boundary, have an even stronger need to cope with potential spillover from either domain.

Trust and Conflict

A clear benefit arising from the copreneurial partnership is the solid foundation of trust that copreneurs derive from their romantic relationship.

The level of trust is difficult, if not impossible, to find in other colleagues. Although certain types of conflict may be avoided due to this trust, the level of closeness that copreneurs experience also means that they confront each other more readily. For many of the couples, business needs also force issues out in the open. Although several couples mentioned that they have developed more effective communication and conflict resolution skills.

Indeed, the complexity of the relationship may at times create the opposite. Whilst the couple may consciously avoid arguing in front of employees, at times it is difficult not to revert to habitual modes of communication that are used in private spheres. There is usually a substantial change when the first employee is hired. The initial introduction of a third party—in most cases, an office manager or administrator—breaks up the intensity of the marital dyad, often providing a buffer between the partners. It also ensures that the couple has a reference point with regard to their behaviour towards each other.

Role Clarity

There is a general consensus that clear roles are needed for a copreneurship to function smoothly. The challenge that couples face, however, is not only juggling the roles of husband and wife versus those of professional partnership. Even in the business, it may not be clear who does what, particularly if the business is small and the partners need to multi-task in order to survive. Typically, roles evolve according to each partner's unique ability, preferred task and/or professionalbackground. This is often the result of an implicit process, rarely discussed openly between partners. The lack of formal communication regarding roles may in fact serve to prolong any existing role and diffusion.

Complementarity or Similarity

Similarity in terms of personality (personal style and character traits) generally points to a higher level of marital stability. Whereas having common values and interests appears to be vital for a well-functioning entrepreneurship, couples may derive great benefit from being dissimilar from each other in other ways. For example, the wife in one couple has no patience for details whereas the husband has a developed sense for the particular; this difference has led them to divide tasks in a way that maximizes contributions based on the specific preferences and strengths of each party. In another couple, the husband describes himself as quiet and introverted whereas the wife is more outgoing and sociable. This allows her to network with external stakeholders and gauge the emotional climate among the employees in a way that he would feel uncomfortable engaging in. At the same time he is able to provide a different perspective based on his more contemplative approach.

Overall, having different skills and abilities seems to be advantageous. Not only is it more efficient in terms of offering a broader ability towards business and client needs, it is also comforting to know that, as a leader, one does not have to be everything. But the challenge is evaluation of the values of the different skills and abilities to determine who is more useful to the continued survival of the business and the use of that to determine remuneration/profit sharing. All these may generate conflict if not properly handled.

As final remarks, copreneurs could be said to experience a high level of togetherness. Working and living together appear to be an active choice which allows these couples to have more time together and develop a deeper relationship. Like all married couples, copreneurs trade for love, sex, status, and life support in their relationship. In addition, copreneurs also trade with their spouses for self-esteem, mastery and achievement. This makes it more challenging, but also rewarding for couples who jointly run a business.

Co-entrepreneurship versus Copreneurship

The prefix *co* is a Latin term which means "together, mutually, jointly, partner or to the same degree." Barnett and Barnett (1984) defined copreneurship as enterprising couples who work in and share ownership of, commitment to, and responsibility for their business. By "couple," it has been stated that this could be a relationship that is married or unmarried, but they jointly share all aspects of the business (2000). Copreneurs are typically located in rural areas (Muske, Fitzgerald and Haynes 2003) and are typically home-based (Fitzgerald and Muske 2002). This allows the business to be family-focused, where the family considerations overlap into the business (Muske, Fitzgerald and Haynes 2009).

Smith (2000) noted that the main reason that couples would enter into a copreneurship relationship is to have greater flexibility between family and work and a more effective result regarding family and work relationships.

Co-entrepreneurship entails two or more venturing partners, regardless of gender and marital status or the ownership and workload arrangements among them (Ponthieu and Caudill 1993). It was Sayers who developed the concept *co-entrepreneurship* in an attempt to expand the definition of copreneurs. In bringing out the differences, copreneurs are described as partners in love and work, composition, status of members, focus and scope.

Challenges to Copreneurship

Couples, married or living together, who go into business together face pitfalls from the financial to the emotional that can lead to dissolution of the relationships. Somebody once remarked that business decisions in the office are not popular, and sometimes when you say "no" to your spouse at work, it becomes something else when you get home (Earnest Bonner, 52, whose ex-wife was his business partner).

(i) In most cases, one member is dominant, and this can cause resentments that undermine the relationship.

(ii) There is usually no second salary to fall back on.

(iii) Boundaries between work and home are always blurred. A consultant, Susan Greer, once remarked that it is always difficult to draw the boundaries between the boardroom and the bedroom.

(iv) There is also the challenge of experiencing delay in decision taking, especially when there a complete difference of opinions.

(v) The practice of purdah; extended family members' interference; absence of trust; cultural belief that sees the husband as owning everything, including the wife, the supposed partner; increasing rate of distrust between couples; polygyny; recognition of cultural dictates/customary expressions, even in the face of a written will, may discourage copreneurship in many of the Nigerian cultures.

Reasons for improving emergence of copreneurships are:

(i) The increasing rate of corporate downsizing, relieving people of their jobs, suddenly now makes copreneurship trend more attractive.

(ii) If there are couples who can complement each other, it is always beneficial starting a copreneurship.

(iii) People are now becoming increasingly interested in controlling their own destiny themselves.

(iv) Copreneurships are formed to avoid taxation. A business classified as sole-proprietorship may be run by a couple.

Benefits

(i) There is usually an opportunity for communication skills, tremendous mutual respect, and the ability to split the load and trust your counterpart to get the job done.

(ii) Working long hours and sacrificing luxuries become much easier when spouses are doing the business together.

(iii)Both partners experience the same ups and downs together, so there will not be any need to justify or account for any strange thing.

(iv)Two heads can mostly be better than one: One of the challenges of *solopreneurship* is that one is doing it all alone.

(v) Split the load without doubling the cost: With a partner, you each take half of the operation rather than immediately needing to hire extra help, keeping startup costs under control. This is not to say that you should not still outsource the activities where neither of you has proficiency.

(vi)Take your best friend to work: For those who are married to their best friend, love to spend lots of time together, and have similar interests and passions, working together can be a perfect scenario. You get to share it all. Shared passion can deepen your relation. When you share a passion, spending time on it together can really strengthen and deepen your relationship with each other. You may have differing outside interests, but for the majority of your day, you are like one mind.

Management of Relationships within Copreneurs

(i) Set healthy boundaries: Some copreneurs establish a rule that outside the office walls discussions about work are taboos. Others choose to develop a more symbiotic relationship, blurring the lines between home and work. There is no right or wrong approach. You have to mutually agree upon the right rules for your relationship. If you are the type who has difficulty "letting go," forcing yourself to leave work at the office will be the best approach. Besides, when you consider that the largest portion of your day is spent at work, you might see the importance of taking a break from it when you are at home. Doing so, you will probably notice that, when you return to work, your perspective on challenges that you left behind is fresher and more productive.

(ii) Create a conflict resolution strategy.

(iii)Plan escapes. Plan work-free escapes.

Technopreneurship

A technopreneur is an entrepreneur who is technology-savvy, creative, innovative, dynamic, dares to be different and takes the unexplored path, and is very passionate about his or her work. Technopreneurs take challenges and strive to lead their lives with greater success. They usually are not afraid of failure. They take failure as a learning experience, a stimulator to view things in another dimension and stride toward the next challenge. They go through an organic process of continual improvement and ways to try to re-define the dynamic digital economy.

Nowadays, improvement in technology and growing interests in entrepreneurial skills are driving many economies to prosperity. Technopreneurs such as Bill Gates (Microsoft), Steve Jobs (Apple) and a number of others have become household names in the world. In Nigeria, there are individuals and/or groups of individuals who are inventing machines to facilitate work in small- and medium-sized enterprises. Cassava processing joints, different mills, and others that use fabricated machines enjoy the innovative ideas of technopreneurs.

Technology startups are usually very small in composition. Some of these companies could involve between only one and four persons. Ability to scale up business is contingent on readiness or ability to grow the size of its core entrepreneurial team. A lot of technology startups develop slogans to make them stand out in consumers' minds.

Business Slogan

This refers to a catch phrase or a small group of words that are in a special way to identify a product. In addition to a trademark, slogans assist the image of a business in the minds of the people. The use of slogans is a survival strategy in the face of competition.

Conditions for adoption of slogans

Slogans are seen to be useful at the time a company is trying to communicate a major shift in strategy. Slogans can also be influenced by societal shifts. For instance, Ford had to drop its famous slogan "Quality is job one" because of the perception that in today's market, no organization toys with quality. It is like stating what makes no difference anywhere. Companies should not use any slogan when unsure of the direction it wants to go.

Quality of a good slogan

(i) A good slogan must communicate or be a mini-vision statement. If slogans are carefully crafted, they can effectively convey a company's key characteristics to variety of audiences; from investors to customers and suppliers to job applicants.
(ii) An effective slogan does not have to be long. The words should be carefully chosen to flow together and for ease of remembrance.
(iii) A good slogan is the one that is a product of both the employees and the management. One approach is to solicit employee suggestions through a contest. This was the technique used by Ford to select its long-lived "Quality is job one" slogan.
(iv) A good slogan stakes out an area that is ignored by rivals. In fact, it makes a slogan unique and appealing.

Benefit

(i) The same memorable message can be used for many purposes in many different media.

Intrapreneurship

Intrapreneurship can as well be defined as entrepreneurship, that is, a process of creating value by bringing together a unique combination of resources to exploit an opportunity. The only difference is that intrapreneurship occurs within an established firm and not in a business startup.

The Schumpeter Effect

The process of entrepreneurship activity reducing unemployment in the economy is termed the "Schumpeter effect." Garofoli (1994) and Audretsch and Fritsch (1994) in their separate studies found that unemployment is negatively related to new-firm startups, that is, as new businesses are established, employability is stimulated and unemployment decreases substantially. In the same vein, Lucas (1978) and Jovanovic (1982) note that high unemployment in the society is associated with a low degree of entrepreneurial activities, that is, where propensity to set up enterprises is low, the rate of unemployment would be very high. The implication of the above assertions is that those who are unemployed tend to remain so because they possess lower endowments of human capital and entrepreneurial talents required to start and sustain new firms to keep them going. A low rate of entrepreneurship culture and skills in any society may be a consequence of the low economic growth, which also reflects higher levels of unemployment (Audretsch 1995).

The Refugee Effect

This process of unemployment fast-tracking entrepreneurship activity has been termed a "refugee effect." This remarkable view dates back at least to Oxenfeldt (1943), who pointed out that individuals confronted with unemployment and low prospects for wage employment often turn to self-employment as a viable alternative. This observation was also an extension of Knight's view that individuals make a decision among three states: unemployment, self-employment and employment. The simple theory of income choice lends credence to refugee effect by suggesting that increased unemployment will lead to an increase in startup business activity on the grounds that the opportunity cost of not starting a firm has decreased (Evans and Leighton 1990; Blanchflower and Meyer 1994). Similarly, Picot *et al.* (1998) and Pfeiffer and Reize (2000) observe that new firms hire the needed employees to work for them, thus helping to reduce the level of unemployment in the society. Evans and Leighton (1990) found that unemployment is positively associated with greater propensity to start a new firm. Many other studies establish that greater unemployment serves as a catalyst for startup activity (Reynolds, Miller and Makai 1995; Reynolds, Storey and Westhead 1994).

References

Audretsch, D. B. (1995) *Innovation and Industry Evolution.* Cambridge, MA: MIT Press.
Audretsch, D. B., and M. Fritsch. (1994) "The Geography of Firm Births in Germany."*Regional Studies*, 28(4), July, 359–365.

Barnett, R., and S. Barnett. (1988) *Working Together: Entrepreneurial Couples*, Berkeley, CA: Ten Speed Press.

Barreto, H. (1989) *The Entrepreneur in Microeconomic Theory*. London: Routledge.

Blanchflower, D., and B. Meyer. (1994) "A Longitudinal Analysis of Young Entrepreneurs in Australia and the United States." *Small Business Economics*, 6(1), 1–20.

Cantillon, R. (2010, 1755) *An Essay on Economic Theory*. Auburn, AL: Ludwig von Mises Institute.

Evans, D. S., and L. Leighton. (1990) "Small Business Formation by Unemployed and Employed Workers." *Small Business Economics*, 2(4), 319–330.

Fitzgerald, M., and Muske. (2002) "Copreneurs: An Exploration and Comparison to other Family Business." *Family Business Review*, 15, 1, pp. 1–15.

Gioacchino, G. (1994) "New Firm Formation and Regional Development: The Italian Case." *Regional Studies*, 28(4), 381–394.

Jovanovic, B. (1982) "Selection and Evolution of Industry." *Econometrica*, 50, 649–670.

Lucas, R. E. (1978) "On the Size Distribution of Business Firms." *Bell Journal of Economics*, 9, 508–523.

Morris, M. H. (1998) *Entrepreneurial Intensity*. Westport, CT: Quorum Books.

Oxenfeldt, A. (1943) *New Firms and Free Enterprise*. Washington, D.C.: American Council on Public Affairs.

Pfeiffer, F., and F. Reize. (2000) "Business Start-ups by the Unemployed: an Econometric Analysis Based on Firm Data." *Labour Economics*, 7(5), 629–663.

Picot, G., M. E. Manser and L. Zhengxi. (1998) "The Role of Self-Employment in Job Creation in Canada and the U.S." OECD-CERFCILN International Conference on Self-Employment, Burlington, Ontario, Canada.

Ponthieu, L. D., and H. L. Caudill. (1993) "Who is the Boss? Responsibility and Business." *Journal of Small Business Management*, 22 (4), pp. 24–30.

Reynolds, P., J. S. David and P. Westhead. (1994) "Cross-National Comparisons of the Variation in New Firm Formation Rates." *Regional Studies*, 28(4), July 443–456.

Reynolds, P., B. Miller and W. R. Maki. (1995) "Explaining Regional Variation in Business Births and Deaths: U.S. 1976-1988." *Small Business Economics*, 7 (5), 389–707.

Schumpeter, J. A. (1981) *History of Economic Analysis*. London: Routledge.

Webster's New Explorer Encyclopedic Dictionary. (2006) Springfield, MA: Federal Street Press.

Internet materials

Familybusinesswiki.ning.com/profile. Accessed March 9, 2010.
Husband and Wife Teams: Challenges and Possibilities of Copreneurship. Posted by Asa Bjornberg on March 9, 2010.

Chapter 2

HISTORY OF ENTREPRENEURSHIP IN NIGERIA

Ogunbameru, O. A.

Introduction

In chapters one, three and four the authors discussed the emergence of entrepreneurship at the global level, but the present chapter focuses specifically on its development in Nigeria.

Rain did not just start yesterday; it is as old as creation itself. In the same vein, entrepreneurship did not start yesterday in Nigeria; its growth has spanned three phases: the pre-colonial phase, the colonial phase, and the post-colonial phase. This chapter presents the historical development of entrepreneurship in Nigeria along these three phases.

The History of Entrepreneurship in Pre-Colonial Nigeria

In pre-colonial Nigeria, the primary sector of the economy was basically subsistence farming. The use of simple technology coupled with unskilled labor barely affected the growth of the economy beyond targeting human survival, with a little exchange of goods where possible. The pre-colonial period was also negatively affected by the absence of essential prerequisites for a formal market economy. The different kingdoms and empires in pre-colonial Nigeria were endowed with natural resources and agricultural products, trade and crafts. The major structure of the economy during this period involved agriculture, fishing, hunting, pastoral activities, and crafts.

This chapter relies on Hoselitz's (1965) definition of an entrepreneur. Hoselitz (1965) submits that "an entrepreneur is an organization leader who guides the action of a private production business, who makes crucial decisions about the use of productive factors of their remuneration in the nature and style of the goods or services to be produced, and the timing and other aspects of production and marketing process".

Agriculture

Agriculture was the mainstay of the Nigerian pre-colonial economy. "As in modern times, in pre-colonial Nigeria, a key factor in the choice of solution was the availability of favourable climate, free of epidemics, fertile land suitable for cultivation and grazing, coastal environment attractive for fishing and safety" (Codestria 1993:15-16). When these factors are lacking, folks resort to migration in search of comfortable living areas. Given these phenomena, the reasons for crop rotation planting in agriculture, grazing and roaming nomadism can be understood. In other words, the ecological factors played a role in human settlements and economic activities (Wooldridge and East 1951:23-24).

The basic tools during the pre-colonial phase were hoes, machetes and sickles. The food crops were yams, okra, vegetables, maize, cocoyams, cassava, and banana, while the cash crops were cocoa, kola nuts, oil palm, and groundnuts. Crops were introduced from one part of Nigeria to the other, and, according to Ogunremi (1996), agriculture really developed in Nigeria naturally and independent of foreign intervention.

Fish Farming

Fishing farming took place both in the fishing activities inland and coastal areas of Nigeria (Ewhurdja Kpor 2008). Fish of numerous types are either sun dried or smoked to preserve them for long or short market (Fakae 2005). Fresh fish was marketed mainly in the areas of short distance, due to the perishable nature and the absence of storage facilities. Fishing on commercial level was transported by canoes and boats. Fishing contributed to the migration of professional fishermen/-women to other parts of the country to improve their economy among the Ilajes, Izons, Itsekins, Efiks, Jukuns, Ijebus, and Awons, among others (Fuchs, Wemer and Wallan 2008).

Hunting

Hunting can be considered as one of the leading economic activities in the pre-colonial Nigeria. It was quite essential because many men and women depended on it for their economic survival in a stage of economic development. Nonetheless, over time, hunting became an essential complement to agriculture (Stride and Ifeka 1971). Hunting in Nigeria during this period was at several levels. At the lower level, hunting included setting traps for birds and small animals like squirrels and monkeys. Another level involved the hunting of large animals, such as crocodiles, elephants, wild pigs, and antelopes, among others. Hunting was a dependable source of meat and animal material, such as skin for shoe and drum making. In addition to its economic value, it also served as a means by which the foot paths and settlements had been developed just before the arrival of the Europeans, who got involved in road construction and settlement of the city. Consequently, these roads and villages later became motorable roads and big towns. Hunters during this phase also served as security by protecting individuals from attacks by enemies or wild animals. Hunters in addition supplied animals and their special parts that have medicinal value among indigenous medicine practitioners (Odegbemi, 2006).

Pastoralism

Pastoralism involved the breeding of animals, especially cattle, goats and sheep, in commercial quantities when going from a fertile land to another. As a result of the infestation of the forest region by the tsetse fly and lack of open spaces in the south, coupled with the swampy nature of the plains, the presence of rivers and streams in the coastal region and the presence of open spaces in the north, grazing was limited mainly by the Fulani in the savannah region of northern Nigeria (Odegbemi 2006). Livestock production was a source of meat for the forest dwellers. The workers demanded the skin to produce leather shoes, bags, shields for war, and arrow quivers (Ogunremi 2006).

Kano, in northern Nigeria, was well-known for such skills. Pastoral activities were of fantastic economic value in the pre-colonial Nigeria.

Crafts

The major arts and crafts included the extraction of salt, soap production, metal work, wood and weaving activities. This is a pointer that indigenous technology was available in Nigeria in pre-colonial Nigeria. The production of salt was of the mineral extraction, which was not obtainable in most areas, but a critical product locally (Ahmed and Nmar 2006). In pre-colonial Nigeria, the production of salt in huge amounts, of course, was limited to coastal areas due to the availability of raw materials like salt water. The production method was the evaporation of sea water either by boiling or sunbathing. Among the coastal dwellers in Nigeria, particularly the Ilaje, Itsekiri and Ijaw, the process consisted of collecting seawater in a significant pot of baked clay until it dried, leaving the white solid at the bottom (Ehinomore 2006).

In the pre-colonial economic enterprise, there was also the production of soap. This was carried out mainly by settlers from the forest region of Nigeria. The main raw materials for the production of soap were palm oil and ashes. These would be boiled together and molded (Stride and Ifeka 1971). In pre-colonial Nigeria, for example, various types of soap were produced. In addition to domestic and commercial applications, the soap also had some other values. The *Ose dudu* (black soap) among the Yoruba, for example, is still utilized to date for healing purposes. Two other essential aspects of pre-colonial Nigeria crafts that deserve attention are metal and wood. A careful study of the history of Nigeria shows that, of all trades, working iron was critical to the economic and political development in the pre-colonial period.

The discovery of iron led to the manufacture of iron tools such as hoes, knives, swords, spears, axes, and the highest productivity impact was on handicrafts, agriculture, fisheries and hunting (Williams 1966). Apart from the economic revolution caused by the smelting of iron, it also equipped most of the leaders with a lot more power and greater political will (Williams 1966). The very first evidence of iron smelting in West Africa is in Nok, a village in central Nigeria, northeast of the confluence of the rivers Niger and Benue and southwest of Jos Plateau (Shaw 1971). The Yoruba, Igbo (Awka men and women specifically), and Uneme (in Benin) were famous in iron-smelting technology in the pre-colonial era.

In pre-colonial Nigeria, Benin and Ile-Ife were famous for bronze casting and became prestigious centres of production. Jos was noted for tin and zinc (Stride and Ifeka 1971). Ife and Benin ranked as famous producers of high quality bronze (Stride and Ifeka 1971).

Organization of the market during this period was influenced largely by the abundant production of farm and non-farm products by men and women. Poor transport systems hampered mobility, production and distribution of goods and services to some extent. Some Western economists had argued that the factors of production had not been well coordinated and that there was no division of labor or specialization in the economy of pre-colonial Nigeria. This appears false and misleading. In traditional African society, division of labor was basically based on sex. For example, coastal dwellers who specialized in repairing fishing nets took an area of specialization, while some men and women specialized in fishing.

In pre-colonial Nigeria, as elsewhere, other elements of production like capital, land and labor were organized and utilized successfully for production. Entrepreneurs in pre-colonial Nigeria were the rulers, chiefs, warlords, and other influential men and women who had sufficient wealth and power to mobilize other factors of production (Ogunremi 2006). For example, Kano potentates organized the production of leather work; Ijebu chiefs organized the production of textiles; Ilaje leaders organized the production of fish; and Ikale leaders organized the production of agricultural crops. Given the general characteristics and lots of sub-sectoral components of the pre-colonial Nigerian economy, it is convincing evidence that the economy was growing progressively and sensitively to innovation just before colonization by British in the nineteenth century. The production system in the Nigerian economy in the pre-colonial period depended heavily on families, community efforts, and professional groups or unions.

In twentieth-century Yorubaland there were constraining environmental forces of warfare and colonialism that provided a context for their ultimate failure to emulate their Asian counterparts (Olukoju 2010). Olukoju (2010) lists five factors that militated against successful entrepreneurship in Yorubaland. First, with the exception of Doherty and Agbaje, none had a clear succession plan within or outside the lineage (Miller 2006). In addition, the businesses of those who died intestate—and even those who left a will— hardly outlived their founders, as acrimonious disputes over sharing of assets effectively destroyed their legacies. Hence, the dissipation of assets and lack of cooperation among several branches of a typical polygynous family ruined many worthwhile businesses. Second, Yoruba entrepreneurs lacked a common focus and platform of action and were generally individualistic. Though Salami Agbaje collaborated with his Ibadan kinsmen to establish a joint stock company, this was the exception rather than the rule. Hence, there was no enduring indigenous chamber of commerce to advance their common interests. When these existed, they were short-lived and fractious. Instead, the leading lights of the indigenous entrepreneurial class strove to join the hitherto Europeans-only Lagos Chamber of Commerce. Third, the basis of their wealth was fragile, consisting of flimsy assets and tied to the fluctuating economic circumstances. This made them vulnerable to the vagaries of global economic dynamics as happened in the inter-war years. Fourth, the absence of a national bank for indigenous entrepreneurs during the period up to 1930, unlike in Egypt, denied the entrepreneurs a reliable source of capital for their businesses. Finally, the concentration on commerce without a commensurate investment in manufacturing was the bane of African entrepreneurship.

In Nigeria before the advent of colonial government, unemployment was a rare phenomenon because the people were highly entrepreneurial and productively engaged. This entrepreneurial engagement was prevalent in Yorubaland of western Nigeria, Hausaland of northern Nigeria, and among the Igbo people of eastern Nigeria. The Ibo ethnic group particularly is to date recognized internationally for its culture of entrepreneurship and enterprise development (Dana 1995).

The History of Entrepreneurship during the Colonial Phase

The compartmentalization of educational, industrial, employment and labour policies in Nigeria probably dates back to the colonial era (Aladekomo 2004). The first colonial policy on education was in 1925. This policy was for Africa and it touched on primary, secondary and adult education. Further policies in 1935, 1940 and 1945 built upon the 1925 policy, modifying it with little additions here and there, the emphasis being on adult education. The colonial educational policy centered on the production of literate nationals, who were required to man positions, which would strengthen the colonial administration. Thus our educational institutions, few as they were, remained factories for producing clerks, interpreters, forest guards and sanitary inspectors, as no special professional nor entrepreneurial skill was envisaged in the educational system (Akinyemi 1987)

Entrepreneurship was formally noticed in Nigeria in 1946 when Ordinance No. 24 of 1945 on a ten-year rolling plan was put in place for the development and welfare of Nigerians. At this time, a Nigerian Local Development Board was established to:

i. set up and operate an experimental processing and development of any produce in Nigeria;
ii. and promote and develop village craft and industrial products. Small scale businesses were planned to achieve a higher level of efficiency by becoming more productive.

Colonial experience had a far-reaching influence on the direction and scope of African entrepreneurship (Olukoju 2010:22). The colonial era, for instance, brought modern transport, currency credit, and banking facilities as well as creating an enabling environment for migration and exchange. However, it had its constraining effects on the economy. For instance, the demonetization of pre-colonial currencies and the abolition of slavery effectively undercut the basis of the wealth and power of the category of entrepreneurs whose wealth had derived from the slave trade and the use of slave and pawn labor (Olukoju 2010). In addition, colonial rule facilitated the influx of European traders into the hinterland, thus reducing indigenous competitors to subsidiary operators, given the overwhelming superiority of the former in capital, organization and links with the imperial power (Olukoju 2010:23).

Cultural values, however, proved too heavy for sustained accumulation. For instance, societal expectations often made it too difficult for the entrepreneur to accumulate or act solely according to the profit motive. The situation in nineteenth-century Ibadan is fairly representative of the Yoruba conception of true wealth, entrepreneurship and the ideal entrepreneurs. First, the society distinguished between the poor (*akuse, oloosi* and *talika*), the rich (*olowo*), the wealthy (*oloro* or *olola*) and the honourable person (*olola*). Second, the Yoruba esteemed the wealthy, who had property and assets (*oloro* or *olola*) above the possessor of mere cash (*olowo*). Third, as society also prioritized honour, a person who combined honour and wealth with generosity—the *borokini* or *gbajumo*—was the ideal entrepreneur (Falola 1997, cited in Olukoju 2010:23).

The History of Entrepreneurship in the Post-colonial Phase

The complete absence of enterprise education in the educational policy has, however, changed in contemporary Nigeria. The industrial policy which came on board only after the Nigerian independence in 1960 initially concentrated on the establishment of big industries, with utter neglect for small-scale business. By so doing, entrepreneurship, which is the bedrock of small-scale business, was unwittingly de-emphasized (Aladekomo 2004:75).

Osorun (2009:16-18) presents a comprehensive development of entrepreneurship in the Nigerian post-colonial phase.

The Nigerian government, especially the Federal Government, have creditably strived to promote and develop entrepreneurship in Nigeria. This has done by instituting or supporting some financial and non-financial bodies, programmes and measures to aid the promotion and development of entrepreneurship in Nigeria.

Some of these bodies and programmes, among others, are:

- Rural Bank Programme (RBP)
- Agricultural Credit Guarantee Scheme (ACGS)
- Nigeria Agricultural and Cooperative Bank (NACB)
- National Directorate of Employment (NDE)
- Nigeria Agricultural Insurance Cooperation (NAIC)
- People's Bank of Nigeria (PBN)
- Community Banks (CBs)
- Family Economic Advancement Programme (FEAP)
- NATIONAL Poverty Eradication Programme (NAPEP)
- Nigerian Agricultural Cooperative and Rural Development Bank (NACRDB)
- Small Industries Credit Scheme (SICS)
- Nigerian Bank for Commerce and Industries (NBCI)
- Bank of Industry (BoI)
- Nigeria Industrial Development Bank (NIDB)
- Small and Medium Industries Equity Investment Scheme (SMIEIS)
- Centre for Management Development (CMD)
- Small and Medium Enterprises Development Agency of Nigeria (SMEDAN)
- Centre for Industrial Research and Development (CIDR)
- National Economic Reconstruction Fund (NERFUND)
- Small Industries Development Agency (SIDA)
- Small and Medium Scale Enterprises Loans Scheme (SMSELS)
- Nigerian Export Import Bank (NEIB)
- Urban Development Bank of Nigeria (UDBN)
- Federal Mortgage Bank of Nigeria (FMBN)
- Centre for Entrepreneurship and Innovation (CEI)
- Centre for Entrepreneurship Development (CED)
- Central Bank of Nigeria (CBN)
- Micro Finance Banks (MFBs)

- Industrial Training Fund (ITF)
- Working for Yourself Programme (WFYP)
- Entrepreneurship Development Centre (EDC)
- Administrative Staff College of Nigeria (ASCON)
- Small Scale Industries Scheme (SSIS)
- Industrial Development Centre (IDC)
- Technology Business Incubation Centres (TBICs) of the
- National Association of Chambers of Commerce, Industry, Mining and Agriculture (NACCIMA)
- Ministry of Science and Technology (Oshorun 2009).

Entrepreneurship development through education has been receiving attention globally. Several attempts have been made through researches, mounting of entrepreneurship courses, programmes in both institutions of learning and entrepreneurship research centers for the purpose of developing both entrepreneurship spirit and culture (Akpomi 2009; Adejimola and Olufunmilayo 2009).The need for apparent change is very desirable and necessary for the country to forge ahead and to meet up with the global challenges. The integration of economies through globalization process means that any government or state that hesitates or vacillates on whether to mobilize the culture will certainly create a standstill, not only to the detriment of its country but to the larger global community.

The mid–70s post-colonial period was marked by the government's involvement in education policy; the government, because of the perceived importance of small-scale industries to the economy, decided to focus attention on the small–medium sector. Thirteen industrial centers and some institutions were set up to support the activities of entrepreneurs in the small and medium industries in the country. The institutions set up were: Nigeria Industrial Bank (NIB), Nigeria Bank for Commerce and Industries (NBCI), and Nigeria Agricultural and Cooperative Bank (NACB). In the 1981 National Policy of Education an attempt was made by the government to link the policy with the issue of self-employment and the industrial policy. But then the main focus was only on primary and secondary schools. The higher education policy was deficient in the sense that it failed to take the issue of self-employment to the tertiary level.

The importance of entrepreneurship to any economy is like that of entrepreneurship in any community: entrepreneurship activity and the resultant financial gain are always of benefit to a country. If you have entrepreneurial skills, then you will recognize a genuine opportunity when you come across one. Entrepreneurship education focuses on developing understanding and capacity for the pursuit of entrepreneurial behaviors, skills and attributes in widely different contexts. Entrepreneurial skills and attributes provide benefits to society, even beyond their application to business activity. Obviously, personal qualities that are relevant to entrepreneurship, such as creativity and a spirit of initiative, can be useful to everyone in their working responsibilities and in their day-to-day existence.

Weber (1930) puts forward the thesis that the Protestant ethic is the spirit of capitalism (Green 1959). Schumpeter (1947), who is, perhaps, believed to be the first major economist to analyze the role of entrepreneurship in economic development, attributed innovation to the entrepreneur. He described entrepreneurship as the engine of economic development. He argued that "to study the entrepreneur is to study the central figure in modern economic history".

In the theory of distribution put forward by Say (1824), a neoclassicial economist, the entrepreneur plays a crucial role, though he or she is not a production factor. Unlike the capitalist, the entrepreneur directs the application of acquired knowledge to the production of goods for human consumption.

Challenges of Entrepreneurship Education in Nigeria

The Nigerian economy, historically, has depended significantly on oil revenues. The following are the most important obstacles facing rapid entrepreneurial development:

(a) rampant political and bureaucratic corruption, together with the absence of social consensus on important macroeconomic policy issues;
(b) poor access to vocational and skills, i.e., development training for rural and urban youths involved in the informal economy;
(c) absence of regulatory mechanisms for effective oversight of enterprise development initiatives, especially those in the MSME sector;
(d) the presence of administrative and trade barriers that curtail capacity building and inhibit access to technical support;
(e) significant infrastructural deficits (especially with regards to roads and electricity) and systematic irregularities inimical to small businesses;
(f) absence of a pro-active regulatory environment that encourages innovative enterprise development at the grassroots level;
(g) and, no doubt, one of the biggest challenges to any entrepreneur is access to capital.

References
Akinjogbin, I. A. (1980) The Economic Foundations of the Oyo Empire. In Akinjogbin, I. A., and S. O. Osoba (eds.), *Topics on Nigerian Economic and Social History*. Ife: University of Ife Press, pp. 35–54.
Aladekomo, O. F. (2004) Nigeria Educational Policy and Entrepreneurship. *Journal of Social Science*, 9(2): 75–83.
Ehinmore, O. M. (2002) Fishing in South-Western Nigeria in the 19th Century: A Study of the Ilaje Fishing Economy. AAU *African Studies Review*, Lagos, First Academic Publishers, Vol. 1, No. 1, p. 56.
Evans-Pritchard, E. E. (1940) *The Nuer: A Description of the Modes of Livelihood and Political Institutions of Nilotic People*. London: Oxford University Press.
Falola, Toyin. (1996) Trade and Market in Pre-colonial Economy.In Ogunremi, G. O., and E. K. Faluyi (eds.), *An Economic History of West Africa Since 1750*. Ibadan: Rex Charles.
Hopkins, A. G. (1973) *An Economic History of West Africa*. London: Longman.
Hoselitz, Bert F. (1965) The Development of African Entrepreneurs. In Jackson, E. F. (ed.), *Economic Development of Africa*. Oxford: Blackwell. Cited in Hopkins, *An Economic History of West Africa*.
Miller, Roger Leroy. (2006) *Economics Today*. Boston, MA: Addison-Wesley Publishers.

Odegbemi, Ariyo. (2006) Cited in Ehinmore, O. M. Pre-Colonial Nigerian Economy: Dynamic or Stagnant? http://www.articlesbase.com/literature-articles/precolonial-nigerian-economy-dynamic-or-stagnant-941809.html.

Ogunremi, G. O. (1996) Traditional Factors of Production in Pre-colonial Economy. In Ogunremi, G. O., and E. K Faluyi (eds.), *An Economic History of West Africa Since 1750*.

Olukoju, A. (2010) Fishing, Migrations and Inter-group Relations in the Gulf of Guinea (Atlantic Coast of West Africa) in the 19th and 20th Centuries. Itinerario, Vol. XXV, *European Journal of Overseas History*, p. 70.

Stride, G. T., and C. Ifeka. (1971) *Peoples and Empires of West Africa*. Hong Kong: Thomas Nelson.

Williams, Dennis. (1966) An Outline History of Tropical African Art. In Joseph, C. A., Nene and Godfrey Brown (eds.), *Africa in the Nineteenth and Twentieth Centuries*. Ibadan: University Press, pp. 60–65.

A detailed discussion and critique of the substantivist and formalist views could be found in Zeleza, J. A. (1993) *Modern Economic History of Africa*, Vol. 1 Senegal: CODESTRIA, pp. 15–16.

Chapter 3

THE CONCEPTS AND PRINCIPLES OF ENTREPRENEURSHIP

Fayomi, A. O.

Introduction

This chapter aims at providing learners with an appreciation and understanding of the elements and concept of entrepreneurship. Specifically, it discusses the concept of entrepreneurship and highlights the various categories into which enterprises can be classified. It further enumerates the roles that people play in enterprise and provides the learners the principles that are critical for building a career in entrepreneurship.

What is an Enterprise?

The word enterprise is used in a wide range of contexts to mean different things. The narrow meaning of the concept relates to business, while the broader meaning suggests a way of behaving that can apply to diverse contexts, including business. Enterprise can broadly be defined as any undertaking or project that involves the organisation of the factors of production for the benefit of an individual, a group of individuals, or the community as a whole. In practical terms, an enterprise refers to any identified idea that is successfully translated into a beneficial activity through systematically planned action. In essence any undertaking can be referred to as an enterprise if it satisfies the condition of idea identification, planning, implementation, successful completion of activity and acceptance of reward. There are essentially two types of enterprise characteristically demarcated by purpose. These include business enterprises and social enterprises.

❖ *Business enterprise* refers to all types of operations involved in the provision of goods, services or both to people, with the anticipated outcome of earning a profit. The scope of business enterprise is very broad and can be applied to any type of firm that is geared towards generating revenue by selling any type of product or providing any type of service.
❖ *Social enterprises* are organizations that are set up with the primary objective of improving human and environmental well-being through the application of business strategies. They also need to be successful, just as business enterprises do, but their success is measured in terms of social benefit rather than profit maximization.

A business enterprise may be private or public. A private enterprise is a business concern that is owned by an individual or group of individuals. Examples include Dangote Group, Global Com, and Greenspring International School. A public enterprise on the other hand is a business concern set up by the government to provide essential goods or services, or both, which may not be adequately provided by private enterprises. Examples include Power Holding Corporation of Nigeria

(PHCN), the various government-owned universities, water corporations, NITEL PLC, etc.

Different Forms of Enterprises

Enterprises are set up basically to solve specific problems and meet identified needs in the society. Because human needs and interests are different, enterprising individuals must identify the specific interests, needs and wants of people and establish appropriate enterprises to satisfy them. Enterprises are classified based on the scale of operation, location, ownership, reward and sector. The terms used to classify enterprises include private, public, formal, informal, individual, community, foreign, small, large, business, social, local, manufacturing and service.

Private enterprises
Private enterprises are business concerns established by individuals or groups of individuals with the major objective of earning profit. They are formed with personal interest and tend to undertake activities with high profitability potential.

Public enterprises
Public enterprises are primarily established with the objective of providing goods or services, or both, which may not be adequately provided by private enterprises to the people. They are formed with social interest. Examples of public enterprises include public educational institutions such as universities and public health centers.

Voluntary enterprises
These are organisations providing utilitarian services for the benefit of the society. Such organisations are not founded on profit motives; rather, they promote cultural or moral values, as the case may be. Membership of voluntary organisations is voluntary, as the name suggests. Individuals subscribe to be members in identification with the beliefs and values of the organisation. Examples of voluntary organisations include all faith-based organisations such Christian Association of Nigeria, Pentecostal Fellowship of Nigeria, etc.

The Concept of Entrepreneurship

The concept of entrepreneurship is fundamental to understanding the role of entrepreneurship in development. Historically, the concept of entrepreneurship can be traced back to the French verb "entreprendre" which means to"take-up" or to "do something". From the conventional scholarly tradition of management research, entrepreneurship is associated with the practice of starting a new business, particularly, a new business that has to do with taking advantage of an existing opportunity in a given market. This viewpoint conceives entrepreneurship behaviour as the activities of individuals who are associated with creating new enterprises only. Though conventional, this viewpoint is limited, as entrepreneurship is also known to exist in established organisations where persons employed in such organisations use entrepreneurial principles and innovation to create value in such organisations. Furthermore, entrepreneurship can occur in the non-profit sector and even in the civil service. It usually involves employing creative and innovative action in the face of risk to exploit opportunities and attain established goals. Consequently, the domain of entrepreneurship involves three important dimensions, namely, risk–taking, innovation, and pro-activity.

In the literature there is no universally acceptable definition of entrepreneurship. However, Schumpeter, who is widely referenced as the founder of modern entrepreneurship theory, provided the framework for understanding entrepreneurship by his theory of "creative destruction". The theory postulates that new firms displace older, less innovative firms through their entrepreneurial mindset. He posited that large organisations tend to resist change, thus motivating entrepreneurially minded individuals to create new firms in order to pursue innovation. He postulated that this creative destruction will generate a higher degree of economic growth and that the new product created would eventually replace older products. Hence, from the viewpoint of Schumpeter, entrepreneurship consists of changing the pattern of production through innovation or through the use of new technology for producing new products or producing an old one in a new way. The concept of entrepreneurship has generated many definitions. However, for our purpose, entrepreneurship will be defined as the process of wealth creation championed by individuals who assume the risk of resources, time and commitment to create value through a product or service.

Who is an Entrepreneur?

"Entrepreneur" is a concept used to describe individuals who generate new ideas, establish an enterprise based on such ideas and make entrepreneurial profit by adding value to the society through such ideas. Though an entrepreneur has often been conceived as a business owner, in practice, an entrepreneur does more than just create a business. A business owner simply makes the decision of starting a business venture as an alternative to paid employment or as an additional source of income to augment salary income. The entrepreneur differs significantly to the ordinary business owner in that he does not maintain the status quo over time, rather, he is committed to growth and constructive change. He is also constantly seeking information and new opportunities, combining resources in unusual ways to achieve unusual results.

Roles of Entrepreneurs in Business

Success in business can be defined in terms of growth, profitability and sustainability. Entrepreneurship literature has revealed that businesses owned or operated by entrepreneurs tend to be more successful. This is because entrepreneurs perform many important roles in a business. Some of these roles include:

Idea generation: Entrepreneurs take the responsibility for making the decisions about what the business will produce and how to produce it. This is based on the need of the market.

Risk taking: Entrepreneurs take moderate and reasonable risk in the pursuit of an identified business opportunity. This is because there is no absolutely safe business idea.

Willingness to take the risk of investing time and resources in the face of uncertainty is an important attribute of an entrepreneur.

Promotion: Entrepreneurs scan the environment, identify opportunities, mobilise resources and implement the business idea. This role is known as business promotion.

Directing: Entrepreneurs employ innovative ideas in directing the activities of the enterprise in order to achieve the set objectives. Such activities include ensuring that the enterprise stakeholders get sufficient returns on their investment through proper management, motivating the employees for optimal performance, and ensuring that the enterprise comply with necessary legal requirements and perform its social responsibilities and obligations.

Shareholding: Entrepreneurs play the role of shareholders when they buy the shares of a business of their choice and therefore become co-owners of such a business. Though this may be regarded as a passive activity in many cases, in the sense that the shareholder has little control over the business (especially when the quantum of share is negligible), there is still an element of risk, pro-activeness and innovation. The entrepreneur takes risks by investing in a business he is not going to run personally. He is also pro-active in the sense that he is deploying resources with the anticipation of a higher return in the future. Furthermore, he is innovative because he has created an additional stream of income. In some cases, however, entrepreneur shareholders influence decisions in the business because of the size of his shares in the company.

Planning: In the face of constantly changing business environment, entrepreneurs must be proactive in running the affairs of their businesses. This is necessary in order not to be destabilised by the changes. Planning involves defining the goals of the enterprise and putting in place the strategies to achieve them. Planning promotes effectiveness and aids informed decision-making processes and revenue allocation in an enterprise. Entrepreneurs discharge planning roles by analysing the present and anticipating the future of their enterprises. They establish specific objectives and actions for their business enterprises.

Organising: Entrepreneurs perform the role of determining the task that is to be performed, who performs the task, how it is to be done, and how the job holders relate to one another in terms of authority and responsibility. Organising involves systematically bringing together the resources of the enterprise in order to achieve the objectives of the organisation.

Co-ordinating: Entrepreneurs perform the co-ordinating role by unifying the activities of the various units of the enterprise in order to realise the established goals of the enterprise. They put systems in place to ensure that the different arms of the enterprise function effectively and efficiently in order to have a good return on the invested capital.

Innovation: Entrepreneurs differ from small business owners in a number of ways; one of such is their passion and commitment to change. While a typical small business owner may maintain its scope and process of operation over years, an entrepreneur is constantly thinking of better and more efficient ways of doing things. Hence, entrepreneurs continue to add value to the product and services of the enterprise to remain competitive and in response to changes in the market. Innovation may take the form of new products, designs, packaging, production processes or even the establishment of new markets.

Principles of Entrepreneurship

Entrepreneurial principles can be described as universal steps that must be followed in building a career in entrepreneurship. The high mortality rate of new entrepreneurial ventures has been attributed significantly to the failure of the promoters of such ventures to observe and operationalise essential principles of entrepreneurship. Taking cognisance of these principles by aspiring entrepreneurs will no doubt facilitate a successful career in the rather challenging field of entrepreneurship. The following are the basic principles that are critical for building a sustainable career in entrepreneurship.

Personal entrepreneurial assessment: The debate on whether entrepreneurs are born is an age-long one. Scholars in the trait school of taught believe that some individuals have certain personality attributes which make them suited to run an enterprise successfully. Such attributes include pro-activeness, commitment, and opportunity recognition, among others. Contemporary management and entrepreneurship studies have however shown that entrepreneurship attributes can both be taught and learnt. In making the decision of whether or not to take up entrepreneurship as a career, the intending entrepreneur must take time to appraise his or her entrepreneurial readiness by assessing his or her skills, personal characteristics and situation. The skills required to start a business include technical skills, business management skills, knowledge of the business line, and negotiation skills. Technical skills are the practical abilities needed to produce the product or provide the services of the business. Prospective entrepreneurs must of necessity possess technical skills in order to be successful in business. Business management skills entail the competencies required to run a business efficiently. These include costing, marketing, and record keeping, among others. Having a good knowledge of the line of business idea is also very important for a prospective entrepreneur. To be successful in business, intending entrepreneurs must be able to identify the market and competitors to prevent avoidable pitfalls. Where the self entrepreneurial assessment by the prospective entrepreneur reveals that he/she is deficient in any of the skills, attitudes and knowledge discussed, effort must be made for personal development in such area.

Business idea generation: A good business idea is a prerequisite to a successful business venture. To transform his/her desire and creativity into a business opportunity, the entrepreneur must find a good business idea. A business idea is the response of an individual, group of individuals or an organisation to meeting perceived needs in the environment. Failure in business in many cases has been ascribed to poorly conceived business ideas. The prospective entrepreneur creatively, pro-actively and systematically generates his/her business idea to achieve success. There are several sources and methods of generating business ideas, some of these include:

Brainstorming: Brainstorming is a creative problem-solving technique. It is known as creative or critical thinking. It usually starts with a question or problem statement. The potential entrepreneur may start the brainstorming process by asking the question: "What are the products or services that I need which are not available in my environment?" The exercise will generate a number of needs that can be met; each of these needs are ideas of potential businesses that the entrepreneur can start.

Hobbies and interests: A hobby is a favourite leisure-time activity. Many people have been able to develop business ideas from their hobbies and interests. For instance, people who enjoy working with computers may think of starting a cyber cafe or a business centre.

Personal skills and experience: The background of potential entrepreneurs plays a crucial role in the decision to start a business as well as the type of business to start. In practice, more than half of successful businesses come from experience in the work place. For example, an apprentice or worker in a furniture company may conceive the idea of starting his own furniture outfit later in life. The skills and experience of an individual who is interested in going into business is perhaps the most important resource in generating business ideas and running a successful business from such idea.

Complaints: Complaints of customers about a product or service may point to the need for another product that can better satisfy the need of customers.

Survey: Every business must be established with the customer in perspective. The needs and wants of the customer can be determined by conducting a survey. This may take the form of formal or informal interview, observation, and questionnaire.

Exhibitions: Attending exhibitions and trade fairs will expose prospective entrepreneurs to new products as well as sales representatives, manufacturers and distributors who may provide information about such products and the modalities for building an enterprise around such products.

Assessing business opportunity: A good business idea is not necessarily a good business opportunity. A business idea becomes a business opportunity when it has the prospect of a good return on investment for the person taking the risk. To be an opportunity, a business idea must be based on identified need, it must be competitive, it must meet desired objectives, and it must be executable, taking into cognisance availability of resources and competencies. To ensure success, prospective entrepreneurs must access their business ideas to establish their worth as viable opportunities. To do this, the entrepreneur must be able to proffer satisfactory answers to the following questions: Is there a ready market for the product or service? Can the idea be executed within the window of opportunity (that is, before other prospective entrepreneurs take advantage of it)? Does the proprietor have the financial resources to execute the idea? Is the idea aimed at meeting a specified and real need? Can the idea yield a reasonable return on invested capital when compared with return on alternative investment opportunities? Can the idea be executed without contravening government policy and procedure?

Preparation of feasibility report: The answers to the above questions can be answered by a well prepared feasibility report. A feasibility report is a decision-making tool that is aimed at assisting the entrepreneur to determine the viability of a business idea before committing his resources into it. A good feasibility report is also a requirement to access bank loans and other financial support from formal organisations.

Preparation of a business plan: A business plan is a concise statement of the business goals and how the goals will be achieved. The business plan compels the proprietor to figure out how to make the business work. It guides every step in business development. A well written business plan will show investors that the business proprietor has carefully thought through what is needed to make the business succeed. Specifically, a good business plan will address seven major things: the concept of the business, the customer, capital, organisation structure, legal structure, business management and plan for growth. The concept of the business is a description of the product or service of the business and how it is different from similar products or services. The customer aspect addresses the question of who will buy the product or service, while capital addresses the questions of how much it will cost to execute the business, how the proprietor will locate the money that the business will need, and how much profit the proprietor can expect. Organisation structure provides information on the profile of key managers and the board of directors. Legal structures describe contract issues, insurance, taxes and relevant government regulations that affect the business. Business management addresses how the activities of the business will be coordinated. It should discuss issues such as production, distribution, operations, purchasing and inventory.

Business communication: The entrepreneur must share information, thoughts or opinions with suppliers, customers, family members, friends, business colleagues and many others. For the communication to be effective, it must be presented in the right tone. A key success factor in business is the ability of the entrepreneur to communicate his/her thoughts in clear and appropriate language which must not be informal, aggressive or too unassertive. Prospective entrepreneurs must learn to communicate effectively.

The six qualities of good communication are:

Brevity: For communication to be effective, it must be devoid of unnecessary words, personal information and other unrelated subjects. The communicator need only identify himself and the reason for the communication.

Organisation: Information must be presented in an easy to follow format. As a rule of the thumb, introduce the subject, add details in a logical order, and close by summarising the main idea.

Clarity: The communicator must include everything the audience needs to understand and act on the message.

Relevance: The right information must be supplied to the right audience. Providing unnecessary facts can be confusing and time consuming.

Courtesy: A good communication should avoid personal attacks and criticism. Rather, respect and positive attitude must be reflected.

Suitability: Different types of communication are required for different situations. The entrepreneur must understand the different forms of communication and the use of each. The common forms of communication include written communication, spoken communication and instant messaging.

Ethics: For sustainable success in entrepreneurship, prospective entrepreneurs must understand and factor in ethical issues that are relevant to their enterprises. Ethics are moral principles and values that should govern actions and decisions in an enterprise. There exist different ethical values in different enterprise/industry sectors. In the simplest terms, business ethics is doing unto others what you want others to do unto you. Ethical practice is important in business because it prevents legal problems, motivates employees, and enhances customers' confidence in the business. Important ethical issues in business include:

Intellectual property: This is artistic and industrial creation of the mind which is protected by law. The owners of such creations are entitled to credit and most of the time some form of payment when their works are used for commercial gain. Artistic creations are protected by copyright, which is the exclusive right to perform, display, copy or distribute an artistic work. Industrial invention is protected by patent, which is the exclusive right to make, use, or sell a devise or process. A trademark on the other hand is a symbol that indicates that the user of a brand or brand name is legally protected and cannot be used by any other business. Violating a copyright, trademark or patent holder's right is known as infringement, and it is punishable under the law.

Confidentiality: Entrepreneurs are privy to much information about their clients and their employees. The duty of the entrepreneur is to respect the confidentiality of the owners of such information when making use of it in the business; otherwise, it might become an ethical issue which might work contrary to the welfare of the business, both in the short and long run.

Corporate social responsibility: Entrepreneurs have legal obligations to provide a safe workplace and fair employment policies for their employees. They also have legal obligations towards their customers to treat them fairly. Furthermore, entrepreneurs have responsibilities towards their environment to protect natural resources.

Growth: Growth is one of the factors that distinguishes entrepreneurship from small business ownership. An economic concern is only qualified to be referred to as an entrepreneurial venture if it fulfills the criteria of innovation and growth. That is, it must be seen to be growing on a sustainable basis over time. Growth in this regard could be in the form of sales, profitability, turn-over and employees. In essence, businesses that maintain the same status quo over time, doing the same thing in the same way over a wide stretch of time, are not an entrepreneurial venture but rather a small business.

References

Acs, Z. J., B. Carlsson and C. Karlsson (eds.). (1999) *Entrepreneurship, Small and Medium Enterprises and the Macro-Economy*. London: Cambridge University Press.

Albert, F. (1999) Entrepreneurship Education and Enterprise Culture: Lessons from Other Countries. Paper presented at the National Conference on Entrepreneurship Education in Nigeria Tertiary Institution, Abuja, Nigeria, March 30–April 1, 1999.

Banfe, C. (1991) *From Zero to Hero*. New York: Van Nostrand Reinhold.

Bechhard, J. P., and J. M. Toulouse. (1998) Validation of a Didactic Model from the Analysis of Training Objectives in Entrepreneurship. *Journal of Business Venturing*.

Bolden, R., and J. Gosling. (2006) Leadership Competencies: Time to Change the Tune? *Leadership* (2): 147–163.

Carrier, C. (1999) The Training Needs of Owner-Managers of Small Businesses with Export Potential. *Journal of Small Business Management*.

Garavan, T. N., and B. O'Cinneide. (1964) Entrepreneurship Education and Training Programmes: A Review and Evaluation, Part 2. *Journal of Small Business Management* 28(1): 70–73.

Gnyawali, D. R., and D. S. Fogel. (1964) Environment for Entrepreneurship Development: Dimensions and Research Implications. *Entrepreneurship Theory and Practice*, Summer: 43–63.

Hatten, S. T. (1996) *Small Scale Business Entrepreneurship and Beyond*. Upper Saddle River, NJ: Prentice Hall.

Chapter 4

THE BEGINNING OF ENTREPRENEURSHIP

Owoeye, O. I. O. and Ajiboye, O. F.

Introduction

Entrepreneurship is an area of academe that deals with an enlarged range of theories and approaches and has been studied in many different ways with very different purposes. Hart (2003) submits that the concepts of 'entrepreneur and entrepreneurship' have become highly desirable labels in recent years, so much so that the definition has been blurred nearly beyond recognition. Researchers from all fields of social sciences—economics, sociology, anthropology, psychology, history, political science and several branches of management sciences—have contributed to this area of study. In addition, the research field of entrepreneurship has been considered to be the target of the most diverse areas of study, and it is developing very fast (Ronen 1983; Sexton and Bowman 1987; Davidson 1989; and Langstrom 2005).

This chapter focuses on the following:
- the definition of entrepreneur and entrepreneurship;
- emergence of entrepreneurship;
- the societal and academic perspectives of the phenomenon;
- the forces behind the emergence of entrepreneurship, as well as
- the emergence of entrepreneurship in Nigeria.

Definition of Entrepreneur and Entrepreneurship

The phenomenon of entrepreneurship is not a new concept in the world. Hindle (2008) states that the word 'entrepreneur' is believed to have been coined in the 19th century (about 1800). An economist, Jean Baptiste Say, defined it as 'one who undertakes an enterprise, especially a contractor, acting as intermediary between capital and labour'. However, Langstrom (2005) believes that the concept 'entrepreneur' was originally a French word that appeared for the first time in the *Dictionaire de la langue francaise* in 1437. The word may have its root in the verb 'entreprendre', which means to undertake something. It was confirmed that the word has been part of the French language since the 12th century, often linked to war-like and risk-taking activities.

Kaplan (2003) and Langstrom (2005) articulate that the word 'entrepreneur' as risk-taking emerged in the 17th century, when it referred to individuals who undertook the risk of a new enterprise. However, not all risk-taking individuals were perceived as entrepreneurs. Entrepreneurial activities involving risk undertaking was usually a function of the volume of the undertakings. Therefore, most entrepreneurs were large contractors working between the state and some competent wealthy persons with the objective of undertaking a major building scheme or supplying the army with equipment. Despite the French linguistic root of the word 'entrepreneur', there has been a long-standing difficulty in how to define the concept 'entrepreneur' and 'entrepreneurship'.

Langstrom (2005) expresses this lack of clear definition as the characteristic of recent entrepreneurship research, thereby making it a complicated, ambiguous and changeable phenomenon as well as a barrier to the development of the research field. Therefore, he furthers his arguments by reviewing some of the definitions of the word 'entrepreneurship' given by some scholars to prove the concept's changeability:

- Morris (1998) found seventy-seven different definitions in a review of journal articles and textbooks over a five-year period.

- Gartner (1990) reviewed the concept as it was understood by academics, business leaders and politicians and listed ninety different attributes associated with the entrepreneur. Some of the definitions are as follows:

  - Entrepreneurship is an act of innovation that involves endowing existing resources with new wealth-producing capacity (Drucker 2005);

  - Entrepreneurship is a process by which individuals pursue and exploit opportunities, irrespective of the resources they currently control (Stevenson 1985);

  - Entrepreneurship is a way of thinking, reasoning, and acting that is opportunity driven, holistic approach, and leadership balanced (Timmons 1997);

  - Entrepreneurship is about how, by whom and with what consequences opportunities to bring future goods and services into existence are discovered, created and exploited (Venkataraman 1997).

However vague the concepts *entrepreneur* and *entrepreneurship*, the problem is not all about the definitions' lack of clarity but, in the concept of this chapter, the emergence of entrepreneurship research and the forces behind it.

Emergence of Entrepreneurship

Busenitz *et al.* (2003) state that the nature of entrepreneurship research and the emergence of entrepreneurship as a legitimate academic pursuit have begun to attract the interest of scholars. Aldrich and Baker (1997, pp. 377–400) claim that the field of entrepreneurship has made only limited progress towards attaining disciplinary status in a normal science framework. Others think that entrepreneurship remains in a theory-building stage (Wiseman and Skilton 1999) and is a 'multidisciplinary jigsaw' characterized by accumulative fragmentalism (Harrison and Leitch 1996:69). The emergence and development of entrepreneurship is not a spontaneous one but a phenomenon that is dependent on the evolving concerns in the economic, social, political, and psychological spheres.

Langstrom (2005) states that, historically, entrepreneurship is one of the oldest human enterprises in the world. Although several books and websites have written about the history of entrepreneurship, Langstrom (2005) provides its details. Langstrom (2005) expressed that to discover or identify new business possibilities and to exploit these possibilities in new ventures for economic gain has always been important in human life. One wave of entrepreneurial activities took place during the last few decades. In the 1970s and 1980s, the world experienced huge structural changes in the shape of oil crises, economic recessions, technological progress, increasing globalization, and political changes, all in favour of a stronger market-oriented ideology.

Historically, the word 'entrepreneur' emerged from the French language paradoxically in the 12th century, when Europe was hooked into the feudal system which hampered entrepreneurship. The situation gradually changed during the Middle Ages, especially in Italy, France and Southern Germany, which were the driving forces in the European countries at that time. The rise of the cities created a platform for entrepreneurship, and it was especially among the merchant class, who supplied raw materials and marketed the finished goods, that entrepreneurship thrived. By the 18th century, feudalism had disappeared, and legal and institutional conditions greatly changed in favour of entrepreneurship and innovation, as evidenced by the burgeoning of the joint stock company and development of the banking system (Wennekers and Thurik 1999; Langstrom 2005).

Entrepreneurship first appeared in the economic science through the writing of Richard Cantillon (approx. 1680–1734) in his work *Essai Sur la Nature du Commmerce en General*, published posthumously in 1775. He endowed the concept with economic meaning and the entrepreneur with a role in economic development as well as work, receiving considerable attention in France. Cantillon observed that the discrepancies between demand and supply in a market created opportunities for buying cheaply and selling at a higher price, thereby bringing equilibrium to the competitive market. His assumption was that the entrepreneur would buy products at fixed price, have them packaged and transported to market, and sell them at unpredictable and uncertain prices. There was an emphasis on risk in Cantillon's analysis because entrepreneurship is about foresight and willingness to assume risk. Cantillon focused on the function of the entrepreneur and made a distinction between an entrepreneur and a capitalist, who provided the capital. He was of the opinion that the entrepreneur makes conscious choices about resource allocation in order to exploit resources so as to achieve as high a financial return as possible.

Changing production conditions, social relations, and a new way of thinking began to emerge in the 18th century; these affected the intellectuals and academic environment. This period coincided with the development of classical theory, which has its origin in Adam Smith's (1723–1790) *Inquiry into Nature and Causes of the Wealth of Nations* (1770/1776). This work influenced the opinion of theorists about the entrepreneur in economic sciences. However, unlike Cantillon, Smith did not distinguish between the entrepreneur as ultimate decision-maker and the capitalist as the provider of the capital; the capitalist emerged the central actor in Smith's analysis. This has been the standard practice among classical economists.

Bentham (1748–1832) criticized Smith for not considering the role of the entrepreneur in society. Bentham's argument is that the entrepreneur was no more than the individual who undertook certain tasks on contractual terms. And J. S. Mills (1806–1873) established the word 'entrepreneur' for more general use than that attributed to it by economists. But French economist Jean Baptiste Say (1767–1873) changed the contemporary trend. Say, in his work *Traite d'economie politique* (1803) (Wikipedia 2013), defines entrepreneurship as a combination of factors of production into an organism. He also provides an empirical description of what the entrepreneur does as well as an analysis of the entrepreneurial function in the economy.

Say perceives the entrepreneur to be a 'broker' who organises and combines means of production with the aim of producing goods. But this adjustment is not just something that occurs by chance; it must lead to the development of a good or a service that provides some form of value or utility at the entrepreneur's own risk.

Late 19th Century

Entrepreneurship was largely ignored theoretically until the late 19th century, when it got an audience in the United States, which was an emerging major industrial power. American economists such as Francis Walker, Fredrick Hawley and John Bates Clark developed the entrepreneurship discussion in the United States. However, of all these scholars, Frank Knight (1885–1972) was the most famous economist who wrote on the work of the entrepreneur with his thesis *Risk, Uncertainty and Profit* (1916, revised 1921), in which he argued that entrepreneurship is mainly characterised by true uncertainty. He made a distinction between three types of future uncertainties:

- Risk exists when outcomes are uncertain, but the outcomes can be predicted with some degree of probability.
- Uncertainty arises when the probability of outcome cannot be calculated.
- True uncertainty occurs when the future is not only unknown but also unknowable, with unclassifiable instances and a non-existent distribution of outcomes (Sarasvathy, Dew, Velamur and Venktaraman 2003).

Knight was later considered a central figure within economics and the founder of the Chicago school of economics. He also published *Economics Organization* (1933), which is considered a classic of microeconomics theory.

20th century

In the 20th century, the understanding of entrepreneurship owes much to the work of the economist Joseph Schumpeter, in the 1930s, and to Austrian economists such as Carl Menger, Ludwig von Mises and Friedrich von Hayek. The influence of these two groups will be assessed in this section.

Schumpeter's Influence

Schumpeter's view of an entrepreneur is a person who is willing and able to convert a new idea or invention into a successful innovation. He called it 'the gale of creative destruction' to replace in whole or in part inferior innovations across markets and industries, simultaneously creating new products and new business models. Entrepreneurship, for Schumpeter, resulted not only in new industries but also in new coordination of currently existing inputs.

It is essential to note that Schumpeter's work and view on entrepreneurship changed over time until about 1940. During this period, he was mainly interested in developing his mode of reasoning about entrepreneurship and integrating these thoughts into his new economic theory. But he encountered a corporate world different from the one found in the Austria of his youth: during the inter-war period in the United States, the corporate scene was dominated by large companies with advanced research departments and not by small firms with clearly distinguishable entrepreneurs. This situation led Schumpeter to focus on innovative activities in existing organisations, while developing a growing interest in economic history. All his new focus found expression in his book, *Capitalism, Socialism and Democracy* (1942), in which he dwelt on the institutional structure of society.

However, Schumpeter's theses were developed at the Research Centre in Entrepreneurial History at Harvard University. The centre was founded by Arthur H. Cole in 1948, and Schumpeter worked at the centre until his death in 1950. Other members of the centre were Hugh Aitken, Fritz Redlich, Alexander Gerschenkron, Talcott Parsons and Thomas Cochran. These researchers at Harvard had a slightly different perception of the nature of entrepreneurship, but they agreed that entrepreneurship consisted of three different dimensions: changes in the economic system; creation of organisation as a prerequisite for the commercialisation of innovation; and the fact that the task of the entrepreneur is to create profits and that this occurs through the production and distribution of goods and services. To be precise, entrepreneurship was related to a certain sector in society. Although the research centre in entrepreneurial history ceased to exist in 1958, Schumpeter's ideas and reasoning still exert much influence.

Austrian Tradition

The tradition emerged at the end of the 19th century and is based on the thoughts of the Austrian economist Carl Menger. Also part of the tradition are Friedrich von Wiesler and Eugen von Böhm-Bawerk, whose ideas were further developed by Austrian economists Friedrich von Hayek (1899–1992) and Ludwig von Mises (1881–1973). But Carl Menger was considered the ideological founder of the Austrian tradition of economic thought. His contribution was at the methodological level, evidenced in the seminal work *Grundsätze der Volkswirtschaftlehre* (*Principles of Economics*) (1871/1981). The general thinking within this tradition is based on the view that the individual is an independent economic entity and that actions, to a great extent, influence the economic conditions in society. The focus of the tradition is on the individual's actions.

For example, in this tradition, Mises (1949/1963) observed that people are not only calculating beings but also alert to making use of opportunities, which caused him to introduce the concept of 'human action' to describe this behaviour. Hayek (1945) stated that knowledge in a market economy is split among different individuals. This is to decentralize and not allow an individual to possess the same knowledge or information as another. This makes the individual unique in the market since the knowledge is obtained through each individual's special situation, occupation, social network and so on, thereby rationalizing the presence of uncertainty leading to market opportunities.

Israel Kirzner is another scholar who stood out in this tradition. Kirzner was a student of Mises and developed the ideas of Mises and Hayek in his book *Competition and Entrepreneurship* (1973). For Kirzner, it is fundamental for an entrepreneur to be alert to identifying and dealing with profit-making opportunities. This is called 'entrepreneurial alertness' and Kirzner's concept of entrepreneurship was dictated by alertness to new entrepreneurial opportunities; entrepreneurs act on these opportunities and information in order to earn money from the difference between supply and demand. Therefore, Kirzner perceives an entrepreneur as someone who is alert to market imperfections as a result of the information about the needs and resources of the different actors and, with the help of this information, coordinates resources in a more effective way as well as creating equilibrium.

The Influence of Behavioural Science on Entrepreneurship

The concept of entrepreneurship has been worked upon to the neglect of the behavioural aspect of man. Evidence prior to World War II indicated that entrepreneurship seemed to be overlooked in economic models as a result of the economic explanations that had focused more on equilibrium models, which seemed not to give room for the entrepreneur (Barreto 1989; Kirchhoff 1994). Another factor was that, since Schumpeter's attention moved away from explanation to developing the concept of entrepreneurship, the concept became an essential factor in economic development. These issues gave rise to a stagnant state, thereby creating a void to be filled as a result of the stagnant state of the field of entrepreneurship.

So, individuals were stimulated to start businesses and create developments in society. This period experienced an individual profile, leading to entrepreneurial success or failure as well as the encouragement of appropriate personalities to engage in an entrepreneurial career. This created an opportunity for behavioural scientists and researchers, especially psychologists, to assume responsibility for continuing the theoretical development of entrepreneurship. Therefore, after World War II, behavioural scientists dominated the research field of entrepreneurship. And one of the first researchers to present empirical studies in the field of entrepreneurship based on behavioural science theory is David McClelland (1917–1998).

David McClelland and the Achieving Society (1961)

McClelland, in his book *The Achieving Society*, published in 1961, discusses the rationale behind some societies developing more dynamically than others. McClelland builds on the sociologist Max Weber's arguments, contained in *The Protestant Ethic and the Spirit of Capitalism* (1904/1970), in which he analysed the interplay between culture and economic development in a society. Weber's main argument is that certain Puritan traits in the Protestant moral code resulted in a combination of thrift, a sense of duty, industriousness and self-denial; all these characteristics also created the platform for the development of capitalism. However, McClelland's viewpoint is that the norms and values that prevail in a particular society, especially with regard to the need for achievement, are of vital importance for the development of that society.

McClelland engages in several experimental studies to demonstrate the link between a nation's need for achievement and its economic development. But he points out that economic development is a complex phenomenon which cannot be explained merely in terms of need for achievement. Therefore, variables such as an individual's relationship motive and need for controls are considered. With these variables, McClelland concludes that economically better developed countries are characterised by a lower focus on institutional norms and a greater emphasis on openness toward other people and their values as well as on communication between people. In other words, entrepreneurs, for McClelland, are those who have a high need for achievement, great self-confidence, and independent problem-solving skills, and who prefer situations that are characterized by moderate risks, follow-ups of results and feedback, and the acceptance of individual responsibility.

There has been a large number of studies that particularly discussed the qualities of the entrepreneur. Some of the individual characteristics assumed to be related to entrepreneurs are (Delmar 2000):

i. Desire for Achievement: This is the most popular characteristic in this tradition, which is from the work of McClelland's study in 1961.

ii. Risk-taking Propensity: This focused on the role of the entrepreneur as an economic risk-taker or risk-bearer in the economic system, which can be traced back to early writings in entrepreneurship in economic science.

iii. Locus of Control: This is developed by Rotter (1961), with the perception that one's goal can be attained through one's own actions or follows from uncontrolled external factors.

iv. Over-optimism: This is reported by Cooper, Woo, and Dunkelberg (1988) that entrepreneurs often show a high degree of over-optimism.

v.   Desire for Autonomy: This quality indicates that the entrepreneur seems to have a high need for autonomy (Sexton and Bowman 1985) and a fear of external control (Smith 1967).

However, for Delmar (2000), there has been an increase in the number of traits from researches, but it has been difficult to link any specific traits to entrepreneurial behaviour. Therefore, research into individual traits has been largely criticised on conceptual and methodological grounds.

The Influence of Sociology and Social Anthropology

Sociology as a discipline and sociologists have contributed immensely to the development of the field of entrepreneurship. This is to assist in understanding how societal context influences the propensity of becoming an entrepreneur and the role of entrepreneurship in the society.

The emergence of entrepreneurship in sociological thinking could be traced to the work of Max Weber. Although his ideas cannot be specifically located in his work, they exist in several different works. Weber analysed how social systems change from one stable position to another. He discussed three (3) types of leadership: bureaucratic, traditional, and charismatic leadership. The charismatic leader has a semblance of an entrepreneur, being a special type of individual with the ability to make other people follow him or her. Weber's argument was that the charismatic leader only functioned effectively as a change agent in the early stages of mankind but not in the capitalistic society. Entrepreneurship, to Weber, played a more important role with the skillful direction of the enterprises that responded to opportunities in the market environment than with the economic operations of a single individual. In his work, *The Protestant Ethic and the Spirit of Capitalism* (1904/1970), he placed a strong emphasis on the religious connections, especially on the impact of the Protestant ethic on entrepreneurship. His view was that this ethic created a positive attitude to work and to earning money, which facilitated the development of capitalism and entrepreneurship. Generally, the field of entrepreneurship in the discipline of sociology is related to other areas in the sociological discourse. Entrepreneurship is related to deviant behaviour (Hoselitz 1963; Young 1971), culture (Landes 1951; Lipset 1967), influence of structural context (Dobb 1948; Moore 1966; Wallerstein 1979) and networks (Granovetter 1985). However, there have been few studies on entrepreneurship in social anthropology but some of the pioneering works in entrepreneurship were done by anthropologists, Fredrik Barth (1963; 1967) and Clifford Geertz (1963). The social anthropologists were mostly interested in the interaction between local entrepreneurship and the social pattern of the individual.

The Forces Behind the Emergence of Entrepreneurship

There are major forces that lead to the emergence of entrepreneurship as well as to the drive behind the continual growth. These are: social turmoil, cognitive development, and social development.

1. Social turmoil

Societal transformation in the 1960s and 1970s raised questions about the efficiency of large systems and the existence of the political will to create the change which was driven by entrepreneurship, industrial dynamics and job creation. Some of the turmoils that encouraged entrepreneurship are:

a. Oil crises which triggered the changes in the world economy and global competition from the Southeast Asian countries as well as technological progress, such as the growth of computers and microprocessors.

b. Most countries experienced recession in their economies and were concerned about unemployment and the belief that the entrepreneurs were the solution to unemployment problems.

c. There were also changes in fashion, especially among young people. This was because smaller firms were perceived as dynamic and creative organizations to work in rather than the large bureaucratic firms.

d. There was also the revival of small enterprises in Europe and United States, supported by a change in political ideology which was pro-market. This was represented by the United Kingdom and the United States in 1979 and 1980 respectively.

2. Cognitive Development of Entrepreneurship

There were limited researches in entrepreneurship until the late 1970s and early 1980s, when there was a proliferation of pioneering researches in it. These works demonstrated the importance of entrepreneurship for societal dynamics and development. Therefore, these studies were hinged on the prevailing societal trends within the political system and academia.

Some of the areas that were focused on entrepreneurship in these pioneering works were on the dynamics of the economy and job creation in the society. Another area of interest in entrepreneurship studies was the interaction between entrepreneurship and regional development, but this was mostly the building of different data bases of information about young and small businesses, making it possible for researchers to identify the patterns in entrepreneurship.

3. Social Development of Entrepreneurship

This had its emergence in the field of management studies. Entrepreneurship gained a stronghold in the United States' business schools. Demands of students concerning entrepreneurship in the 1970s led schools like Harvard and Stanford to introduce entrepreneurship courses at the early stage. However, other universities gradually capitalised on this demand in the early 1970s. Most importantly, the business schools in the United States were sensitive and responsive to this demand.

The second factor in the social development of entrepreneurship was the inflow of money from wealthy alumni and foundations whose wealth was often founded on successful entrepreneurship chairs, centres and awards.

Another factor was the increasing interest in entrepreneurship on the part of politicians and policy-makers, which led to the initiation of several government support programmes across the United States and Europe to stimulate entrepreneurship scholarships and education.

Entrepreneurship in Nigeria

Entrepreneurship originated in Nigeria when production exceeded consumption levels, which resulted in the barter system, or double coincidence of wants. This is what made producers realize that if they had surplus, the people would not have to wait for double coincidence of wants. Now, the exchange of products and services is done freely in the Nigerian market. Lately, total commercialization of the act came into being.

Entrepreneurship started when people produced more products than they needed; as such, they had to exchange these surpluses. For instance, if a blacksmith produced more hoes than he needed, he exchanged the surplus he had with what he did not have but needed; maybe he needed some yams or goats and so on: he would look for someone who needed his products to exchange with. By this way, producers came to realize that they could concentrate in their areas of production to produce more and then exchange for what they needed.

Through this exchange of products, entrepreneurship started. A typical Nigerian entrepreneur is a self-made man, who might be said to have a strong will to succeed; he might engage the services of others, like friends, mates, in-laws and so on, to help him in his work or production. Availed by this, Nigerians in the olden days were able to engage in entrepreneurship. Early entrepreneurship was characterized by production or manufacturing, in which case the producer most often started with a small capital, most of it from his own savings. Early entrepreneurship started with trade by barter even before the advent of any form of money.

The Modern Stage

Modern entrepreneurship in Nigeria started with the coming of the colonial masters, who brought in their wares and made Nigerians their middlemen. In this way, modern entrepreneurship was conceived. Most of the modern entrepreneurs were engaged in retail trade or sole proprietorship.

One of the major factors that have in many ways inhibited entrepreneurship development in Nigeria is the value system that had been brought about by formal education. For many decades, formal education had been the preserve of the privileged. With formal education, people had the opportunity of being employed in the civil service, because in those days the economy was large enough to absorb the prestigious occupations and their goods. As such, the system made Nigerians dependent on the colonial masters.

Again, the contrast between Nigerians and foreign entrepreneurs during the colonial era was very detrimental, and the competitive business strategy of the foreign entrepreneurs was ruinous and against the moral standards established by the society. They did not adhere to the philosophy of 'live and let live'. For instance, the United African Company (UAC),which was responsible for a substantial percentage of the import and export trade of Nigeria, had the policy of dealing directly with producers and refused to make use of the services of Nigerian entrepreneurs. The refusal of the expatriates to utilize the services of local businessmen inhibited their expansion and acquisition of necessary skills and attitudes. Because of this, many companies and organisations eventually folded up. Those that folded up built up resentment against business, which became demoralising to other prospective entrepreneurs. As a result, the growth of entrepreneurship in the country was slowed down. But, with more people being educated and the fact that the government could no longer employ most school leavers, economic programmes meant to encourage individuals to go into private business and be self-reliant were initiated.

Such economic policies that are geared towards self-reliance for individuals are programmes like Open Apprenticeship Scheme, Graduate Employment Programs and so on, and other policies that encourage or make it easy for entrepreneurs to acquire the needed funds. Such financial institutions as Peoples Bank of Nigeria, Funds for Small Scale Industries (FUSSI), Co-operative Societies, and so on were established to assist entrepreneurs in Nigeria.

References

Aldrich, H. E.,and T. Baker. 1997. Blinded by the cites. Has there been progress in entrepreneurship research? In Sexton and   Smilor, eds., *Entrepreneurship*. Chicago, IL: Upstart.

Barth, F. 1967. Economic Spheres in Darfur. In Firth, R., ed., *Themes in Economic Anthroplology*. London: Tavistock.

Barreto, H. 1989. *The Entrepreneur in Microeconomic Theory: Disappearance and Explanation*. London: Routledge.

Busenitz, L. W., P. West, G. Shepherd, D. Nelson, T. Chandler and A. Zackarakis. 2003. Entrepreneurship in Emergence: Past Trends and Future Directions. *Journal of Management:* 29, 3, 285–308.

Carl, M. 1948/2007. *Principles of Economics*. Auburn, AL: Ludwig von Mises Institute.

Cooper, A. C., C. Y. Woo and W. C. Dunkelberg. 1988. Entrepreneurs' Perceived Chances of Success. *Journal of Business Venturing:* 3, 97–108.

Davidsson, P. 2001. Towards a Paradigm for Entrepreneurship Research. Paper at the XV RENT Conference, Turku, England.

———. 2003. The Domain of Entrepreneurship Research. In Katz, J., and D. Shepherd, eds., *Advances in Entrepreneurship, Firm Emergence and Growth*, Vol. 6. Greenwich, CT: JAI Press.

Delmar, F. 2000. The psychology of the entrepreneur. In Carter, S., and D. Jones-Evans, eds., *Enterprise and Small Business*. Harlow: Pearson Education.

Dobb, M. 1946. *Studies in the Development of Capitalism*. London: Routledge.

Drucker, P. 1985. *Innovation and Entrepreneurship*. New York: Harper and Row.

Geertz, C. 1963. *Peddlers and Princes: Social Change and Economic Modernization in Two Indonesian Towns*. Chicago: Chicago University Press.

Gartner, W. B. 1988. "Who is an Entrepreneur?" Is the wrong question. *American Journal of Small Business*: 11–32.

———. 1990. What are we talking about when we talk about entrepreneurship? *Journal of Business Venturing:* 5, 1, 15–29.

Granovetter, M. 1985. Economic Action and Social Structure: The Problem of Embeddedness. *Journal of Sociology:* 91, 3, 481–599.

Hayek, F. 1945. The use of knowledge in society. *American Economic Review*: 35, 519–530.

Hoselitz, B. F. 1963. Entrepreneurship and Traditional Elites. *Explorations in Entrepreneurial History:* 1, 2, 36–49.

Kirchhoff, B. A. 1994. *Entrepreneurship and Dynamic Capitalism*. Westport, CT: Praeger.

Kirzner, I. M. 1973. *Competition and Entrepreneurship*. Chicago: University of Chicago Press.

Knight, F. H. 1916/1921. *Risk, Uncertainty and Profit*. New York: Houghton Mifflin Press.

———. 1933. *Economic Organizations*. Chicago: University of Chicago Press.

Landes, D. 1951. French business and the businessman: a social and cultural analysis. In Earle, E. M., ed., *Modern France*. Princeton, NJ: Princeton University Press.

Langstrom, H. 2005. *Pioneers in Entrepreneurship and Small Business Research*. New York: Springer Business and Business Media Inc.

Lipset, S. M. 1967. Values, Education, and Entrepreneurship. In Lipset, S. M., and A. Solari, eds., *Elites in Latin America*. London: Oxford University Press.

McClelland, D. C. 1961. *The Achieving Society*. Princeton, NJ: Van Nostrand.

Moore, B. 1966. *The Social Origins of Dictatorship and Democracy*. Boston: Beacon Press.

Morris, M. H. 1998. *Entrepreneurial Intensity: sustainable advantages for individuals, organizations, and societies*. Westport, CT: Quorum.

Rotter, J. B. 1966. Generalised Expectations for Internal Versus External Control of Reinforcement. *American Psychological Association, Psychological Monographies*, p. 80.

Sarasvathy, S., N. Dew, S. R. Velamur, and S. Venkataraman. 2003. Three Views of Entrepreneurial Opportunities. In Acs, Z. J., and D. B. Audretsch, eds., *Handbook of Entrepreneurship Research*. Dordrecht, NL: Kluwer Academic Publishers.

Schumpeter, J. A. 1942. *Capitalism, Socialism and Democracy*. New York: Harper and Row.

Sexton, D. L., and N. Bowman. 1985. The Entrepreneur: A Capable Executive and More. *Journal of Business Venturing:* 1, 129–140.

Smith, A. 1776/1977. *Inquiry into the Nature and Causes of the Wealth of Nations*. Chicago: University of Chicago Press.

Smith, N. R. 1967. The Entrepreneur and His Firm. *Bureau of Business Research*. East Lansing, MI: Michigan State University Press.

Stevenson, H. H., and J. C. Jarillo. 1990. A Paradigm of Entrepreneurship: Entrepreneurial Management. *Strategic Management Journal*: 11, 17–27.

Timmons, J. A. 1997. *New Venture Creation*. Homewood, IL: Irwin.

Venkataraman, S. 1997. The Distinctive Domain of Entrepreneurship Research. In Katz, J. A., ed., *Advances in Entrepreneurship, Firm Emergence, and Growth,* Vol. 3. Greenwich, CT: JAI Press.

Wallerstein, I. 1979. *The Capitalist World Economy.* Cambridge, UK: Cambridge University Press.

Wennekers, S., and R. Thurik. 1999. Linking Entrepreneurship and Economic Growth. *Small Business Economics:* 13, 1, 27–55.

Say, J.-B. 1803. *Traite d'economie politique.* In Wikipedia, http://en.wikipedia.org/wiki/ Entrepreneur. Downloaded January, 2013.

Young, F. V. 1971. A macro sociological interpretation of entrepreneurship. In Kilby, P., ed., *Entrepreneurship and Economic Development.* New York: Free Press.

Chapter 5

THEORIES OF ENTREPRENEURSHIP

Akinbami, C. A. O.

Introduction

The terms 'entrepreneur' and 'entrepreneurship' are often used interchangeably. Entrepreneurship is an outcome of a complex balancing of opportunity initiatives, risks and rewards. Entrepreneurship is a process by which people pursue opportunities, fulfilling needs and wants through innovations, without regard to the resources they currently control. Although a key element of economic development is that the 'people of the country' must be major participants in the process that brings about changes in structures of economic and population growths along with consumption patterns, entrepreneurship is still a vital ingredient of economic development. Through the process of entrepreneurship, it is possible to augment the scope of capital formation, employment generation and facilitation of industrialisation in a country. Consequently, entrepreneurship acts as a powerful tool of employment generation, raising productivity through innovation, facilitating transfer of technology, playing a key role in commercialising new products, redistributing wealth and income, earning foreign exchanges, promoting social welfare, and the like (Alam and Hossan 2003).

The entrepreneur is the person who starts his own business. Richard Cantillon (1680–1734) was the first of the major economic thinkers to define the entrepreneur as an agent who buys means of production at certain prices to combine them in a new product. He classified economic agents into landowners, hirelings, and entrepreneurs, and considered the entrepreneur as the most active among these three agents, connecting the producers with customers. Jean-Baptiste Say (1767–1832) improved Cantillon's definition by adding that the entrepreneur brings people together to build a productive item.

Peter F. Drucker opined that 'an entrepreneur is one who always searches for change, responds to it and exploits it as an opportunity'. He laid emphasis on two important factors—innovation and resource—that led to the emergence of entrepreneurship. According to him, innovation is the real hub of entrepreneurship as it creates resource. A thing is a regarded as resource when its economic value is recognised. For example, mineral oil was considered worthless until the discovery of its use. Similarly, purchasing power was considered an important resource by an American innovative entrepreneur who invented installment buying. According to Drucker, successful entrepreneurship involves increased value and satisfaction obtained from a resource by the consumer. New values are created, material is converted into a resource, or existing resources are combined in a new or more productive configuration. Entrepreneurship is the practice which has a knowledge base. Entrepreneurship is not confined to big businesses and economic institutions; it is equally important to small businesses and non-economic institutions. Entrepreneurship behaviour rather than personality trait is more important to enhance entrepreneurship. The foundation of entrepreneurship lies in concept and theory rather than in intuition. Thus, Drucker has given his views that 'an entrepreneur need not be a capitalist or an owner. A banker who mobilises other's money and allocates it in areas of higher yield is very much an entrepreneur though he is not the owner of the money'.

Entrepreneurship is an evolved phenomenon. With the advancement of science and technology, it has undergone changes and emerged as a critical input for socio-economic development. The exact definition of 'entrepreneurship' still remains a vague concept, though various entrepreneurship theories have defined the concept. Theory is not merely bookish. Theory helps us to comprehend phenomena better. Researchers are always using theories to explain phenomena. Bull *et al.* (1995) have defined a theory as 'a set of interrelated constructs or concepts, definitions and propositions' that presents a systematic view of phenomena by specifying relations among variables with the purpose of explaining and predicting phenomena. Consequently, understanding a theory helps one to apply it in practice more effectively. The origins and determinants of entrepreneurship span a wide spectrum of theories and explanations (Brock and Evans 1989; Carree 1997; Carree, Van Stel, Thurik and Wennekers 2001; Gavron, Cowling, Holtham and Westall 1998; OECD 1998; Verheul *et al.* 2001). At present there are a number of entrepreneurship theories for the development of entrepreneurship. Bull *et al.* (1995) further state that entrepreneurship theory essentially consists of a new combination causing discontinuity, which will occur under the following conditions:

- task-related motivation, that is, some vision or sense of social values embedded in the basic task itself that motivated the initiator to act;
- expertise, that is, the present know-how, together with confidence to be able to obtain the know-how needed in the future;
- expectation of gain for self,which can be either economic and/or psychic benefits; and
- a supportive environment.

This chapter attempts to bring out what theories explain and motivate entrepreneurial drive. Various writers have developed various theories on entrepreneurship and popularized the concept among the common people. These theories propounded by various writers can be categorised mainly as: sociological theories, economic theories, cultural theories, and psychological theories.

Sociological Theories

There are some theories based on sociological and anthropological aspects. This is because socio-cultural factors have a substantial influence in creating an entrepreneur as well as entrepreneurship (Katz *et al.* 1991) The sociological theory of entrepreneurship holds social cultures http://www.brighthub.com/office/entrepreneurs/articles/73851.aspxas the driving force of entrepreneurship. The entrepreneur becomes a role performer in conformity with the role expectations of the society, and such role expectations are based on religious beliefs, taboos, and customs. The following theories explain how sociological factors accelerate the growth of entrepreneurs:

- Theory of religious beliefs
- Theory of social change

These theories are some of the works of Max Weber, who is the father of sociology. Max Weber (1864–1920) held religion as the major driver of entrepreneurship. The important elements of Weber's theory include spirit of capitalism, adventurous spirit, Protestant ethic and inducement of profit. The right combination of discipline and an adventurous free-spirit define the successful entrepreneur. According to him, entrepreneurism is a function of religious beliefs, and religion shapes the entrepreneurial culture. He emphasised that entrepreneurial energies are exogenously supplied by means of religious beliefs. The important elements of Weber's theory can then be seen, first, in the spirit of capitalism, and capitalism is an economic system in which economic freedom and private enterprise are major players, hence the emergence of entrepreneurial culture. Second, the adventurous spirit, in which Weber also made a distinction between the spirit of capitalism and adventurous spirit. According to him, the former (spirit of capitalism) is influenced by strict discipline, whereas the latter (adventurous spirit) is affected by free force of impulse. Entrepreneurship culture is influenced by both factors. Third, in Protestant ethic, according to Max Weber, the spirit of capitalism can be grown only when the mental attitude in the society is favourable to capitalism. Lastly, in inducement of profit, Weber introduced the new businessman into the picture of tranquil routine in which the spirit of capitalism intertwined with the motive of profit, resulting in the creation of a greater number of business enterprises.

Although this theory suited the British rulers, who desired to encourage European entrepreneurship in India, it was vehemently criticised by many researchers because of its unrealistic assumptions.

The Theory of Social Change proposed by Everett E. Hagen (1963) asserted that in a traditional society continuous technical progress is encouraged, and this theory exhorts the following features which presume the entrepreneur's creativity as the key element of social transformation and economic growth. The theory further revealed a general model of the society which considers the interrelationship among the physical environment, social structure, personality and culture. Hagen was of the opinion that the followers' syndrome on the part of the entrepreneur should be discouraged, because according to him the solution to economic development does not lie in imitating Western technology but in being creative. In his book, *How Economic Growth Begins*, he revealed that historic shift is the crucial force which can bring about social change in technological progress, thereby leading to the emergence of the entrepreneurial class from different communities. Consistent with the historic shift is the social group that plunges into rigorous entrepreneurism and experiences the status withdrawal or withdrawal of status respects. Hence, Hagen's creative personality is the admixture of Schumpeter's innovation and McClelland's high need for achievement. But Hagen's analysis fails to provide policy measures for backward countries, which are striving for economic development, as he identifies status withdrawal as the causal factor in the emergence of creative personality. Hagen's thesis of disadvantaged minority groups has its own limitations. For instance, there are many disadvantaged minority groups in India which have not supplied a good number of entrepreneurs. Briefly put, E. E. Hagen's theory:

- reveals a general model of the social interrelationship among the physical environment, social structure, personality and culture;
- thinks economic theories are inadequate;
- finds political and social change the catalysts for entrepreneurs;
- rejects followers' syndrome imitating Western technology;
- considers technology an integral part of the socio-cultural complex;
- proposes historic shift as a factor initiating change.

Another anthropological theory, named Marginal and Tension Theory, which was introduced by Robert Park in 1928, stated that a marginal man is one whose fate has condemned him to live in two societies. The two societies are not merely different but antagonistic cultures, like occidental and oriental cultures. Sometimes, for their existence, marginal men engage themselves in business because the marginal man cannot be accepted widely in any society. So, from the group of marginal men, there is a likelihood of creating more entrepreneurs (Islam and Mamun 2000).

All these reveal some variables for entrepreneurship development. These variables are:

- need for achievement;
- withdrawal of status;
- training for changing individual's mentality, thinking and attitude, etc.;
- risk-taking mentality;
- self-confidence, extreme belief in one's ability and power;
- creative ability;
- authority or personal power;
- inherent goodness of work, self-restraint in the case of consumption profit; and
- social marginality.

All these variables are found from existing prominent theories of entrepreneurship. These psychological and sociological variables are the qualitative type, and they play stimulative roles in an individual towards becoming an entrepreneur. These variables explain only the initial stage of entrepreneurship development process, that is, why and when an individual acts as an entrepreneur. But these variables do not explain the post-initial stage of the entrepreneurship development process. As a result, we don't find any guidelines relating to how entrepreneurs use their resources (capital, skill, risk-taking ability, etc.) and overcome their barriers (coordination, knowledge) from these models (Alam and Hossan 2003).

Economic Theories

Entrepreneurship and economic development are interdependent. Economic development takes place when a country's real national income increases over all periods of time, wherein the role of entrepreneurs is an integral part. Schumpeter's Theory of Innovation/ Theory of Entrepreneurship is a pioneering work of economic development. 'Development' in his sense implies that carrying out a new combination of entrepreneurship is basically a creative activity. According to Schumpeter, an entrepreneur is one who perceives the opportunities to innovate, i.e., to carry out new combinations of enterprise. In his views, the concept of new combination leading to innovation covers the following cases:

- the introduction of new goods, that is, ones with which consumers are not yet familiar, of a new quality;
- the introduction of new methods of production;
- the opening of new markets;
- the conquest of a new source of supply of raw materials; and
- the carrying out of new organisation.

In view of the above, Schumpeterian theory of entrepreneurship has the following features:

- Distinction between invention and innovation: Schumpeter makes a distinction between innovation and invention. Invention means creation of new things and innovation means application of new things for practical use.
- Emphasis on entrepreneurial function: Schumpeter has laid emphasis on the role of entrepreneurial functions in economic development. In his views, development means basic transformation of the economy that is brought about by entrepreneurial functions.
- Presentation of disequilibrium situation through entrepreneurial activity: The entrepreneurial activity represents a disequilibrium situation, a dynamic phenomenon and a break from routine or a circular flow or tendency towards equilibrium.
- Entrepreneurialism dream and the will to found a private kingdom: The motives of creating things and applying them for practical purposes inspire the entrepreneur to undertake innovation.

It should be noted that Schumpeter's theory of innovation is criticised on the following grounds:

- The theory has the scope of entrepreneurism in the sense that it has included the individual businessman along with the directors and managers of the company. Schumpeter's innovating entrepreneurs represent the enterprise with research and development (R and D) and innovative character, but the developing countries lack these characters.
- The theory emphasises innovation and excludes the risk-taking and organising aspects.
- Schumpeter's entrepreneurs are large-scale businessmen who introduce new technology and/or new methods of production.
- Schumpeter's entrepreneursare large-scale businessmen, who are rarely found in developing countries, where entrepreneurs are small-scale businessmen, who need to imitate rather than innovate.

- Schumpeter remained silent about why some economies had more entrepreneurial talents than others.

However, despite the above criticisms, Schumpeterian theory is regarded as one of the best theories in the history of entrepreneurial development.

In his Theory of Achievement/Theory of Innovation, McClelland (1917–1988) identifies two characteristics of entrepreneurship as:

- doing things in a new and better way;
- decision-making under uncertainty.

He stressed that people with high achievement orientation (need to succeed) were more likely to become entrepreneurs. Such people are not influenced by money or external incentives. They consider profit to be a measure of success and competency.

McClelland further opines that a person has three types of needs or motives for accomplishing things at any given time, which are:

- need for achievement (get success through one's own efforts);
- need for power (to dominate, influence others);
- need for affiliation (maintain friendly relations with others).

Although the need for achievement and need for power drive entrepreneurship, the need for achievement is the higher priority for entrepreneurs.

David McClelland considers entrepreneurs as people who do things in a better way and make decisions in times of uncertainty. The dream to achieve big things overpowers monetary or other external incentives.

McClelland also conducted what is known as the Kakinada experiment in America, Mexico and Mumbai. In this experiment, young adults were selected and put through a three-month training programme. The training aimed at inducing the achievement motivation. The course contents consisted of:
- trainees were asked to control their thinking and talk to themselves, positively;
- they should imagine themselves in need of challenges and successes for which they had to set planned and achievable goals;
- they should strive to get concrete and frequent feedback;
- they should try to imitate their role models/those who performed well.

From the results of this experiment, he was able to conclude that:

- traditional beliefs do not inhibit an entrepreneur;
- suitable training can provide necessary motivation for an entrepreneur;
- the achievement motivation has a positive impact on the performance of the participants.

Finally, it was the Kakinada experiment that made people realise the importance of Entrepreneurial Development Programme (EDP) towards inducing motivation and competence in young, prospective entrepreneurs.

Frank Knight (1885–1972) first introduced the dimension of risk-taking as a central characteristic of entrepreneurship. He adopted the theory of early economists such as Richard Cantillon and J.-B. Say and added the dimension of risk-taking. This theory considers uncertainty as a factor of production and holds the main function of the entrepreneur as acting in anticipation of future events. The entrepreneur earns profit as a reward for taking such risks.

Alfred Marshall in his *Principles of Economics* (1890) held land, labour, capital, and organisation as the four factors of production, and considered entrepreneurship as the driving factor that brings these four factors together. According to him, the characteristics of a successful entrepreneur include:

- thorough understanding of the industry;
- good leadership skills;
- foresight on demand and supply changes; and
- the willingness to act on such risky foresights.

The success of an entrepreneur, however, depends not on the possession of these skills, but on the economic situations in which the entrepreneur operates.

Many economists have modified Marshall's theory to consider the entrepreneur as the fourth factor itself instead of organisation, and which coordinates the other three factors.

Mark Casson (1945) holds that entrepreneurship is a result of conducive economic conditions. In his book *Entrepreneurship, an Economic Theory,* he states that the demand for entrepreneurship arises from the demand for change. He states that the economic conditions that encourage or discourage entrepreneurshiphttp://www.brighthub.com/office/entrepreneurs/articles/73616.aspxinclude:

- taxation policy;
- industrial policy;
- easy availability of raw materials;
- easy access to finance on favourable terms;
- access to information about market conditions;
- availability of technology and infrastructure;
- marketing opportunities.

Joseph Schumpeter's innovation theory of entrepreneurship (1949) holds an entrepreneur as one having three major characteristics: innovation, foresight, and creativity. He believes that entrepreneurship takes place when the entrepreneur:

- creates a new product;
- introduces a new way to make a product;
- discovers a new market for a product;
- finds a new source of raw materials;
- finds new ways of making things or organisation.

Schumpeter's innovation theory, however, ignores the entrepreneur's risk-taking ability and organisational skills, and places undue importance on innovation. This theory applies to large-scale businesses, but economic conditions force small entrepreneurs to imitate rather than innovate.

Other economists have added a dimension of imitating and adapting to innovation. This entails successful imitation by adapting a product to a niche in a better way than the original product innovators' innovation.

Israel Kirzner (1935) holds that spontaneous learning and alertness are the two major characteristics of entrepreneurship, and entrepreneurship is the transformation of spontaneous learning to conscious knowledge, motivated by the prospects of some gain. Kirzner considers the alertness to recognise opportunity more characteristic than innovation in defining entrepreneurship. The entrepreneur either remedies ignorance or corrects errors of the customers. His entrepreneurship model holds that:

- the entrepreneur subconsciously discovers an opportunity to earn money by buying resources or producing a good and selling it;
- the entrepreneur finances the venture by borrowing money from a capitalist;
- the entrepreneur uses the funds for his entrepreneurial venture;
- the entrepreneur pays back the capitalist, including interest, and retains the 'pure entrepreneurial profit'.

Harvey Leibenstein (1922–1994) considers entrepreneurs as gap-fillers. The three traits of entrepreneurship, according to him, include:
- recognising market trends;
- developing new goods or processes in demand but not in supply; and
- determining profitable activities.

Entrepreneurs have the special ability to connect different markets and make up for market failures and deficiencies.

For Peter Drucker (1909–2005) innovation, resources, and an entrepreneurial behaviour are the keys to entrepreneurship. According to him, entrepreneurship involves:

- increase in value or satisfaction to the customer from the resource;
- creation of new values;
- combination of existing materials or resources in a new productive combination.

How Economic Factors Influence Entrepreneurship

The nature of the economy is a major factor that influences entrepreneurship. The following reveals the interrelationship between the economy of a nation and entrepreneurial activities.
- The general purchasing power of the people, which manifests itself in the income levels and economic prosperity of a region, plays a major role in the success of entrepreneurial ventures.
- During times of economic slowdown or recession, the purchasing power declines and people remain reluctant to invest, affecting entrepreneurship adversely.

- In a subsistence economy, most of the people are engaged in agriculture, consuming most of their output and bartering the rest for simple goods and services. Entrepreneurial opportunities are few in such scenarios.

Availability of Resources as a Major Factor that Affects Entrepreneurship

Other critical factors that influence entrepreneurship include the availability of resources such as capital, human assets, raw materials, infrastructure, and utilities.
- Capital remains indispensable for the purpose of starting an enterprise. The availability of capital allows the entrepreneur to bring together other factors and use them to produce goods or services.
- The importance of human assets or employees can never be underestimated. No enterprise succeeds without a skilled and committed workforce.
- The very existence of the business depends on the availability of raw materials.
- Physical infrastructure and utilities such as good roads, parking lots, communication facilities, and power all play a crucial factor in the seamless functioning of a business.

Cultural Theories

The popular perception of entrepreneurship is of a heroic individual or an economically successful firm (Cole 1959; Collins *et al.* 1964; Schumpeter 1934). However, this fundamental attribution error continues to erode in the face of increasing evidence showing that individuals and entrepreneurship are socially embedded in network structures (Aldrich and Zimmer 1986; Casson and Della Giusta 2007; Johannisson 1988) which are situated within a specific cultural context (Hofstede 2001). Hence, the need to analyse the social and cultural factors that influence the decisions to create new businesses.

Since societies are endowed by nature with different physical environments, members of society must adopt environmentally relevant patterns of behaviour to achieve success. These environmentally relevant patterns of behaviour lead to the formation of different cultural values in different societies, some of which influence the decision to create new businesses. Thus, culture, as distinct from political, social, technological or economic contexts, has relevance for economic behaviour and entrepreneurship (Shane 1993; Shapero and Sokol 1982).

One of the difficulties in examining cultural effects in relation to entrepreneurial activity is the lack of a precise and commonly understood definition of culture (McGrath *et al.* 1992). Anthropologists suggest that culture is related to the ways in which societies organise social behaviour and knowledge (Hall 1973; Kroeber and Parsons 1958). Cultural values are defined as the collective programming of the mind which distinguishes the members of one human group from another and their respective responses to their environments (Hofstede 1980).

Several studies have stressed the influence of cultural factors on entrepreneurship from different perspectives. Hayton *et al.* (2002), in their literature review, link culture and entrepreneurship to three broad streams of research. The first focuses on the impact of national culture on aggregate measures of entrepreneurship such as national innovative output or new businesses created. The second stream addresses the association between national culture and the characteristics of individual entrepreneurs. The third explores the impact of national culture on corporate entrepreneurship. Accordingly, when an individual creates a business in a specific cultural environment, this business reflects that cultural environment, for example, characteristics such as strategic orientation and growth expectations for the business.

Much of the research in entrepreneurship that considers cultural variables has followed Hofstede's (1980, 2001) seminal work, showing how culture is manifested in various forms, and how cultural values at individual or societal levels are influenced by national culture. According to this view, cultural differences across societies can be reduced to four quantifiable dimensions, which are stated as:

- uncertainty avoidance,
- individualism,
- masculinity, and
- power distance.

The dimension of uncertainty avoidance represents preference for certainty and discomfort with unstructured or ambiguous situations. Individualism stands for a preference for acting in the interest of one's self and immediate family, as distinct from the dimension of collectivism, which stands for acting in the interest of a larger group in exchange for their loyalty and support. Power distance represents the acceptance of inequality in position and authority between people. Masculinity stands for a belief in materialism and decisiveness rather than service and intuition. Using Hofstede's (1980) concept of culture, researchers have in general hypothesised that entrepreneurship is facilitated by cultures that are high in individualism, low in uncertainty avoidance, low in power-distance and high in masculinity (Hayton *et al.* 2002).

Anthropologists view entrepreneurship as well as other social processes as cultural processes (e.g., Greenfield and Strickon 1986; Stewart 1991). The important roles of norms and traditions have been demonstrated in various researches. Although society norms generally do not inhibit entrepreneurship, they can influence, in some cases, the entrepreneurial process. From an anthropological perspective, attention to social and cultural factors that are related to the creation of a new business has provided interesting contributions to the understanding of entrepreneurship, especially through the study of social constraints (Garlick 1971; Kennedy 1988; Wiewel and Hunter 1985) and collective approaches (e.g., family business, community-centered business, ethnic or organisational entrepreneurship) to business formation and growth (Benedict 1968; Davis and Ward 1990; Kleinberg 1983; Parker 1988).

Advocates of cultural theories point out that entrepreneurship is the product of culture. Entrepreneurial talents come from cultural values and cultural systems that are embedded in the cultural environment. Hoselitz's Theory explains that the supply of entrepreneurship is governed by cultural factors, and minority groups in a cultural context are the spark-plugs of entrepreneurial and economic development. In many countries, entrepreneurs have emerged from a particular socio-economic class. He emphasises the role of culturally-marginalised groups like Jews and the Greeks in medieval Europe, the Chinese in South Africa and the Indians in East Africa in promoting economic development. Various writers lay emphasis on various aspects of culture that interface with entrepreneurial capability:

a) Hoselitz's Theory

Hoselitz explains that the supply of entrepreneurship is governed by cultural factors and that minority groups are the spark-plugs of entrepreneurial economic development. His theory places emphasis on:

i) Marginal men – They are reservoirs of entrepreneurial development. Their ambiguous positions from a cultural or social perspective make them creative.

ii) Emphasis on skills – Entrepreneurial people are those who possess extra-ordinary skills such as managerial and leadership skills, and, of course, personal traits.

iii) Contribution of social classes – The socio-economic background of specific classes makes them entrepreneurs. For instance, family patterns in France, Protestants in UK/USA, and Parsees in India.

How Cultural Factors Influence Entrepreneurship

As stated before, culture refers to the customary practices and beliefs that have a significant impact on the basic values, perceptions, preferences, and behaviours of people. What makes some entrepreneurs tick while others fail? Why do people in some cultures and regions display a better entrepreneurial spirit compared to people in other cultures or areas? The following give an overview of the major factors that reveal the intervening influences of culture on entrepreneurship:

- People traditionally who are engaged in businesses have a pro-business attitude and disdain working as employees.
- Many people fall outside the establishment and remain unsuited for the traditional job market due to a strong culture of independence or other reasons.
- Business school students come under the missionary zeal of teachers who exhort them to become entrepreneurs even if the opportunity cost is very high.
- The culture of consumerism, in which people desire material goods, encourages entrepreneurship within the area as returns from a business become more than returns from a job.
- People engaged in jobs and other services pressure their children to find secure jobs and crush their entrepreneurship spirit at a very early age.
- A culture of thrift, in which people spend less and save for a rainy day, discourages entrepreneurship within the local community as the returns from a business become less attractive compared to returns from a job.
- Cultures where people are averse to risk and do not attach much importance to hard work and persistence are not conducive to entrepreneurship.

How Political Environments Support or Suppress Entrepreneurship

The political culture also has its effects on entrepreneurship. The following are some of the ways in which the political environment influences entrepreneurship (Nayab 2011):

- Unstable political conditions, in which government policies change frequently, discourage business as investors fear for the safety of their investments.
- Government support for economic development through infrastructure development, facilitation, industrial parks and the like all encourage entrepreneurship.
- High taxes that cut into returns usually discourage entrepreneurs. On the other hand, tax holidays to encourage business attract start-ups.
- The availability of infrastructure and utilities such as good roads, power, communication facilities, and lack of corruption and bureaucratic delays in obtaining such utilities encourage entrepreneurship.
- Economic freedom in the form of favourable legislation and few hurdles to start and operate businesses encourage entrepreneurship.
- While most businesses accept laws that are related to the safeguarding of labour rights and the environment, some countries have retrograde laws that make compliance very difficult and time-consuming. Such legal hurdles create a barrier to entrepreneurship.

Psychological Theories

Psychological theories centre around the psychological characteristics of the individual in a society. Psychological characteristics affect the emergence of entrepreneurs in the society. The essence of psychological or personal theory is the difference in individuals' attitudes. According to this theory, the difference in attitude, i.e., the internal attitude and ability to judge and forecast the situation, lead a man to become a successful entrepreneur. Some important theories of this field are discussed below.

David McClelland's theory on the need for achievement is the most important of all the various psychological theories on entrepreneurship. In his theory, McClelland emphasised the relationship of achievement motivation or need for achievement to economic development via entrepreneurial activities. He wrote that 'the presumed mechanism by which the need for achievement level translates itself into economic growth is the entrepreneurial class. If the need for achievement level is high, there will presumably be more people who behave like entrepreneurs' (Islam 1989). According to McClelland, one would expect a relatively greater amount of entrepreneurship in a society if the average level of need for achievement in that society is relatively high. Because having a high need for achievement encourages an individual to develop challenging goals, the entrepreneur works hard to achieve desired goals and uses skills and abilities needed to accomplish them (Islam 1989). Moreover, it is the inner drive of individuals that propels them to work more and to achieve something for their own interest by taking personal risk (Islam and Mamun 2000). Need for achievement then reflects a strong goal orientation, and an obsession with the job or task to be done. So entrepreneurship becomes the link or intervening variable between need for achievement and economic growth. Consequently, McClelland advocates increasing the level of need for achievement in a society in order to stimulate entrepreneurship and economic growth (Islam 1989). Furthermore, according to McClelland, entrepreneurs are activated by the high extent of achievement motivation and a desire to do well, not so much for the sake of social recognition or prestige, but for an inner feeling of personal accomplishment. This longing for fulfillment induces people to be entrepreneurs (Islam and Mamun 2000). He also suggests that the need for achievement level can be increased in an individual through training and by creating the appropriate culture.

In the theory of withdrawal of status respect, Everett Hagen's argument is that certain social changes are the cause of psychological changes in a group or in an individual. He believes that the initial condition leading to eventual entrepreneurial behaviour is the loss of status by a group or collectivity (Islam 1989). According to Hagen, loss of status can occur in one of the four ways:

- the group may be displaced by force;
- it may have its valued symbols denigrated;
- it may drift into a situation of status inconsistency; and
- it may not be accepted in a new society.

The outcomes from or reactions to the loss of status are retreatism, ritualism, innovation, reformism and rebellion. Among these reactions, retreatism is important for entrepreneurship because it is characterised by psychological repression or the trauma associated with the status loss. The suppressed rage resulting from the loss of status ultimately emerges in a later generation, in which the standard of achievement is being held up by mothers within the group and passed on to their sons. Consequently, the son's opportunity for becoming an innovator is increased and entrepreneurship becomes a feasible outlet for such tendencies (Islam 1989). However, this theory has been criticised for two major reasons. The first reason is that this theory is post-hoc; this implies that Hagen discovered instances of the withdrawal of status respect by looking first at situations in which economic growth occurred and then by looking for status losses that might have preceded that growth. The second criticism has centered on the long period of time, because as much as five or more generations are required for the withdrawal of status respect to result in the emergence of entrepreneurship.

Motive-Acquisition theory, which is a revised version of McClelland's need for achievement theory, expresses the view that mentality, personality, thinking power, attitude, etc., are not in-born but that they are flexible and change with situations. So this theory advocates in favour of frequent training and development programmes to influence and motivate an individual towards a goal by changing his/her thinking, mentality, attitude, etc. (Islam and Mamun 2000).

Risk-taking theory, which is introduced by Richard Cantillon and John Stuart Mill, defines entrepreneurship as a mentality to take moderate or calculated risks, because people taking a very big risk also have a great responsibility. Then, to perform this responsibility, people have to take initiatives, and these initiatives result in entrepreneurship.

Another psychological theory of entrepreneurship, named Creativity or Innovation Theory, highlights the physical performance as the determinant that is used to evaluate whether an individual is creative or not, because the creative individual uses his talents and thinking ability to create new and fundamental ideas or views and also to find out techniques that will bring new ideas into practice. On the contrary, Power Motivation Theory has laid emphasis on the authority to do a certain task properly. For entrepreneurship development in particular, personal power, which is related to self-interest, is essential.

Internal-External Locus of Control theory, introduced by Professor J. D. Rotter of Ohio University, highlights the self-confidence of a person, the dependency on fortune and external environment for becoming an entrepreneur. According to this theory, internal locus of control, i.e., self-confidence and extreme belief in one's ability and power, motivates individuals in a society to take initiatives for innovation, which is very helpful for the individuals and society (Islam and Mamun 2000). On the other hand, Independence Motivation Theory is similar to Internal-External Locus of Control Theory, which also emphasises the independent thinking of entrepreneurs. This theory expresses the contention that people having independent thinking, self-confidence and self-controlling ability can avoid social condemnation for becoming an entrepreneur.

How Entrepreneurial Skill and Psychological Orientation Affect Entrepreneurship

All other factors notwithstanding, the success of an entrepreneurial venture depends on the entrepreneur. The entrepreneur is the leader and driver of the venture, and he requires the following skills and orientation to achieve success (Barclay and Boston 1989; Kotler and Armstrong 2004):
- hard work and persistence;
- ability to manage and minimise risk;
- ability to draw up a comprehensive business plan, and having a contingency plan ready;
- a strong need-orientation that provides the inclination to achieve things.

With collapsing trade barriers bringing in greater opportunities and job security passé, the conditions for entrepreneurship are better now than ever before.

Other Theories

The Knowledge Spillover Theory of Entrepreneurship

This is a new theory of entrepreneurship which postulates that the creation of new knowledge expands the technological opportunity set. Therefore, entrepreneurial activity does not involve simply the arbitrage of opportunities but the exploitation of knowledge spillovers not appropriated by incumbent firms. The Knowledge Spillover Theory of Entrepreneurship (Acs *et al.* 2006) shifts the fundamental decision-making unit of analysis in the model of economic growth away from exogenously assumed firms to individual agents with endowments of new economic knowledge. Agents with new knowledge endogenously pursue the exploitation of knowledge, suggesting that the stock of knowledge yields knowledge spillovers and that there is a strong relationship between such spillovers and entrepreneurial activity. If incumbent firms appropriated all the results of R and D, there would be no knowledge spillover.

There are several implications of these findings. First, the theory helps us bridge the gap between the subjective literature on entrepreneurship and the objective literature on the sources of opportunity. Entrepreneurship theories need to be able to explain where opportunities come from, how knowledge spillovers occur, and how occupational choice arises in the context of existing corporations that lead to new firm formation. Prevailing theories of entrepreneurship are not able to answer these questions. Second, the theory helps us to better understand the contradictions in Smith's *Wealth of Nations* between increasing returns (the pin factory) and how the market economy can harness self-interest for the common good, leading each individual to an end which was not part of his intention (the invisible hand). The real challenge in endogenous growth theory is not that the firm will not invest enough in new knowledge, but how to balance increasing returns with competition. The Knowledge Spillover Theory of Entrepreneurship provides an explanation for the relationship between the role of the individual in the economy and the firm.

HBS (Harvard Business School)

The HBS considers that entrepreneurship is the outcome of the combination of internal and external forces. According to Chetty (2010):

Internal forces are the individual's traits and qualities, viz. :
- intelligence,
- skill,
- knowledge,
- intuition,
- exposure and experience.

External forces are the surrounding conditions, viz. :
- economic,
- political,
- social and cultural,
- legal frame-work.

Stable government, external security, law and order, and legal process are the influencing factors.

Conclusion

This chapter reviewed various entrepreneurship theories such as sociological, psychological, economical, cultural and contemporary. The sociological theories see the entrepreneur as a role performer conforming to the expectations of the society, which are based on religious beliefs, taboos, and customs.

The economic theories reveal that an entrepreneur must possess certain characteristics such as innovation, foresight and creativity, and the ability to employ these characteristics to operate in different markets to make up for market failure and deficiencies.

Cultural theories show that individuals and entrepreneurship are socially embedded in network structures which are situated within a specific cultural context. Cultural theories see entrepreneurship as a product of culture.

Generally, the psychological theories deal with individual traits that will enhance the ability to make appropriate judgements and take necessary and timely decisions; these will lead to successful entrepreneurship practices.

The contemporary theories generally provide explanation for the relationship between the role of the individual in the economy and the firm. They also help to bridge the gap between subjective literature in entrepreneurship and the objective literature in sources of opportunity.

However, analysis of the various entrepreneurship theories reveals that, while economists differ on the force that drives entrepreneurs or the central characteristics of entrepreneurship, they remain unanimous that entrepreneurship is a distinct concept and a central factor of the economic activity.

References

Acs, Z. J., D. B. Audretsch, P. Braunerhjelm and B.Carlsson. (2006) The Knowledge Spillover Theory of Entrepreneurship. CESIS, Electronic Working Paper Series, Paper No.77.

Alam, J., and M. A. Hossan. (2003). Linking between Franchising Networks for Entrepreneurship and Economical Development—Looking for a New Model. Paper presented at the EMNet-Conference on Economics and Management of Franchising Networks, Vienna, Austria, June 26–28, 2003. www.univie.ac.at/EMNET

Aldrich, H. E., and C. Zimmer. (1986) Entrepreneurship through Social Networks. In: Sexton, D., and R. Smilor (eds.), *The Art and Science of Entrepreneurship*. New York: Ballinger, 3–23.

Barclay, M. J., and S. Boston. (1989) Factors Influencing International Entrepreneurship in the Hospitality Industry. *Journal of Hospitality and Tourism Research*, Vol. 13, No. 3, 547.

Benedict, B. (1968). Family Firms and Economic Development. *Southwestern Journal of Anthropology,* 24:1–19.

Brock, W. A., and D. S. Evans. (1989) Small Business Economics. *Small Business Economics* (1), 7–20.

Cantillon, R. (1755) Essai sur la nature du commerce en general. London. (Reprinted for Harvard University Press, Boston: G. H. Ellis, 1892.)

Carree, M. A. (1997) Market Dynamics, Evolution and Smallness. Amsterdam: Thesis Publishers and Tinbergen Institute.

———, A. Van Stel, A. R. Thurik and A. R. M. Wennekers. (2001) Economic Development and Business Ownership: An Analysis Using Data of 23 Modern Economies in the Period 1976-1996. *Small Business Economics*.

Casson, M., and M. Della Giusta. (2007) Entrepreneurship and Social Capital: Analysing the Impact of Social Networks on Entrepreneurial Activity from a Rational Action Perspective. *International Small Business Journal* 25(3):220–244.

Chetty. (2010) http://www.projectguru.in/publications/theories-of-entrepreneurship.

Cole, A. (1959) *Business Enterprise in its Social Setting*. Cambridge, MA: Harvard University Press.

Collins, O. F., D. G. Moore and D. B. Unwalla. (1964) *The Enterprising Man*. East Lansing: Michigan State University Business Studies.

Davis, D. R., and M. D. Ward. (1990) The Entrepreneurial State: Evidence from Taiwan. *Comparative Political Studies* 23:314–333.

Garlick, P. C. (1971) *African Traders and Economic Development in Ghana*. London: Oxford University Press.

Gavron, R., M. Cowling, G. Holtham and A. Westall. (1998) *The Entrepreneurial Society*. London: Institute for Public Policy Research.

Greenfield, S. M., and A. Strickon. (1986) Introduction. In: Greenfield, S. M., and A. Strickon (eds.), *Entrepreneurship and Social Change*. Lanham, MD: University Press of America, 4–18.

Hall, E. T. (1973) *The Silent Language*. New York: Anchor.

Hayton, J. C., G. George and S. A. Zahra.(2002) National Culture and Entrepreneurship: A Review of Behavioural Research. *Entrepreneurship Theory and Practice* 26(4): 33–52.

Hofstede, G. (1980) *Culture's Consequences: International Differences in Work-related Values*. Beverly Hills, CA: SAGE.

———. (2001) *Culture's Consequences: Comparing Values, Behaviors, Institutions and Organizations across Nations*, 2nd ed. Thousand Oaks, CA: SAGE.

Islam, M. M. (1989) Theories on Entrepreneurship. In: Habibur, Rahman (ed.), *Entrepreneurship*. Bangladesh: University Grand Commission (English version).

Islam, N., and Z. M. Mamun. (2000) *Entrepreneurship Development: An Operational Approach*. Bangladesh: The University Press Limited.

Johannisson, B. (1988) Business Formation: A Network Approach.*Scandinavian Journal of Management* 4(3-4): 83–99.

Katz, J. A. (1991) The Institution and Infrastructure of Entrepreneurship. *Entrepreneurship Theory and Practice* 15(3).

Kennedy, P. (1988) *African Capitalism: The Struggle for Ascendancy*. New York: Cambridge University Press.

Kirzner, I. M. (1973) *Competition and Entrepreneurship*. Chicago: University of Chicago Press.

———. (1999) Creativity and/or Alertness: A Reconsideration of the Schumpeterian Entrepreneur. *Review of Austrian Economics*, Vol. 11, pp.5–17.

Kleinberg, J. (1983) Where Work and the Family are Almost One: The Lives of Folkcraft Potters. In: Plath, D. W. (ed.), *Work and Lifecourse in Japan*. Albany, NY: State University of New York Press, 215–247.

Kotler, P., and G. Armstrong. (2004) *Principles of Marketing*. Englewood Cliffs, NJ: Prentice Hall.

Kroeber, A. L., and T. Parsons. (1958) The Concepts of Culture and Social System. *American Sociological Review* 23: 582–83.

Leibenstein, H. (1968) Entrepreneurship and Development. Papers and Proceedings of the Eightieth Annual Meeting of the American Economic Association. *The American Economic Review*, Vol. 58, No. 2, pp. 72–83.

McClelland, D. (1961) *The Achieving Society*. Princeton, NJ: Princeton University Press.

McGrath, R. G., I. C. Macmillan, E. Ai-Yuan Yang and W. Tsai. (1992) Does Culture Endure or Is It Malleable? *Journal of Business Venturing* 7:441–458.

Nayab, N. (2011) Factors Having an Impact on Starting and Operating a Business. Edwards,Ginny (ed.).
http://www.brighthub.com/office/entrepreneurs/articles/73616.aspx

Organization for Economic Co-operation and Development. (1998) *Fostering Entrepreneurship: the OECD Jobs Strategy*. Paris: OECD.

Parker, B. (1988) Moral Economy, Political Economy, and the Culture of Entrepreneurship in Highland Nepal. *Ethnology*27: 181–194.

Say, J.-B. (1803) *A Treatise on Political Economy*, 4th ed. Paris: Deterville (reprinted by Lippincott, Grambo and Co., Philadelphia, 1855).

———. (1828) *Cours complet d'économie politique pratique*, Vol. 6. Paris: Guillaumin (reprint 1840).

Schumpeter, J. A. (1911) *The Theory of Economic Development: An Inquiry into Profits, Capital, Credit, Interest and the Business Cycle*. Translated by Opie, Redvers, 1934. Cambridge: Harvard University Press.

———. (1934). The Theory of Economic Development. *Harvard Economic Studies Series* Vol. XLVI.

———. (1939) *Business Cycles*. New York: McGraw-Hill.

Shane, S. (1993) Cultural Influences on National Rates of Innovation. *Journal of Business Venturing* 8:59–73.

Shapero, A., and L. Sokol. (1982) The Social Dimensions of Entrepreneurship. In: Kent, C., L. Sexton and K. Vesper (eds.), *Encyclopedia of Entrepreneurship*. Englewood Cliffs, NJ: Prentice Hall, 72–90.

Stewart, A. (1991) A Prospectus on the Anthropology of Entrepreneurship. *Entrepreneurship Theory and Practice* 16(2):71–91.

Verheul, I., S. Wennekers, D. Audretsch, and R. Thurik. (2001) An Eclectic Theory of Entrepreneurship: Policies, Institutions and Culture. Tinbergen Institute Discussion Paper, TI 2001-030/3, Erasmus Universiteit Rotterdam, Universiteit van Amsterdam and Vrije Universiteit Amsterdam.

Wiewel, W., and A. Hunter. (1985) The Interorganizational Network as a Resource: a Comparative Case Study on Organizational Genesis. *Administrative Science Quarterly* 30: 482–496.

Chapter 6

BUSINESS STATISTICS

Titilayo, A.

Introduction

The purpose of this chapter is for students, business practitioners, and other readers of cognate concerns to have a basic and first-hand understanding of business management and for them to know the basic application and importance of statistics in it.

Contemporary experiences have proven that applications of theories without empirical instances are nothing but a baseless argument that could be faulted without stress. That is, in the modern day, be it in the physical, natural or social sciences' perspective, no application of theory could stand the test of time without the application of empirical ideas and realities.

Collection of empirical ideas and realities (observation, modeling and verification) in any field of human endeavour without further analytical processing that will always involve statistical application and understanding would do no good or have any logical and sensible meaning at the end. Business studies and management is one principal discipline that cannot be divorced from the general umbrella of social science. It is an essential arm of life: analysis cannot be done without a good reference to or explanation of human behavior. Statistics extends to almost every realm of human endeavor. The above explanation, therefore, makes the application of statistics in business management as important an issue as the vein is to functional human bodies for the transferring of blood.

Statistics is such an important, valuable, viable and interesting aspect of life that its study cannot be overemphasized. If applied appropriately, statistics gives meaning to all the day-to-day activities of our lives. Consciously or unconsciously, every living soul takes decisions in one area of life or the other, at every minute of his or her life, but the one taken with the application of a good statistics, no matter how simple it might look, will always yield a better conclusion and invariably good results.

But despite a very wide use of well-applied statistics to decisions, many students, most especially in the social and business world, have a phobia against statistics, probably because of its mathematical proclivity. Attempts will be made in this chapter not to over-labour them with mathematical jargon but with attention to basic facts that are needed to have a good understanding of how to arrive at good and accurate business decisions. Concepts of descriptive and inferential statistics—that will enhance understanding of business data collection, analysis, summary and presentation—and how raw, "scattered" information can be gathered to make up organized data that will provide meaningful and better business information—which will come out to help students and business managers in making better business—will be discussed decisions.

It is, therefore, pertinent at this juncture to note that before any individual or corporate body or organization can have any meaningful, rich and interesting statistics ready for decision making, a good and well-conducted research or study must have taken place.

Take for instance,
- ✓ Fifty-four percent of Sand A Consulting firm's clients are based in North Central Nigeria.
- ✓ Twelve percent of the subscribers to the recently introduced bundle plan for internet connection of GIN-GIN Communication Ltd. are complaining of poor signals and therefore wish to drop the product for any other alternative available.
- ✓ The recent occurrence in some parts of the country has caused a 27% drop in the profit margin of my clients.
- ✓ Unemployment rate in some parts of the country has increased by 5% due to the recent threats to life.
- ✓ An increase in crime rate in the country of about 15% has been statistically ascribed to the recent politically and religiously ignited crisis in some parts of the country.
- ✓ Close to seven out of ten consumers of the product were very satisfied in the first five years of production, but the satisfaction rate dropped to two out of ten thereafter.

If one looks at the above reports, one will note that none of these would have come to being without a previously conducted research or study, either by the authors of those reports or via secondary-sourced data.

What is business statistics?

The best way to do a good judgment to the definition and introduction of business statistics is by answering the question: *What is statistics*? Having diverse meanings, the word "statistics" can be used in different ways. On a broad scale, the *Oxford Advanced Learner's Dictionary* defines statistics as the science of collecting and analysing information in form of numbers. This could be stated in another way: statistics is a systematic arrangement of information or facts in numerical figures towards the arrival at a meaningful and intelligent conclusion. In other words, statistics is a meaningful, useful science, whose broad scope of applications to individual, business or government decisions and to the physical and social sciences are almost limitless. In a concise term, statistical analysis is an attempt to generalize reports from collected data or information. The usefulness of statistics in business management can be discerned in the following: understanding the presentation and description of business information, knowing how to draw business conclusions from information gathered from sub-sets (samples) of a large population, understanding the basis for business improvement and forecasts, and being able to arrive at logical and sensible decisions and conclusions. These collected information or data, from which reports are generated, could either be qualitative or quantitative.

Scope of statistics

As stated in the first paragraph of this chapter, statistics is extensively wide, and its scope cannot be discussed in a book chapter. Despite the extensiveness of the subject, the scope can be discussed under these two subheadings:

1. **Mathematics statistics:** This is the ritualistic method of data collection, processing, classification, tabulation, presentation, analysis, interpretation and reporting. It is an area of statistics where inferences could be made for a logical conclusion.
2. **Applied statistics:** This is a branch of statistics that can be divided into other sub-groups: descriptive applied statistics, scientific applied statistics, and business applied statistics.
   - **Descriptive applied statistics** – This is deployed basically to make or give a descriptive information from an observation or data gathered.
   - **Scientific applied statistics** – This is the basic application of statistics in scientific research in order to arrive at a logical conclusion as it relates to a particular theory. For example, biometry and biostatistics in the area of medical and biological sciences.
   - **Business applied statistics** – This concerns application of statistics in the area of business management, forecast and prediction.

Uses of statistics: In clear terms, the basic use of statistics is to be able to have concise, precise and never useless information that could stand the test of time, where a logical and scientific conclusion that supports or debunks an existing idea or theory could be inferred.

Sampling and Sampling Distribution

It is important to note that *inference* is a watch-word in statistics as a science. People generalise and make inferences for a general population (whole) having been equipped with processed information derived from samples (parts); that is, making inferences for a universal set (whole population) with information or data gathered from sub-sets (sample/part) of the universal set. To have reliable statistics from which inferences of the whole will be made, the entire population of interest (target population) under each study must be known and defined adequately. But most times there is always the need to take some units (sample) from the whole population to represent the universal population.

The sample (which could be randomly or purposively selected) are a selected set of elements that are formed from the whole population to represent the characteristics or parameters of the entire or whole population. There is always a need for a sample in a research study or investigation, most especially when the population is large. The cost implication and time frame required to attend to all the elements of the entire population (which at times might be *infinite*) in an investigation always necessitate the call for sample selection.

Commitment of errors (sampling error) is an evil that must be averted in choosing samples in any study. Serious attention must be paid to drawing a truly representative sample of the entire population of interest. The closer a sample is to the whole (population of interest), the less the likelihood of committing sampling error. In an effort to reduce the probability of committing sampling error, a researcher or investigator should apply the use of random sampling more than any other sampling methods. An open (unbiased) mind must always be the mind of whoever will be selecting the sample from the population of interest in order to reduce the sampling error to the barest minimal level.

Obtaining a Reliable Random Sample

The importance of unbiased and reliable samples from a target population cannot be over-emphasized in a social research study. It is the basis upon which the statistical inferences of the conclusion that has to do with the entire population would be drawn. So, proper attention has to be placed on obtaining a reliable sample for any study, making sure that the sample represents adequately and proportionately all the elements of the entire population.

The first material needed for a random sample to be obtained is the good idea of having a list of the whole population (otherwise called a *frame*). Having the *frame* will allow a researcher to draw a representative sample for the population of interest. This selection can be drawn with the aid of a *computer system*, by randomly generating the numbers of the elements to be included in the sample. Another method is the use of *table of random sample*. These two ways give every element of the population of interest equal chance or probability of being selected in the sample for the study.

Descriptive and Inferential Statistics

Having known the difference between *population* and *sample*, differentiating between *descriptive statistics* and *inferential statistics* will be easy.

Descriptive statistics is the statistical description or conclusion about a population which is arrived at using data gathered from the entire group or population. *Inferential statistics,* which is also known as inductive statistics, is the statistical information, report or conclusion arrived at by using data gathered from the sample which was taken from the universal population to represent the larger population. While *parameter* (e.g., population mean μ, population variance σ^2, and population standard deviation σ) is the descriptive measure of the population, the descriptive measure of a sample is statistic (sample mean x, sample variance s^2, and sample standard deviation s). The basic advantage of inferential statistics is the ability it has to make conclusions for a whole population without having to go through the rigor of collecting data from the whole population.

Data Collection Methods

Sources of data and *data collection methods* are two phrases that are always mistakenly used interchangeably in social research methodology textbooks. A researcher could decide to source for a set of data either primarily or secondarily or both. Stating this has not given the correct and detailed data collection method in the methodology section for the data used for such study. Basically, primary and secondary sources are the two sources of data, and this is just to state how a researcher came about the data employed for the study. If a set of data for a study is generated by the researcher or investigator, such set of data is referred to as primarily sourced data. But if a set of data is "borrowed" from another source (already collected) to be used by a researcher, such data source is referred to as secondary source. Variables in a primary or secondary source of data could take both or either qualitative or quantitative data collection method. This could be with structured questionnaires, in-depth interviews, focus group discussion, case study and panel discussion.

Data are derived from variables. Variables are measurements which are gotten from individual characteristics or attributes. Variables can be *discrete* or *continuous,* likewise are data (*discrete* or *continuous variable*).

Discrete and Continuous Distribution

Obtaining level or state of possibility or probability of happening is an essential aspect in the discussion of *discrete and continuous variable* or *data.* If the possible outcome or value of possible outcome of a certain occurrence within an event takes the value of whole number, one talks of discrete variable. It is usually assumed that a certain occurrence or value of occurrence can never happen. Discrete variables or data usually produce values that are *nonnegative whole numbers.* For instance, in answering the question "How many customers picked an Android-powered product on a certain business day from TeTo shopping mall from 100 randomly selected customers for the particular business day?" The values of the best answer for this question is within the value of 0,1,2,3,4,5,6,7,8,9,10,11,12,13,- - - - - - -100 customers. It is assumed that such value can never include 0.5, 0.75 customer. It has to be a whole, counted number and not measured.

Some other examples of investigation or research that can produce discrete variables are:

1. Randomly selected vehicle with 6-cylinder engine truck in the car shop.
2. Selecting those that wear Nike singlet out of 100 randomly selected undergraduate students of an institution.
3. Out of 1000 randomly selected PHCN customers in Nigeria, how many are using pre-paid electrical meter billing system?

Continuous variable on the other hand considers every point within an interval. It takes into cognizance every decimal point within an interval. It deals mostly with certain characteristics of an element such as time, height, weight, length and volume. A continuous variable can easily become a discrete variable by recoding such continuous variable into a discrete variable.

As mentioned earlier on, the possible outcome of an observation can be arranged into distributions. There are two types of such distributions: *discrete distributions* and *continuous distributions.* Discrete distributions are formed from discrete random variables while continuous distributions are formed from continuous random variables. Among the various types of discrete distribution are:

*Binomial and Poisson distributions:*Binomial is a type of discrete distribution that has been in place for many decades. For any proper and accurate performance of binomial distribution, certain assumptions must be considered, namely:

i. The total number of observations or trials must be known.
ii. The observation or trial can only take one of the two (2) instances of outcome, for example, good or bad, male or female, moving or not moving, success or failure. The outcome of the binomial discrete variable must be properly dichotomized.
iii. Each layer or category of the trial must be independent of the other.
iv. The probability of the occurrence (*p*) or not (*1-p*) must be known or stated clearly.

More often than not, the terms *success* and *failure* are used in binomial distribution. The outcome of interest is usually referred to as success *(p)* while the alternate outcome *(q)* is referred to as failure.

Formula for the calculation of binomial discrete distribution –

$$P(x) = {_nC_x}.p^x.q^{n-x} = \frac{n!}{x!(n-x)!}.p^x.q^{n-x}$$

Where
p = the probability of getting success (desired result) in each of what or one trial
q = 1-p = the probability of failure (alternate result)
x = the number of desired successes
n = the number of trials allowed or given (sample size)

Example:

A study of petrol powered engine motor vehicles revealed that 70% of all motor vehicles plying a major road in town were using petrol. If 30 cars are selected randomly yesterday, what is the probability that exactly 20 have petrol engines?
Solution:

$$P(x) = {_nC_x}.p^x.q^{n-x} = \frac{n!}{x!(n-x)!}.p^x.q^{n-x}$$
p =70%=0.7
q = 1-q= 1-0.7=0.3
x =20
n = 30

$$P(x) = {_{30}C_{20}}.0.7^{20}.0.3^{30-20} = \frac{30!}{20!(30-20)!}.0.7^{20}.0.3^{10}$$
P(x)=30045015.(0.00079792266297612).(0.0000059049)
P(x)=0.141561701 = 0.1416

Result: If 70% of all motor vehicles plying a major road in town use petrol, and 30 cars are selected randomly, 14.16% (4 cars) of the randomly selected cars would be using petrol.

Poisson distributions: Poisson distribution has a lot of similarities to and differences from binomial distribution. While binomial considers the likelihood of occurrence between success and failure from a given or known number of observations or trials, Poisson distribution focuses mainly on the number of certain possible occurrences within a *given, stated or speculated time interval or continuum.* Poisson distribution needs not to know the sample size, like binomial distribution, for its calculation or probability of occurrence.

For instance, as stated in the above example, where the probability of petrol-powered cars among 30 randomly selected is of interest: in the case of Poisson, the interest will be the number of petrol-powered cars that will randomly ply the road on a *particular time, day or within a particular given time interval.* Poisson distribution describes occurrence of rare (mostly unknown) events, maybe to encourage or to avert such occurrences.

For any proper and accurate performance of Poisson distribution, certain assumptions and attributes must be considered and taken into consideration, namely:

i.   It is a discrete distribution.
ii. It describes rare (mostly unknown) events.
iii. All the occurrences are independent of one another.
iv. Description of occurrence over a time interval or period.
v.   Occurrences can range from level zero to any positive number or digit (infinity).

Formula for the calculation of binomial discrete distribution:

$$P(x) = \frac{\lambda^x . e - \lambda}{x!}$$

Where
$x = 0, 1, 2, 3, 4 \ldots \ldots \ldots$
$\lambda = long\text{-}run\ average$
$e = 2.718282$

Example:
If in a mechanic workshop, cars for normal servicing check-up arrive randomly on every Wednesday at an average of three customers every five minutes, what is the probability of exactly seven customers arriving in a five minutes interval on March 7, 2012, which happened to be a Wednesday?

Solution:

x = seven customers per four minutes, the probability of seven customers randomly arriving during a five minutes interval when the long-run average has been three customers per five minutes interval is as follows:

$$P(x) = \frac{\lambda^x . e^{-\lambda}}{x!}$$

$P(x) = \frac{(3^7). (e^{-3})}{7!} = \frac{(2187). (0.04978706)}{7.6.5.4.3.2} = \frac{(2187).(0.04978706)}{5040} = 0.02160$

Note: remember that e = 2.718282

Result:
If the workshop averages three customers every five minutes, the probability of seven customers arriving during any five minutes interval is 0.02160

Levels of Data Measurement

Business researchers or any other researchers should always be mindful of the use of figures in their measurement of statistics in their data analysis. What the figure 2 in a variable stands for might not necessarily mean the same thing or represent in another variable, no matter how close the two variables are. Take for instance, a parcel or letter weighing 2 is not the same as an officer of a corporation that was ranked 2 in an assessment exercise. While three parcels with each weighing 2 will be 6, three officers ranking 2 in an assessment exercise will not be on the same footing with an officer that was ranked 6 in the same assessment exercise. Therefore, attention should be paid to the phenomenon, circumstance or object represented by the numerical figure. The phenomenon, circumstance or object will determine the levels of data measurement.

There are four common types of data measurement levels:

1. Nominal
2. Ordinal
3. Interval
4. Ratio

Nominal levels of data measurement: Nominal levels are just numerical representation only, not in reality. For instance, if I am allocated jersey number 2 on a football field and somebody else is wearing jersey number 4, it does not mean that the man with jersey number 4 plays twice more than me with jersey number 2. Nominal level is just to distinguish, differentiate or classify; it does not have much importance attached to the numerical figure each entity or individual is given. Female workers in a business outfit who are allocated 2 and their male counterparts that are given 1 for computation's sake will never by the nominal numbers receive twice as much as the male counterparts with

1. The figures 1 and 2 are only used to differentiate or identify, most especially when computing statistics.

Ordinal levels of data measurement: This level of measurement is rather more sensitive than nominal levels. It could otherwise be described as a number that means or stands for the actual position the object has taken, most especially in a series. For instance, if, in a study, the spending profile of all the units of a manufacturing company was rated as follows:

not important – 1
somewhat important – 2
moderately important – 3
very important – 4
extremely important – 5

After the analysis of the collected data, the unit of the company that scores 5 will not be ranked as the same with that other unit that scores 3 or 2. Unlike the nominal level, there is importance attached to the numerical position or score in this type of measurement; but at the same time, one common similarity between nominal and ordinal levels of measurement is that one numerical figure or position does not necessarily mean double or triple the other numerical figure or position. Just as 2 for female does not mean twice as big a human being for a woman as her male counterpart represented by 1, so is the unit with total score of 4 not twice that other unit with total score of 2 in the above example.

Interval levels of data measurement: Interval level of measurement attaches importance to numerical figures allocated to objects or phenomenon, but in its own case the difference between numerical figures in a series is the same and measurable. If in an aptitude test four candidates (A, B, C and D) scored 15, 25, 30 and 0 respectively, it could be said that candidate B scored 10 marks more than that of candidate A, while it is also correct to state that candidate C scored 15 marks more than candidate A. But it should be noted that for candidate D that scored 0 it did not mean that such candidate did not exist but that the value of the candidate's score is zero (0).

Ratio levels of data measurement: ratio level of data measurement is more or less the same as that of interval level of data measurement. The main difference between interval and ratio levels of measurement is that ratio level of data measurement takes zero (0) value as the complete absence of the element that is ascribed zero (0) while in interval level of data measurement zero (0) stands for a candidate that scores nothing, that is, zero (0).

Categorical and Quantitative Variables

A clear distinction exists between categorical and quantitative variables, but the beauty of it is that quantitative variables could be regrouped and thereby made categorical. Whether a variable is categorical or quantitative must be known for a meaningful statistical analysis to be performed on such variable or data, simply because the statistical analysis relevant for a particular variable depends on whether such variable is categorical or quantitative. For instance, it will be wrong to perform some arithmetic functions like addition, subtraction or arithmetic mean (average) on categorical variables (if 1 is representing male and 2 is representing female), it will be so wrong to now be adding or subtracting 1 from 2 and be interpreting the result which will be 1 as representing a male.

Central Tendency and Its Measurements

The central tendency is the central propensity of the set of measurement (of a set of data) to cluster around a certain numerical value. Though the most popular and easy-to-understand measurement of central tendency is arithmetic mean, there are other measurements of relative positions of points within a data set or a population—median, mode, range, percentile, quartile and interquartile.

Mean: The mean of a set of observation is otherwise called its average. This is the sum (addition) of all the observations (measurements) divided by the total number of observations (measurements) contained in the data set.

Percentile: At times, it becomes important or it might be of interest to define the position a particular score or number takes in an observational result. Then, given a magnitude arrangement, most especially of a set of numerical observations, it becomes easy to define or know the boundaries—the range (lower limit and upper limit). Therefore, the position a particular numerical result takes is defined in terms of *percentile.* An instance is: a marketing research outfit is interested in writing a proposal but needs to categorize a particular business outfit among its peers. If, at the end of the investigation, the position of the total score of that business outfit compared with others is defined as *percentile;* if the position of the total score of that business outfit is put at 70th percentile, that means that 70% of its peers received a total score less than such business outfit in the investigation.

> The *Pth* percentile of a set of data (scores) obtained in an investigation is that value below which lies *P%* (p percent =) of the numbers arranged in magnitude order in the group. Placement of *Pth* percentile is given by $(n+1)P/100$. Where n = the number of data points.

Quartiles: In any percentile arrangement, there are some positions that are conventionally taken as having more important positioning than others. Any of such positions is known as *quartile.*

> 25th percentile – (1st quartile) is also known as lower quartile. This is the value at the position or point that could be described as the first quarter after all the observations must have been arranged according to magnitude.

> 50th percentile – (2nd quartile) is also known as middle quartile, the median. This is value at that position or point that breaks all the observations into half (two equal parts, which lie half the data).

75th percentile – (3rd quartile) is also known as upper quartile. The value at the point below which lies 75 percent of the set of data arranged in magnitude.

They are regarded as important because they break down the observed data set arranged in magnitude into quarters.

The scores of 10 students in a dictation test—21,24,26,27,28,23,25,29,22,20—are a good example. To find the first, second and third quartiles of the score, one needs to arrange the set of data into magnitude (from smallest to largest), thus: 20, 21, 22, 23, 24, 25, 26, 27, 28, 29. Then . . .

1st quartile (25th percentile) is the value of the score in the position $(n+1)(25/100)=(10+1)(0.25)=(11)(0.25)= 2.75$, which is equal to 21.75;

2nd quartile (50th percentile) is the value of the score in the position $(n+1)(50/100) = (10+1)(0.5) = (11)(0.5) = 5.5$, which lies in between scores 24 and 25 = 24.5;

3rd quartile (75th percentile) is the value of the score in the position $(n+1)(75/100) = (10+1)(0.75) = (11)(0.75) = 8.25$, which is equal to 27.25.

Interquartile: It is the range of values between the third quartile and the first quartile. Basically, it can be called the walk-away distance between the third quartile and the first quartile. It is otherwise known as the value of middle 50% (half) of the data set.

Mode: It the number or number of values which occur with the most or greatest frequency.

Median: At times it might be of importance or interest to know the middle point or the value that stands in the middle point of a series of numbers or values. This is simply done by arranging the numbers or the values in ascending order and then looking for the one (number or value) that stands at the middle, that is, the number that divides the set of data into two equal parts. It is easy to find the median for an odd number of observations. After arranging the set of data (number of observations) in ascending order, the one that divides the set into two equal parts is known as the median (middle point) of such set of observations. To calculate median for an even number of observations, after the ascending order arrangement, the two values or points that fall in the middle will be added after which the result will be divided by 2.

Index Numbers

Index numbers or statistics in the business world are numerical facts, figures and indicators that assist business operators and other stakeholders to understand a series or a variety of basic business and economic situations over a period of time. Every nation of the world collects and compiles series of indexes and statistics. These indexes and statistics are essential for all nations and individual organizations to be able to monitor and measure the state of business and economic activities over a given period of time (base period or starting point and current period or another reference year). It is also important for good business judgment and economic decisions. Though there are many indexes that serve as indicators, the best known and commonly used is price index (price variability), that is, changes in prices of an item or group of items over a given period of time.

Price Relative Index (PRI): To compare the price of an item in the base year to the price of that particular item in another or current year, PRI is the simplest method. This is calculated thus:

$$\text{PRI in period } t = \frac{Price\ in\ period\ t}{Base\ period\ price} (100)$$

Take for instance the unit price of a gallon of sealed water over a period of 10 years

Year	2000	2001	2002	2003	2004	2005	2006	2007	2008	2009
Price	230	210	209	207	222	248	257	280	285	300

Taking year 2000 as the base year, the price relative indexes for each year through 2009 are calculated and shown in Table 2 thus:

Year	2000	2001	2002	2003	2004	2005	2006	2007	2008	2009
PRI	100	91.3	90.9	90.0	96.5	107.8	111.7	121.7	123.9	130.4

The interpretation of the relative price index per year in Table 2 shows that the price of a gallon of sealed water in year 2001 was 8.7% below that of the price in the previous year (2000). As indicated in Table 2, with 130.4 price relative index in 2009, this shows a 30.4% increase in the price of a gallon of sealed water relative to the price in year 2000.

Aggregate Price Index (API): This is the index calculated to study the changes in the prices of a group of items combined together. It is usually an indicator to measure the general market or economic conditions in an economic working system.

$$API_t = \frac{\sum P_{it}}{\sum P_{io}} (100)$$

Where
$\sum Pit$ = *summation of unit prices of all the items in period t*
$\sum Pio$ = *summation of unit prices of all the items in the base period*

In a situation where the interest is the changes in the general market, API is the best indicator that can be used to study and describe the market or price situation. The prices of some consumable food items such as yam, beans, rice, and bread can be used to explain this.

Items	Unit Prices	
	2002	2012
Bread	150	210
Beans	330	480
Yam	250	320
Rice	750	1050

$$\text{API}_{2012} = \frac{210 + 480 + 320 + 1050}{150 + 330 + 250 + 750}(100)$$

$$\text{API}_{2012} = 139.2$$

A 139.2 Aggregate Price Index of the listed consumable items shows a 39.2% increase in the market price of the listed items over a period of 10 years (between year 2002 and year 2012).

References

Aczel, A., and J. Sounderpandian. (2008) *Aczel-Sounderpandian Complete Business Statistics* (7th edition). New York: McGraw-Hill/Irwin.

Adebowale, S. A. (2006) *Statistics for Engineers, Managers and Scientists.* Lagos: Alfredo Graphics Ltd.

Anderson, Sweeney and Williams. (2011) *Statistics for Business and Economics.* Stamford, CT: South-Western Cengage Learning.

Black, Ken. (2010) *Business Statistics for Contemporary Decision Making* (6th edition). Hoboken, NJ: John Wiley and Sons, Inc.

Fabayo, J. A. (2009) *Quantitative Techniques for Economic and Management Decisions.* Ibadan: Intec Printers Ltd.

Gupta, Sapna. (2009) Business Statistics. Jaipur, India: Biyani Shikshan Samiti. http://www.gurukpo.com.

McClave, J. T., and T. Sincich. (2000) *Statistics.* Upper Saddle River, NJ: Prentice-Hall, Inc.

Spiegel, Murray S., and Larry J. Stephens. (2008) *Statistics.* (Schaum's Outline Series). New York: The McGraw-Hill Companies, Inc.

Chapter 7

COMPETENCIES FOR ENTREPRENEURIAL SUCCESS

Ogunbameru, O. A. and Adekunle, A. R.

Introduction

The concept of competence has mainly been applied in the world of business, and more specifically in the field of recruiting and selecting new employees (Stoof 2005). In the domain of entrepreneurship, previous research has studied models of competency in order to examine entrepreneurs' competencies regarding the importance of initiating and succeeding in new business (Bird 2002).Entrepreneurs, on the one hand, consider that decision making is the most important competency when embarking on an entrepreneurial venture, whereas scholars are in favor of identifying business opportunities. Competency approach has become an increasingly popular means of studying entrepreneurial characteristics. Competency can be studied from its inputs (antecedents to competencies), process (task or behaviour leading to competencies), or outcomes (achieving standards of competence in functional areas) (Mole *et al*. 1993).

The Meaning of Competence

There is no single definition of competence. The definition of competence is lacking a theoretical framework to date because of its complexity. The following ten definitions provide different ways by which competence can be defined, from a very broad to more specific ways:

1. "The ability of implementation, especially of something physical, mental or financially, in as a legal power to achieve something. It is either a natural or an acquired skill or talent" (www.answers.com).
2. "Competencies are a mix of knowledge, skills and attitudes" (Lans *et al*. 2008).
3. It is often believed that competencies are "a combination of knowledge, skills and attitudes which are required by employees in their jobs or tasks" (Stoof 2005).
4. Gibb (1990:21) defines competence as "an ability to perform certain tasks for which knowledge, skills, attitudes and motivations are necessary".
5. According to Boyatzis (1982:21), "a job competency is an underlying characteristic of a person in that it may be a motive, trait, skill, aspect of one's self-image or social role, or a body of knowledge which he or she uses".
6. Spencer and Spencer (1993:9) define a competency as "an underlying characteristic of an individual that is causally related to criterion-referenced effective and/or superior performance in a job or situation".
7. Competency is an underlying characteristic of a person in that it may be motive, traits, skills, aspect of one's self-image, a body of knowledge, set of skills and

cluster of appropriate motives/traits that an individual possesses to perform in his/her business (Anderson 2012).

8. "Skills, knowledge, behaviours and attitudes required to perform a role effectively" (Brophy and Kiely 2002).
9. "A cluster of related knowledge, attitudes, and skills that: (1) affects a major part of one's job, (2) correlates with performance on the job, and (3) can be improved via training and development" (Parry 1998).
10. "The set of behaviour patterns that the incumbent needs to bring to a position in order to perform its task and functions with competencies" (Tett, Gutterman, Bleier, and Murphy 2000).

The four important facets of competencies common to these definitions are:
➤ Competencies include overall characteristics of an individual that are related to the effective performance of a given job.
➤ Competencies are manifested in the individual's behaviour, and are therefore observable and measurable.
➤ Competencies facilitate the accomplishment of goals and objectives.
➤ Competencies are resources in the organization that can be fostered and nurtured. Understanding business success as arising from competency provides an approach to intervention (Bird 1995; Burgoyne 1993; Parry 1998). Training programs for entrepreneurship could achieve their aim of developing entrepreneurial competencies. In addition to providing a focus for intervention, McClelland (1973) suggests that the competency approach is valuable insofar as being able to reduce the bias of the traditional personality approach. However, research to date typically does not distinguish entrepreneurial competencies from managerial competencies. The identification of the specific competency requirements of the entrepreneur therefore remains an important research task. (Sadler-Smith *et al.* 2003).

Despite the relative differences in the definitions, we can conclude that the term *competence* is a broad concept that consistently associates knowledge, skills, attitudes and motivations as dimensions that competent entrepreneurs must be able to use in order to deal with the tasks and problems related to their entrepreneurial actions (Onstenk 2003).

Frequently Asked Questions (FAQ) About Competence

The following are the frequently asked questions when discussing competence:

1. "What competencies for entrepreneurship should individuals be able to manifest when facing an entrepreneurial venture?"
2. "What competencies for entrepreneurship should universities and colleges address in their curricula for undergraduate and graduate programmes?"
3. "What competencies should policy makers, educators and other stakeholders address in their policies in order to predict venture outcomes?"

There is a relationship between entrepreneurs' competencies and their expected causal relationship with venture initiation and success (Bird 1995). Mansfield, McClelland,

Spencer, and Santiago (1987) submit that the identification of relevant entrepreneurial competencies should provide insight into the field of entrepreneurship and that such competencies might predict business formation and success within and across cultures. It can also help educators and policy makers design appropriate mechanisms to foster entrepreneurial activity in their communities. The former can adapt their courses and curricula to better prepare students and possibly increase their confidence and motivation for successful business startups and the survival of profitable enterprises. Accordingly, competence-based education and training can be designed to promote entrepreneurial activity among university students. Policy makers, on the other hand, can reorient their practices and policies to stimulate the diffusion and development of entrepreneurship.

According to Chandler and Jansen (1992), for example, one of the primary roles of business founders is related to scanning their environments, choosing potential opportunities, and taking advantages of those opportunities by formulating the required strategies. Business founders must assume three predominant roles in their businesses. These are the entrepreneurial, managerial and technical-functional roles. These abilities are identified as entrepreneurial competencies (Chandler and Hanks 1994). The managerial role demands the interaction of the business founders with their environment for the acquisition and use of resources. The technical-functional role requires the founder to function effectively in tasks related to the technical field within a certain industry. A competency approach seems to be a more effective tool in predicting firm performance than entrepreneurial experience alone (Bird 2002).

Importance of Competence
Proper entrepreneurial competencies are required to successfully start, operate and ensure the survival of a new business in the marketplace. This is shown in Table 7:1.

Table 7:1 Importance of Entrepreneurs' Competencies

Competencies
Identifying business opportunities
Evaluating business opportunities
Decision making
Identifying and solving problems
Networking
Oral communication abilities
Coping with uncertainties
Innovative thinking
Team building abilities
Deal making and negotiation
Dealing with failure
Coping with stress
Calculated risk taking
Intuitive thinking
Having a different view of the market
Team working abilities
Analytical thinking
Writing communication abilities
Language learning abilities

Source: Izquierdo *et al*. (2005)

Ten Competencies for Entrepreneurial Success

The ten competencies for entrepreneurial success are: integrity, conceptual thinking, risk taking, networking, strategic thinking, commercial aptitude, decisiveness, optimism, customer sensitivity and people focus.

1. **Integrity**
   What Is Integrity?
   Integrity is an uncompromising adherence to doing what is right and proper. It encompasses the following:
   • Honesty, reliability, and fairness in business practices; and is
   • an essential element of successful business relationships.
   • Integrity is as much about what to do as it is who to be.
   • Personal integrity of the owner

The most important characteristic of successful entrepreneurs is integrity. "Personal integrity is the measure of how a person is in action, how a person embodies his/her beliefs, how a person can hold and carry forth a vision and mission." (Mansfield *et al.* 1987).

Integrity does not only mean that you must be honest with those people around you, it also means that you must be true to yourself in all things. Being honest with yourself means that you provide a service to the best of your ability, you keep your promises to yourself, you know yourself and you value yourself.

It is a simple fact that entrepreneurs without integrity never succeed in the long term. They're too busy in the short term trying to screw their employees and their customers to provide a good service, and sooner or later it catches up with them and they fail.

There are certain actions that should be taken to commit oneself to high integrity. These are:

- Analyse some ethical decisions you have made in the past and give your reasons for deciding to do what you did.
- Discuss with others the ethical implications of the decision you have made and evaluate how they might affect the people around you.
- Read a book on ethics and integrity in business.
- Become aware of the importance of ethical awareness and the high standards of integrity required to become a millionaire and a successful entrepreneur.
- Commit to always being absolutely honest with yourself and others.

Eight Integrities of Entrepreneurship

Robert Kiyosaki (2011) lists eight integrities of entrepreneurship that are required to be implemented in all businesses which want to grow from a small to a big business. These are: mission, team, leader, product, legal, systems, communication, and cash flow.

Figure 7.1: 8 Integrities of Entrepreneurship

Source: http://fenesi.com/wp-content/uploads/2011/11/bi_triangle.jpg

Robert Kiyosaki (2011) points out that *8 Integrities of Entrepreneurship* are required to be implemented in all businesses which want to grow from being a small business to a BIG business (500+ employees).

Mission: It is very important that you have a Spiritual Mission for your business. Your company has to have a meaning to the clients/customers whom you are targeting and not just making money. The spiritual mission of a company acts as the foundation of the business. It has to be firm, and also it is the reason for existence. Most businesses usually set their mission statements to outline *what they do* rather than *why they do it*. As an entrepreneur, you must make sure you don't confuse the two.

Team: Teams represent power. Let's be sincere: it's hard to run a business as an individual. The team is more important than the individual. Most successful businesses have always attributed their success to the strong and united teams they have.

Leader: Leaders are role models. Leadership is earned. It is earned through trust, respect, experience, and competence.

Product: A product without a strong 8-I triangle behind it will probably not be a successful product. When coming up with your products, make sure that you have your *Mission* put in place first, then come up with great products.

Legal: Every business needs lawyers. Lawyers and laws are important in protecting your product and the rest of your 8-I triangle.

Systems: A business is a system of systems. It needs a system that operates efficiently and effectively. It needs professionals to operate it.

Communication: A business needs strong sales, PR, marketing, web and HR communications. Information technology is essential to businesses today.

Cash flow: A business must have accurate and clear accounting. A business with poor accounting systems is a poor company; hence, you need an accountant.

Personal integrity is the measure of how a person is in action, how a person embodies his or her beliefs, how a person can hold and carry forth a vision and mission. But most importantly, it is what followers follow over the long term, and the key is the long-term. Followers will intellectually, emotionally and intuitively measure the integrity of their leader(s) against their own values and their doctrines of fairness, and will over time decide to what measure they place their fate in the hands of their leader(s) (Steward 2009).

2. Conceptual Thinking

Conceptual thinking is...the ability to perceive and imagine, predict and hypothesize, and to conclude and reflect. Conceptual thinking means that the entrepreneur is prepared to use fresh approaches; comes up with crazy ideas that may just work, leading to radical change or significant improvements; and takes time to listen to new ideas without pre-judgment (Anderson 2012).

Conceptual thinking is one step further of philosophy. Philosophy, by definition, is: Investigation of the nature, causes, or principles of reality, knowledge, or values, based on logical reasoning rather than empirical methods. While philosophy can lead to new concepts, it is more about explaining them and why and how they work. Also, a conceptual thinker can be considered a philosopher, as it takes understanding of other concepts to be able to create your own.

There are specific words often used to describe or label a conceptual thinker:

- Ambitious
- Independent
- Perfectionist
- Entrepreneur
- Philosopher
- Intellectual
- Leader

3. Risk Taking

Risk taking involves trying something new—and possibly better—in the sense of stretching beyond what has been done in the past. The constant challenge is to learn how to assess choices responsibly, weighing the outcomes against one's values and responsibilities (Anderson 2012).

> One of the more important players in the free market is the entrepreneur. In the free market the skills and risks which the entrepreneur is willing to take can be fully exploited by both producers and consumers to their advantage. Entrepreneurship manifests itself in many ways. Entrepreneurs start businesses, develop new procedures for the production and distribution of goods, act as middlemen between markets and are a source of information. The entrepreneur is also characterised by an alertness for opportunities which have been ignored or unseen by others. These opportunities are almost always accompanied by some profit. (Cooray 1996)

Liles (1974) speculated about what he believed is at risk in a new venture. He suggested that in becoming an entrepreneur an individual risks financial well-being, career opportunities, family relations, and psychic well-being. The personal financial obligations that the entrepreneur makes as an individual could jeopardize his future standard of living. Moreover, because the entrepreneur is likely to have devoted himself to the venture at a personal level, the failure of the venture becomes, in effect, the failure of the individual and therefore can have major emotional consequences. Realizing that the financial and emotional consequences of failure could be devastating, Liles suggested that the potential entrepreneur is well advised to analyze carefully the risks associated with his specific business proposal and then to determine whether or not he is willing to undertake them.

4. Networking

This is a key business activity which can provide access to information, expertise, collaboration, sales, and careful planning. Networking is an essential skill for most business people but especially for entrepreneurs. The strong association between the entrepreneur as a person and his or her business demands that entrepreneurs get out into the world and create and maintain business relationships. Here are some tips and resources to help you improve your networking skills and extend your reach.

Dan Schawbel (2009) lists the top 10 social networks for entrepreneurs. Each helps entrepreneurs succeed by providing them with the guidance, tools and resources they need to setup their company and gain exposure.

- ***Entrepreneur Connect***

Social networks provide the opportunity to create your own profile, explore the community, share ideas with other entrepreneurs and network. However, unlike most social networks, this one frowns upon too much self-promotion and applauds idea sharing.

This network can be used to connect to service providers, suppliers, advisers and colleagues. It also allows you to start your own blog and possibly have it appear on the main page.

- ▪ *PartnerUp*

This is a social network for entrepreneurs who are searching for people and resources for business opportunities. Anyone can join, but business partners, co-founders, executives and board members will get the most out of this one. In this network, you can ask or offer advice, find commercial real estate and find service providers for your business, like accountants and marketers.

- ▪ *StartupNation*

Most social networks neglect the content aspect that makes StartupNation so useful. With articles, forums, blogs, on-demand seminars, and podcasts, entrepreneurs will be better prepared for their ventures and have the resources required to make better business decisions.

There is a wide range of topics being discussed on StartupNation today, such as business planning, marketing and web-based business. If you're an entrepreneur or hope to become one, this site is definitely one you can't miss out on.

- ● *LinkedIn*

LinkedIn networking is very useful for anyone who's either searching for a job, is trying to network with like-minded individuals, or building a company. LinkedIn offers many resources for entrepreneurs.

- ▪ *Biznik*

Biznik brands itself as a social network that "doesn't suck." The Biznik community is composed of freelancers, CEOs, and the self-employed. Like the other networks, this is a place for you to share ideas instead of posting your resume. It is mandatory for all members to use their real names and provide real data, and Biznik editors actually review all profiles to ensure compliance with that policy.

- ▪ *Perfect Business*

Perfect Business might be the perfect social network for meeting many serious entrepreneurs, experts and investors from a variety of industries. The type of people you'll find are potential business partners, potential clients and advisers.

- ▪ *Go BIG Network*

The Go BIG Network embraces job seekers, in addition to funding sources, service providers and entrepreneurs. In this social network, you post requests for help, which are then routed to other people in the network who can answer your questions or support you. Members of this social network can search through profiles of other members, contact them or post a request (a classified ad) to talk about what they are looking for (such as a business partner).

- *Cofounder*

The Cofounder network is made up of idea makers, entrepreneurs, programmers, web designers, investors, freelancers and executives. The primary purpose of joining this network is to start a new web venture. Unlike most of the social networks already listed here, Cofounder is a strictly private network, which means that you can't view member profiles before you register for an account.

- *The Funded*

The Funded is an online community of entrepreneurs who research, rate and review funding sources. Entrepreneurs can view and share terms sheets to assist each other in finding good investors as well as discuss the inner workings of operating a business. General benefits of this site include viewing facts, reviews and commentary on funding resources, and accessing RSS feeds of the most recent public comments by members.

- *Young Entrepreneur*

Young Entrepreneur is a great starting point for you. This community appears as a discussion forum, with topics such as e-commerce, search engine optimization, marketing, IT and Internet, and franchising.

Seven Tips for Networking. Colleen DeBaise (2012) submits that networking goes hand in hand with running a successful business. These are:

- **Resist the urge to arrive late.** It's almost counter-intuitive, but showing up early at a networking event is a much better strategy than getting there on the later side. It's easier to find other people who don't have conversation partners yet.
- **Ask easy questions.** Don't wait around the edges of the room, waiting for someone to approach you. If you're not a natural extrovert, you're probably a very good listener—and listening can be an excellent way to get to know a person.
- **Ditch the sales pitch.** Remember, networking is all about relationship building. Keep your exchange fun, light and informal—you don't need to do the hard sell within minutes of meeting a person. The idea is to get the conversation started. People are more apt to do business with—or partner with—people whose company they enjoy.
- **Share your passion.** Win people over with your enthusiasm for your product or service. Leave a lasting impression by telling a story about why you were inspired to create your company. Talking about what you enjoy is often contagious, too. When you get other people to share their passion, it creates a memorable two-way conversation.
- **Smile.** By smiling, you'll put your nervous self at ease, and you'll also come across as warm and inviting to others. Remember to smile before you enter the room, or before you start your next conversation. And if you're really dreading the event? Check the negative attitude at the door.
- **Don't hijack the conversation.** Some people who dislike networking may overcompensate by commandeering the discussion. Don't forget: the most successful networkers (think of those you've met) are good at making other

people feel special. Look people in the eye, repeat their names, listen to what they have to say, and suggest topics that are easy to discuss. Be a conversationalist, not a talker.

○ **Remember to follow up.** It's often said that networking is where the conversation begins, not ends. If you've had a great exchange, ask your conversation partner the best way to stay in touch. Some people like email or phone; others prefer social networks like LinkedIn. Get in touch within 48 hours of the event to show you're interested and available, and reference something you discussed, so your contact remembers you.

5. Strategic Thinking

Creating something from nothing—dubbed *bricolage*—is an act of deliberate thinking. Creating a whole new business venture is an act of strategic thinking. Thinking is the ultimate human resource that involves moving from one state of knowledge to a better one (de Bono 1982). Thinking also involves memory, plans, ideas, and possibilities (Haye 1994). Thinking can be classified into two types: vertical thinking and strategic thinking. Vertical thinking is employed here to mean logical thinking, mathematical thinking, analytical thinking, and rational thinking. As Hussey (2001) points out, there is no rigid sequence to whether bright ideas precede or follow analytical activities. Vertical thinking is sequential, disciplined, and rule-based, and in it the individual moves in the thinking process forward by sequential steps, each of which must be justified (de Bono, 1970).

On the other hand, the term strategic thinking is used in the paper to refer to thinking that is lateral, critical, and creative. There is no consensus on a definition for strategic thinking. For example, Liedtka (1998) defines strategic thinking in terms of five attributes: a system of holistic view, a focus on intent, time-based, hypothesis-driven, and intelligently opportunistic. Dixit and Nalebuff (1991, p. 3) define strategic thinking as "the art of outdoing an adversary, knowing that the adversary is trying to do the same to you". Larson and Hansen (2005, p. 1) define it as "a distinct form of pragmatic reasoning". We, however, view strategic thinking as referring to "sensible ideas, thoughtful analyses, and sound decisions".

The brain is divided into two hemispheres: The left hemisphere, which performs the vertical thinking as defined above, and the right hemisphere, which performs the strategic thinking as stipulated above. Both brain segments are deemed crucial for proper human functioning, because they complement each other. As Pink (2006) elaborates, although the power of the left-brain is necessary, it is not sufficient, and it must be augmented with the capabilities of the right-brain if rapid progress is to take place.

Strategic thinking is proactive and reflective. It is valuable to all mankind, and especially necessary to those individuals who wish to become successful entrepreneurs. Strategic thinking enables entrepreneurs to navigate with self-assurance in a dynamic, competitive environment. The benefits of this type of thinking skills are well recognized. Barnett and Berland (1999) indicate that strategic thinking capability can help businesses identify ways to develop confident forecasts, and to reduce the uncertainty of business decisions. Graetz (2002) declares that strategic thinking is seen as central to creating and sustaining competitive advantage. Additionally, strategic thinking can assist entrepreneurs in other areas, including the following:

- Preparing for the future;
- Seeing the bigger picture;
- Anticipating threats;
- Making sensible business decisions;
- Solving challenging problems;
- Understanding environmental trends;
- Envisioning opportunities;
- Identifying market needs for the intended venture;
- Positioning the venture for success;
- Avoiding excessive risk;
- Building alliances;
- Assembling the right resources; and
- Managing for results.

6. Decisiveness

1. Decisiveness is the willingness to make decisions, even in the face of complexity or uncertainty. It means weighing the information that is available to us and using our judgment to choose among the possibilities. To be decisive we must clear about our values and goals.

2. Decisiveness means taking the risk that we may be wrong, but knowing that perfect clarity is rarely available and indecision can be costly. It also means taking responsibility for the outcome of the decision.

The desirable man/woman, the one whom the corporation promotes and the world respects, is decisive. The decisive person is calm and cool under pressure; s/he's a take charge kind of person; he/she has purpose and direction; he/she is the man/woman with the plan. On the other hand, the indecisive man/woman makes little or excruciatingly slow progress in life because s/he is always standing shilly-shally, unable to decide which way to go.

The indecisive person is also the restless one. He or she labors under the delusion that not making a decision will allow him or her to remain safe in the current position. Yet he or she fails to understand that life is like standing in the midst of a river in which one is continually fighting the current. If one ceases to paddle, one will simply be swept downstream.

Just making decisions isn't enough, because the person who makes all poor decisions isn't very successful or popular either. A person needs to be both skilled in decision making and in making the right decisions at the right time.

How to Make a Good Decision

There are four major ways to making a good decision.

- ✓ **Get as much information as possible.** Whenever you're faced with a big decision, this is the first step you should always take. Don't just sit and stew about it day after day, waiting somehow for the stars to align and for the answer to come to you. Instead, find out as much information as possible about all of the options you have before you.

✓ **Make a list of pros and cons.** Take a piece of paper, make some columns and list the pros and cons of each potential decision. The pro column for one might be much longer than the others. Even if it's not that obvious, the process of really thinking through the positives and negatives can lead to your "a-ha" moment.

✓ **Imagine yourself down each road.** Sometimes when we're making a choice, we only imagine the results of that decision in the abstract. Sit or lie down somewhere quiet and really try to imagine your life after making each of your possible choices. Think about what you're doing and how you're feeling. Which scenario gives you a sense of peace? Which one makes you happy just thinking about it? And which one leaves you feeling a little empty?

✓ **Think about past decisions.** It's often been said that those who don't understand history are doomed to repeat it. This is as true for our personal lives as it is for the world. Sometimes we make the same screwy decisions over and over again.

Think about the bad decisions you made in the past: is there a common denominator? Did you bail out on what you're really passionate about because you thought you wanted prestige, only to wish you had followed your dream? Then don't make another decision based on your pride. Have you made bad choices based simply on your insecurity? Make sure that's not behind the way you're leaning now.

7. Commercial Aptitude
Commercial aptitude assessments have been designed for use with sales and counter staff in retail, banking and financial services. Each test is shorter than the industry standard whilst maintaining robust reliability and validity.

Why are Aptitude Assessments used?
Employers often use aptitude assessments as part of their assessment procedures for the selection and development of staff. They are powerful predictors of performance at work.

Assessments help you to:

- demonstrate your strengths;
- be assessed fairly on job relevant criteria;
- find out more about your strengths and development needs;
- make future career decisions based on your abilities.

Differences between Pessimists and Optimists

When bad events happen, pessimists tend to explain the calamity as:

- **Permanent** – Behind on earnings: "We're never going to hit our numbers." The pessimist believes that he's hit the iceberg, so the team is doomed. There is no point in problem-solving at this point, since the ship is going down anyway.
- **Pervasive** – Mad at your accountant: "Accountants are such losers." This is the tendency to explain all people or things in a category as bad even if only one is bad.

On the other hand, a little tweak in explanatory style when bad things happen and you become an optimist:

- **Temporary** – Behind on earnings: "This is a bad quarter, but next quarter we have a few things in the pipeline to make up for this quarter." The optimist looks for options when things are bad, making the situation a temporary negative. This keeps them and others motivated.
- **Specific** – Mad at your accountant: "I need to get a new accountant. This one's not working out." The optimist doesn't throw all bad people and things into the same category. They are specific about who or what is bad, and then they go find a good one.
  Optimistic people work harder. Pessimism severely hinders a person's ability to engage in life-improving acts. To a successful entrepreneur, this should be obvious.

Optimism is the propensity to look at the bright side of any situation and expect the best possible outcome from any series of events. People who feel optimism live their lives expecting positive outcomes and events. Optimism is powerfully motivational; optimism is one of the cornerstones of success.

Strategies to Improve Optimism
1. Paint a Positive Future
- By occasionally envisioning your long-term dreams, you will keep your mindset positive. This is especially important when something negative has happened. Imagining yourself in a Spanish vacation home or mailing a large donation to your favorite charity will instantly recharge your optimism.

Forget the Snooze
- By hopping out of bed on the first alarm sound, your day will already be headed in the right direction. Additionally, by waking up faster, you will be less drowsy throughout the day. Tiredness naturally leads to pessimism.

Breathe More Deeply and Drink Water—Lots of It
- More oxygen to your brain will allow you think more clearly. Most people have shallow, tiny breaths that do little for them. Deep breaths, on the other hand, will help boost positive thoughts.
- Along the same lines of breathing more deeply, drinking clean, cool water will give you an instant rush of positive energy.

Ditch the Downers
- Depressants are optimism killers. Everything from alcohol to negative people can significantly decrease your willingness to succeed. I'm not saying to stop drinking your nightly glass of red wine or to avoid your friends and family. What is necessary, though, is to tread lightly when around anyoneor anything that will lower your mood and optimism.

Meditation
- Countless generations of humans would agree with this one. By sneaking away for 15 minutes a day, your optimism and energy will surge. Meditation is a huge subject; however, to start, head to a dark room, sit in an upright position and clear

your mind. Keep your eyes slightly open and focus only on your breath. Be sure to set an alarm for 15–20 minutes, or you will unknowingly let a lot of time pass.

Give Yourself Some Me-Time

- Joining a yoga class, playing video games, reading a fictional book or any other activity that allows you to escape the world for a few hours will do wonders for your mindset. Hopefully, your me-time includes exercising. Remember: *Motion Creates Emotion.*

Forget the News

- The local and national news is the worst activity you can partake in when striving to stay optimistic. News organizations trap people into a world of fear and uncertainty—exactly what you do not need. Think I'm wrong? Well, what did learning that a little girl was murdered in a neighboring state do for you? If you didn't know it, are you better or worse off psychologically? You have enough on your mind. Forget the news.

To summarize, forget the negative and *surround yourself with everything positive*. Your success as an entrepreneur is directly relational to your optimism. So be sure to stay as positive as possible.

8. Persistence

Persistence is the biggest key to success as an entrepreneur. Persistence is a vital characteristic of successful entrepreneurs. Driven by an indomitable spirit, successful entrepreneurs never give up on their dreams of building a viable business. There is no impediment too great. This unflagging attribute is a key characteristic of triumphant business builders.

9. Customer Sensitivity

The entrepreneur builds trust and long-term relationships with customers, generates an expectation of high level of customer service, and regularly exceeds customer expectations.

10. People Focus

The entrepreneur creates common purpose with colleagues through shared vision and values, walks the talk, sees and values the best in others, builds the total capability of the immediate and wider team, and always considers the principles of inclusiveness in planning and dealing with others.

Conclusion

Despite the relative differences in the definitions, we can observe that the term *competence* is a broad concept that consistently associates knowledge, skills, attitudes and motivations as dimensions that competent entrepreneurs must be able to use in order to deal with the tasks and problems related to their entrepreneurial actions. Entrepreneur competences which are actually learnable and measurable knowledge, skills and attitudes are the base for construction of individuals' beliefs, potential reactions, expectations, and attitudes about their potential performance and of their views on the feasibility of possible entrepreneurial ideas, and as such they positively affect entrepreneurial intentions.

References

Anderson, K. (2012) Cultural Competence. http://aea365.org/blog/?p=7822.

Barnett, William F. Jr., and Terrance P. Berland. (1999) Strategic Thinking on the Front Lines. *McKinsey Quarterly* 2, 118–124.

Bird, B. (1995) Toward a Theory of Entrepreneurial Competency. *Advances in Entrepreneurship, Firm Emergence, and Growth.* JAI Press, 2, 51–72.

————. (2002) Learning Entrepreneurship Competencies: The Self-Directed Learning Approach. *International Journal of Entrepreneurship Education* I, 203–227.

Boyatzis, R. E. (1982) *The Competent Manager: A Model for Effective Performance.* New York: John Wiley & Sons.

Brophy, M., and T. Kiely. (2002) Competencies: a new sector. *Journal of European Industrial Training* 26(2/3/4):165–176.

Burgoyne, J. (1988) Competency Approaches to Management Development. Lancaster Centre for the Study of Management Learning, Lancaster, UK.

Chandler, G. N., and E. Jansen. (1992) The founder's self-assessed competence and venture performance. *Journal of Business Venturing* 7(3), 223–236.

————, and S. H. Hanks. (1994) Founder Competence, the Environment, and Venture Performance. *Entrepreneurship Theory and Practice* 18(3), 77–89.

Cooray, Mark. (1996) The Entrepreneur, Risk Taking and the Profit Motive. *From Bondage to Freedom.* http://www.ourcivilisation.com/cooray/btof/chap15.htm.

Debaise, Colleen. (2012) Seven Tips for Networking. http://www.entrepreneur.

de Bono, Edward. (1970) *Lateral Thinking.* New York: Harper & Row, Publishers.

————. (1982) *De Bono Thinking Course.* New York: Facts on File Publications.

Dixit, Avinash K., and Barry J. Nalebuff. (1991) *Thinking Strategically.* New York: W. W. Norton & Company.

Gibb, A. (1990) Training the trainers of small business. *Journal of European Industrial Training,* 14, 17–25.

Graetz, Fiona. (2002) Strategic Thinking Versus Strategic Planning: Toward Understanding the Complementarities. *Management Decision* (40) 5/6, 456–462.

Hayes, Nicky. (1994) *Psychology.* United Kingdom: Hodder Education.

Hussey, David. (2001) Creative Strategic Thinking and the Analytical Process: Critical Factors for Strategic Success. *Strategic Choice* (10) 4, 201–213.

Kiyosaki, Robert. (2011) Do You Have 8 Integrity of Entrepreneurship In Your Business? http://fenesi.com/do-you-have-8-integrity-of-entrepreneurship-in-your-business/.

Lans, T., R. Wesselink, H. J. A. Biemans, and M. Mulder. (2008) Work-related lifelong learning for entrepreneurs in the agri-food sector. *International Journal of Training and Development* 8, 72–88.

Larson, Reed, and David Hansen. (2005) The Development of Strategic Thinking: Learning to Impact Human Systems in a Youth Activism Program. *Human Development* (48) 6, 327–349.

Liedtka, Jeanne M. (1998) Linking Strategic Thinking with Strategic Planning. *Strategy and Leadership* (26) 4, 30–35.

Liles, P. R. (1974) Who Are the Entrepreneurs? *MSU Business Topics* 22, pp. 5–14.

Mansfield, R. S., D. C. McClelland, L. M. Spencer, and J. Santiago. (1987) The identification and assessment of competencies and other personal characteristics of entrepreneurs in developing countries, Final Report: Project No. 936-5314. *Entrepreneurship and Small Enterprise Development*, Contract No. DAN-5314-C-00-3065-00. Washington, DC: United States Agency for International Development.

Mole, V., S. Dawson, D. Winstanley, and J. Sherval. (1993) Researching managerial competences. Paper presented to British Academy of Management Annual Conference, Milton Keynes, September.

Onstenk, J. (2003) Entrepreneurship and education. *European Educational Research Journal* 2 (1), 74–89.

Parry, S. B. (1998) Just What Is a Competency? *Training* (6), 58–61.

Pink, Daniel H. (2006) *A Whole New Mind*. New York: Riverhead Books.

Sadler-Smith, E., C. W. Allinson, and J. Hayes. (2003) Learning preferences and cognitive style: some implications for continuing professional development. *Management Learning* Vol. 31, No. 2, pp. 239–256.

Schawbel, Dan. (2009) Top 10 Social Networks for Entrepreneurs. http://mashable.com/2009/03/12/entrepreneur

Spencer, L. M., and S. M. Spencer. (1993) *Competence at Work: Models for Superior Performance*. New York: John Wiley & Sons.

Steward, B. (2009) The Future of Entrepreneurial Businesses. http://andrewbarden.wordpress.com/category/entrepreneur/

Stoof, A. (2005) Tools for the Identification and Description of Competencies. Thesis Dissertation, Open Universiteit Nederland.

Tett, R. P., H. A. Guterman, A. Bleier, and P. J. Murphy. (2000) Development and Content Validation of a "Hyperdimensional" Taxonomy of Managerial Competence. *Human Performance* 13 (3), 212.

Chapter 8

ENTREPRENEURSHIP: A TOOL FOR BLISSFUL RETIREMENT

Adeigbe, Y. K.

Introduction

Events surrounding the post-work life experiences of retirees in Africa, and especially Nigeria, today confirm the need for self-sustenance as a pre-requisite for quality existence in life after retirement. This is more so when one realizes all the sufferings retirees experience as a result of either non-payment or irregular availability of monthly pensions. This trend emerged in the period immediately preceding the early 1990s. Pensioners have been severally reported to have died while endlessly waiting to be paid. If governmental agencies could be failing to make peoples' welfare the priority it deserves, then there is the need for individuals to source their survival legitimately elsewhere in retirement to prevent hardship.

The above picture, therefore, presents the acute need for entrepreneurship as a tool for good living in retirement, which is the focus of this write-up.

What is Entrepreneurship?

Entrepreneurship is an effort at beginning a company, organizing business deals, and taking of risks with an aim to make profits, using knowledge or education acquired (Omolayo 2006).

Entrepreneurship may thus be seen as the possession of the requisite knowledge, skills and aptitude towards making a conscious effort to be creative in the production process and to attract profit.

Omolayo (2006) opines that entrepreneurship can be seen as "the process of bringing together creative and innovative ideas andcoupling these with management-organization skills in order to combine people andmoney resources to meet an identified need and create wealth". Nwangwu (2007) was also quoted by Omolayo (2011) to have written that entrepreneurship is the process of bringing together the factors of production, which are land, labour, capital and managerial personnel, with a view to providing productive goods or services to serve human consumption.An entrepreneur, according to Robert and Michael (2002), can be defined as the one involved in the following: (1) initiative taking, (2) the organizing and reorganizing of social and economic mechanisms to turn resources and situations to practical account; and (3) the acceptance of risk or failure. They hold that, to an economist, an entrepreneur is one who brings resources, labour, materials, and other assets into combinations that make their value greater than before, and also one who introduces changes, innovations, and a new order. To a psychologist, such a person is typically driven by the need to obtain or attain something, to experiment, to accomplish, or perhaps to escape the authority of others. To one businessman, an entrepreneur appears as a threat, an aggressive competition, whereas, to another businessman, the same entrepreneur may be an ally, a source of supply, a

90

customer, or someone who creates wealth for others as well as finds better ways to utilize resources, reduce waste, and produce jobs others are glad to get. The duo went ahead to define entrepreneurship as "the dynamic process of creating incremental wealth. The wealth is created by individuals who assume the major risks in terms of equity, time, and/or career commitment or provide value for some product or service. The product or service may or may not be new or unique, but value must somehow be infused by the entrepreneur by receiving and locating the necessary skills and resources" (Robert and Michael 2002).

The ability, drive, willingness and conscious effort of an individual or a group to acquire the requisite technical know-how and apply it to the creative production of goods and services with a view to making profit can therefore be called entrepreneurship.

Entrepreneurship plays the important role of giving growth to new jobs and assisting the individuals as well as the society ultimately to sustain themselves and thus gives the required life-line to the welfare of all and sundry in a nation. This points to the essential need for entrepreneurship in the lives of human beings. The need for retirees to embrace entrepreneurship as a panacea to suffering in retirement is, therefore, a golden rule.

Entrepreneurship seems to be becoming more important all the time, and it is mainly put forward as an avenue to creating growth and new jobs, not least in order to include the increasing number of people who are excluded from the labour market (Berglund and Holmgren 2006).

An entrepreneur could be defined as someone who acquires or possesses ability and converts this to the production of economic goods and services that are required by human society, with an intention to make profit.

What is Retirement?

Retirement has been described as a process of work-role transition in which an individual withdraws from routine work performance due to old age, ill health, redundancy, or because of the necessity to leave work, having completed the official employment years in a particular working system (Akinboye 1998). Akinade (2006) also describes the concept of retirement as the terminus of a person's active primary earning life, a stage when one transits from a period in which one works for money to anomadic one in which money works for one.

According to Ogunbameru (1996), the retiree is bound to experience some problems in retirement. These include deterioration of health, rolelessness, loss of peer group, reduction or loss of income, loss of status, manifestation of negative emotional life with feelings of carrying a big burden, fears, and anger. One may also add that a person who leaves service, voluntarily or otherwise, but who has always planned for such an inevitable occurrence of being out of work one day, may not experience so much of the negative socio-economic or psycho-personal emotions that result from loss of work. It is, therefore, necessary that entrepreneurship is embraced as a way out of the problems usually faced by retirees in life after work.

Adeigbe (2011) reports that retirement-benefits administration and financing still create a lot of problems for the Nigerian society. He says retirees experience complete non-payment of monthly stipends (called *pensions*), unnecessary delay in payment of gratuities (now called *lump sum*) by authorities, or irregular payment of accruals needed for survival. For the wise, therefore, entrepreneurship and life in retirement should be taken as Siamese twins.

Acquiring Entrepreneurship Skills

The acquisition of skills involved in entrepreneurship requires conscious effort and the resolve to be self-actualized.

A study, commissioned by the World Bank in 2002 and carried out by Halfdan Farstad, reveals that informal micro-, small- and medium-sized enterprises (MSMEs) are important providers of decentralized employment, create income and contribute to poverty reduction. This does not exclude the retirees in our own situation; there is just the need to stimulate and evolve more of self-sustenance programmes tailored towards profitable self-reliance as an entrepreneur. Through this, one would become an employer of labour instead of waiting for a retirement stipend that may be irregular or not sufficient for survival.

Arogundade (2011) reports that the need for entrepreneurship education started emerging in the mid-1980s, stressing that the reason for this was because, before this period, unemployment and poverty were not issues of national concern as they are currently. This need has now extended to the retirees because of the need not to rely on returns from retirement, which may either not come at all or be irregular.

Tracing the current trend of uncertainty that heralded in the need for self-employment, it was reported by Arogundade (2011) that Kolawole and Omolayo (2006) discovered that political instability and inconsistencies in the social–economic policies of successive governments were said to have led to the emergence of a high level of unemployment in Nigeria, while the collapse of the economy, leading to youth and graduate unemployment as well as early retirement of able-bodied men and layoff of workers, had started since the 1980s (Arogundade 2011).

It could therefore be argued that, given these various unexpected and sudden losses of sources of the means for survival as well as myriad disappointments in collection of monthly stipends by retirees at the end of the month, learning to start one's own business that will guarantee some profits and hence an average level of good quality living in retirement is desirable. This is more so when we are in a situation in this part of the world where the full monthly take-home pay of workers hardly gets home because of continuous rises in the prices of goods and services—no thanks to galloping inflationary trends. Government is even currently fighting to withdraw from subsidies in whatever form, including that on petrol, the major Nigerian export. The populace, and especially the retirees, are therefore fully on their own. This view is held because there is no longer any way to transfer part of the load back to government for retirees, either by asking for more salaries or higher allowances. If it comes at all, the retirement stipend is now fixed. The way out, therefore, is a self-reliant effort at self-sustenance, which entrepreneurship provides.

Many individuals have been noted to be having difficulties developing their business ideas to the level of commercialization with a view to creating profitable ventures of their own due to lack of requisite technical know-how and appropriate information.

A list of steps to follow in acquiring entrepreneurship skills is presented in the theoretical framework contained in Figure 8.1.

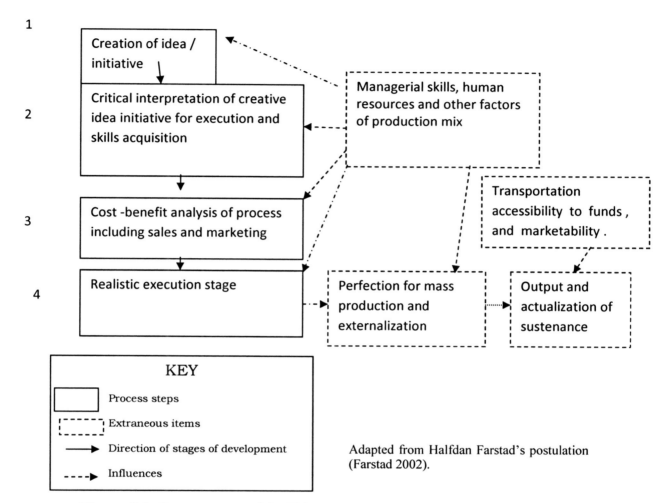

Figure 8.1: Entrepreneurship Skills Acquisition Processes Model

Source: (C) Adeigbe, Y. K.

From the above model, the steps for entrepreneurship skill development and execution are:

(a) generation of creative entrepreneurship ideas or initiative;
(b) critical examination and interpretation of generated idea or initiative;
(c) engaging in a cost-benefit analysis of the product idea, with a view to perfecting sales and marketing strategies;
(d) actual execution of idea or initiative for concrete production, including budgeting, cash control and marketability;
(e) perfection of goods or services for mass production and profitability;
(f) final output and attainment of self-sustenance.

It is pertinent to note that the success of entrepreneurship drive is largely based on a value-added approach to creativity, because it is through this that the emerging entrepreneurship will take leadership position and control of the market.

In some situations, new members of a sales situation may add home delivery, attractive packaging or higher quantity of product offered without any adverse effect on competitive pricing, to snatch quality customers from the market. Aggressive publicity and personal contact do help the green entrepreneur to quickly stabilize and be a leader in sales.

However, it should be noted that there are areas of adverse experiences, which one should neverallow to lead to depression if one must succeed. These include capital problems, theft by staff and (or) machinery disappointment, among others. An entrepreneur who produces sachet water, for instance, may take some time before taking full control of the situation since he cannot solely be involved in all facets of production, marketing and accounting. Any emerging lapse must be considered as never to be allowed to lead to high disappointment, which may cause the juvenile entrepreneur to abandon the self-sustained idea.

Some Small-Scale Production Ideas That a Retiree May Engage in

1. Bakery or bread-making factory
2. Soap-making factory
3. Poultry or fish farming
4. Product distribution and marketing, e.g., sales of printing papers or photographic materials
5. Sachet water factory
6. Transport business
7. Block-making factory
8. Candle or chalk production
9. Day care, nursery or primary school ownership
10. Insurance agency
11. Bookshop ownership
12. Mechanized farming.

References

Adeigbe, Y. K. (2011) Psycho-personal Predictors of Fear of Retirement Among Public Servants in Osun State, Nigeria. An unpublished PhD Thesis.

Akinade, E.A. (2006) *Towards a Successful and Joyful Retirement.* Ibadan: Olu-Akin Press.

Akinboye, J. O. (1998) *Happy Retirement.* Ibadan: Dot Kamerun (Nig) Ltd.

Arogundade, B. B. (2011) Entrepreneurship Education: An Imperative for Sustainable Development in Nigeria. *Journal of Emerging Trends in Educational Research and Policy Studies (JETERAPS)* 2(1): 26–29.

Berglung, Karin, and Carina Holmgren. (2006) At the Intersection of Entrepreneurship Education Policy and Practice: on conflicts, tensions and closures. A paper presented at the 14th Nordic Conference on Small Business Research, 11th–13th May, 2006, in Stockholm.

Farstad, Halfdan. (2002) Integrated Entrepreneurship Education in Botswana, Uganda and Kenya. A review commissioned by the World Bank. Oslo, Norway: National Institute of Technology.

Nwangwu, I. O. (2007) Higher education for self-reliance: an imperative for the Nigerian economy. NEAP Publication, p. 1–8.

Ogunbameru, O. A. (1996) Retirement: On the need for planning policy at the Local Government in Nigeria. *Ife Social Sciences Review* 13 (2),1 and 2, p. 78–83.

Omolayo, B. (2006) Entrepreneurship in Theory and practice. In Omotosho, F., T. K. O. Aluko, O. I. Wale Awe, and G. Daramola (eds.), *Introduction to Entrepreneurship Development in Nigeria.* Ado-Ekiti: UNAD Press.

Robert, D. H., and P. P. Michael. (2002) *Entrepreneurship.* New York: McGraw-Hill.

Chapter 9

EMERGING ISSUES IN ENTREPRENERSHIP AND OPPORTUNITY RECOGNITION AS THE BEDROCK OF A MARKET-DRIVEN ECONOMY

Adegbite, S.A.

Introduction

Entrepreneurs generally identify opportunities for new products, new markets and new process creations. Although technology changes generate a range of opportunities, not every entrepreneur is able to discover these opportunities. Only entrepreneurs who recognize that opportunities exist and value them can earn profits from these opportunities.

Concept of Entrepreneurship

In the theoretical history of entrepreneurship, scholars and researchers from multiple disciplines such as anthropology (Steward 1991), psychology (Shaver and Scott 1991), sociology (Reynolds 1991), economics (Kirchoff 1991), management (Stevenson 1985) and technology (Roberts 1991; Litvak and Maule 1999) have grappled with a diverse set of interpretations and definitions of entrepreneurship. Also, in the last century, many researchers have identified entrepreneurship with the function of uncertainty and risk bearing; identification and recognition of opportunities; coordination of productive resources; the introduction of innovation; and the provision of technical know-how (Burnet 2000).

The necessity of entrepreneurship for production was first recognized by Alfred Marshall in 1890 when he asserted in his treatise, *Principles of Economics*, that there are four factors of production, i.e., land, labour, capital and organization. Entrepreneurship, both technological and commercial, is the driving element behind a modern organization. The skills associated particularly with entrepreneurship are rare and limited in supply, and the ability of entrepreneurs are so great and so numerous that very few people can exhibit them all in a very high degree (Marshall 1890). Other researchers such as Penrose (1963) posit that entrepreneurial activity involves identifying opportunities within the economic system and filling market deficiencies through input-completing activities, including the process of identifying, developing and bringing a vision to life. This vision may be an innovative idea, an opportunity, or a better way of doing something. The end result of this process is the creation of a new technology-based venture or the expansion of an existing one, carried out under conditions of risks and considerable uncertainty.

Technological and Commercial Entrepreneurship

In recognition of the considerable risks and uncertainty associated with entrepreneurship, Afonja (1999) made a clear distinction between technological entrepreneurship and commercial entrepreneurship. The former involves product manufacture or the provision of technical services while the latter involves trading, buying and selling or provision of non-technical services. The prerequisites for success and risk factors involved differ significantly for the two types of entrepreneurship. Similarly, Joseph Schumpeter's (1934) definition of technological entrepreneurship placed emphasis on innovative skills for the creation of new products, new production methods, markets and new forms of organization. It was further suggested that wealth is created when such an innovation results in new demand.

From this point of view, the function of the technological entrepreneur involves combining the various input factors in an innovative manner to generate value that will exceed the cost of input factors and generate profit. The technological entrepreneur is an innovator who implements change within the markets through the carrying out of new combinations (Schumpeter 1943). The combinations can take several forms, including the introduction of a new product, a new method of production, opening of a new market, the discovery of a new source of supply of raw materials, and the creation of a new organization. In this context, Schumpeter equated technological entrepreneurship with innovation and the combination of resources.

The Entrepreneurial Process

Bygrave and Hofer (1991) characterized the entrepreneurial process as involving all the activities and actions associated with the perceiving of opportunities and the creation of organizations to pursue them. Bygrave (1995) and Carton *et al.* (1998) further explain that entrepreneurial process involves applying new management concepts and techniques, standardizing the product, designing processes and tools, analyzing the work to be done and setting required standards (Drucker 1985). Bygrave (1995) argued that the role of an entrepreneur is that of an innovator, which involves the ability to combine various inputs into new innovations in order to satisfy unfulfilled market demand. In this context, innovation could be technological, process, market, product, factor or even organizational innovations (Di Massi 1999).

The underlying concepts of entrepreneurship are the key dimensions of innovativeness, risk-taking, pro-activeness and opportunity recognition. Innovativeness is a creative, unusual or novel solution to problems and needs. These solutions can take the form of new technologies and processes as well as new products and technical services (Covin and Slevin 1991). Risk-taking involves the willingness to commit significant resources to opportunities having a reasonable chance of costly failure. These risks are typically manageable and calculated. Pro-activeness is concerned with implementation, with doing whatever is necessary to bring an entrepreneurial concept to fruition (Covin and Slevin 1991). The process usually involves considerable perseverance, adaptability and a willingness to assume some responsibility for failure. To the extent that a manufacturing industry demonstrates some amount of innovativeness, risk-taking and pro-activeness, it can be considered an entrepreneurial process and the person behind it an entrepreneur.

In addition, Stevenson (1983) described entrepreneurship as management pursuing opportunities without reference to resources currently controlled (Brown and Eisenhardt 1995). Before an opportunity can be considered worthy of pursuit, it must first be recognized. It was Kirzner (1973) who first identified the central importance of the discovery of opportunities to entrepreneurship. He argued that entrepreneurs find and exploit opportunities by taking advantage of economic disequilibrium by knowing or recognizing things that others do not. Prior customer and market knowledge and responses to specific problems have been considered to be the key antecedents to opportunity recognition (Hills and Schrader 1998; Shane 2000). As a response to economic disequilibrium, opportunity recognition has been theorized as an event dependent on opportunity alertness, the ability to notice, without search, opportunities that have hitherto been overlooked (Kirzner 1979). Opportunity alertness, as the necessary antecedent to opportunity recognition, an element of the entrepreneurial process, is thus arguably the cornerstone of a firm's entrepreneurial behavior.

Entrepreneurial Opportunities

Perhaps one of the most important characteristics of entrepreneurs is the ability to see an opportunity that others may not, a gap in the market that needs to be filled, and the resources to exploit it. It consists of a specific combination of handling risks, content and market. This trait, according to Afonja (1999), is largely intuitive but can also be cultivated. Spotting an opportunity and a gap in the market may involve the creation of a completely new market. But most successful entrepreneurs are people who come up with better ways to serve an existing market or find better ways of doing something that exists already.

Specifically, they can find opportunities by looking for better ways to accomplish a task through inventions, creative imitations, new services and new products. They perform these tasks by exploring a segment of the population which could respond to a new or improved product targeted to lifestyle or needs, delivering a cheaper product or service than that which is currently available in the market, applying a new technology to solve customers' problems in a different way, or finding a business location which is more convenient for customers (Gibbs 1998). Other scholars also discuss the centrality of opportunity recognition for entrepreneurship. For instance, Kirzner (1973) argues that the process of discovery, that is recognizing and exploiting things that others do not, is a proximate issue of entrepreneurship. Vesper (1996) suggests a search approach in identifying new venture opportunities. Stevenson *et al.* (1999) posit that technical entrepreneurship is driven mainly by perceptions of opportunity. Timmons *et al.* (1987) maintain that opportunity recognition should be viewed as the most important steps in the entrepreneurial process. Christensen *et al.* (1997) defined opportunity recognition as either perceiving a probability to create a new business or significantly improving the position of existing business.

The literature discussed above is convincing based on the fact that the ability to recognize a new venture opportunity is a critical first step in the entrepreneurial process. However, taken together, the researchers appear to imply that individuals recognize entrepreneurial opportunities by showing how network entrepreneurs, that is, individuals who recognized entrepreneurial opportunities through their personal networks, identified significantly more opportunities than sole entrepreneurs who believe that the business idea is strictly their own.

What is Opportunity Recognition?

The origin of opportunity recognition has its roots in the classic entrepreneurship literature. However, much of this early literature attempted to explain the process of new firm creation and growth, with an almost exclusive focus on the entrepreneur's traits and personalities. Authors attempted to explain how these 'special' qualities endowed entrepreneurs with a unique ability or driving force to create and nurture new businesses. Many such driving forces were proposed, including the need for achievement (McClelland 1961), locus of control (Rotter 1966), or an extraordinary ability to transform markets through innovation (Schumpeter 1934).

Opportunity recognition has subsequently emerged as a field of entrepreneurship research in its own right (Gaglio 1997; Venkataraman 1997; Shane and Venkataraman 2000; Hills and Shrader 1998; Hills et al. 1999; Koen and Kohli 1998; Singh et al. 1999; Zietsma 1999; Craig and Lindsay 2001; Shepherd and De Tienne 2001). Kirzner (1973) suggested that entrepreneurs possessed or obtained specialized knowledge and could use it to create or exploit opportunities. This is reinforced in later studies by Kaish and Gilad (1991) and Busenitz (1996), where entrepreneurs were shown to be more active in seeking opportunity than corporate managers. Hills and Shrader (1998) and Zietsma (1999) also found that the successful entrepreneurs had high levels of entrepreneurial alertness. Timmons (1999) proposed that successful entrepreneurs have the capacity to see what others do not. Opportunity recognition is a skill highly relevant in the field of technology, where some huge product innovations have largely involved the transfer of a 'low-value' technology from one business sector to another where it becomes 'high-value' (Christensen 1997).

The most comprehensive review of opportunity recognition is by Gaglio (1997), drawing upon the earlier research proposing opportunity recognition as a long deliberate process. A four-stage process is proposed, involving pre-vision, vision, elaboration and eventual launch decision. However, this model fails to include the extremely important refinement stage, a critical part of any market entry. The most recent study of opportunity recognition processes used by entrepreneurs is directly based upon technology businesses. Shane (2000) demonstrates that just one technology can spawn multiple business opportunities. Shane (2000) surveyed eight entrepreneurs, who have all exploited very different market manifestations originating from one original technology patent, and proposed a simple model of opportunity recognition based on two key components: technological invention and prior experience. He argues that the ability of an entrepreneur to recognize the market value of a particular technological innovation is based on the entrepreneur's ability to recognize the value of the invention in the market based on the previous experience he or she has in solving customer problems in related markets. The issues explored are:

i. Building understanding of the sources of information used by entrepreneurs to identify opportunities (Hills 1995);
ii. The importance of social networks in opportunity recognition (Julien 1995; Singh et al. 1999);
iii. The structure of the opportunity recognition process (Hills et al. 1999);

iv. The role of personal intuition in the conception development and execution of opportunities (Baker *et al*. 2001; Craig and Lindsay 2001); and

v. The specific role of prior knowledge and the importance of knowledge of customers and markets (Shepherd and De Tienne 2001).

In Zahra's (1991) study, three antecedents of corporate entrepreneurship are developed. These are external environment, grant strategy, and organizational related variables. External environment not only offers new opportunity but also reinforces organization to be adaptive and innovative (Meyer 1982; Zahra 1991). In addition, external environment serves as a variety of resources for new product development, such as suppliers, competitors, customers, distributors, alliances, partners, universities and so on (Huber 1991; Salter and Narver 1995; Zahra 1991). Opportunities emerge from dynamic environment and industry change. Furthermore, new niches and markets are developed by shift or change from social, technological, economic and political environment (Zahra 1991). This means that entrepreneurial opportunity recognition is one of the corporate entrepreneurship activities.

Stevenson and Gumpert (1985) also propose that entrepreneurial opportunity is influenced by the two factors referred to as "entrepreneur's opportunity matrix." One is the extent of entrepreneur's desired future state, such as change and growth, and the other is the entrepreneur's own self-perceived power and ability to realize goals. They stress that sometimes entrepreneurs might not necessarily desire to have breakthrough innovation. As a result, entrepreneurs usually utilize existing resources and technology with slight modification to develop a new market or accommodate the newly perceived market segment. That means that what opportunities bring to innovation is the activity to reconfigure the resources in organization.

Steven and Gumpert (1985) point out the following external pressures, which stimulate opportunity recognition, including technology, consumer economics, social values and political action and regulatory standards. That is, how managers perceive external environment changes have impact on the organizational development (Daft and Weick 1984: Meyer 1982; Steven and Gumpert 1985). Gaglio and Katz (2001) from a psychological perspective also argue that entrepreneurial alertness influences the opportunity identification process. It is the psychological scheme of alertness that decides individual's perception of opportunities and interpretation of external stimulus. Gaglio and Katz (2001) and Steven and Gumpert (1985) did not mention "prior knowledge" in their study about entrepreneurs' perceptions and discoveries of opportunities. Shane and Venkataraman (2000) suggest that information corridors and cognitive properties are two main factors that determine whether entrepreneurs discover particular opportunities. These two factors, information corridors and cognitive properties, can be explained in Shane's (2000) empirical study, which concludes that prior knowledge and experiences are the antecedents of entrepreneurial opportunity recognition. Both information corridors and cognitive properties put emphasis on mental disposition, which frames an individual's recognition of new opportunities. The information an individual possesses can be viewed as one's prior knowledge and experiences. Therefore, the cognitive properties in valuing opportunities are dependent on the prior information one possessed.

Similarly, Ardichvili, Cardozo and Ray (2003) have constructed a theoretical model and propositions that influence the entrepreneurial opportunity recognition process. The theoretical model comprises five factors affecting the core process of entrepreneurial opportunity recognition, such as entrepreneurial alertness, information asymmetry and prior knowledge, social network, personality traits, and types of opportunity itself. The personality traits include optimism, self-efficacy and creativity. These traits are similar to those found in traditional entrepreneurship studies, which focus on the roles and function of entrepreneurs in opportunity recognition.

Furthermore, Ozgen (2003) examines factors in the entrepreneurial opportunity recognition process from three perspectives. These are environmental context, social context and personal context. Under environmental context, information flow and knowledge acquisition play critical roles in creating opportunity. It was argued that access to industry-related information could update an individual's knowledge base and provide insights in recognizing new opportunities. In the same vein, social perspective was defined as interpersonal networking, which also plays a positive role in the entrepreneurial opportunity recognition process. Prior knowledge is examined as one factor having impact on the mental process of entrepreneurs. It shapes the individual's mental process in organizing information and identifying information relevant to existing schemes. Prior knowledge contains prior work experiences and education training. Hence, prior knowledge and experiences have been discussed most frequently in studying factors influencing entrepreneurial opportunity recognition. Shane (2000) has explored eight enterprises through in-depth case studies and states that entrepreneurial opportunity recognition means the entrepreneurs have the ability to recognize new knowledge to exploit new products and technology, including knowledge of markets, knowledge of ways to serve markets, knowledge of customer problems, and knowledge of technology. Therefore, entrepreneurial opportunity recognition may lead to better deciphering and understanding other new knowledge or technology for innovation.

However, entrepreneurs easily fail to identify and recognize the possible opportunities for new processes, new products, new markets, or new process creations. Kirzner (1973) indicates that the distribution of information in society influences the discovery of entrepreneurial opportunities. In other words, although technology changes generate a range of opportunities, not every entrepreneur is able to discover these opportunities. Venkataraman (1997) proposes that opportunities do not appear in a well-packaged informational form. That is, the process of discovering opportunities depends on people's ability and willingness to scan the environment. External pressures, for example, change in technology, stimulate opportunity recognition. Nevertheless, people might not be able or willing to pay attention to these, which may lead to loss of opportunity (Stevenson and Gumpert 1985).

Models of Opportunity Recognition

Based on different assumptions, numerous models have been developed for identification and exploitation of entrepreneurial opportunities.

Plummer *et al.* Model

In Figure 1, Plummer *et al.* (2007) state that opportunity is discovered when an entrepreneur finds that the optimum use of a set of resources has not been made: an entrepreneurial opportunity is recognized. Thereafter, the decision to exploit the opportunity is based on the entrepreneur's evaluation that the opportunity's expected value (i.e., profit) will exceed the opportunity cost paid in its exploitation; individuals will differ in their evaluations, and some will exploit the opportunity while others will not (Plummer 2007). An entrepreneur estimates the value of the resources based on his knowledge and perception. Even in the case of a fixed expected value, different people may not gain the same evaluation results. Finally, as part of the exploitation base, the mode of exploitation is selected based on a combined assessment of the nature of the opportunity itself, the competitive environment, and the potential for appropriating the returns for the entrepreneur's efforts.

The element Plummer *et al.* (2007) introduced is the idea that the exploitation process includes deciding the best strategy for exploiting the opportunity, given the characteristic of the opportunity and the nature of the environment. They call this the entrepreneurial strategizing portion of the exploitation phase, and suggest that it involves a determination of the optimal set of actions, decisions, and commitments to be made to maximize the returns from the exploitation of the opportunity. They refer to this as the strategy-opportunity-environment fit.

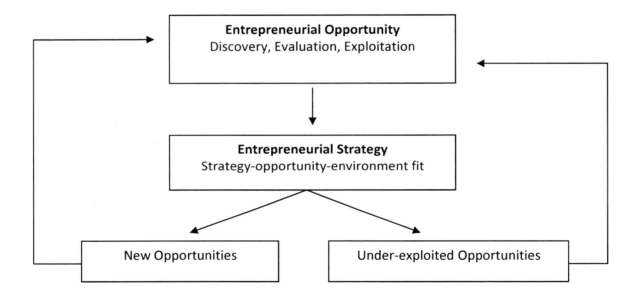

Fig. 9.1: Plummer *et al.* Model (Plummer 2007)

In summary, whether or not entrepreneurial activity creates a new opportunity, the entrepreneur's effort is also very likely to make the original opportunity available for other entrepreneurs to pursue.

Ulwick's Model

Emphasizing the role of customer satisfaction in the organization success, Ulwick (2002) believes that organizations should apply a suitable method to gather customers' ideas and needs. The reason why many organizations are not able satisfy their customers is that they listen to them in a wrong way. Customers should not be expected to offer effective final solutions, since they are not experts of the field. The best way is to ask them about the value sought and the final results they are looking for, and then the organization takes the responsibility for innovating and fulfilling the identified need. Ulwick (2002) emphasizes that organizations should follow a procedure in gathering customers' ideas, based on the final result, not solutions. He introduces a five-step model as follows:

(a) **Customer Interview:** Planning interviews with customers based on the results and final situation they are looking for. In this step, the target product or service should be analyzed, and customers show "importance" and "satisfaction" from the current situation.

(b) **Deriving desired results:** Results of the previous stage should be analyzed and evaluated carefully to make sure they are all targeted needs, not solutions.

(c) **Organization:** The results are categorized and organized, and a list is prepared.

(d) **Ranking the Results:** The gathered results are then quantified. Since the pursuit of unimportant opportunities will waste an organization's resources, each of the items from the first step will be graded in order to identify the most important opportunities.

(e) **Utilizing the results for innovation:** Using the list of ranked results provided in the previous stage, the organization will be able to identify the most promising opportunities for developing new products and services.

In summary, Ulwick's model perception of what customers are looking for is more valuable and important than finding out their solutions. The innovation process starts with recognition of what results customers are looking for and ends in offering products or services they would choose.

Ardichvili, Richard, and Sourav Model

Ardichvili, Cardozo and Ray (2003) developed a model to help understand the process of entrepreneurial opportunity identification (Fig. 2). Describing the process, these researchers point to personality traits, social networks and prior knowledge as the initiators of opportunity identification which cause entrepreneurial alertness (Ardichvili *et al*. 2003).

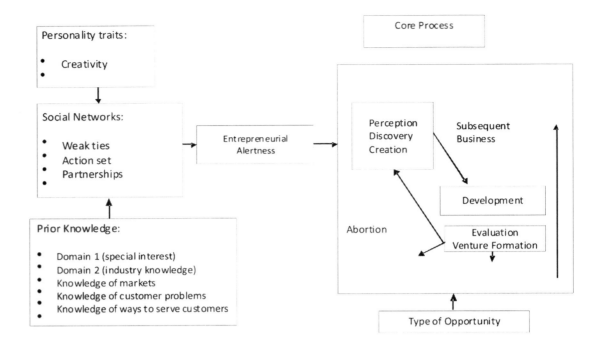

Fig. 9.2: Ardichvili *et al.* Model (2003)

Review Questions

1. Define entrepreneurship and explain why entrepreneurship is necessary for production.
2. Briefly explain the following:
    i. Technological entrepreneurship
    ii. Commercial entrepreneurship
    iii. Entrepreneurial process
3. Discuss between the following recognition models:
    i. Plummer (2007)
    ii. Ulwick (2002)
    iii. Ardichvili *et al.* (2003)

References

Afonja, A. A. (1999) "Materials, Energy and Environment," an Inaugural Lecture. Faculty of Technology, University of Ife, Ife, Nigeria.

Ardichvili, A., C. Richard, and R. Sourav. (2003) "A theory of entrepreneurial opportunity identification and development." *Journal of Business Venturing* 18(1), 105–123.

Baker, T., A. S. Miner, and D. T. Eesley. (2001) "Fake it until you make it: Improvisation and New Ventures." A paper presented at the Babson College Entrepreneurship Research Conference, Babson College, Wellesley, MA. *Frontiers of Entrepreneurship Research.* http://digitalknowledge.babson.edu/fer/.

Brown, S. L., and K. M. Eisenhardt. (1995) "Product Development: Past Research, Present Findings, and Future Directions." *Academy of Management Review* 20, 343–378.

Burnett, D. (2000) "Hunting for Heffalumps: The Supply of Entrepreneurship and Economic Development." In Technopreneurial.com, *History of Entrepreneurship Theory*, pp. 1–3.

Busenitz, L. (1996) "Research on Entrepreneurial Alertness." *Journal of Small Business Management* October, 35–44.

Bygrave, W. D. (1995) "Mom-and-Pops, High Potential Start-Ups, and Intrapreneurship: Are They Part of the Same Entrepreneurship Paradigm?" In Katz, J. A., and R. H. Brockhaus (eds.), *Advances In Entrepreneurship, Firm Emergence and Growth*. Greenwich, CT: JAI Press, 1–20.

————, and C. W. Hofer. (1991) "Theorizing about Entrepreneurship." *Entrepreneurship Theory and Practice* Vol. 16, pp. 13–22.

Carton, R. B., C. W. Hofer, and M. D. Meeks. (1998) "The Entrepreneur and Entrepreneurship: Operational Definition of their Roles in Society." Paper presented at the Annual International Council for Small Business Conference, Singapore. Athens, GA: The University of Georgia, Terry College of Business, pp. 1–10. http://www.sbaer.uca.edu/research/icsb/1998/32.pdf.

Christiensen, C. M. (1997) *The Innovators Dilemma: When Technologies Cause Great Firms to Fail*. Boston, MA: Harvard Business School Press.

Covin, J., and D. P. Slevin. (1991) "A Conceptual Framework of Entrepreneurship as a Firm Behaviour." *Entrepreneurship Theory and Practice* 16(1):7–25.

Craig, J., and N. Lindsay. (2001) "Quantifying 'gut feeling' in the Opportunity Recognition Process." A paper presented at the Babson College Entrepreneurship Research Conference, Babson College, Wellesley, MA. *Frontiers of Entrepreneurship Research*. http://digitalknowledge.babson.edu/fer/.

Daft, R. L., and K. E. Weick. (1984) "Toward a Model of Organizations as Interpretation Systems." *Academy Management Review* 9, 284–295.

Di Massi, P. (1999) "Defining Entrepreneurship."
Generated at e-mail pauljude@centrin.net.id.

Drucker, P. (1985) *Innovation and Entrepreneurship: Practice and Principles*. New York: Harper and Row.

Eason, G., B. Noble, and I. N. Sneddon. (2005) "On certain integrals of Lipschitz-Hankel type involving products of Bessel functions." *Phil. Trans. Roy. Soc. London* Vol. A247, pp. 529–551.

Gaglio, C. M. (1997) "Opportunity Identification Review, Critique and Suggested Research Directions." *Advances in Entrepreneurship, Firm Emergence and Growth* Vol. 3, pp. 139–201.

————, and J. A. Katz. (2001) "The Psychological Basis of Opportunity Identification; Entrepreneurial Alertness." *Small Business Economics* 16(2), 95–111.

Hills, G. E. (1995) "Opportunity Recognition by Successful Entrepreneurs." A paper presented at the Babson College Entrepreneurship Research Conference, Babson College, Wellesley, MA. *Frontiers of Entrepreneurship Research*. http://digitalknowledge.babson.edu/fer/.

————, and R. C. Shrader. (1998) "Successful Entrepreneurs' Insights into Opportunity Recognition." A paper presented at the Babson College Entrepreneurship Research Conference, Babson College, Wellesley, MA. *Frontiers of Entrepreneurship Research.* http://digitalknowledge.babson.edu/fer/.

————, C. Rodney, G. T. Shrader, and T. Lumpkin. (1999) "Opportunity Recognition as a Creative Process." A paper presented at the Babson College Entrepreneurship Research Conference, Babson College, Wellesley, MA. *Frontiers of Entrepreneurship Research.* http://digitalknowledge.babson.edu/fer/.

Hornsby, J. S., and D. F. Kuratko. (1994) "A Proposed Research Model of Entrepreneurial Motivation." *Entrepreneurship Theory and Practice* 18(3), 29–42.

Huber, G. P. (1991) "Organizational Learning: The Contributing Processes and the Literatures." *Organization Science* 2, 88–115.

Julien, P. (1995) "New Technologies and Technological Information in Small Business." *Journal of Business Venturing* 10(6), 459–475.

Kaish, S., and B. Gilad. (1991) "Characteristics of Opportunities Search of Entrepreneurs versus Executives: Sources, Interests, General Alertness." *Journal of Business Venturing* 6 (1), 45–61.

Kirchhoff, B. (1991) *Entrepreneurship and Dynamic Capitalism: The Economics of Business Firm Formation and Growth.* Westport, CT: Praeger Press.

Kirzner, I. M. (1973) *Competition and Entrepreneurship.* Chicago: University of Chicago Press.

Koen, P. A., and P. Kohli. (1998) "Idea Generation: Who comes up with the most Profitable Products?" A paper presented at the Babson College Entrepreneurship Research Conference, Babson College, Wellesley, MA. *Frontiers of Entrepreneurship Research.* http://digitalknowledge.babson.edu/fer/.

Litvak, I. A., and C. J. Maule. (1999) "Comparative Technical Entrepreneurship: Some Perspectives." *Journal of Economics,* Carlton University, Department of Economics, pp. 31–8.

Marshall, A. (1890) *Principles of Economics.* Oxford, UK: Oxford University Press.

Meyers, A. D. (1982) "Adopting the Environmental Jolts." *Administrative Science Quarterly* 27, 515–537.

Ozgen, E. (2003) "Entrepreneurial Opportunity Recognition: Information Flow, Social and Cognitive Perspective." Unpublished Doctoral Dissertation, Rensselaer Polytechnic Institute, Troy, NY.

Penrose, E. (1963) *The Theory of Growth of the Firm.* New York: Wiley Press.

Plumber, L. A. (2007) "An essay on the origins of entrepreneurial opportunity." *Small Business Economics* 4, 363–379.

Reynolds, P. (1991) "Nascent Entrepreneurship in Northern Europe." In EIM (ed.), *Entrepreneurship in the Netherlands.* The Hague/Zoetermer: EIM/EZ.

Roberts, E. B. (1991) "How to Succeed in a New Technology Enterprise." *Technology Review,* December, 1970, p. 22.

Rotter, J. B. (1996) "Generalized Expectancies for Internal versus External Locus of Control of Reinforcement." *Psychological Monographs* 80, 1–28.

Schumpeter, J. (1934) *The Theory of Economic Development.* Cambridge, MA: Harvard University Press.

————. (1943) *Capitalism, Socialism and Democracy.* New York: Harper and Row Press.

Shane, S. (2000) "Prior Knowledge and the Discovery of Entrepreneurial Opportunities." *Organization Science* 11, 448–469.

————, and S. Venkataraman. (2000) "The promise of entrepreneurship as a field of research." *Academy of Management Review* 25 (1), 217-226.

Shaver, K. G., and L. R. Scott. (1991) "Person, Process, Choice: The Psychology of New Venture Creation." *Entrepreneurship Theory and Practice* 16(2), 23–45.

Shepherd, D. A., and D. R. De Tienne. (2001) "Discovery of Opportunities Anomalies, Accumulation and Alertness." A paper presented at the Babson College Entrepreneurship Research Conference, Babson College, Wellesley, MA. *Frontiers of Entrepreneurship Research.* http://digitalknowledge.babson.edu/fer/.

Singh, R. P., G. E. Hills, R. P. Hybels, and G. T. Lumpkin. (1999) "Opportunity Recognition through Social Network Characteristics of Entrepreneurs." A paper presented at the Babson College Entrepreneurship Research Conference, Babson College, Wellesley, MA. *Frontiers of Entrepreneurship Research.* http://digitalknowledge.babson.edu/fer/.

Stevenson, H. (1985) "A New Paradigm for Entrepreneurial Management." In Kao and H. Stevenson (eds.), *Entrepreneurship: What it is and how to teach it.* Boston, MA: HBR Press.

————, and D. E. Gumpert. (1985) "The Heart of Entrepreneurship." *Harvard Business Review* 63(2), 85–95.

————, and J. C. Jarillo-Mossi. (1986) "Preserving Entrepreneurship as Companies Grow." *The Journal of Business Strategy* 7, 10–23.

Timmons, J. A. (1999) *New Venture Creation: Entrepreneurship for the 21ˢᵗ Century.* Singapore: McGraw-Hill.

Ulwick, A. (2002) "Using Customers' Ideas for Innovation." Translated by Kamelia Ehtechame Akbari. *Gozide Modiriat Journal* 17.

Venkataraman, S. (1997) "The Distinctive Domain of Entrepreneurship Research." *Advances in Entrepreneurship, Firm Emergence and Growth*, Vol. 3. pp. 119–138.

Vesper, K. H. (1996) *New Venture Experience.* Seattle, WA: Vector Books.

Zahra, S. A. (1991) "Predictors and Financial Outcomes of Corporate Entrepreneurship: An Exploratory Study." *Journal of Business Venturing* 6, 259-285.

Zietsma, C. (1999) "Opportunity Knocks or Does It Hide?" A paper presented at the Babson College Entrepreneurship Research Conference, Babson College, Wellesley, MA. *Frontiers of Entrepreneurship Research.* http://digitalknowledge.babson.edu/fer/.

Chapter 10

GENERAL OVERVIEW OF KEY SUCCESS FACTORS IN SETTING UP A SMALL BUSINESS

Opatola, M. O.

Introduction

According to Steve Ma Reyna, success, they say, is "where preparation and opportunity meet." The questions that come to one's mind are: How does one define and measure success in one's business? How does one know if the business is a success? Can one tell if one is on or off course? And if one is off course, what corrective action(s) can be taken?

An important part of planning your business entails knowing the key things that can tell you when you have reached your goals. Called key success factors, these are indicators or milestones that measure your business achievements and help determine how well you are progressing towards your goals and objectives. Without determining your key success factors, you run the risk of needing to make expensive changes of direction later on, as you have not aligned your objectives to the success of your business. You must sit down and think what you really need to do to make your dream business a success.

The process of setting up your key success factors need not be tedious or difficult. Simply ask the question: "What are the key things that, if I do them well, will ensure my success as a business?"

General Overview of Key Success Factors in Setting up a Small Business

This chapter will enable learners to identify and describe the key variables which might determine success in setting up a small business. At the same time, the learners will be able to develop an awareness of what is required to avoid failure or minimize the risks. An awareness of the factors which might determine success will not only enable the learners to assess themselves in terms of readiness and suitability to venture into business but also help them to prepare or equip themselves for self-employment. It must be noted that *entrepreneur* is the essential ingredient in setting up a business in a free-market setting. He or she takes the initiative and the risk of setting up and organizing the business. One also needs all four factors or components in the framework for success, i.e., two or even three is not a good recipe for success. Therefore, all the four components must be acquired or developed.

Importance of Entrepreneurship in the Society

a.) Employment: Entrepreneurs create employment for themselves and other people. They are employers, and hence they assist in solving the unemployment problem.

b.) Local resources: When entrepreneurs utilize local resources, the value of these resources increases.

c.) Decentralization and diversification of business: Entrepreneurs are able to identify business opportunities and locate these businesses in suitable areas, including rural areas.

d.) Promotion of technology: By being creative, entrepreneurs are able to contribute to the utilization and development of technology.

e.) Capital formation: Entrepreneurship increases capital formation and investment.

f.) Promotion of an entrepreneurial culture: By projecting successful images, entrepreneurs become models that can be copied by young people.

Meaning of Key Success Factors (Critical) in Setting up a Small Business

Critical Success Factors (CSFs) are the critical factors or activities required for ensuring the success of a business. The term was initially used in the world of data analysis and business analysis. Critical Success Factors have been used significantly to present or identify a few key factors that organizations should focus on to be successful. As a definition, critical success factors refer to "the limited number of areas in which satisfactory results will ensure successful competitive performance for the individual, department, or organization."

Factors Contributing to Successful Growth of a Start-up Enterprise (Aspen Institute, 2006)

a.) Scaling-up does not happen by accident, rather it requires a clear and consistent focus by the organization's board and management;

b.) Leadership and good management are essential to taking an organization to scale;

c.) Market knowledge and information are critical to scaling-up;

d.) Marketing of products or services which is active and proactive is an element of successful scale-up;

e.) The ability to create a diversified yet complementary set of products is important for scaling;

f.) Scale-up can take place at the product level, but this is a process rarely seen at the community development finance level;

g.) Geographic expansion is also critical;

h.) Partnership, mergers and other approaches to strategic restructuring often play a key role in expanding geographic coverage or expanding/adding product lines;

i.) Partnerships also require considerable commitment and negotiation, which can be intense and time consuming;

j.) Replication can also be a path to greater scale, but successful replication is difficult;

k.) Standardization may be a necessary precursor to growth;

l.) Investments in technology play a role in expanding services, increasing efficiency and cost savings;

m.) Significant investment in infrastructure—the basic systems, technologies and resources to a program—will be critical to successful growth;

n.) New staff and management skills and capacities are needed at different points in the growth process;

o.) Organizations focused on scale-up use performance measurement to guide decision making;

p.) Organization scale-up takes time and money;

q.) Significant growth requires substantial investment of capital; growth without adequate financing can in fact endanger an organization's sustainability;

r.) The legal or regulatory environment can also play a key role in driving or facilitating expansion or growth to scale;

s.) The funding environment is also critical to supporting scale.

Factors which Lead to Start-up Business Failure

a.) Inadequate planning of the business;

b.) Insufficient initial capital for start-up period and development stages due to inadequate planning;

c.) Mistaken estimate of market demand for product or service;

d.) Lack of management ability;

e.) Failure to select and use appropriate outside professional advisors;

f.) Inability to market product or services effectively;

g.) Over-dependence on a single individual or on a predicted specific event;

h.) Failure to understand capital requirements of a growing business;

i.) Poor timing of expenditures due to poor planning;

j.) Expedient rather than reasoned decision-making.

Meaning of Small Business

A business is small if the owner has direct lines of communication with the operating managers and has personal contact with a large proportion of the work force, including key personnel. Such a business is individually owned and operated and employs not more than fifty people (this number may differ from one country to another). The elements constituting the meaning of small business are independent management, owner-supplied capital, operating mainly within a local area, and of relatively small size within an industry.

Small Enterprise Strengths

a.) **Personal touch:** Customers will often pay a premium for personalized attention. In fact, in many industries where product and price differences are minimal, the human factor emerges as a prime competitive advantage.

b.) **Greater motivation:** Key management of a small enterprise normally consists of the owner(s). Consequently, they work harder, longer and with more personal involvement. Profits and losses have more meaning to them than salaries and bonuses have to the employees of a larger company.

c.) **Greater flexibility:** A small enterprise has the prime competitive advantage of flexibility. A big business cannot close a plant without opposition from organized labor, or even raise prices without possible intervention from the government, but a small enterprise can react quickly to competitive changes. A small enterprise also has shorter lines of communication. Its product lines are narrow, its markets limited and its factories and warehouses close by. It can quickly spot trouble or opportunity and take appropriate action.

d.) **Less bureaucracy:** Grasping the big picture is difficult for executives of large companies. This "management myopia" leads to redundant actions and bureaucratic inefficiencies. In a small business the whole problem can be understood readily, decisions can be made quickly, and the results can be checked easily.

e.) **Unobtrusive (less conspicuous):** Because it is not quite as noticeable, the small company can try new sales tactics or introduce new products without attracting undue attention or opposition. Large companies are constantly faced with proxy battles, antitrust actions and government regulations. They are also inflexible and hard to change or restructure.

Weaknesses of Small Enterprises

a.) **Financial limitations:** Balancing "cash in" and "cash out" is a struggle, especially when trying to expand. Instead of receiving the red carpet treatment by financiers when asking for a loan, the small businessperson is often made to feel like a second-class citizen. Small enterprises can't use credit as a selling tool as readily as companies with large financial reserves. Additionally, many small enterprises have trouble staying afloat while waiting for their products to win acceptance in the marketplace.

b.) **Staffing problems:** Small companies cannot pay top salaries and provide the opportunities and status normally associated with a big company job. Small enterprise owners must also concentrate on the day-to-day problems of running the business and generally have little time left to think about objectives.

c.) **Higher direct costs:** A small enterprise cannot buy raw materials, machinery or supplies as cheaply as a large company, or obtain a large producer's economies of scale. So per unit production costs are usually higher for a small enterprise, but overhead costs are generally somewhat lower.

d.) **Too many eggs in one basket:** A large diversified company can take a licking in one sector of its business and still remain strong. This is not so for the small business with only a few product lines. A small company is vulnerable if a new product doesn't catch on, if one of its markets is hit by a sharp recession, or if an old product suddenly becomes obsolete.

e.) **Lack of credibility:** The public accepts a large company's products because its name is well known and usually respected. A small enterprise must struggle to prove itself each time it offers a new product or enters a new market. Its reputation and past successes in the marketplace seldom carry weight.

Different Categories of Key Success Factors in Small Business

Your business plan must contain a list of key success factors for your business. Jan B. King, in her book *Business Plans to Game Plans: A Practical System for Turning Strategies into Actions*, offers a number of key success factors applicable for any start-up small businesses. Below are some of them:

(i) Sell each unit at a profit – Evaluate each and every product that you sell and determine if you are selling it profitably. If not, you may need to identify how to make its current sales profitable, whether by reducing your costs for that product or increasing its price.

(ii) Continue to reduce overhead costs – A lower overhead should be a continuing objective for your business. You can cut costs by evaluating your insurance needs, reducing your reliance on outside consultants and service providers, or cutting out unnecessary supplies and equipment.

(iii) Develop new products while maintaining the high quality of existing products – Ensure that your products are created or chosen in response to the needs of your customers. Ask for customer feedback through surveys or direct interaction with them to find out what items they need and expect from your business.

(iv) Find and retain high-value customers – The 80-20 rule of business states that 80 percent of your business will come from 20 percent of your customers. It is therefore critical that you exert the extra effort to ensure that you retain the business of your top customers.

(v) Create and maintain the highest level of customer satisfaction – A very important success factor needed to sustain your business is to provide the best service to your customers. Satisfied customers are more likely to come back to you. Better yet, give your customers more than they expect.

The above are but a few of the key success factors that you can use for your business. Your key success factors must encompass all the important areas of your business, from finance, marketing and product development, to sales and customer service and human resources. As a small and home business owner, understanding what you must do to make your business a success is the first step to your path to entrepreneurial success. Other key success factors are listed below.

Key Success Factors of an Entrepreneur or Business Owner

- adaptable
- accountable
- action-oriented
- collaborative
- contributing
- driven
- disciplined
- energized
- engaging
- having integrity
- initiative
- innovative
- resourceful
- building relationships
- risk-taker
- self-motivated
- self-confident
- service-oriented

Geared with the above success factors, entrepreneurs are focused on their goals according to the business plan time frame, and avail themselves to the utmost of their resourceful mindsets to create the businesses of their dreams.

Other Views on the Factors that Contribute to the Success of an Enterprise

According to Duncan (1991), a key ingredient for business success is the skill of an entrepreneur in identifying a market niche and developing a venture for that niche. This is supported by another, similar study by DeHayes *et al.* (1990), who found that the most frequent reason for success among businesses was their ability to identify and focus on one or a few market niches. Other reasons for success included the ability of lead entrepreneurs who know the "craft" of the industry and the ability of companies to develop and sustain a technology advantage in their industry.

A study by Steiner *et al.* (1988) also suggested that developing a competitive advantage through specialization in products, markets or customers was a key factor in the success of small manufacturing firms. Prescott (1986) reported that developing a specialty or a niche could be vitally important for small business.

In a study amongst Jamaican entrepreneurs, Huck *et al.* (1991) found technical knowledge and customer relations to be the competencies most important for the success of small businesses. In an article published by *The Economist* (1991), Wilkin and Sons, which produces the famous Tiptree jams, was reported to have been successful by spotting a trend in the market well before its competitors; the company was also obsessed with quality and was very close to its customers. McCormack (1989) agreed that one of the most important factors to a successful business was a commitment to quality, which to him was the only absolute competitive edge. The journal *Profit-Building Strategies for Business Owners* (1989, 1990, 1991) identified that one of the factors in building a successful business was the ability to deal effectively with customer complaints. The success and failure of a small enterprise also depended on the owner's personal qualities and the way the business was managed. A successful business owner must know how to get and manage the business, be dollar-conscious, follow a good credit policy, have flexibility and have financial intelligence.

A profile on Joseph Maurelli, President and CEO of Techmatics Inc. (1988), revealed that he attributed his successful business to a strong company foundation, which was essential to achieving future company's objectives. Foley (1987) reported in an unpublished PhD thesis three factors of particular importance which were found to be consistently important for successful business. These were: a written business plan, the development of new products, and a strong sales and market team. Pollock (1989) and Barkham (1989) (also unpublished PhD theses) identified factors such as skill, attitudes and the gathering of market information as factors contributing to the success of an enterprise. Pollock, in particular, found that women proprietors placed a greater value on the quality of life and hence preferred long-term stability to rapid business growth. Moussavi (1988) in his unpublished PhD thesis stated that experience on the part of the owners/managers contributed to the survival of businesses.

Also of importance is the ability of the entrepreneur to communicate effectively. Evans (1986) emphasized that a firm's success in competing in a hostile environment was attributable to top management's involvement in all phases of the operation and to upgrading human resources. Campbell (1991) identified twelve keys for a successful business, amongst which were a clear mission statement and corporate value system, a customer-oriented policy, a competitive strategy and personal commitment from top management. Gaskill *et al.* (1989) identified six keys to a successful business, which included people power, a business plan, a study of the competition, measurement of performance, resistance to becoming too comfortable with progress, and efficient financial reporting systems. Beam *et al.* (1989) reported that, to be truly successful, small-business owners must have a missionary zeal about their product or service, be willing to be personally involved in it, be willing to stick with the business, be able to define the market clearly and pay attention to details.

Mraz (1989) stated that thorough planning was vital to starting a successful business; finding customers, vendors, employees and financial resources should be thought out in advance. Entrepreneurs should link up with venture capitalists who could fund new businesses. Ibrahim *et al.* (1986) indicated that personality attributes, managerial skills, interpersonal skills and environmental characteristics were perceived to be success factors in small businesses. Blanchard (1991) stated that, to be successful, the business owner needed to follow the four principles, namely, ensure that sales exceed expenses, collect outstanding bills, take care of customers, and take care of employees.

According to Schilit (1986), some guidelines to a successful business venture were, amongst other things, develop a common value system, ensure adequate capitalization (by using debt and equity financing), develop a formal business plan, monitor the business environment continually, retain a marketing orientation, encourage entrepreneurial thinking throughout the company, and delegate authority.

Basic Components and explanation of Key Success factors (MAIR) in small business

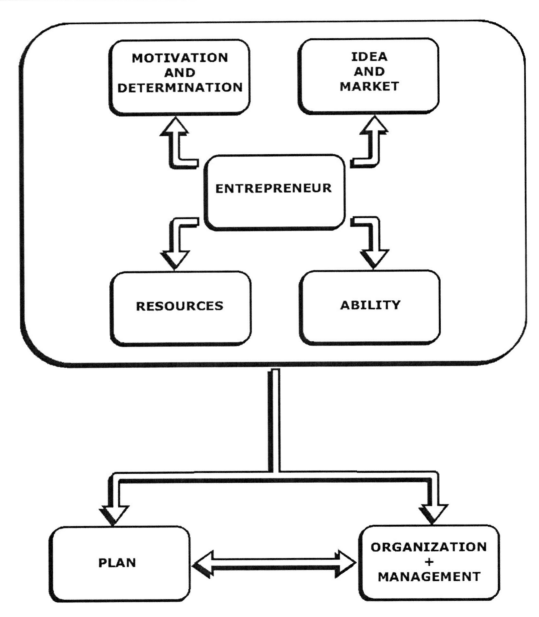

Figure 10.1: Key Success Factors in Setting Up a Small Business

Adapted from A. A. Gibb (1981)

Key Success Factors in Setting up a Small Business

The questions that come to mind are: How can one become an entrepreneur? And how can one set up a successful business? Unfortunately, however, no foolproof answer or formula has been identified as yet. Notwithstanding this, success—according to the literature, observations and experience—depends on that peculiar ability to spot opportunities in the market and act on them by organizing the necessary resources to offer something attractive to customers and take on the attendant risks. This is the essence of entrepreneurship in a business context. **The crucial ingredient in the whole process is the entrepreneur.** He/she takes the initiative and also bears the risk in creating and/or organizing an attractive offer of value to potential customers. Notwithstanding the above, the following factors from the MAIR model (adapted from A.A. Gibb 1981) are important determinants for success: Motivation and Determination, Abilities, Idea and Market, and Resources. In order to turn the above components into reality, the would-be entrepreneur needs a plan. And once the business is set up, it would need to be managed. The acronym—MAIR—may help you remember these factors more easily. These are explained in turn.

Idea and Market

The important issue to be determined here is the viability of the idea, project, product or service to be offered. In other words, does the idea, product or service meet a need or want for which there are customers who can afford it and are willing to use/purchase it in sufficient quantities to make the whole project worthwhile (i.e., return a profit, in a business context)? How is the proposition to be offered more desirable or better than what is currently available, and how will competitors react?

Motivation and Determination

It is widely acknowledged that, to be successful, the individual or group needs to be highly motivated and determined to set up the business to make it succeed. This will be reflected, for example, in how persistent they are in overcoming obstacles that might get in the way, how they go about seeking information and how they act on opportunities. Additional indicators might be their commitment and attitude to work (quality, efficiency, and long hours), previous attempts to set up a business, and the support of family or partners.

Ability

Another important question is whether the individual or others involved have particular abilities—these may be knowledge, technical or managerial skills of relevance to the business or project. One way of making up for any lack in this area could be to team up with people who have the necessary expertise or to buy it in.

Resources

Finally, the extent to which the person(s) involved can acquire or organize resources in adequate measure will not only influence performance but also, in some cases, determine whether they start at all. Examples here include capital, cash, premises, materials, equipment and labor. The availability of infrastructure (e.g., utilities like electricity, telephone, roads) and support services might also be important.

Business plan

In order to turn the above four components into reality, a plan is required. In business, this is normally referred to as a Business Plan. On the whole a business plan should show four main things, namely:

a.) where you currently are with your idea, project or business;
b.) what you wish to do;
c.) how you propose to go about it;
d.) and that the project is worthwhile.

Organization and Management

The business then needs to actually start operating and, once this is done, it needs to be managed. In setting up the business, or before starting to operate, there may be legal or other statutory requirements to be met. There may be a need to consult professionals such as lawyers, accountants and/or staff from small business support agencies for advice. The whole business and the process need to be managed, and how well this is done—in particular, finding and dealing with customers, management of cash and finances, marketing, handling employees, dealing with suppliers, control systems—will all affect performance.

Key Success Factors in Setting up a Small Business – Example of an Internet Café

Resources
➢ Desktop PCs, all networked
➢ Dial-up, broadband or wireless connection
➢ Account with an Internet Service Provider (ISP) or satellite provider
➢ Software to manage transactions and accounts
➢ Desks and chairs
➢ Air conditioners or fans
➢ Staff to run/supervise

Ability
➢ IT or computing knowledge and skills
➢ Ability to install software and do routine maintenance and repair
➢ Book-keeping and basic organization
➢ Ability to teach/train clients in basic computing and internet browsing

> Familiarity with internet search engines/e-mail

Motivation and Determination
> Able to work or operate long hours for 6 or 7 days a week
> Innovative
> Able to use influential strategies
> Problem-solver
> Takes initiative
> Concern for efficiency

Idea and Market
> Viability: number and nature of internet or cyber-cafés in the neighbourhood or within, say, a 3 km radius—the fewer the better
> Speed and prices vis-à-vis other cafés in area—should be competitive
> Number of people living and/or working in the area—the more, the better
> Profile of people living or working in the area: low- to middle-income best—not so rich as to be able to afford their own PCs and internet connection, but not so poor as not to be able to afford the service
> Nice ambience—with soft drinks and snacks for sale and background music in a well-ventilated room
> Provision of ancillary services for sale, such as fax, printing, photocopying, sale of diskettes, CD-ROMs, etc.

Self Assessment Exercise

(i) What is meant by Key (Critical) Success Factors in a small business?

(ii) List the items that constitute Success Factors in a small business as you understand them from the class lecture.

(iii) Discuss the basic Components of Key Success Factors in a small business.

(iv) Explain MAIR.

Summary

This chapter discusses an overview of the meaning of Key Success Factors, items that constitute success, its components, and the meaning of the acronym MAIR.

Tutor Mark Assignment

Write short notes on the following:

(i) Key Success Factors in a small business
(ii) A small business
(iii) Items that constitute Key Success Factors in small business

(iv) Basic Components of Key Success Factors in small business
(v) MAIR

Each question attracted marks.

References

Aspen Institute. (2006) Lessons Regarding Scale: Findings from a Literature Review by the Aspen Institute/FIELD and the Association for Enterprise Opportunity. Aspen Institute.

Beam, Henry H., and Thomas A. Carey. (1989) Could You Succeed in Small Businesses? *Business Horizons* 32(5):1989, 65–59.

Blanchard, Ken. (1991) Keep to the Basics. *Executive Excellence* 8(10):1991, 20.

Campbell, Regi. (1991) Twelve Keys for Entrepreneurial Success. *Business and Economic Review* 37(3):1991, 19–22.

DeHayes, Daniel W., and William L. Haeberle. (1990) University Alumni Small Business Research Program: A Study of Emerging Businesses. Centre for Entrepreneurship and Innovation, Indiana University, Bloomington.

Duncan, Ian. (1991) An Introduction to Entrepreneurs. *CMA Magazine* 65(9):1991, 32.

Evans, Joh. H. III, and Frank C. Evans. (1986) A Small Manufacturer's Success Story. *Management Accounting* 68(2):1986, 47–49.

Foley, Paul. (1987) Marketing Management Policies and Small Businesses: An Investigation of the Factors Contributing to Small Business Success. PhD Thesis. Council for National Academic Awards (UK).

Gaskill, Gary T., and J. Michael Hyland. (1989) Starting and Managing a Small Business. *Management Accounting* 71(6):1989, 28–31.

Gibb, A. A. (1981) A workshop approach for stimulating new enterprise development. Durham, UK: Durham University Business School.

Huck, John F., and Thaddeus McEwen. (1991) Competencies Needed for Small Business Success: Perceptions of Jamaican Entrepreneurs. *Journal of Small Business Management* 29(4), 1991, 90–93.

Ibrahim, A. B., and I. R. Goodwin. (1986) Perceived Causes of Success in Small Business. *American Journal of Small Business* 11(2):1986, 41–50.

McCormack, Mark H. (1989) Starting Your Own Business. *Modern Office Technology* 34(9):1989, 12–14.

Moussavi Barab, Mir Ayoub. (1986) Success and Failure in Small Business: Manufacturing Firms in California. PhD Thesis, United States International University.

Mraz, Stephen J. (1989) Advice from Entrepreneurs. *Machine Design* 61(9):1989, 125–128.

Pollack, Marilyn Frasier. (1989) Controlling Their Own Success: Women and Business Ownership. PhD Thesis, Rutgers State University of New Jersey.

Prescott, Eileen. (1986) How to be Small and Successful. *Public Relations Journal* 42(2):1986, 31–32.

Schilit, W. Keith. (1986) Guidelines for Entrepreneurial Success. *Advanced Management Journal* 51(3):1986, 44–48.

Steiner, Michael P., and Olaf Solem. (1988) Factors for Success in Small Manufacturing Firms. *Journal of Small Business Management* 26(1):1988, 51–56.

Further Readings

Brazell, James L. (1991) Starting a Small Business. *Business and Economic Review* 37(4):1991, 10–14.

Duchesneau, Donald A., and William B. Gartner. (1990) A Profile of New Venture Success and Failure in an Emerging Industry. *Journal of Business Venturing* 5(5): 1990, 297–312.

Duncan, Leon A. (1992) The Real World of the Entrepreneur. *Agency Sales Magazine* 21(5):1992, 60–62.

Flahvin, Anne. (1985) Why Small Business Fail. *Australian Accountant* 55(9):1985, 17–20.

Gaskill, Gary T., and J. Michael Hyland. (1989) Starting and Managing a Small Business. *ManagementAccounting* 71(6):1989, 28–31.

Ghosh, B. C., and Tan Teck Meng. (1995) An Exploratory Study of Strategic Planning Among SMEs. Working Paper, Dorset Business School, February.

Gibb, Allan, and John Ritchie. (1982) Understanding the Process of Starting Small Businesses. *European Small Business Journal* l(l):1982, 26–45.

Hebert, R. E., and A. N. Link. (1989) In Search of the Meaning of Entrepreneurship. *Small Business Economics* 1(l):1989, 42.

Holt, D. H. (1992) *Entrepreneurship: New Venture Creation.* Englewood Cliffs, NJ: Prentice-Hall.

How Creative Thinking Can Bring Success to a Small Business. *Profit-Building Strategies for Business Owners* 18(3):1988, 23–24.

Kets de Vries, Manfred F. R. (1977) The Entrepreneurial Personality: A Person at the Crossroads. *Journal of Management Studies* 14(1):1977, 34–57.

Lauzen, Leo G. (1985) Small Business Failures are Controllable. *Corporate Accounting* 3(3):1985, 34–38.

Nelson, Carol. (1986) Starting Your Own Business: Four Success Stories. *Communication World* 3(8):1986, 14–16.

Palmer, Susan S. (1988) CEO Profile: Combining Courage and Intuition. *Small Business Report* 13(4):1988, 37–41.

Plotkin, Harry M. (1990) Portrait of a Successful Small Business Owner. *Small Business Reports* 15(l):1990, 15–19.

Silver, A. David. (1983) *The Entrepreneurship Life: How To Go For It and Get It.* New York: John Wiley.

———. (1988) Portrait of the Entrepreneur. *Accountancy* (UK), 102 (1134):1988, 77–80.

Six Factors that Separate Business Winners from Losers. *Profit-Building Strategies for Business Owners* 20(5):1990, 3–5.

Smallbone, David. (1990) Success and Failure in New Business Start-ups. *International Small Business Journal* 8:1990, 34–47.

Special Characteristics You Need to Succeed in Your Own Business. *Profit-Building Strategies for Business Owners* 19(1):1989, 21–22.

Steck, Robert N. (1985) Why Business Fail. *D and B Reports* 33(6):1985, 34–38.

The Road to Success: What Thriving Small Business Have in Common. *Profit-Building Strategies for Business Owners* 19(12):1989, 3–5.

Wood, Dorman. (1989) Why New Businesses Fail and How to Avoid Disaster. *Corporate Cashflow* 10(8):1989, 26–27.

WorldBank. (1978) Employment and Development of Small Enterprises. Sector Paper, Washington, DC, February.

Yee, Wah Chin. (1991) The Entrepreneur as a Risk Manager. Paper presented at the World Conference on Entrepreneurship and Innovative Change, Nanyang Technological University, July 3–5, 1991, 177–180.

Chapter 11

BUSINESS OPPORTUNITIES FOR SMALL AND MEDIUM ENTERPRISES

Kolawole, T. O. and Zaggi, H. Y.

Introduction

A small business, also called a store by some in the United States, is a business that is privately owned and operated, with a small number of employees and a relatively low volume of sales. Small businesses are normally privately-owned corporations, partnerships, or sole proprietorships. Small businesses are common in many countries, depending on the economic system in operation. Typical examples include convenience stores, other small shops (such as a bakery or delicatessen), hairdressing, tradesman's work, law, accounting offices, restaurant business, guest houses, photography store, small-scale manufacturing, and online business, such as web design and programming, etc. Globally, people understand well that micro-, small and medium enterprises (MSMEs) are the engine for growth and poverty reduction.

Meaning of Small/Micro Business

A microbusiness is loosely defined as a small enterprise (typically fewer than five employees, usually only one or two) which frequently has only a very limited reliance on the traditional commercial banking loans that many other businesses rely upon for their day-to-day activities. The year 2010 was a banner year for those microbusinesses—with the recent economic downturn, more people than ever are starting their own microbusinesses in an effort to create their own job security in an uncertain economy (European Commission 2003).

A microbusiness (or micro-business) is a very small business, started with minimal resources, and operating without business loans or major overhead. Microbusinesses are ideal for teens who want to save for college while gaining business skills. Microbusinesses can also be a good way to try out a possible career or to supplement income in a flagging economy. The legal definition of *small* varies by country and by industry, ranging from fewer than 15 employees under the Australian Fair Work Act 2009, 50 employees in the European Union, and fewer than 500 employees to qualify in the US. Small businesses can also be classified according to other methods, such as sales, assets, or net profits (Department of Trade and Industry 2001).

A micro-enterprise (or microenterprise) is a type of small business, often registered, having five or fewer employees and requiring seed capital of not more than $35,000. The term is often used in Australia to refer to a business with a single owner-operator and having up to twenty employees. The European Union EU defines micro-enterprises as those that meet two of the following three criteria and have not failed to do so for at least ten years:

i. fewer than 10 employees;

ii. balance sheet total below EUR 2 million;
iii. turnover below EUR 2 million (Edmiston 2007).

The term micro-enterprise connotes different entities and sectors, depending on the country. Generally speaking, in developed countries, micro-enterprises comprise the smallest end (by size) of the small business sector, whereas in developing countries, micro-enterprises comprise the vast majority of the small business sector, a result of the relative lack of formal sector jobs available for the poor. These micro entrepreneurs operate micro-enterprises not by choice but out of necessity (Storey 1994).

Micro-enterprises add value to a country's economy by creating jobs, enhancing income, strengthening purchasing power, lowering costs and adding business convenience. Because micro-enterprises typically have little or no access to the commercial banking sector, they often rely on micro-loans or micro-credits in order to be financed. Micro-finance institutions often finance these small loans, particularly in the Third World. Those who found micro-enterprises are usually referred to as entrepreneurs (Shanker and Joseph 1996).

The terms micro-enterprise and micro-business have the same meaning, though traditionally, when referring to a small business financed by micro-credit, the term micro-enterprise is used. Similarly when referring to a small, usually legal business that isn't financed by micro-credit, the term micro-business is used (Dent 2012).

Characteristics of Small Businesses

Size definitions: The legal definition of *small* varies by country and by industry. In the United States, the Small Business Administration establishes small business size standards on an industry-by-industry basis, but generally specifies a small business as having fewer than 500 employees for manufacturing businesses and less than $7 million in annual receipts for most non-manufacturing businesses. The definition can vary by circumstance—for example, a small business having fewer than 25 full-time equivalent employees with average annual wages below $50,000 qualifies for a tax credit under the healthcare reform bill, Patient Protection and Affordable Care Act. In the European Union, a small business generally has under 50 employees. However, in Australia, a small business is defined by the Fair Work Act 2009 as one with fewer than 15 employees. By comparison, a medium-sized business or mid-sized business has under 500 employees in the US, 250 in the European Union and fewer than 200 in Australia. In addition to number of employees, other methods used to classify small companies include annual sales (turnover), value of assets and net profit (balance sheet), alone or in a mixed definition. These criteria are followed by the European Union, for instance (headcount, turnover and balance sheet totals). Small businesses are usually not dominant in their field of operation (European Commission 2003).

Demographics: According to a survey run in the United States among businesses having <500 employees in late 2010, about 50% of minute/micro-businesses are owned by women.

Franchise Businesses: Franchising is a way for small business owners to benefit from the economies of scale of the big corporations (franchiser). McDonald's restaurants, TrueValue hardware stores, and NAPA Auto Parts stores are examples of a franchise. The small business owners can leverage a strong brand name and purchasing power of the larger company while keeping their own investment affordable. However, some franchisees conclude that they suffer the *worst of both worlds*, feeling they are too restricted by corporate mandates and lack true independence. Also, in some chains, such as the aforementioned TrueValue and NAPA, franchisees may have their own name alongside the franchise's name (Edgcomb and Klein 2005).

Advantages of Small Business

A small business can be started at a very low cost and on a part-time basis. Small business is also well-suited to internet marketing because it can easily serve specialised niches, something that would have been more difficult prior to the internet revolution which began in the late 1990s. Adapting to change is crucial in business and particularly small businesses; not being tied to any bureaucratic inertia, it is typically easier to respond to the marketplace quickly. Small business proprietors tend to be intimate with their customers and clients, which results in greater accountability and maturity (Fox and Murray 2004).

Independence is another advantage of owning a small business. One survey of small business owners showed that 38% of those who left their jobs at other companies said their main reason for leaving was that they wanted to be their own bosses. Freedom to operate independently is a reward for small business owners. In addition, many people desire to make their own decisions, take their own risks, and reap the rewards of their efforts. Small business owners have the satisfaction of making their own decisions within the constraints imposed by economic and other environmental factors. However, entrepreneurs have to work very long hours and understand that ultimately their customers are their bosses.

Several organisations in the United States also provide help for the small business sector, such as the Internal Revenue Service's Small Business and Self-Employed One-Stop Resource (Grasmuck and Rosario 2000).

Opportunities in Micro Business

Micro-business possibilities are nearly endless. This is corroborated with the findings of Karen Dent (2012). Small and micro-businesses in the northeast of the UK are worried about the future of the region's economy as they face higher costs and falling revenues. The new research by the Federation of Small Businesses (FSB) found that both sales and others fell in the last six months, while a number faced higher costs and predicted that these will increase further over the next six months. The regional survey found the majority of FSB members in the northeast (63%) are not confident about the future of the local economy. This had a knock-on effect on investment, with almost eight out of ten saying it has stopped them taking on staff. However, the following are the top micro-business opportunities and trends for the future (many of which are relatively safe bets), several of which hinge on key current technology trends (Bryan 2010).

- **Social Media:** With each passing quarter, more emphasis is being placed on the web presence of any business. Not only should a business have its own web address, but it should also have a blog, a Twitter account, and a Facebook page. These are all required if a business wants to stay relevant and seem accessible to an increasingly tech-centered consumer base. More businesses are even carefully finessing their YouTube presence and paying programming proficient developers to create iPhone and Blackberry apps. This is the perfect opportunity for a web and technology savvy micro-business entrepreneur, who can easily capitalise on the lack of technical prowess of other business owners.

- **Clean Energy and Energy Efficiency:** Expect climate change legislation to make its way through the Senate and create a plethora of business opportunities for micro-businesses involved in the clean energy, efficiency, and conservation sectors.

- **Health Care:** Health care reform is expected to create a whole new market frontier for savvy micro-business leaders—the trick is to keep a keen eye on the actual contents of the final bill, which has been in a constant state of flux.

- **Services for New Businesses**: With the rapid increase in the number of small businesses showing no signs of slowing, supporting micro-businesses for these businesses will become necessary for the firms that can afford them.

- **E-commerce:** Increasingly, consumers are taking their dollars directly to the internet. This is great news for micro-business operators with online stores or an otherwise strong web presence. The World Wide Web is a much easier place to compete with industry giants, and it offers a much wider base of potential customers from all over the world. The social media sites have made connecting with these customers easy and often completely free.

- **Federal Contracting:** The American Recovery and Reinvestment Act (ARRA) has made available a good deal of funds for appropriate projects—micro-business owners in the construction industry can still find plenty of work this year through contracting or subcontracting opportunities (Edgcomb and Klein 2005).

Business Opportunities in Medium-Scale Entrepreneurship

Medium enterprise, also called medium-sized businesses (MBs), and variations thereof are companies whose headcount or turn-over falls below certain limits. The abbreviation SME occurs commonly in the European Union and in international organisations, such as the World Bank, the United Nations, and the WTO. The term *small and medium businesses* or SMBs are predominantly used in the USA. In most economies, smaller enterprises are much greater in number than large companies. SMEs are often said to be responsible for driving innovation and competition in many economic sectors.

Meanings and Categorisation of SMEs

The issue of what constitutes a small or medium enterprise is a major concern in the literature. Different authors have usually given different definitions to this category of business. SMEs have indeed not been spared the definition problem that is usually associated with concepts which have many components. The definition of firms by size varies among researchers. Some attempt to use the capital assets while others use skill of labour and turn-over level. Others define SMEs in terms of their legal status and method of production. Storey (1994) tries to sum up the danger of using size to define the status of a firm by stating that in some sectors all firms may be regarded as small, whilst in other sectors there are possibly no firms which are small. The Bolton Committee (1971) first formulated an *economic* and *statistical* definition of a small firm.

In a global context, a general definition of SMEs, using size and scale of operation, is not easy, but within the fixed co-ordinates of national boundaries, it might be relatively easier. At the 13th Council meeting of the National Council on Industry held in July, 2001, micro-, small and medium enterprises (MSMEs) were defined by the Council as follows:

- ➤ **Micro/Cottage Industry:** An industry with a labour size of not more than 10 workers, or total cost of not more than N1.50 million, including working capital but excluding cost of land.
- ➤ **Small-Scale Industry:** An industry with a labour size of 11-100 workers or a total cost of not more than N50 million, including working capital but excluding cost of land.
- ➤ **Medium-Scale Industry:** An industry with a labour size of between 101-300 workers or a total cost of over N50 million but not more than N200 million, including working capital but excluding cost of land.
- ➤ **Large-Scale Industry:** An industry with a labour size of over 300 workers or a total cost of over N200 million, including working capital but excluding cost of land.

Under the "economic" definition, a firm is said to be small if it meets the following three criteria:

- It has a relatively small share of the market place;
- It is managed by owners or part owners in a personalized way, and not through the medium of a formalised management structure;
- It is independent, in the sense of not forming part of a large enterprise.

Under the "statistical" definition, the Committee proposed the following criteria:

- The size of the small firm sector and its contribution to GDP, employment, exports, etc.
- The extent to which the small firm sector's economic contribution has changed over time;

- Applying the statistical definition in a cross-country comparison of the small firms' economic contributions.

The Bolton Committee applied different definitions of the small firm to different sectors. Whereas firms in manufacturing, construction and mining were defined in terms of number of employees (in which case, 200 or less qualified the firm to be a small firm), those in the retail, services, wholesale, etc., were defined in terms of monetary turn-over (in which case the range is 50,000–200,000 British Pounds to be classified as small firm). Firms in the road transport industry are classified as small if they have five or fewer vehicles.

There have been criticisms of the Bolton definitions. These centre mainly on the apparent inconsistencies between defining characteristics based on number of employees and those based on managerial approach. The European Commission (EC) defined SMEs largely in terms of the number of employees as follows:

- firms with 0 to 9 employees: micro enterprises;
- 10 to 99 employees: small enterprises;
- 100 to 499 employees: medium enterprises.

Thus, the SME sector is comprised of enterprises (except agriculture, hunting, forestry and fishing) which employ fewer than 500 workers. In effect, the EC definitions are based solely on employment rather than a multiplicity of criteria. Second, the use of 100 employees as the small firm's upper limit is more appropriate, given the increase in productivity over the last two decades (Storey 1994). Weston and Copeland (1998) hold that definitions of size of enterprises suffer from a lack of universal applicability. In their view, this is because enterprises may be conceived of in varying terms.

Size has been defined in different contexts, in terms of the number of employees, annual turn-over, industry of enterprise, ownership of enterprise, and value of fixed assets. Van der Wijst (1989) considers small and medium businesses as privately held firms with 1–9 and 10–99 people employed, respectively. Jordan et al.(1998) define SMEs as firms with fewer than 100 employees and less than €15 million turn-over. Michaelas et al.(1999) consider small those independent, private limited companies with fewer than 200 employees, and López and Aybar (2000) considered companies with sales below €15 million as small. According to the British Department of Trade and Industry, the best description of a small firm remains that used by the Bolton Committee in its 1971 Report on Small Firms. This stated that a small firm is an independent business, managed by its owner or part-owners, and having a small market share (Department of Trade and Industry 2001).

UNIDO also defines SMEs in terms of number of employees by giving different classifications for industrialized and developing countries (Elaian, 1996). The definition for industrialized countries is given as follows:

- Large: firms with 500 or more workers;
- Medium: firms with 100-499 workers;
- Small: firms with 99 or fewer workers.

The classification given for developing countries is as follows:

- Large: firms with 100 or more workers;
- Medium: firms with 20-99 workers;
- Small: firms with 5-19 workers;
- Micro: firms with fewer than 5 workers.

In Nigeria, the Central Bank of Nigeria defined Small and Medium Enterprises in Nigeria on the basis of asset base and number of staff employed. The criteria are asset base of between N5 million and N500 million and staff strength of between 11 and 300 staff.

Finally, the EC definition did not assume that the SME group is homogenous; that is, the definition makes a distinction between micro-, small-, and medium-sized enterprises. However, the EC definition is too all-embracing to be applied to a number of countries. Researchers would have to use definitions for small firms, which are more appropriate to their particular *target* group (an operational definition). It must be emphasized that debates on definitions turn out to be sterile unless size is a factor, which influences performance. For instance, the relationship between size and performance matters when assessing the impact of a credit programme on a target group (Storey 1994).

It is clear from the various definitions that there is not a general consensus over what constitutes an SME. Definitions vary across industries and also across countries. It is important now to examine definitions of SMEs given in African context. According to the new definition, an enterprise is 'any entity engaged in an economic activity, irrespective of its legal form'. The wording is not new. It reflects the terminology used by the European Court of Justice in its decisions. By being formally included in the recommendation, the scope of the new SME definition is now clearly marked out. Thus, the self-employed, family firms, partnerships and associations that are regularly engaged in an economic activity may be considered as enterprises. It is the economic activity that is the determining factor, not the legal form.

What are the new thresholds?

(Art. 2)
Once you have verified that you are an enterprise, you have to establish the data of your enterprise according to the following three criteria:

- Staff head-count,
- Annual turn-over,
- Annual balance sheet.

Comparing the characteristics of your business with the thresholds for the three criteria will allow you to determine whether you are a micro-, small- or medium-sized enterprise. It is necessary to note that, while it is compulsory to respect the staff head-count thresholds, an SME may choose to meet either the turn-over or balance sheet ceiling. It does not need to satisfy both and may exceed one of them without losing its status.

The new definition offers this choice since, by their nature, enterprises in the trade and distribution sectors have higher turn-over figures than those in manufacturing. Providing an option between this criterion and the balance sheet total, which reflects the overall wealth of an enterprise, ensures that SMEs that are engaged in different types of economic activity are treated fairly.

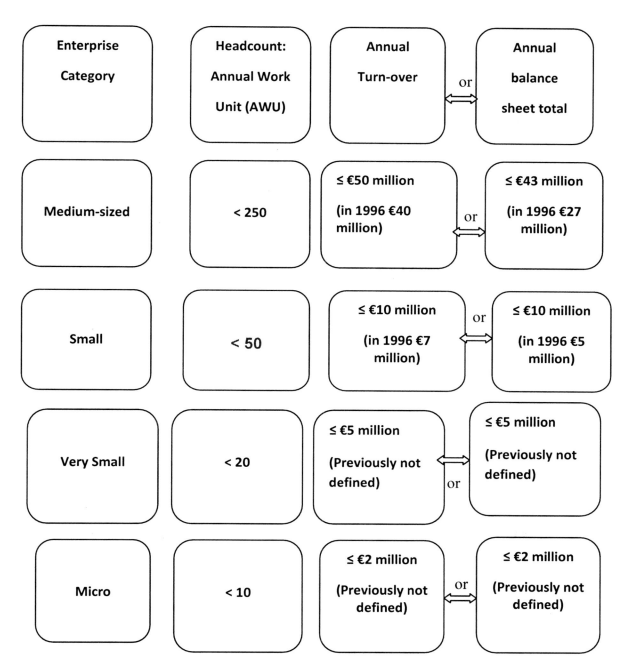

Fig. 11.1 Classification of SMES

Source: Adapted from Falkena *et al.* (2001)

The above framework of classification and indices of defining SMEs classified SMEs into four (4) major categories, which include micro-, very small, small and medium enterprises. It also globally accepted the head-count of each category, annual turn-over, and annual balance sheet total expected from each classification of the SMEs.

This is a standard framework of SMEs as it helps one to remove the definition cloud surrounding SMEs.

Benefits of Supporting Local Business

By opening up new national-level chain stores, the profits of locally owned businesses greatly decrease, and many businesses end up failing and having to close. This creates an exponential effect. When one store closes, people lose their jobs, other businesses lose business from the failed business and so on. In many cases, large firms displace just as many jobs as they create. Not only that: it also increases the costs of taxes. Instead of increasing a community's revenue, big businesses actually shift money away from the community. Independent businesses depend on the many resources that a community can supply. They hire architects, contractors, hardware stores, interior designers, local advertisement agencies, accountants, business attorneys, and insurance companies. Local businesses are also more likely to supply locally produced products than are chains, ultimately benefiting their community. Large corporations on the other hand eliminate the need for local goods and services (Milchen 2002).

A lack of diversity can decrease the revenues in a community. When towns are interesting, they attract people from out of town. More personality and individuality can lead to more tourists, which in turn leads to money placed directly into the community. The diversity of businesses is also important to the individuality of consumers. Oftentimes, independent retailers can adjust the products that they sell in order to fit the needs of their consumers and the unique tastes of their community. Local businesses are also more likely to support unique, new, and/or controversial products. Local bookstores can provide controversial books and can support small authors or local authors. The same idea helps out with local art and music. Bookstores and music shops are more likely to support local art and music than the mainstream stuff that large corporations provide. Business chains decrease a community's individuality because they ultimately choose what products reach their customers. This greatly narrows what products are available and shrinks diversity.

Marketing the small business: Finding new customers is the major challenge for small business owners. Small businesses typically find themselves strapped for time, but in order to create a continual stream of new business, they must work on marketing their business every day. Common marketing techniques for small business include networking, word of mouth, customer referrals, yellow pages directories, television, radio, outdoor (roadside billboards), print, email marketing, and internet. Marketing through electronic media like TV can be quite expensive and is normally intended to create awareness of a product or service. Another means by which small businesses can advertise is through the use of *deal of the day* websites such as Groupon and Living Social. These Internet deals encourage new visitors to small businesses (Edmiston 2011).

Sources of funding

Small businesses use several sources available for start-up capital:

a. Self-financing by the owner through cash, equity loan on his or her home, and/or other assets;

b. Loans from friends or relatives;
c. Grants from private foundations;
d. Personal savings;
e. Private stock issue;
f. Forming partnerships;
g. Angel investors;
h. Banks;
i. SME finance, including collateral-based lending and venture capital, given sufficiently sound business venture plans.

General Opportunities for SMEs in Nigeria

It is important to have a strong understanding of identified opportunities. It is essential to conduct market research, thus having an understanding of the market within which your business will operate, the industry, competitors and so forth. You should also have a strong understanding of your potential customers' needs and wants. It is important to determine whether or not they will be receptive to your new idea, product or service. It is also important to conduct a feasibility analysis to determine whether your identified opportunity is feasible, or has the potential to start a business. This is determined by analysing the opportunity's technical, marketing and economic feasibility. You will also need to analyse your abilities, skills and resources, and determine whether or not they are adequate to exploit the opportunity

A number of opportunities are open to all and sundry to exploit in Lagos, Nigeria. That includes foreigners and expatriates from any country of the world. Residents of Lagos, Nigeria, are generally welcoming people. With that, there will be little or no ill-treatment meted out to anyone wishing to start or commence a productive venture in this part of the world. Paulipopo (2012) identifies the following viable opportunities for businesses to thrive in Nigeria. They are:

Real Estate: One area that offers vast opportunities is real estate. Prices of houses and rent in Lagos are growing so fast that in two or three years' time they could be almost twice as high as they are currently going for. This is because Lagos is a densely populated area with a fast-growing population and an ever-expanding economy, so that owning property in this part of the world does not only make you a landlord but possibly financially independent. Houses and rents are not cheap in this part of Nigeria, especially in prime locations like Ikoyi, Lekki, Ikeja and Victoria Island.

Transportation: With a large population needing to commute on a day-to-day basis, there are vast opportunities for investors to provide commuter transportation services to the population. People commute to their work places from Mondays to Fridays; and even on Saturdays, when most people do not work, there are still many social functions taking place around the state. That means big business for transport services, especially road transportation.

Commercial Services: Provision of commercial services such as technology infrastructure and equipment like Information and Technology (IT) facilities for commercial and non-commercial purposes to a teeming population is just one area of commerce that the population of Lagos, Nigeria, can do with. Life in Lagos, Nigeria, is so hectic that services which alleviate stress will be affectionately patronized.

Education: Educational services such as provision of secondary and boarding facilities, university placement and admission services, excursion services, among others, exist to offer quality academic training for Nigeria's bright future assets (its children and youths).

Commerce: Trade and commerce are very much thriving ventures in Lagos, Nigeria. There exist large markets and commercial centers contributing to the growth and development of the state and Nigeria at large.

Labour: Compared to developed economies, labour in Lagos is very cheap, with average monthly salaries for regular staff employed in the formal sector falling within the range of N30,000 and N100,000 (roughly between $200 and $700). Most people earn below N100,000 a month, but in industries such as telecoms, oil and gas (especially the upstream sector but also the downstream sector, from where we have petroleum exploration, petroleum refinery and marketing), banking and finance as well as media services (especially public relations and advertising), there are people who earn much more than that, in some cases as much as N3,200,000 ($20,000 a month).

Tourist Attractions: A number of tourist attractions exist in Lagos, Nigeria, such as Badagry Beach, Wools Worth Park, and the Silverbird Galleria; even very busy locations like markets and bus stops are also tourist destinations.

Infrastructure: There has been a massive improvement in infrastructural development in Lagos, Nigeria, starting especially in 2007, following the assumption of office by the incumbent governor, Raji Fashola. Road and transportation systems have improved tremendously with the introduction of massive transit systems like the Bus Rapid Transport system (BRT), repair and construction of street lights along major highways, upgrading of public schools, and repair of water supply systems, improved refuse and sewage deposal, and beautification of the state.

Information and Communication Technology (ICT): It is a must for all SMEs to be linked up with the modern technological revolution. That is, SMEs depending on the capital base of the business must endeavour to adopt some level of relevant ICT facilities in order to change work design, process and structure, which will enhance work performance and high productivity. This means SMEs must be intensive ICT users like Seven-Up Bottling Company (SBC) and Frigo-glass Cool Division (FCD) (Kolawole 2004; Duncombe and Heeks 2001).

Challenges of Micro-/Small and Medium Enterprises

Udechukwu (2003) identified the enormous problems of SMEs in Nigeria and they range from:

(1) Inadequate and inefficient infrastructural facilities, which tend to escalate costs of operation, as SMEs are forced to resort to private provisioning of utilities such as road, water, electricity, etc.;

(2) Lack of adequate credit for SMEs, traceable to the reluctance of banks to extend credit to them, owing, among other things, to poor documentation of project proposals as well as inadequate collateral by SME operators;

(3) Bureaucratic bottlenecks and inefficiency in the administration of incentives, which discourage rather than promote SME growth;

(4) Weak demand for products, arising from low and dwindling consumer purchasing power and lack of patronage for locally produced goods by those in authority;

(5) Incidence of multiplicity of regulatory agencies and taxes, which has always resulted in high cost of doing business, and poor management practices and low entrepreneurial skill, arising from inadequate educational and technical background of many SME promoters.

Questions for Discussion

1. What is small/micro-business?
2. Mention the characteristics of small/micro business.
3. List the advantages and opportunities of micro/small business.
4. Identify the general opportunities of SMEs in Nigeria.
5. What are SMEs and what are the standard indicators for categorizing SMEs?
6. State the benefit of supporting local small businesses and their challenges.

References

Birch, D. (1979) The job generation process. Unpublished Report, Massachusetts Institute of Technology, prepared for the Economic Development Administration of the U.S. Department of Commerce, Washington, D.C.

————. (1987) *Job Creation in America: How our smallest companies put the most people to work*. New York: The Free Press.

Bolton, J. E. (1971) Report of the Committee of Inquiry on Small Firms. London: Her Majesty's Stationery Office.

Bryan. (2010) Top Micro-Business Opportunities For 2010. Available on-line.

Cabal, M. (1992) Microempresas y pequeñas empresas en la Republica Dominicana: Resultadados de una encuesta nacional. Santo Domingo: Fondomicro.

Dent, Karen. (2012). Smaller businesses hit hard by rising costs. http://www.nebusiness.co.uk/business-news/latest-business-news/2012/04/24/smaller-businesses-hit-hard-by-rising-costs-51140-30822110/.

Department of Trade and Industry. (2001) Small and Medium Enterprise (SME) – Definitions. *Economics*, 12, 113–130. Available on-line at: http://www.dti.gov.uk/SME4/define.htm. Retrieved 2013-05-16.

Duncombe, Richard, and Richard Heeks. (2001) Information and Communication Technologies and Small Enterprises in Africa. Results of a research project undertaken by IDPM in co-operation with the Botswana Institute for Development Policy Analysis. Institute for Development Policy Analysis, Manchester, UK.
http://www.sed.manchester.ac.uk/idpm/research/is/ictsme/summary/summary.pdf.

Edgcomb, Elaine, and Joyce Klein. (2005) Opening Opportunities, Building Ownership: Fulfilling the Promise of Microenterprise in the United States.
http://fieldus.org/Publications/index.html#2002Dir. Retrieved 2008-09-29.

Edmiston, K. (2007) The Role of Small and Large Businesses in Economic Development. *Economic Review* 92.2:73–97. Academic Search Complete. Web. 18 Mar. 2012.

———. (2011) The Role of Small and Large Businesses in Economic Development. *Economic Review* 1 (2010): 1-93. KansasCityFed.org. Web. 25 Oct. 2011.

European Commission. (2003) Recommendation 2003/361/EC: SME Definition.
http://ec.europa.eu/enterprise/enterprise_policy/sme_definition/index_en.htm. Retrieved 2009-04-05.

Falkena, H., I. Abedian, M. Blottnitz, C. Coovadia, G. Davel, J. Madungandaba, E. Masilela, and S. Rees. (2001) SMEs' Access to Finance in South Africa: A Supply-Side Regulatory Review. The Task Group of the Policy Board for Financial Services and Regulation. www.finance.gov.za/documents/smes.

Fox, W. F., and M. N. Murray. (2004) Do Economic Effects Justify the Use of Fiscal Incentives? *Southern Economic Journal* Vol. 71, no. 1, pp. 78–92.

Grasmuck, S., and E. Rosario. (2000) Market Success or Female Autonomy? Income, Ideology, and Empowerment among Microentrepreneurs in the Dominican Republic. *Gender and Society* 14(2):231–255.

Hope, J. B., and C. M. Patrick. (2007) The Relationship Between Employee Turnover and Employee Compensation in Small Business. *Small Business Research Summary* 308:1–44. Web. 21 Mar. 2012.

Internal Revenue Service.Small Business Health Care Tax Credit for Small Employers.
http://www.irs.gov/uac/Small-Business-Health-Care-Tax-Credit-for-Small-Employers.

———. Small Business and Self-Employed One-Stop Resource. Irs.gov. 2010-10-25. http://www.irs.gov/businesses/small/. Retrieved 2010-11-13.

Jordan, J., J. Lowe, and P. Taylor. (1998) Strategy and Financial Policy in U.K. Small Firms. *Journal of Business Finance and Accounting* 25(1/2), pp. 1–27.

Kolawole, T. O. (2004) Adoption and Use of Information and Communication Technology (ICT) in Selected Manufacturing Industries in Ibadan, Oyo State, Nigeria. An Unpublished Master's Thesis in Department of Sociology and Anthropology, Obafemi Awolowo University, Ile-Ife.

Lepoutre, J., and Aimé Heene. (2012) Investigating the Impact of Firm Size on Small Business Social Responsibility: A Critical Review. *Journal of Business Ethics* 67.3 (2006): 257-273. JSTOR. Web. 3 Jan. 2012.

Lohr, Steve. (2010). Small-Business Forces Unite. *The New York Times*, Special, Jan. 15, 1980. http://select.nytimes.com/gst/abstract.html?res=F40C1FFA3E5C12728DDDAC0 994D9405B8084F1D3. Retrieved 2010-11-13.

Longenecker, Justin G., Carlos W. Moore, J. William Petty, and Leslie E. Palich. (2008) *Small business management: launching and growing entrepreneurial ventures* (14th ed.). Mason, OH: South-Western Cengage Learning.

López-Garcia, J., and C. Aybar-Arias. (2000) An Empirical Approach to the Financial Behaviour of Small and Medium Sized Companies. *Small Business Economics*, 14, pp. 55–63.

Milchen, J. (2002) The Benefits of Doing Business Locally. AMIBA | The American Independent Business Alliance. http://www.amiba.net/home/benefits-local-business

Mitchell, S. (2003) The Multiplier Effect of Local Independent Business Ownership. AMIBA | The American Independent Business Alliance. Santa Fe Independent Business Report, Santa Fe Independent Business and Community Alliance.

Msme.gov.in. (2007) Home Page for Ministry of Agro and Rural Industries. http://msme.gov.in/msme_aboutus.htm. Retrieved 2010-12-09.

Munoz, J. M. (2010) *Contemporary Micro-enterprise: Concepts and Cases*. Cheltenham, UK: Edward Elgar Publishing.

Official Journal of the EU. Recommendation by the European Commissionconcerning the definition of micro, small and medium-sized enterprises 2003/361/EC dating from 060503, Annex Article 2. http://eur-lex.europa.eu/LexUriServ/ LexUriServ.do?uri=OJ:L:2003:124:0036:0041:EN:PDF.

Paulipopo. (2012) Business and Investment opportunities in Lagos Nigeria. http://paulipopo.hubpages.com/hub/Lagos-Nigeria-Business-and-Investment-opportunities.

Portfolio.com. (2011) Small-Biz Snapshot: Women-owned Companies. http://www.portfolio.com/business-news/2011/11/17/acbj-women-owned-business-insights-2011?ana=e_pft.Retrieved 2011-12-21.

Rural Income Diversification Project in Tuyen Quang Province. Project Completion Report (PCR) and Validation, 2010. http://www.ifad.org/evaluation/public_html/ eksyst/doc/validation/2011/vietnam_rural.pdf.

Scorerochester.org.(2010) Funding Sources for Small Business. http://www.scorerochester.org/help/funding/sources.php. Retrieved 2010-11-13.

Shanker, M. C., and Joseph H. Astrachan. (1996) Myths and Realities: Family Businesses' Contribution to the US Economy—A Framework for Assessing Family Business Statistics. *Family Business Review* 9.2 (1996): 107–123. http://fbr.sagepub.com/content/9/2/107.full.pdf.

Storey, D. (1994) *Understanding the Small Business Sector*. London: Routledge.

Udechukwu, F. N. (2003) Survey of Small and Medium Scale Industries and Their Potentials in Nigeria. Central Bank of Nigeria (CBN), No.4.

United States Small Business Administration. Size Standards. http://www.sba.gov/category/navigation-structure/contracting/contracting-officials/eligibility-size-standards.

United States Small Business Administration, Office of Advocacy. The Small Business Economy. A Report to the President: 2001, Table A.3. http://www.sba.gov/sites/default/files/files/sb_econ2001.pdf.

———. The Small Business Economy.A Report to the President: 2008. http://www.sba.gov/advo/research/sb_econ2008.pdf. Retrieved 2010-11-13.

———. Characteristics of Small Business Employees and Owners. http://www.sba.gov/advo/stats/ch_em97.pdf. Retrieved 2010-11-13.

———. Frequently Asked Questions. Jan. 2011. http://www.sba.gov/sites/default/files/sbfaq.pdf. Retrieved 2012-03-21.

Van der Wijst, D. (1989) Financial Structure in Small Business. Theory, Tests and Applications.Lecture Notes in *Economics and Mathematical Systems* Vol. 320, New York: Springer-Verlag.

Weston, J. F., and T. E. Copeland. (1998) *Managerial Finance*. New York: CBS College Publishing.

World Bank. Surveying Businesses on Tax Compliance Costs. https://www.wbginvestmentclimate.org/uploads/SBTCC_Consolidated_Web.pdf. Retrieved 2011-10-17.

Chapter 12

WHO IS AN ENTREPRENEUR? LEADERSHIP TRAITS OF AN ENTREPRENEUR

Adebayo, A. A.

Introduction

The term entrepreneur is a loanword from French and was first defined by the Irish-French economist, Richard Cantillon. The term first appeared in the French dictionary, *Dictionnaire Universel de Commerce* of Jacques des Bruslons, published in 1723 (Shane 2003). He defined entrepreneur as the person who pays a certain price for a product to resell it at an uncertain price, thereby making decisions about obtaining and using the resources while consequently admitting the risk of enterprise. *Webster's New International Dictionary* (1961) defines an entrepreneur as "the organizer of an economic venture, especially one who organizes, owns, manages and assumes the risk of business." *Funk and Wagnall's Standard Dictionary* (1958) offers a similar definition. It states that the entrepreneur is "one who undertakes to start and conduct an enterprise or business, assuming full control and risks." However, over time, various scholars have defined the term in different ways. Here are some prominent definitions:

- 1803: Jean-Baptiste Say: An entrepreneur is an economic agent who unites all means of production—land of one, the labour of another, and the capital of yet another—and thus produces a product. By selling the product in the market, he pays rent of land, wages to labour, interest on capital, and what remains is his profit. He shifts economic resources out of an area of lower and into an area of higher productivity and greater yield.
- 1934: Schumpeter: Entrepreneurs are innovators who use a process of shattering the status quo of the existing products and services to set up new products and new services.
- 1961: David McClelland: An entrepreneur is a person with a high need for achievement. He is an energetic and moderate risk taker.
- 1964: Peter Drucker: An entrepreneur searches for change, responds to it and exploits opportunities. Innovation is a specific tool of an entrepreneur; hence, an effective entrepreneur converts a source into a resource.
- 1971: Kilby: Emphasizes the role of an imitator / entrepreneur, who does not innovate but imitates technologies innovated by others. Are very important in developing economies. (Shane 2003)
- 1975: Albert Shapero: Entrepreneurs take initiative, accept risk of failure and have an internal locus of control.
- 1975: Howard Stevenson: Entrepreneurship is "the pursuit of opportunity without regard to resources currently controlled." (Shane 2003)

- 1983: G. Pinchot: Entrepreneur is aperson who works within an already established organization. (Shane, 2003)
- 1985: W.B. Gartner: Entrepreneur is a person who started a new business where there was none before. (Reynolds 2007,p. 231)

Furthermore, Glueck (1980) opines that "Entrepreneurs are individuals who start a business from the scratch," and Marriotti (2000) says, "Entrepreneurs are people who constantly discover new markets and try to figure out how to supply those markets efficiently and make a profit." Consequently, an entrepreneur has an eagle eye to see available opportunities where others are seeing problems. An entrepreneur has the ability to see and evaluate business opportunities and to gather necessary resources in order to take advantage of the identified opportunities for profit making.

The concept of entrepreneurship as an organized knowledge came into being about hundred years ago, although the economists from Adam Smith to Marshall were talking about it but without assigning it the name of entrepreneurship. They used terms like *employer, the master, the merchant* and *the undertaker* for carrying out different entrepreneurial activities now comprising entrepreneurship (Murthy 1989). Considerable attention has focused on the definition of the term "entrepreneur." For instance, as stated earlier above, Schumpeter (1959) considered the entrepreneur as an innovator. He writes that entrepreneurship is the "carrying out of new combinations we call enterprise"; the individuals whose function is to carry them out we call entrepreneurs. The new combination focuses on five aspects: the introduction of new goals, new methods of production, opening up of new markets, new sources of supply of raw material, and new industrial organizations. Say (1964) uses the term *entrepreneur* to refer to someone who creates and then, perhaps, operates a new business firm, whether or not there is anything innovative in those acts. Baumol (1993) sees the "Schumpeter" type as an innovating entrepreneur and the "Say" type as the firm-organizing entrepreneur. People who get ideas for creating a new business, bring that business into existence and then carry on the work of the enterprise, are entrepreneurs (Jena 1989). Precisely: an entrepreneur is one who undertakes to organize, manage, and assume the risks of a business. Even a small business unit is an entrepreneur and his activities are the entrepreneurship.

Entrepreneurship is a human activity which plays a major role in economic development. Its history is as old as human history, as it indicates to the spirit of enterprise. Such a spirit transforms the man "from a nomad to a cattle rearer, to a settled agriculturist, to a trader and an industrialist" (Murthy 1989). An entrepreneur is a person, while entrepreneurship is the process of its actual working. Entrepreneurship is also consistently equated with the establishment and management of small business enterprises. In the United States, the entrepreneur is often defined as one who starts his own, new and small business (Drucker 1985).

Modern literature on economic development classifies the term entrepreneurship in four broad categories: the innovating, the imitating, the Fabian and the drone entrepreneurship (Williams and Bultrick 1969). Innovating and imitating entrepreneurship are generally available in developed countries and very rare and limited in developing countries. Developing countries have in them the Fabian and drone types of entrepreneurship.

The reason for the backwardness of the developing countries lies in the fact that they are deficient in innovating and imitating entrepreneurs, whereas those are found in abundance in developed countries. Entrepreneurship has been a major factor in the economic growth of the West, of Russia and of Japan in Asia, and it was undoubtedly of innovating and imitating type, which made the process of development smooth and fast there. This brings to mind the question that has captured the imagination of scholars regarding the phenomenon of entrepreneurship: "Are entrepreneurs born or made?" Many people believe that entrepreneurs possess innate, genetic talents. However, experts generally agree that most entrepreneurs are not born; rather, the environment, traning, family tradition, etc., help in the development of successful entrepreneurs (Jha 1989).

The role played by entrepreneurship in the development of Western countries has made the people of developing countries very much conscious of its importance in the programme of rapid economic development. People have begun to realize that, for achieving the goal of development, it is necessary to increase both the quantitative and qualitative entrepreneurship in the country. The qualitative entrepreneurship implies the stress on innovating, and the quantitative implies the stress on imitating entrepreneurship. Both of them contribute stimulus for development. It is also known that even though a country has resources—labour, technology, capital and raw material, etc.—these remain under-explored in the absence of the active and enthusiastic entrepreneurs, who have the ability to organize the various factors of productions. Innovating entrepreneurs are rarely found in developing countries. In the past, these countries have depended largely on developed countries for their manufacturing requirements. But now they are planning to develop as early as possible, for which they require modern kinds of innovating and imitating entrepreneurs. Fabian entrepreneurs do not want to take huge risks, and they do not believe in making big changes, unless, of course, it becomes inevitable for their existence. Drone entrepreneurs go on using their own traditional techniques, even at a loss.

How Do Entrepreneurs Emerge?

There are two theories about how entrepreneurs develop in any given society. These are often called supply and demand theories. The supply theory holds that entrepreneurs are born, not made. That is, some people by virtue of their personality are imbued with entrepreneurial traits, some of which John G. Burch (1986) describes as the desire to achieve and to be independent.

On the other hand, the demand theory, which is now generally more dominant, holds that entrepreneurs emerge out of a combination of entrepreneurial opportunities and people who are well positioned to take advantage of such opportunities. Thus, anyone who encounters the right conditions might become an entrepreneur, if he finds himself in a position where he finds a valuable problem that he can solve. Scholars studying the demand theory try to understand the conditions under which entrepreneurs appear, particularly in understanding how differences in the information on how various people have created entrepreneurial opportunities, and how environmental factors such as access to capital, competition, etc., change the rate of entrepreneurship.

Classification of Entrepreneurs

Entrepreneurs are generally known not to operate their businesses the same way. That is, entrepreneurial activities are substantially different depending on the type of organization and creativity involved. Their modes of operation are classified as follows:

1. *Innovative entrepreneurs:* Such entrepreneurs introduce new goods or new methods of production or discover new markets or reorganize the enterprise.
2. *Imitative or adaptive entrepreneurs:* Such entrepreneurs don't innovate; they copy the technology or technique of others.
3. *Fabian entrepreneurs:* Such entrepreneurs display caution and skepticism in experimenting with any change in their enterprises. They change only when there is a serious threat to the very existence of the enterprise.
4. *Drone entrepreneurs:* Such entrepreneurs are characterized by a diehard conservatism and may even be prepared to suffer the losses.

Sources of Finance for Entrepreneurs

The take-off of any business enterprise requires finance. The following are some of the avenues or sources through which the necessary financing could be obtained.

1. *Personal Resources:* Personal savings or resources (in cash or kind) of the owner is the single most important sources of a small firm's initial capital. More often, the small business owner is obliged to stake a reasonable amount of his or her personal resources, irrespective of the size of the new business. When personal savings are insufficient for take-off of a proposed business, inherited and/or personal assets (moveable or unmovable) accumulated over time can be very helpful. Selling some or all of them can go a long way to augment the initial capital raised from the savings. Alternatively, some of the assets may be useful in the firm to constitute a source of capital.
2. *Family and Friends:* Family members and friends are another source of start-up capital if they believe in the business idea. In some cases, the initiator of the business idea may be required to repay part or all of what is obtained from these sources. There is also the possibility that the only immediate cost is a promise of reciprocating their gesture in the future. Whether repayment will be made later or not, they expect to be recognized as having been part of the firm's success story.
3. *Partners or Business Associates:* Borrowing from the adage "two heads are better than one," it could be inferred that two or more owners in a business are better than a sole owner. This is because, by admitting one or more interested people into the business as part owners, the firm increases its financial resources. Additionally, chances are that if the business owners-managers are prudent and selective in their choice of these people, their skills and expertise will complement each other, thereby saving the

cost of hiring people with such skills or expertise. In other words, they can increase their firm's capital base by inviting other people to join in partnership rather than running them as a sole proprietary concern.

4. *Informal Financial Markets:* In the small business firm's locality there may also be wealthy individuals who are willing to lend money if the owner-manager is well-known to them or introduced by someone known to them. Usually their conditions are stiffer than those of the family members and friends. The cost of borrowing is higher depending on the owner-manager's relationship with the individual lender and his/her ability to shop for the cheapest bargain. The urge to use this source of capital may be irresistible for reasons such as accessibility and flexibility, among others. Yet unless the owner-manager has exhausted other possibilities, apart from making sure that his/her business will be able to pay its way, it may be ill-advised to use this source. Other sources which operate along somewhat similar lines include the Rotating Savings and Credit Associations, Trade Associations and Co-operatives. However, in most cases, a very important condition for accessing funds from these sources is membership.

5. *Banks:* Contrary to the misconception among small business owners, a large number of banks are excellent sources of capital for small businesses. Provided a firm can meet a bank's needs for a well-articulated business plan, cash projections and collateral, chances are that the banks will make funds available. In Nigeria, banks which are sources of capital for firms are commercial banks, merchant banks, the Nigeria Bank for Commerce and Industry (NBCI), the Nigeria Industrial Development Bank (NIDB) and the Nigerian Agricultural and Cooperative Bank (NACB)—for those engaged in agriculture or agro-allied business ventures. Until 1996, commercial banks were mandatorily required to reserve 20% of their loans and advances for small businesses. Although they have the discretion as to what percentage of these loans goes for business start-ups, expansion purposes and working capital needs of firms, commercial banks will usually give favourable considerations to viable business proposals. It is hoped that in the future, banks will eventually take up ownership scale in small and medium enterprises (SMEs). When this materializes, these firms will be able to increase their capital via equity participation by banks.

6. *Specialized Funding Facilities:* The National Economic Reconstruction Fund (NERFUND); the World Bank Loan Scheme for SMEs, managed by the Central Bank of Nigeria; and the African Development Bank Loan Scheme for Export Stimulation in the SME sector are specialized funding schemes established by the Federal Government in conjunction with international financial institutions and governments for small- and medium-scale enterprises in Nigeria. The NERFUND Scheme is implemented through commercial and merchant banks designated as participation banks (PBs). Detailed information on the operation institutions of each scheme is available at the participating banks and the

supervising institutions. This is a veritable source of capital for new business start-ups, business expansion, modernization, restructuring or revival of existing businesses and export-oriented small business activities. It is important, however, to point out that the African Development Bank Loan Scheme for SMEs has been phased out, while the African Development Bank Loan Scheme for Export Simulation has been transferred to the Nigerian Export-Import Bank (NEXIM).

7. *Leasing:* Another source of finance which can be exploited by a small firm is leasing. Contrary to the perception among some small business owner-managers, the leasing technique as a financing option is not a preserve of large businesses. Small- and medium-sized businesses can also venture leasing in order to enjoy its attendant benefits. Indeed, leasing releases for a small firm's expansion funds that would have been tied down in items like vehicles, equipment and other machineries. Apart from the few equipment-leasing firms in Nigeria presently, merchant and commercial banks do participate in leasing activities.

8. *Sub-Contracting:* Although not yet a common feature in the Nigerian industrial landscape, sub-contracting can serve as a source of finance for small firms. Depending on the small firm's relationship with its parent/client firm (usually a large scale firm), it is possible for it to be advanced money to finance the production of goods, which will be supplied later to the parent/client firm. This is similar to trade credit, which is a spontaneous source of financing for small firms that may not qualify for short-term financing from other sources. Thus, a small firm, which fails the credit test of banks, may still be able to meet a shortfall in its capital requirements by relying on its suppliers to buy on credit. However, the amount that can be derived from this source fluctuates with the small firm's purchases, and it is subject to any limit that may be imposed by the supplier(s).

Leadership Traits of an Entrepreneur

1. *Disciplined:* These individuals are focused on making their businesses work and eliminate any hindrances or distractions to their goals. They have overarching strategies and outline the tactics to accomplish them. Successful entrepreneurs are disciplined enough to take steps every day toward the achievement of their objectives.

2. *Confidence:* Entrepreneurs do not ask questions about whether they can succeed or whether they are worthy of success. They are confident with the knowledge that they will make their businesses succeed. They exude that confidence in everything they do.

3. *Open-Minded:* Entrepreneurs realize that every event and situation is a business opportunity. Ideas are constantly being generated about workflows and efficiency, people skills and potential new businesses. They have the ability to look at everything around them and focus it toward their goals.

4. *Self-Starter:* Entrepreneurs know that if something needs to be done, they should start it themselves. They set the parameters and make sure that projects follow that path. They are proactive, not waiting for someone to give them permission.

5. *Competitive:* Many companies are formed because entrepreneurs know that they can do a job better than another. They need to win at the sports they play and need to win at the businesses that they create. These entrepreneurs will highlight their own companies' track records of success.

6. *Creativity:* One facet of creativity is being able to make connections between seemingly unrelated events or situations. Entrepreneurs often come up with solutions which are the synthesis of other items. They will repurpose products to market them to new industries.

7. *Determination and Optimism:* Entrepreneurs are not thwarted by their defeats. They look at defeat as an opportunity for success. They are determined to make all of their endeavors succeed, so will try and try again until it does. Successful entrepreneurs do not believe that something cannot be done.

8. *Strong People Skills:* The entrepreneur has strong communication skills to sell the product and motivate employees. Most successful entrepreneurs know how to motivate their employees so the business grows overall. They are very good at highlighting the benefits of any situation and coaching others to their success.

9. *Strong Work Ethic:* The successful entrepreneurs will often be the first persons to arrive at the office and the last ones to leave. They will come in on their days off to make sure that an outcome meets their expectations. Their mind sare constantly on their work, whether they are in or out of the workplace.

10. *Passion:* Passion is the most important trait of the successful entrepreneurs. They genuinely love their work. They are willing to put in those extra hours to make the business succeed because there is a joy their business gives which goes beyond the money. The successful entrepreneur will always be reading and researching ways to make the business better. Successful entrepreneurs want to see what the view is like at the top of the business mountain. Once they see it, they want to go further. They know how to talk to their employees, and their businesses soar as a result.

11. *Acceptance of Responsibility:* Entrepreneurs are morally, legally and mentally accountable for their ventures. Since the buck stops at his desk, he takes responsibility for whatever happens to the enterprise.

12. *Ability to Lead:* Entrepreneurs are individuals who have the charisma to carry others along to achieve a set goal, have good human relations, and are responsive to suggestions and criticisms.

13. *Hardworking and focused:* Entrepreneurs are hardworking people. They make no distinction between office hours and private hours. They are not easily discouraged while carrying out a task and are mentally attached to their job always. To demonstrate how hardworking they are, they can carry out the work of a messenger in their organization to make sure that there are no lapses and delays in achieving the organizational goal.

14. *Risk Taking:* All entrepreneurs take risks in the process of making things happen by venturing into virgin areas where there is little or no precedent to emulate.

While embarking on any venture, they are always conscious of the fact that they are taking risks which may either be successful or fail.

15. *Accountability:* Entrepreneurs keep records of all their activities in such a way that they can explain and proffer answers to any questions raised about their business activities anytime. They are also interested in profit-making and in what they can also achieve with the profit made from their businesses.

16. *Adaptability:* Entrepreneurs are usually moderately flexible in their approach to life. They usually do not have difficulty adjusting to changing circumstances. They are people who tolerate ambiguity and do not feel uncomfortable in ambiguous situations. They usually find it convenient running businesses in areas where market change is constant and rapid.

Obstacles to Entrepreneurship Development in Nigeria

There are myriad problems facing entrepreneurship development in Nigeria. Some of them are:

(a) *Inadequate Capital Base:* This has been identified to be one of the major factors affecting entrepreneurship development in Nigeria. The relationship between finance and any business enterprise cannot be over-emphasized. There seems to be a very high positive relationship between finance and entrepreneurial development of a country. Akode (2004) lamented that government's dwindling fiscal budget/expenditure has been a major constraint facing adequate provision of infrastructural facilities. For a greater entrepreneurship development, adequate funds should be made available for early-stage financing of entrepreneurial activity from the government and from the private sector.

(b) *Insufficient Education:* Education plays a vital role in entrepreneurship. Education should be geared towards fostering entrepreneurship for better participation in the economy after graduation. Nigerian education is too bookish, theoretical and "white-collar job"-oriented. Nwangwu (2007) opined that the failure of tertiary education to inculcate the above philosophy in students has led to wastages in terms of both human and natural resources. This is because the youth and graduates from tertiary institutions are not equipped with the skills with which to exploit the natural resources that abound in Nigeria. All these factors have rendered the pursuit of self-reliance among our graduates difficult to retain.

(c) *Unhealthy Macro-Economic Environment:* Healthy entrepreneurship requires the creation of a stable macro-economic environment and structural policies to produce well-functioning markets. This means that government needs to create competitive markets, efficient capital markets, flexible labour markets, a reasonable tax regime, simplify the administrative burden of government, and reduce the cost of firm closure and bankruptcy. Nigeria's macro-economic environment is unhealthy and unstable for virile entrepreneurship development.

(d) *Fear of Failure:* In Nigeria, the fear of failure reduces the rate at which people embark on entrepreneurial activity. To succeed in life, one must be ready to take risks—"No risk, no business."

(e) *Cloudy Political Climate:* A stable political environment promotes entrepreneurial activities and also encourages investors to come, whereas an unstable political climate drives away investors. During the military era in Nigeria, Nigerians preferred to have a chain of business in overseas countries rather than in their own country.

(f) *Inadequately Designed Government Programmes and Policies:* Government programmes/policies, if well designed, also promote entrepreneurship. Countries like the USA have a wide range of programmes to assist businesses. In some cases, some programmes are targeted to different areas of business, such as agricultural farms, high-tech enterprises, and manufacturing, among others. There is a clear role for government in fostering entrepreneurship at the national, state and local government levels. This is not the case with Nigeria.

(g) *Low-Level Infrastructural Development:* The development of infrastructure generally enhances welfare and fosters economic growth. As a result, the adequacy of infrastructure determines a country's success in diversifying production, expanding trade, coping with population growth, reducing poverty, and improving environmental conditions. Therefore, a good infrastructure is the *sine qua non* for high productivity and entrepreneurial activities. The level of infrastructural development in Nigeria is still very low, and this has been affecting to a very high extent the level of productivity.

Conclusion and Recommendations

The importance of entrepreneurs and entrepreneurship in any country cannot be over-emphasized. It is the engine for the economic growth of any country. The countries that have a flair for entrepreneurship and have created a favourable business climate for it have been witnessing monumental growth in their economies over the years. Any country that stifles or stagnates the private sector does so at its own peril. In Nigeria, for some time, entrepreneurship has not been given a prominent priority in the economic arena. As a matter of fact, many frustrated entrepreneurs have relocated their businesses to Ghana and other countries where the economic climate is favourable for their ventures.

It is therefore recommended that the government should create an economic-friendly environment for business to thrive so as to encourage individual participation in business. This could be done when government gives needed financial assistance, creates a peaceful political climate, improves on infrastructure, and installs favourable tax policies, among other things. This will go a long way toward encouraging entrepreneurs, and it would bring about a drastic reduction in youth unemployment as well as improved economic growth.

References

Akode, T. O. (2004) An Analysis of the Role of Infrastructure in Nigeria Economic Development (1990-2000). *Journal of Economics and Social Studies* 4, pp. 17–27.

Drucker, P. F. (1985) *Innovation and Entrepreneurship.* London: Heinemann.

Glueck, W. (1980) *Business Policy and Strategic Management.* Tokyo: McGraw-Hill.

Ilesanmi, O. A. (2000) *Entrepreneurial Development.* Ilorin: Kola Success Publication.

Jha, S. M. (1989) The Constraint in Entrepreneurial Renaissance. In Uddin, Sami (ed.), *Entrepreneurship Development in India.* Delhi: Mittal Publication, p. 109.

Kolapo, F. (2004) *Entrepreneurship in Nigeria.* Lagos: DOJOS Publication.

Kolawole, T. O. (1997) Entrepreneurship Concepts. In Olaleye, O. A. *et al.* (eds.), *Entrepreneurship.* Akure: STECOM Publishers.

————. (2004) Adoption and Use of Information and Communication Technology (ICT) in Selected Manufacturing Industries in Ibadan, Oyo State, Nigeria. An Unpublished Master's Thesis in Department of Sociology and Anthropology, Obafemi Awolowo University, Ile-Ife.

Lepoutre, J., and Aimé Heene. (2012) Investigating the Impact of Firm Size on Small Business Social Responsibility: A Critical Review. *Journal of Business Ethics* 67.3 (2006): 257-273. JSTOR. Web. 3 Jan. 2012.

Lohr, Steve. (2010). Small-Business Forces Unite.*The New York Times*, Special, Jan. 15, 1980.
http://select.nytimes.com/gst/abstract.html?res=F40C1FFA3E5C12728DDDAC0 994D9405B8084F1D3. Retrieved 2010-11-13.

Longenecker, Justin G., Carlos W. Moore, J. William Petty, and Leslie E. Palich. (2008) *Small business management: launching and growing entrepreneurial ventures* (14th ed.). Mason, OH: South-Western Cengage Learning.

Marriotti, S. (2000) *The Young Entrepreneur's Guide to Starting and Running a Business.* New York: Three Rivers Press.

Murthy, N. (1989) Entrepreneurship in Small Towns. In Uddin, Sami (ed.), *Entrepreneurship Development in India.* Delhi: Mittal Publication, p. 4.

Nwangwu, Ig. O. (2007) *Higher education for self Reliance: An imperative for the Nigerian economy.* Melbourne, Australia: NEAP Publication.

Omolayo, B. (2006) Entrepreneurship in Theory and Practice. In Omotosho, F., T. K. O. Aluko, O. I. Wale-Awe, and G. Adaramola (eds.), *Introduction to Entrepreneurship Development in Nigeria.* Ado-Ekiti: UNAD Press.

Owualah, S. I. (1999) *Entrepreneurship in Small Business Firms.* Lagos: G. Mag Investment Limited.

Reynolds, Paul D. (2007) *Entrepreneurship in the United States.* New York: Springer.

Shapero, A. C. (1981) Self-renewing economies. *Economic Development Commentary* 5 (April), 19–22.

Schumpeter, J. A. (1934) *The Theory of Economic Development.* Cambridge, MA: Harvard University Press. Reprinted 1959.

————. (1950) *Capitalism, Socialism and Democracy.* New York: Harper and Row.

Shane, S. (2003) *A General Theory of Entrepreneurship: the Individual-Opportunity Nexus.* New York: Edward Elgar.

Tandon, B. C. (1973) *Environment and Entrepreneur.* Allahabad: Chug Publication.

Timmons, J. (1999) *New Ventures Creation, Entrepreneurship in the 21st Century.* New York: Irwin McGraw-Hill.

Wale-Awe, O. (2005) *StrategicEntrepreneurship Development.* Lagos: Culgal Creations and Publications.

Weber, M. (1904)*The Protestant Ethic and the Spirit of Capitalism.* New York: Routledge.

Williams and Bultrick. (1969) *Economic Development—Change and Entrepreneur.* Cambridge: Cambridge University Press.

Chapter 13

THE ENTREPRENEURIAL PROCESS

Ologunde, A. O.

Introduction

Who is an entrepreneur?

The definition of an entrepreneur has evolved over time as the economic structure has become more complex. Today, entrepreneurship is defined as the process of creating something different by devoting necessary time and efforts, taking into account the accompanying financial, psychic, and social risks, and receiving the resulting monetary rewards and personal satisfaction. The study of entrepreneurship has relevance today not just because it helps entrepreneurs to better fulfill their personal needs but because of the economic function of new ventures. More than increasing national income by creating new jobs, entrepreneurship acts as a positive force in economic growth by serving as the bridge between innovation and application.

An entrepreneur is a person who takes advantage of a business opportunity by assuming the financial, material and psychological risks of starting or running a company (Hatten 1997). The entrepreneur sees the opportunity, takes it and assumes the risk of starting the business. The term entrepreneur, a French word, translates literally to "go-between" but originally referred to men who organized and managed exploration expeditions and military manoeuvers. The term has evolved over the years into a multitude of definitions but most include the following functionalist concepts:

- **Creation:** A new business is started.
- **Innovation:** The business involves a new product, process, market, material, or organization.
- **Risk assumption:** The owner of the business bears the risk of potential loss or failure of the business.
- **General management**: The owner of the business guides the business and allocates the business' resources.
- **Performance intention**: High levels of growth and/or profit are expected. (VanderWerf and Brush 1989)

All new businesses require a certain amount of entrepreneurial skill. The degree of entrepreneurship involved depends on the measure of each of those concepts that are needed.

Entrepreneurship and Small Business Management

Entrepreneurship involves the start-up process, whereas small business focuses on running a business over a long period of time. While one cannot study one without the other, they are different. In managing a small business, most of the "entrepreneuring" was done a long time ago. Of course, a good manager must always look for new ways to please customers, but the original innovation and actual starting of the business make way for more stability in the maturity stage of the business.

The manager of a small business needs perseverance, patience and critical thinking skills to deal with the day-to-day challenges that arise in running a business over a long period of time. Achieving stability, however, must not put an end to entrepreneurship. As the business grows, the small business manager must maintain the opportunity-seeking, creative, daring, and innovative entrepreneurial spirit that made the business start successfully in the first place. To do this, the manager must develop an appropriate control system, emphasize responsibility not just authority, create and nurture teams and teamwork, promote continuous adaptive organizational change and encourage functional excellence in all positions.

The entrepreneurial process, which is the stages of a business' life, consists of five stages. They are:

A. conducting opportunity analysis;

B. developing the plan and setting up the company;

C. acquiring financial partners and sources of funding;

D. determining the resources required and implementing the plan; and

E. harvesting the venture.

A. Conducting opportunity analysis:

This is the first stage of the entrepreneurial process. It involves developing ideas and business opportunities. The entrepreneurial process begins with an innovative idea for a new product, process, or service, which is refined. You can come up with a totally new idea or build an already existing idea by re-designing, extending, re-segmenting, improving, re-differentiating (i.e., re-pricing), adding value or re-packaging existing ideas. It is also possible to create a business from a hobby. Figure 13.1 describes where ideas for opportunity originate.

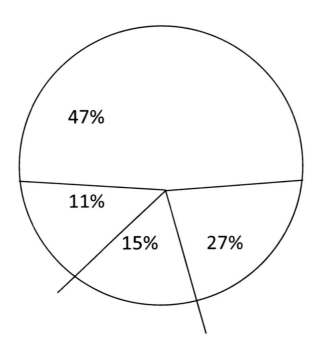

Fig 13.1: Where ideas for opportunity originate

Source: Kaplan 2003, p.22

Key:
47% - present work environment
27% - secondary sources: brainstorming, trade publications, idea brokers, venture capital
    firms, technology transfer agencies
15% - improving existing technology, product or service
11% - vision of opportunity

The time span for the innovation stage may be months or even years before the potential entrepreneur moves on to the next stage, when issues proceed from thinking to doing—a triggering event. When a triggering event occurs in the entrepreneur's life, he or she begins bringing the organization to life. This event could be loss of a job, the successful gathering of resources, or some other factors that set the wheels in motion. In this stage, the founder identifies the opportunity and creates a vision for the company. If there is no vision for the venture, the new idea remains just a dream.

Assessing the Risks and Rewards

The fact that entrepreneurs need plenty of encouragement and support while they develop a business idea cannot be over-emphasized. In turning their idea into a concrete business, entrepreneurs will face hard facts and cold realities. They soon realize that what happens in real life is quite different from what they think. However, if they have adequate information from research, they can more easily decide whether the venture is worth going into or not. Many businesses (10%) fail and fold up within ten years; 85% actually fail within five years. Business failure extends beyond just bankruptcy. Many businesses lack the resources/investment needed to carry them through the start-up process (typically six months to a year between opportunity analysis and opening the doors for business). Many others die because of poor business planning at the initial stages, lack of business resources, lack of management expertise, dearth of experience, lack of financial stability, poor financial control, lack of inventory control and the inability to make entrepreneurial transition. Many start-up owners start their businesses as part-time and never make emotional and partial investment needed to ensure continued success. Many businesses are never legally registered since they do not intend to grow or transfer ownership.

Entrepreneurs have different motives, and this is why different outcomes spell personal success to different people. Some are not interested in running the business for a long time because of the risks involved. Some are not interested in growing but prefer to be stable. Different motives require different strategies. Sonfield and Lussier (1997) developed the Entrepreneurial Strategy Matrix (ESM) for small businesses. The ESM was developed to suggest strategies for new and ongoing entrepreneurial ventures that will lead to optimal performance in response to the identification of different combinations of innovations and risks. The matrix answers the questions:

- What venture situation are you in?
- What are the best strategic alternatives for a given venture?

Innovation being the creation of something new and different, the newer and more different the product or service is, the higher the innovation. Risk is defined as the probability of a major financial loss. The entrepreneur determines the chances of the entrepreneurial venture failing and how serious the financial loss would be. The entrepreneur will feel the same amount of loss differently. In order to effectively combine innovation and risk, a four-cell matrix as shown in figure 13.2 is desirable.

The ESM also suggests appropriate strategies for each cell, which are presented in figure 13.3. Thus, entrepreneurs use the matrix (fig 13.2) to identify which cell their firms are in. Then, based on their cell, they utilize the appropriate strategies suggested for their matching cell in figure 13.3.

	The Entrepreneurial Strategy Matrix: Independent variables		
INNOVATION (creating a unique and different product/service)	High	I-r High innovation Low interest	I-R High innovation High Risk
	Low	i-r low innovation low risk	i-R low innovation high risk
	Low High		
	Risk (probability of financial loss)		

Fig 13.2: The entrepreneurial strategy matrix

Source: Lussier 2000, p. 132

The Entrepreneurial Strategy Matrix: Appropriate Strategies

INNOVATION	High	I-r • Move quickly • Protect innovation. • Lock in investment and operating costs via control systems, contracts, etc.	I-R • Reduce risk by lowering investment and operating costs. • Maintain innovation. • Outsource high investment operations. • Joint venture options.
	Low	i-r • Defend present position • Accept limited payback. • Accept limited growth potentials.	i-R • Increase innovation, develop a competitive advantage. • Reduce risk. • Use business plans and objective analysis. • Minimize investment. • Reduce financing costs. • Abandon venture.
	Low	**RISK**	high

Fig 13.3: The entrepreneurial strategy matrix: appropriate strategies

Source: Lussier 2000, p. 132

Preparing an Opportunity Analysis

The entrepreneur must conduct a most thorough inquiry into the potential of the idea/opportunity, otherwise known as the opportunity analysis. Preparing an opportunity analysis helps in identifying which business ideas have real commercial potential or otherwise. To evaluate a business opportunity, review the sequence of events in Fig. 13.4.

DOES THE OPPORTUNITY

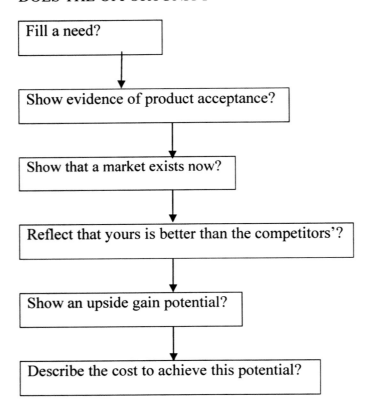

Fig 13.4: Evaluating an opportunity.

Source: Kaplan 2003, p. 27

Fig. 13.5 shows the factors that help entrepreneurs create opportunities for their business.

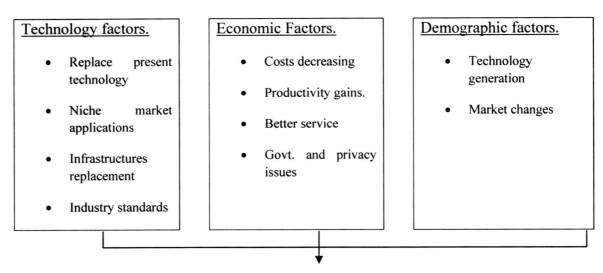

```
┌─────────────────────────────────────────────────────────────────┐
│                                                                   │
│   Questions Entrepreneurs Must Ask Themselves                     │
│                                                                   │
│      • Will these factors continue?                               │
│                                                                   │
│      • For how long?                                              │
│                                                                   │
│      • What is the market size, growth and outlook?               │
│                                                                   │
│      • Will these lead to other opportunities?                    │
│                                                                   │
└─────────────────────────────────────────────────────────────────┘
```

Fig 13.5: Factors that create opportunity

Source: Kaplan 2003, p. 27

Another important step the entrepreneur must take while preparing an opportunity analysis is to investigate the need through market research. It is important to identify, measure, and document the need for the product or service. During the research, the entrepreneur needs to know by asking preliminary questions: Will the product or service benefit customers? Will customers prefer this product or service to the competitors'? Is the product unique enough to be patented and get a significant head start on competition? How much will the cost of production be? How much will be needed in future, and how much will the customers be willing to spend on the product? How will the product be advertised? How will it be distributed? How will it be transported? Can required employees be attracted?

The entrepreneur must also identify secondary sources to support preliminary research. He/she should consult directly with existing business owners and experts in the same field and ask pertinent key questions and get advice. The entrepreneur must write a report after analyzing the data: What do the data reveal? How can they be interpreted? The final report will ensure that a record exists for the future. To ensure that the market research is done with limited funds and costs, an entrepreneur can use search engines, web-pages and online databases. The entrepreneur should use the telephone instead of mail surveys and door-to-door interviewing, avoid research in high-cost cities, test more than one product at a time and avoid collecting unnecessary data.

B.   **Developing the Plan and Setting Up the Company**

The second stage of the entrepreneurial process is to formulate the business plan. A business plan is a written document of 25 to 40 pages in length that describes, like a roadmap does, where a business is heading and how it hopes to achieve its goals and objectives. Developing a business plan is very important in securing capital and growing the business. Entrepreneurs often find that developing a business plan forces them to be disciplined in their thinking and planning activities. A properly prepared business plan will also help entrepreneurs to consistently establish and meet goals and objectives for their employees, investors and management. In addition, the plan provides a basis for measuring actual performance against expected performance. The plan also acts as a vehicle for communicating to others what it is that the business is trying to accomplish.

The business plan shows how all the pieces of the company fit together to create a viable organization that is capable of meeting its goals and objectives. It must also communicate the company's distinctive competence to anyone who might be interested. Preparing a business plan takes considerate time, effort and resources. Therefore, for it to be worthwhile, the plan must be useful to employees, management and potential investors. Putting down on paper where the company is in terms of its product offerings, its customer base, its relative competitive position, its financial requirements and resources, and its organization forces management to identify opportunities and threats, recognize the strengths and weaknesses of the company, reconcile conflicting views and arrive at a set of agreed-upon goals, objectives and strategies for the company in a systematic and realistic way. In short, a good business plan ensures the success of the company as it serves as a blueprint for building a company. It provides a means to determine whether the business is viable, raise capital for the business, project sales, expenses and cash flows for the business, provide a roadmap for future operations, explain to employees their responsibilities as well as company expectations, improve and assess company performance, plan for a new product development, and prevent oversight.

The single most important reason for preparing a business plan is to secure capital. Investors need to know the parameters, time-tables and expected future revenue streams. A business plan helps to define the often-asked who, what, why, where, when and how of the business. It is a tool for establishing the direction of the company and for establishing the action steps that will guide the company through the start-up period. Without a business plan, managers run the risk of proceeding blindly through a rapidly changing business environment. Hence, failure is imminent.

Target the Plan to Selected Groups

Entrepreneurs must consider which groups are relevant to their needs and send a plan only to the appropriate groups. These include;

- Bankers – to provide loans;
- Business brokers – to sell the business;
- New and potential employees – to learn about the company;
- Investors – to invest in the company;
- Suppliers – to establish credit for purchases.

Types of Plans

Business plan: An entrepreneur should use a business plan when he/she needs to describe the business in detail in order to attract potential investors, strategic partners or buyers.
Executive summary plan: This is a two-to-five page document that contains the most important information about the business and its directions. It is often used to gauge

investor-interest and to find strategic partners. It can only be used to attract key employees and to persuade friends to invest in the business.

<u>Action plan</u>: An implementation or action plan is a document the management team uses to implement the plan. It consists of a time-table and a list of tasks that should be accomplished within a certain time-frame.

Differences between Business Planning and Strategic Planning

A business plan addresses the operations of the business and how the business will accomplish its strategies. A business plan is generally written to test the feasibility of a business idea, to acquire financing, co-ordinate the start-up phase, and to get the business organized. Strategic planning concentrates more on internal and external factors which concern long term issues that will affect the business for about three to five years. It matches the direction of the business with the changes that occur within its environment.

Strategic planning addresses strategic growth—where the business is going. Business planning addresses operational growth—how it will get there. Strategic planning looks outward from the business at the long term prospects for its products, markets, competition, etc.; it requires the entrepreneur to broaden his/her thinking and forces him/her to counter the realities of the competitive world with concrete plans instead of wishful thinking. Business planning on the other hand is more detailed and focuses on the internal concerns, such as capital, personnel and marketing.

These two plans will eventually converge, as long-term strategic goals will be strongly influenced by operational decisions that were made when the business was started.

The Components of a Business Plan

A business plan should be tailored to fit your particular business. Write the plan yourself, though you may seek assistance from lawyers, accountants and or consultants. In 40 pages or less, it should contain your strengths clearly and in a logical order. The contents vary from business to business but should contain as many of the following sections as appropriate for your type of business.

The major components of a business plan include:

- Cover page;
- Table of contents;
- Executive summary;
- Company and industry;
- Products or services;
- Marketing research and evaluation;
- Marketing plan;
- Manufacturing and operation plan;
- Management team;
- Timeline;
- Critical risks and assumptions;
- Benefits to community;

- Financial plan;
- Appendix.

Cover page should include the name of the business, its address and phone number and the date the plan was issued so that potential investors can locate you to ask additional questions or send a check.

Table of contents makes the business plan easy to read. An orderly table of contents will allow the reader to turn directly to the desired sections.

Executive summary gives a one-to-two page overview of your entire plan. This is the most important section of the plan because readers do not want to wade through 35–40 pages to get the essential facts. If you do not capture the reader's attention here, the person is certainly not likely to read the rest of the plan. Just explain everything simply in two pages. Though it is the first section of the plan, it should be written last. The executive summary should include:

i.   Company information;
ii.   Market opportunity;
iii. Financial data.

Timeline outlines the inter-relationship and timing of the major events planned for your venture. In addition to helping you calculate your business needs and minimize risks, the timeline is also an indicator to investors that you have thoroughly researched potential problems and are aware of deadlines. Your time schedule should be realistic and attainable.

Critical risks and assumptions: Identifying and discussing potential trends, problems or risks you think you may encounter will show the reader that you are in touch with reality. This section gives you an opportunity to establish alternate plans in case the unexpected happens. If investors discover unstated negative factors, your credibility and the business may be questioned. Possible contingencies to anticipate are: unreliable sales forecasts, competitors' ability to underprice or to make your product obsolete, unfavorable industry-wide trends, appropriately trained workers not as available as predicted, erratic supply of products or raw materials, and anyone of the 10,000 other things you didn't expect.

Benefits to Community: You should imagine that your business will have an impact on many other people besides yourself. You must describe the potential benefits that the formation of your business could provide to the community. The economic, social and human development impact on the community must be spelt out.

Appendix: Supplemental information and documents not crucial to the plan, but of potential interest to the reader, are presented in the appendix. Information such as résumés of workers and principal managers, advertising samples, etc., can be included.

Steps Involved In Writing the Business Plan

The five steps involved are:
Step 1: Identify the objectives.

The entrepreneur must determine his/her audience, what they want to know and how they will use the information. Entrepreneurs think about competitive conditions, new opportunities and advantageous situations as they write the plan. The plan can be used to encourage investors to gain better understanding of business objectives and determine whether the business is worth the risk. The plan can also be used to familiarize sales reps, suppliers and others with the company's operational goals.

Step 2: Draft the outline.

Once the objectives have been identified, the entrepreneur should draft the outline that would provide enough details the audience will understand.

Step 3: Review the Outline.

Review the outline to identify areas that should be presented in even greater detail. Follow up on areas where you did not have sufficient information while doing the draft outline.

Step 4: Draft the plan.

A great deal of research is needed before enough information can be gathered to start drafting the business plan. Most entrepreneurs begin by collecting historical financial information about their company, which they use in preparing their initial drafts of proposed financial statements and projections. This enables them to know which strategies will work from a financial perspective before investing many hours in writing out a detailed description of the plan.

The business plan should contain eight sections. Section 1 should contain the **executive summary,** which is the last element to be prepared since it is a summary of the entire business plan. The executive summary must be able to stand on its own, describing the product and the market it will serve. It must contain its competitive advantages, everything that will be done to develop the product, the legal form of operation of the company, year of formation, principal owners and the key personnel. Finally, it must contain a highlight of the important financial information about the business, including its sales, profits, cash flow and return on investment.

Section 2 will contain detailed information about the company, industry, the product(s) and service(s) as well as the growth plan. The market analysis section (3) describes the market size and trends, the target customers and competition. Section 4 of the business plan describes in detail the marketing and sales plan. It describes the marketing strategy, pricing, sales plan, advertising and promotion, channels of distribution as well as the operations plan. Section 5, the operating plan, contains information about the product development, manufacturing plan plus maintenance and support. Section 6 describes the management team, its organization chart, key management personnel, policy and strategy for employees, board of directors and the advisory board.

In Section 7, the financial plan section, the entrepreneur demonstrates the ability of the business, showing the realistic first-year projections of income statements and balance sheets by each month as well as the quarterly projections for the next three years. Entrepreneurs should also keep detailed notes on the assumptions made in the draft so that they can later add footnotes to accompany the statements. The last section (8), which by no means is the last to be prepared, sets out the financial requirements, amounts, training terms and details about the uses of funds (capital expenditure, working capital, etc.).

Step 5: Plan review and updates.

The entrepreneur should have a professional review the draft for completeness and effectiveness. The plan must then be updated at least every six months and as objectives change.

Setting up the Company

One of the most important decisions entrepreneurs must make is how they will legally structure or organize their business. Before deciding how to organize a company, entrepreneurs must identify the legal structures that will best meet the short- and long-term requirements of their business. Factors to consider include tax laws, liability situations the capital needs and the ease of organizing them. Because there are significant tax and non-tax differences between the forms, entrepreneurs should carefully consider the results and requirements of each form to ensure that the business form they choose best meets their requirements. There is no single best form of ownership (sole proprietorship, partnership, co-operations); what is best depends on the circumstances particular to the business. To determine the form of ownership, an entrepreneur must be prepared to answer the following questions:

1. How big do you think this business can potentially become?
2. How much control do you need in the decision-making process of the company? Are you willing to share ideas and potential profits with others who can help build a more successful business?
3. How much capital is needed to start the business? Can you raise all of it alone?
4. What tax considerations are important? What sources of income are there and how are they to be sheltered?
5. In case of failure, to what extent are you willing to be personally responsible for debts created by the business?
6. Is it important that the business continue should you die or become incapacitated?
7. Who will be the sole or major beneficiary of the business success? Do you mind taking all the risks and in turn expect to reap all the benefits if you are successful?
8. Can you put up with the time-consuming bureaucratic red tape associated with the more complicated forms of ownership?
9. What is your emotional reaction to the government's regulations and the accompanying paper-work requirements?

Another factor to consider is the location of the business. Consider how important the location of your business is to your customers. If your customers come to your business, your location decision is critical, but if your business goes to them or if you do not meet with them face-to-face, your location is a less critical decision.

In deciding where to locate your business, you should consider the price and availability of land and water, the labour pool, accessibility to customers and suppliers, closeness of completion, adequacy of transportation and public attitude towards your business, taxes and regulations, your personal preference about where you want to live, financial incentives offered and the quality of life available.

C. Sources of Funding

The third stage of the entrepreneurial process is sourcing for funding. Finding money to start your business can be a real challenge. Entrepreneurs have a number of options when it is time for them to secure funding. To increase their chances of obtaining funding, entrepreneurs must know what funding sources are available to them and what the requirements of these sources are. What sources are best and most likely to help will depend on many different factors, including how much money is required, when it is needed, and when it can be repaid. The most common/ traditional sources of funding available to entrepreneurs are:

1. Equity financing (no set repayment schedule): need not be repaid but supplied by investors in exchange for an ownership position in the business and so does not create a constraint upon the cash flows of the business. However, equity providers demand a voice in management, thus reducing the entrepreneur's autonomy. The most common sources of equity financing are: personal funds, family and friends, partners, venture capital firms, small business investment companies, angels and stock offerings.

Personal funds: Most new businesses are originally financed with their creditor's personal assets. Cash, savings accounts and checking accounts are the most obvious sources of equity funds. Additional sources are the sales of stocks, bonds, real estate or other personal investments.

Family and Friends are more willing to risk capital in a venture owned by someone they know. Relationships will, however, become strained if the business is not successful and the funds cannot be repaid.

Partners: Acquiring one or more partners is another way to secure equity capital. Many partnerships are formed to take advantage of diverse skills or attributes that can be contributed to the business, expand the amount of equity capital, and enable borrowing more funds as a result of the cumulative creditworthiness of the partners versus that of only one entrepreneur.

Venture capital firms: These are groups of individuals or companies that invest in new or expanding firms, but it is not easy obtaining capital from them. Most of them have investment policies that outline the preferences relative to industry, geographical location, investment size and investment maturity. These firms look for businesses with potentials for rapid growth and high profitability. They provide funds in exchange for an equity position, which they hope to sell out within five to ten years or less. They rarely invest in retail operations.

Angels: An angel is a wealthy and experienced individual who has a desire to assist in growing a business. Most of them are self-made entrepreneurs who want to help sustain the system that allowed them to become successful. They are an excellent source of funding and can be the best option for entrepreneurs to pursue. Angels invest their own money, unlike the venture capitalists who invest mostly institutional funds and invest later in a company's life. Angels always review potential deals carefully, examine business plans, desire a strong management team, and look at financial reviews and analysis. Angels also expect the companies they invest in to go public or be acquired within five to seven years. They want an equity stake and a return of 20–35% on their investment, and some request a seat on the Board of Directors (Lorsch *et al.* 2001).

Stock offerings: Selling company stock is another method of obtaining equity financing. This is to be considered carefully because the entrepreneur will lose a portion of ownership of the business. Private placements and public offerings are the two types of stock sales.
Private placements involve selling stock to a selected group of individuals. Sales may be in any amount.
Public offerings involve selling of stock to the general public. Sales are always governed by regulations that can be both costly and time-consuming. To qualify, companies must be in good financial health and be able to attract an underwriter (typically a stock brokerage firm or investment banker) to help sell the stock offering. However, companies must make financial disclosures to the public; otherwise they can be sued for withholding or misrepresentation of information by the shareholders.

2. The second major source of financing a business is **debt financing**.
    These are loans borrowed from creditors and must be repaid. This can be a constraint to the future cash flows generated by the business. It creates the risk of becoming technically insolvent if repayment is not made on time. Continued non-repayment of debt will ultimately lead to bankruptcy of the business. Its three important parameters include: the amount of principal to be borrowed, the loan's interest rate and the loan's time to maturity. Until the debt is repaid, the creditor has a legal claim on a portion of the business' cash flows. The most common types of debt financing are:

Bank Loans: Many companies depend on bank loans. Commercial banks are the backbone of the credit market, offering the widest assortment of loans to creditworthy small businesses. They remain the primary source of debt financing for small businesses. The type, maturity, and other terms of each loan, however, are uniquely a function of the financial strength or creditworthiness of the borrower.
Commercial Finance Companies extend short- and intermediate-term credit to firms that cannot easily obtain credit elsewhere. They are willing to take a bigger risk than the commercial banks, so their interest rates are often considerably higher.
Insurance Companies also provide entrepreneurs with loans based on the amount of money paid in premiums on an insurance policy that has a cash surrender value.
Government loans: Governments at all levels give assistance through various programs to entrepreneurs, especially in specific sectors of the economy to stimulate

economic activities. This is to assist entrepreneurs to become profitable and create jobs. The loan programs of the government are usually tied to their economic development.

3. Other major sources of debt servicing are:

Trade Credit: Trade creditors supply goods or service to a business only to receive the payments at a later date with no interest charged. It is like a free loan.

Venture Capitalists provide funds for the growth of a business. Many of them are not interested in funding business at an early stage since they must liquidate their investments and provide cash returns to their investors over a comparatively short period of time. Some of them focus on specific industries or stages of investment such as when a company is planning to go public and requires financing until the event takes place. Venture capitalists can also be a valuable asset to a company in terms of their contacts, market expertise and business strategy. It is essential, therefore, for entrepreneurs to locate potential investors whose skills, experience and reputation complement their company and whose objectives are in close alignment with their own.

Debt Factoring: Here, the lender buys up the debt of the company, advances 60–80% upfront, and takes over the responsibilities of collecting from the borrower's clients. The factor charges a discount of between 2–4% that can increase to 15% or more if payments are overdue for several months.

Leasing: This is a contract agreement whereby a finance company purchases the durable goods needed by a company and rents them out to the company for a specific period of time. The rent payment includes some amount of interest. This activity allows entrepreneurs to have the use of state-of-the-art equipment at a fraction of the cost.

D. Determining the Resources Required and Implementing the Plan.

This is the fourth stage of the entrepreneurial process. It is very important that entrepreneurs know what assets are required to start their business and how these assets will be financed.

This knowledge is termed *initial capital requirements*. The process of determining initial capital requirements begins with identifying the short-term and long-term assets necessary to get the business started. Once you have this list of required assets, you can then determine how to pay for them.

Defining Required Assets: Before starting a business, each business needs a set of short-term and long-term assets. Typical short-term assets include cash and inventory, prepaid expenses (such as rent, insurance paid in advance), and a working capital (cash) reserve with which to pay bills, especially in the first year of operation when the business is not yet profitable.

The most common long-term assets are buildings and equipment, land, patents and all that the business needs to operate before opening its doors.

Implementation: This is the juncture of the entrepreneurial process when the organization is formed. Risks increase at this stage because a business is now formed. The innovation goes from being an idea in the head to committing resources to bring it to a reality. After opening its doors to produce original work of some potential value, usually referred to as intellectual property, implementation of the company's plan is concentrated on managing intellectual property, preparing the business for growth, and managing financial operations.

Managing intellectual property: Among the provisions by government to protect the various forms of intellectual properties are copyrights, trademarks, patents and trade secrets. The purpose of granting protection for intellectual properties is to encourage the advancement of "science and useful arts" by offering rewards to those who make such advancements. Protecting intellectual property provides profits or some form of competitive advantage to the entrepreneur. Intellectual properties, like other forms of property, may be used, bought, sold, licensed or otherwise transferred.

Copyrights are instruments of legal protection given to authors of original works of writing, arts, musical composition, photography and architectural design, expressed and recorded in a fixed medium—in print, by brush stroke, or disk, etc. The owner of the copyright has the exclusive right to reproduce, distribute, sell, publicly display and publicly perform his or her protected work or a newer derivative work based upon the protected work.

Trademarks are useful tools (name, symbol, motto, jingle, etc.) employed by commercially active entities to distinguish their products and the sources of these products from one another. They are some sort of brand, representing a company and what it is associated with. It is meant to affect the decisions of consumers or users of a produce at a glance.

Patents grant their holders the right to exclude others from making, selling, using or offering for sale the patented invention for a specific period of time, usually about 20 years. This is to give competitive advantage from which to profit or secure financial compensation for allowing others to participate. This is to encourage invention and technological progress.

Trade secrets can be any useful or vital information not shared with the general public. The information is not generally known, but it is valuable to the success of an entrepreneurial entity. Coca-Cola is a good example of a company that has maintained a trade secret for over 100 years and continued to reap economic benefits from it. It has succeeded in keeping the formula for its popular soft drink Coke secure from outside discovery. Trade secrets can be enjoyed by their owners for a limitless number of years but can, however, be lawfully employed by another party if development takes place independently and without any infringement. Even Coca-Cola's valuable trade secret might one day be reproduced and used competitively by an outside party.

Preparing the Business for Growth: Most businesses succeed or fail based on the performance of the entrepreneur and the management team. The drive of the entrepreneur and the strength of the management team are what breathe life into a business. Boards of directors as well as outside sources like accountants, consultants and venture capital firms can also be used by the entrepreneur because of their skills, access to additional resources, contacts and valuable services that can help prepare the organization for growth. An informal board of advisors can provide direction and expertise in a variety of areas, such as financing, product development and technical issues.

Another critical factor in preparing the organization for growth is that the entrepreneur should be familiar with human resource planning and staffing practices so as to be able to build broader human resource management capabilities beyond the management team and advisors, as the organization progresses.

The entrepreneur must decide which recruitment sources will be most effective for the company's needs, what is the most effective type of interview to be used in determining whether the graduates' skills and experience match the job, and how well the applicants' qualities will match the spirit and culture of the new company.

Another factor to consider is how to manage the employees' performance. The employees' skills, knowledge and abilities influence their performance. Performance is also influenced by various organizational and entrepreneurial constraints. For new ventures, factors such as capital and resources affect employee behaviour and performance.

Companies need to implement a performance evaluation system based on attributes, behavior, results, 360-degrees feedback, or some combination best suited to the needs of the new venture. Employees must also be provided with appropriate feedback on their performance.

A final factor in preparing the organization for growth is to provide appropriate performance incentives. These can range from small recognition for a job well-done and other types of on-the-spot rewards to more complex incentives such as bonuses and stock options. Communication with employees is important to convey what needs to be done to encourage continuous interest and effort.

Managing Financial Operations: Being able to understand financial statements, analyze them, prepare budget and cash flow forecasts and manage cash, assets and profits will help entrepreneurs measure financial performance and contribute to the success of their business. The entrepreneur will have to plan operations and make a variety of decisions using financial information gathered from the company's balance sheets, income statements, and statements of cash flows.

The **balance sheet** itemizes the company's assets, liabilities and shareholder's equity and gives a detailed picture of the company's stand at a particular time. The **income statement** itemizes revenues and expenditures during an accounting period, showing income or loss. The **cash flow statement** itemizes receipts and expenditures, resulting in increased or decreased cash.

These statements uncover important trends and overall performance, giving management direction as to what adjustments need to be made to the business' operations. Financial ratios can also be used to check overall performance. Ratios indicate strengths and weaknesses in the business. Financial ratios involve taking certain numbers from your financial statement to compute key ratios which can be compared to industry averages or historical figures from your own business to help you make financial decisions.

Accurate financial information is needed to know the financial health of the business. To make effective management decisions, the entrepreneur must know things like how quickly the inventory is turning over, which items are not moving, how much the firm owes, when debts are due, and how much taxes are owed. Good records are needed to answer these questions and many others. Accurate financial records also allow the entrepreneur to identify problems before they become threats to the business.

E. Harvesting the Venture

Harvesting a business can be thought of as picking the fruit of years of labour. In the harvest stage, the owner removes himself from the business. This last stage is a time that should be planned for carefully. It is like beginning with the end in mind, which is one of the keys to becoming effective in life. Entrepreneurs spend so much time creating a business that many do not plan for a successful exit. Exit plans should be developed early in the business cycle because a time will come when the stress of managing the business will become too great, when the entrepreneur will no longer be able to meet the financial expectations of investors, if new technologies affect product revenues or if competitors are gaining in market share and the company is losing its market position.

Harvest can take one of many forms. There are several ways an entrepreneur can realize the value he/she has created. The most common are:

Selling an equity stake to a strategic partner: The business can be sold to another individual, who will step into the position of manager; ownership of the business could be transferred to its employees via an Employee Stock Ownership Plan (ESOP); the business can be sold to the public via an Initial Public Offering (IPO); the business could be merged with another existing business to form an entirely new business. Finally, the harvest could be due to failure, in which case the doors are closed, the creditors paid, and the assets liquidated. Selling an equity stake to a strategic partner by establishing a strategic alliance can attract needed capital and substantially increase the value of the venture and, therefore, be an excellent exit option. Selling the business option may be risky in a weak economy. Entrepreneurs may have to agree to long-term payment plans that include a stock-for-stock exchange, resulting in stock price declines.

Merging is another alternative to growing the business, especially when a company loses its competitive advantage in the market place. A buy-out means the entrepreneur sells the business to its partners or management team. If the business has a positive cash flow or assets, the financing can be accomplished. However, when the managers or partners do not have sufficient capital, realizing the gain potential can be a problem. The entrepreneur can also obtain a harvest option by going public. This option can be the most profitable strategy for the entrepreneur but it takes a great deal of time, expense, and financial commitment.

Conclusion

In this chapter, we have seen that all new businesses require a certain amount of entrepreneurial skill. An entrepreneur being the person who creates, innovates, and assumes the risks involved as well as manages the business. The entrepreneurial process, which is the stages of a business' life, has been extensively discussed and it consists of five stages. They are: 1) conducting opportunity analysis, 2) developing the plan and setting up the company, 3) acquiring financial partners and sources of funding, 4) determining the resources required and implementing the plan, and 5) harvesting the venture.

References

Covey, S. (1989) *The Seven Habits of Highly Effective People.* New York: Simon and Schuster.

Drucker, P. (1985) *Innovation and Entrepreneurship: Practice and Principles.* New York: Harper and Row.

Guidelines for Entrepreneurs, pamphlet,Colorado Small Business Development Center.

Hatten, S. T. (1997) *Small Business: Entrepreneurship and Beyond.* Upper Saddle River, NJ: Prentice-Hall, Inc.

Hisrich, Robert. (1990) Entrepreneurship/ Intrapreneurship. *American Psychologist* Feb. 1990, p. 209.

Kaplan, Jack M. (2003) *Patterns of Entrepreneurship.* Hoboken, NJ: John Wiley and Sons, Inc.

Lorsch, J. W., S. Z. Andargachew, and K. Pick. (2001) Unbalanced boards. *Harvard Business Review* Feb. 2001.

Lussier, R. N. (2000) *Management Fundamental Concepts. Applications. Skills Development.* Mason, OH: South-Western College Publishing.

Sahlman, W. A. (1997) How to write a Great Business Plan. *Harvard Business Review* July 1, 1997, pp. 2–5.

Sonfield, M., and R. N. Lussier. (1997) The Entrepreneurial Strategy Matrix: A model for New and Ongoing Ventures. *Business Horizons* Vol. 40(May/June 1997), pp. 73–77.

Timmons, J. A. (1991) *Planning and Financing the New Venture.* Acton, MA: Brick House Publishing Company.

VanderWerf, P., and C. Brush. (1989) Toward Agreement on the Focus of Entrepreneurship Research: Progress without Definition. Proceedings of the National Academy Management Conference, Washington, D.C.

Chapter 14

EXPERTISE FOR SUCCESSFUL ENTREPRENEURSHIP

Jegede, C. T.

Introduction

The world is in the midst of an entrepreneurial revolution. The rates of new venture start-ups, patents, technology licenses, new product and service introductions and other indicators of entrepreneurial activity are at a high globally (Zahra 1993; Alarape 2010). The whole world is now in an entrepreneurship era, and developing nations cannot be an exception if they wish to join the league of industrialized nations of the world by the year 2020. It is a democratic revolution in that it involves every person: men and women, young and old, from all walks of life and backgrounds. In western Nigeria today, women and young girls are creating small enterprises and trades in the informal sector at a faster rate than anyone in the country (Jegede 2012). Unfortunately, the educational system, as it is in developing nations, is inadequate to drive the process because it is not addressing urgent and dire needs of the immediate communities. There are serious questions of relevance of the developing world's educational system. It merely teaches youths to obey instructions and reproduce facts as given to them by their lecturers without reflecting on what is being taught (Akinwumi 2011). Products of such educational systems are unable to contribute to the socio-economic and industrial development of the nation. Industries are complaining that skills of graduates from such educational systems do not meet their needs. This gap has resulted in a large army of graduates of varying educational cadres roaming the streets unemployed in many nations of the developing world (Low 2001).

Jegede (2012) observed that enterprise education has been prescribed as a sure panacea for filling this gap. Since students are being trained to contribute to national socio-economic development after graduation, they should consider themselves as student entrepreneurs in their various fields of study. This is the concept of nascent entrepreneurship. It works best when students are given a sense of belonging, by allowing them to study under real-life situations and learning on the job (Akinwumi 2011). This will no doubt close the gap between experiences in the classroom and workplace. Past studies in entrepreneurship courses (Angus and Pedro 2004; Abereijo 2011; Jegede 2012a) have revealed that students are eager to learn entrepreneurship; however, teachers, lecturers and students are yet to understand what teaching and learning concepts in entrepreneurship are all about. This gap needs to be addressed for teachers, lecturers and students to understand the most vital factors that are necessary for entrepreneurs to be successful in life. This chapter is an attempt in this direction. It attempts to fill this gap by describing those success factors among others that promote entrepreneurship. Specifically, the chapter aims at highlighting and elucidating the main success factors and competencies that are *sine qua non* for successful entrepreneurship activities.

Though some studies (Aldrich 1979; Bruyat and Julien 2001; Covin and Miles 1999; Drucker 1985; Galbraith 1970; Gartner 1985) have deliberated on the process of entrepreneurship that borders on the recognition of key success factors, challenges, dilemmas and, ultimately, solutions, nevertheless no solution seems to last long in an entrepreneurial milieu whose underpinning is "creative destruction" (Schumpeter 1935). To understand the process involved in this creative destruction, it is vital to critically examine the definition of entrepreneurship, discuss the entrepreneurial decision-making process, explain the competencies for successful entrepreneurship, and elucidate the key success factors in setting up a small enterprise so as to gain necessary skills and insight into some factors that are still vital for its creativity in any situation.

The Definition and Significance of Entrepreneurship

Entrepreneurship is more than something one does at a point in time. It is a process. It involves taking decisions and making concrete plans to venture into an enterprise. It is a way of life, of wanting to start an enterprise and manage it successfully (Bruyat and Julien 2001). It is a set of activities culminating in starting and running a business or trade (Stevenson and Jarillo 1990). It is a philosophy of life that believes in creativity and planning before starting a business (Jegede 2012a). It is a philosophy of life summed up in the equation "PROFIT* = SALES – COST" and not "SALES – COST = PROFIT**" (Jegede 2012b).

> ➤ *The first equation assumes the entrepreneur is focused, objective, determined, knowledgeable with concrete plans on what he wants to do, but
> ➤ **the second equation assumes the business man has no idea of what he wants to do; therefore he relies completely on fate, chance or luck.

Entrepreneurship in literature is sometimes explained as the next step after innovation and invention. It is the process that brings innovation or invention to consumers (Drucker 1985). It may be argued also that entrepreneurship starts with either innovation or invention (Jegede 2012b). The debate is still going on whether entrepreneurship encompasses innovation and invention or not. To a common business man, entrepreneurship incorporates innovation, invention and commercialization, but for academic purposes the three concepts are distinct and must be treated separately. Entrepreneurship is therefore a unique concept. It is a process, an undertaking by both an individual (entrepreneurship orientation) and a team activity (intra-entrepreneurship or corporate entrepreneurship) in a firm (Covin and Miles 1999). The challenge to each individual is to discover his or her own entrepreneurial potential and find ways to capitalize on that potential. The challenge is to build an entrepreneurial career that might include starting ventures, working for high growth ventures, taking over a family business, entrepreneuring in a large company, and/or pursuing social and non-profit entrepreneurship.

Whatever form of entrepreneurship one undertakes, entrepreneurship is the quality of being enterprising and full of initiative. It is the practice of starting or undertaking new business. Entrepreneurship, according to Shane and Venkataraman (2000), is "the pursuit of opportunity without regard to resources currently controlled, and starting or undertaking new business". At the heart of any entrepreneurial venture is an entrepreneur doing it alone or heading a team or coalition group in large company

(Galbraith 1970). These are the individuals with the vision, the tenacity, perseverance, the adaptability, and the passion to successfully implement a novel concept. Entrepreneurs are the agents of change and, according to Stevenson and Jarillo (1990), the "dreamers and doers," the people who see a better way and do whatever it takes to make that better way happen either socially or commercially. Much of what can be learned from them involves not so much their idea, but how they made it happen, how they overcame the obstacles and the negatives, how they found resources when there were none, how they brought along the team members, how they dealt with personal and ethical conflicts, and more regarding implementation and growth (Stopford and Baden-Fuller 1990).

Clarification of the Entrepreneurship Concept

Entrepreneurship, being a new field of study, is seldom used interchangeably with other concepts in the field of management. This practice seldom causes confusion among students, literates and practitioners. The affected concepts include *entrepreneurship, enterprise* and *small and medium enterprises* (Johan 2003).

The concept of 'enterprise' refers to either big and small businesses or trades. However, not all enterprises or businesses are involved in entrepreneurship. In developed nations, many firms are involved in entrepreneurial activities, but in developing nations few of the big, medium and small enterprises are involved in *intrapreneurship*/corporate entrepreneurship or entrepreneurship orientation (Jegede 2012b). The concept of 'intrapreneurship or corporate entrepreneurship' refers to the practice of entrepreneurship in big enterprises, which usually occur in groups called coalition group (Galbraith 1970; Stopford and Baden-Fuller 1994). These are groups of knowledgeable people in the companies that usually hold informal meetings with the chief executive officer (CEO) to determine courses of action before being discussed at the periodic management meetings. Entrepreneurship orientation refers to the art of entrepreneurship by an individual in a small enterprise which is usually a one-man business. The words 'entrepreneurship' and 'innovation' are seldom used distinctly by experts. This is because *innovation* may occur without necessarily *commercializing* it. *Innovation* and invention may occur in a research institute while *commercialization* of it occurs in a small enterprise. Some experts argue that innovation without commercialization is not entrepreneurship. However, when innovation happens simultaneously with commercialization, it becomes entrepreneurship. A good example of this assertion is the case of Late Steve Jobs, an entrepreneur who succeeded with computer technology. In America, his peers refer to him as the creative genius of the digital age and a technology idol; however, he is remembered as the first and the most successful entrepreneur globally during his days. Though he was neither an engineer nor a programmer, he was a technology whiz entrepreneur and a creative mastermind and a visionary.

Rather than spending his time in scientific laboratories designing and implementing information technology programming codes, he tried to understand what exactly is required by the people and learnt the product as a marketer. He was immensely successful as an entrepreneur not because he was efficient with technology; instead, because he was a very good observer, he aptly understood the consumers' mindset. The business lessons and ideologies preached by Late Steve Jobs are golden rules which could be applied universally in the teaching of entrepreneurship studies.

He understood the role and responsibilities of an entrepreneur. As a successful entrepreneur, he did not only react responsively to the marketing environment but brought overall revolution to the computer industry. He had his own creative ways to transform an industry. Therefore, Late Steve Jobs saw the significant role of an *entrepreneur* as an *innovator* and always tried to drive the entire market and consumers' outlook towards a particular product.

Another school of thought argues that when innovation occurs and it is put into use in a non-enterprise/business environment like government offices, it is not entrepreneurship (Gartner 1989). Events and time have proved this idea wrong because all institutions, either public or private, are now being referred to as 'enterprise'. Hence, entrepreneurship can now occur in any organised institution (Jegede 2012b). It is important to note that entrepreneurship is the practice of starting or undertaking a new organisation. Some competencies are therefore necessary for this to happen. It is thus important to identify and describe the key competencies required in setting up a successful small business. This is because, in considering self-employment or setting up a business as a career option, we should be aware of what it takes to become a successful entrepreneur (Sykes 1986). With such awareness, we can then develop or acquire the necessary competencies. But before then, we need to consider the process of decision making that eventually leads to the decision to start a business. The decision-making process is among the key issues that need to be learnt for a successful entrepreneurship.

Entrepreneurial Decision-Making Process

Given the novelty of entrepreneurship study, one important question that keeps recurring in business circles is how a person arrives at the decision to begin a business or run a successful business. In other words, what are the forces or factors that stimulate a person to venture into entrepreneurship and manage it successfully? One major attribute among others that has been found in literature to be responsible for this action is the ability to conceive thoughts and fruitful ideas through well structured plans to arrive at entrepreneurial decisions. These thoughts and ideas, however, usually originate from circumstances which according to Manu, Nelson and Thiongo (2005) could be categorized under the following headings, namely:

➢ displacement factor or change from current situation,
➢ role of a mentor or a credible example/model,
➢ possession of the necessary entrepreneurial competencies, and
➢ an enabling environment.

Displacement factor

For many people, the decision to start a business comes about following displacement at the working place. Many others tend to start businesses in areas similar to environments in which they have previously worked. This is called displacement factor/event or change from current situation.

The displacement of a potential entrepreneur arises from a sequence of events which result in his/her decision to begin to set up a business. According to Manu, Nelson and Thiongo (2005), the immediate manifestation of this could be: losing a job due to reorganisation, being unable to find a suitable job because of economic meltdown or structural adjustment programme of the government and/or tribal prejudice, or a refugee in a new environment who needs to start life from scratch. Other examples include the returning expatriate who has enjoyed rewards and status abroad not available in his/her home country and, more importantly, executives in large companies or organizations who were frustrated in their jobs and retired.

Role of the mentor/credible model

The role of the credible model or mentor is best illustrated by the occupation of the parents of the incipient or nascent entrepreneur. Research indicates that between 25% and 34% of entrepreneurs' parents (particularly fathers) were the owners of small businesses, and that, if farmers and independent professionals are considered as small business owners, this figure rises to 54%. Credibility as a motivational impetus, however, is not confined solely to families but also extends to peers and friends. Thus, for example, one of the reasons cited for the development of 'Silicon Valley' in the U.S. was the example provided by engineers leaving large organizations to successfully establish their own. The role of the credible model would also appear to explain why entrepreneurship is highly identified within certain ethnic and national groups, for example, Ibos in Nigeria; Jews, Lebanese, Koreans in the U.S.; and many Asian groups in the U.K.

Possession of entrepreneurial competencies for running a good business

The term competency is defined according to Manu, Nelson and Thiongo (2005) as: a body of **knowledge**, a set of **skills**, and cluster of **traits in** a particular personality. The presence of all or any of these in an individual makes entrepreneurial activities easier for the person. However, it is suggested that the presence of the three competencies is best achieved divinely by nature and may never be acquired through training or nurturing. Jegede (2012) concluded in his studies that every man is born and endowed with a gift (entrepreneurial seed), but such a gift is at times not visible or discovered but nurtured by teaching and learning. This teaching and learning process centres mainly on the competencies required for successful entrepreneurship.

The first competency, **knowledge**, refers to a set or body of information stored and recalled at an appropriate time. Knowledge in the context of business may manifest in the form of information, or familiarity with aspects, such as:

- a business opportunity,
- the market,
- customers,
- competitors,
- production processes,
- technical matters,
- business management,
- sources of assistance.

Knowledge of business or trade, however, is not enough for setting up and operating a business, just as reading or learning about flying, driving or fishing will not on its own enable you to fly a plane, drive a car or catch fish in the sea.

Skills refer to the ability to apply knowledge correctly. This can be acquired or developed through practice, e.g., flying, driving or fishing. In the field of management, it is possible to distinguish between skills of a **technical** and **managerial** nature. They relate to abilities to perform tasks or functions in areas such as:

Technical
• Engineering
• Computing
• Carpentry
• Mechanics
• Catering

Managerial
• Marketing (including selling)
• Financial management
• Organization
• Planning
• Leadership

Knowledge and skills are relatively easy to acquire or develop. They can be nurtured. By contrast, traits take time to develop and are not so easily changed or acquired. A trait is more of nature and can hardly be changed except by divine intervention.

Traits refer to the aggregate of peculiar qualities or characteristics which constitute the individuality of a person (Hornaday and Aboud 1971). There are 14 personal entrepreneurial characteristics (PECs) documented in literature (Manu, Nelson and Thiongo 2005) which appear to depict the behaviour of successful entrepreneurs; namely, a successful entrepreneur:

• Takes initiative
• Is persistent
• Is concerned for high quality
• Is oriented to efficiency
• Solves problems in original ways
• Takes calculated risks
• Is persuasive

• Sees and acts on opportunities
• Personally seeks information
• Is committed to fulfilling contracts
• Plans systematically
• Demonstrates self-confidence
• Is assertive
• Uses influential strategies.

Enabling environment

For entrepreneurship to grow, it needs an enabling environment, depicted by the willingness of the government to promote and support entrepreneurial activities. Favourable industrial policy needs to be in place to motivate and encourage potential entrepreneurs. Such government policy must reduce the risk involved in starting new capital-intensive enterprises and also promote human development programmes in the areas of entrepreneurial capital. However, given the novelty of the entrepreneurship subject, many experts still doubt if the subject can be learned, and they talk less of identifying key competencies to be learned in mastering the subject. So many controversies have come up in an attempt to understand the nature of entrepreneurship. This misunderstanding is often labeled as the "Nurture-Nature controversy" in entrepreneurship studies. To this school of thought, entrepreneurship is an in-born thing (by Nature) that cannot be learned (nurtured). This school of thought has been labeled *externals* while another school of thought believes that it can be learned/nurtured, and therefore labeled as *internals* (Rotter 1966). The difference between the two can be explained through their relative method of handling their *locus of control*.

Locus of Control refers to the extent to which an individual believes in fate and his or her ability to control fate. Individuals who have an external locus of control believe that the outcome of an event is outside their control and view fate as mainly determined by external forces and luck. On the other hand, individuals with an internal locus of control believe that personal actions do affect the outcome of an event. Thus, individuals with an internal locus of control are goal- and profit-oriented. They are focused, objective, and thus propelled, motivated and encouraged to pursue entrepreneurial activities, despite the challenges, because they believe that they control their fate (Rotter 1966).

Apart from the competencies of an entrepreneur, there are other vital factors, called the key success factors, in entrepreneurship discipline. These factors enable business men and women to spot the key variables which determine success in setting up a successful small business. At the same time, they develop an awareness of what is required to avoid failure or minimize the risks. An awareness of the factors which might determine success will not only guarantee the success of the business but enable individuals to equip and assess themselves in terms of readiness and suitability to venture into business.

Key Success Factors in Setting Up a Small Trade or Business

Many times we are confronted with questions like: How do I become an entrepreneur? How can I set up a successful business? However, it is difficult to give a method or blueprint from literature, as an answer to these questions because no correct systematic procedure has been identified yet as universal to starting a business that will guaranteea full success story. In spite of this, success, according to Manu, Nelson and Thiongo (2005), depends on that peculiar ability to spot opportunities in the market and act on them by organizing the necessary resources to offer something attractive to customers and taking the attendant risks. This is the essence of entrepreneurship in a business context. The crucial ingredient in the whole process is the entrepreneur. He/she takes the initiative and also bears the risk in creating and/or organizing an attractive offer of value to potential customers. He or she plans a course of action by taking some proactive decisions. The entrepreneur's ability to do this successfully depends, according to Manu, Nelson and Thiongo (2005), on four factors, namely: Motivation, Ability, Idea and Resources. The acronym—MAIR—may help in remembering these factors more easily. These are explained in turn below.

Motivation and Determination

It is widely acknowledged that, to be successful, the individual, in the case of small enterprise, or the coalition group, in the case of big enterprise, needs to be highly motivated and determined to set up the business. This will be reflected, for example, in how persistent the would-be entrepreneurs are in overcoming obstacles that might get in the way, how they go about seeking information, and how they act on opportunities. Additional indicators might be their commitment and attitude to work such as quality, efficiency, long hours, previous attempts to set up a business, and the support of their family or partners (Hoy and Verser 1994). Most of the time, profit is the best source of motivation, in line with the first equation that 'PROFIT = SALES – COST'.

Ability

Another important question is whether the individuals involved have particular abilities such as knowledge and technical or managerial skills of relevance to the business or project. One way of making up for any lack in this area could be to team up with people who have the necessary expertise.

Idea and Market

The important issue to be determined here is the viability of the idea, project, and product to be offered. In other words, does the idea, product or service meet a need or want for which there are customers who can afford it and are willing to use/purchase it in sufficient quantities to make the whole project break even? How is the proposition to be offered more desirable or better than what is currently available, and how will competitors react?

Resources

Finally, the extent to which the person(s) involved can acquire or organize resources in adequate measure will not only influence performance but also, in some cases, whether they start at all. Examples here include capital, cash, premises, materials, equipment and labour. The availability of infrastructure (e.g., utilities like electricity, telephone, roads), a business plan and support services might also be important. The business plan is a tool for transforming these factors into success.

In order to turn the resources into reality, a proactive decision-making process and a plan would be required. Every proactive decision taken must be documented in the business plan. These decisions are taken in respect of the identification of the basic resources. These are mainly men, money and materials (the "3 Ms"). The information to be collected on the 3 Ms consists of the following:

On materials, it will be necessary to survey relevant natural resources available in the remote and immediate environment to ascertain an adequate and continuous supply of raw materials. While scanning the immediate environment, it will be necessary to check if the machineries required to produce the goods are available locally. It may be vital to focus the scanning antennae on some research institutes and universities within the locality. Others include trade missions, embassies, magazines, trade fairs and journals. Taking decisions on the type of premises required for the business is also important.

On money, the business plan will evaluate financial sources from family, friends, relations and personal savings. Others include state Ministry of Commerce and Industry, Development Banks, venture capital firms and private finance houses.

On men resources, it is necessary to scan the environment for availability of different types of labour required. These include skilled, semi-skilled and unskilled labour. The skilled labour is important to the success of the enterprise. It is responsible for the organization and management of the enterprise. The men are generally responsible for the main components of the plan, namely, marketing, operation, organisation and financing. Generally speaking, the information collected on the 3 Ms will be used to explain the following, namely:

- where you currently are with your idea, project or business;
- what you wish to do;
- how you propose to go about it;
- and that the project is worthwhile.

As soon as the business plan is in place, and the resources are put in place, operation can start. In setting up the business, or before starting to operate, there may be legal or other statutory requirements to be met. There may be a need to consult professionals such as lawyers, accountants and/or staff from small business support agencies for advice. The whole business and the process need to be managed, and how well this is done—in particular, finding and dealing with customers, management of cash and finances, marketing, handling employees, dealing with suppliers, control systems—will all affect performance. How well this is done depends on the decision-making process in starting and running business.

Conclusion

Entrepreneurship is defined as the quality of being enterprising and full of initiative. It entails the practice of starting or undertaking new business. It is stressed that the entrepreneur is the essential ingredient in setting up a business in a free-market setting. He/she takes the initiative and the risk of setting up and organizing the business. He or she also bears the risk in creating and/or organizing an attractive offer of value to potential customers. There is no foolproof guideline for success in setting up a successful small business. Success depends on that peculiar ability to spot opportunities in the market and act on them by organizing the necessary resources to offer something attractive to customers and taking the attendant risks.

The key issues in being a successful entrepreneur border on some environmental factors and competencies of an individual including possession of knowledge, cluster of some entrepreneurial traits and skills. However, it is noted that possession of only one or even two of these competencies is unlikely to be sufficient to start and run a successful business. In the same vein, the lack of one or more of these competencies is not the end of the world as far as starting a business is concerned, for most of the competencies can be developed or acquired over time. For example, running a partnership form of organisation may make a team of two or more people compensate for the lack of all of these competencies in one person. In summary, there are basically three key competencies required for successful entrepreneurship, namely, Knowledge, Skills and Traits.

It is noted that one or two competencies only are not enough for success. All the three competencies,can be acquired or developed with time.

Also, the following factors from the MAIR model are important determinants for success:

❖ Motivation and Determination
❖ Abilities
❖ Idea and Market
❖ Resources

In order to turn the above components into reality, you need a plan, a feasibility study, if the business is yet to start. Once the business is set up, it would need to be well managed through a plan, a business plan.

Fourteen (14) Personal Entrepreneurial Characteristics of successful entrepreneurs were identified and these transcend race, culture and nationality. Major factors that push entrepreneurs into action to start business were categorised into:

− Displacement factor
− Possession of the necessary entrepreneurial competencies
− Role of the credible model and
− Enabling environment

ASSIGNMENTS:

1. Have the students list their own competencies on the board. Then ask them to select one business idea to which they could apply these competencies.
2. Divide the class into groups, in which each individual would present and justify his/her competencies and ideas.
3. Conduct a brainstorming exercise: Ask the class to list what they consider to be the key factors which can determine success in setting up a small business. List the responses on a board.
4. **Either** conduct a brainstorming session **or** divide the class into groups: Ask the students to come up with as many explanations as possible as to how and why individuals (or groups) can start their own business. List the responses on a board.
5. Ask the students to list people they know in their area who have started businesses as a result of the factors presented, justifying their choice in each case.
6. Let the students write an essay on "What skills would be important for an entrepreneur?"
7. Let the students write another essay on "Why is entrepreneurship important in Nigeria?"
6. Finally, get the students to complete the quiz on the WORKSHEET on "Entrepreneurial Decision-making Process Audit". Have them rate themselves, and explain the significance of the scores.

ENTREPRENEURIAL DECISION-MAKING AUDIT QUIZ

For each question below, unless indicated otherwise, please circle the answer that corresponds most to your views. Please be objective and honest with yourself; there is no right or wrong answer for this exercise (Adapted from George, Robert and John 2005).

1. How or where do you see yourself in 20 years' time, in terms of career or occupation (please state your response clearly):

2. List the names and occupations of 3 people whom you consider to be particularly good examples of who/what you would like to be in life:
(a)
(b)
(c)

3. Do you have any relatives who are running their own businesses?
(a) Yes
(b) No

4. Are you native of another state?
(a) Yes, I was born outside this state
(b) Yes, one or both of my parents were born outside this state
(c) No

5. Are you a member of a minority group in this state?
(a) Yes
(b) No

6. Has any of your parents ever been self-employed?
(a) Yes, for most of their working life
(b) Yes, for a limited period of time
(c) No

7. All things being equal, would you prefer to be self-employed or employed?
(a) I would prefer to be employed by a firm
(b) I would prefer to be self-employed

8. Would you say it was impossible, difficult or easy for you to start or help your parents in business at the present time?
(a) Impossible
(b) Difficult
(c) Easy

9. Do you think there is presently support in this state (e.g., help with finance, premises, infrastructure such as roads and electricity) for you to start your own business?
(a) Yes
(b) No

10. Which of these corresponds to your position in your family?
(a) Youngest child
(b) Middle child
(c) Oldest child
(d) Other

11. Please indicate your marital status (if applicable)
(a) Single
(b) Divorced/Separated/Widowed

(c) Married

12. Please indicate your age group

(a) Under 15

(b) 15 – 29

(c) 30 – 39

(d) 40 – 49

(e) 50 or over

13. Please indicate your highest level of formal education:

(a) Completed JS 3

(b) Completed SS 1or SS 2 education

(c) Vocational level diploma

(d) Bachelor's degree, professional qualifications, or higher

14. Do you have work experience in business?

(a) Yes, I have worked with my relative in farm/petty trading

(b) Yes, I have worked in SMEs

(c) No

15. Have you ever been punished for bad business malpractice?

(a) Yes

(b) No

16. Have you ever started or managed a petty trading business?

(a) Yes

(b) No

17. Do you think men and women have equal access to business opportunities and support services in this country?

(a) Yes

(b) No

18. What is your sex:

(a) Male

(b) Female

Quiz Score

Listed below are the scores to be given to each of the questions of the quiz on ENTREPRENEURIAL DECISION-MAKING AUDIT. The significance of the scores is also given. Please score yourself, referring to your answers on worksheet.

Question Marks

1. Award 2 points, if you intend to start and run your own business
Award 1 point in total for all other responses
2. Award 2 points in total, if any of these are entrepreneurs or are running their own petty businesses
Award 1 point in total for all other responses
3. (a) 2 points
(b) 1 point
4. (a) 3 points
(b) 3 points
(c) 1 point

5. (a) 2 points
(b) 1 point
6. (a) 3 points
(b) 2 points
(c) 1 point
7. (a) 1 point
(b) 2 points
8. (a) 1 point
(b) 2 points
(c) 3 points
9. (a) 2 points
(b) 1 point
10. (a) 2 points
(b) 2 points
(c) 3 points
(d) 1 point
11. (a) 1 point
(b) 2 points
(c) 3 points
12. (a) 1 point
(b) 2 points
(c) 3 points
(d) 2 points
(e) 1 point
13. (a) 2 points
(b) 2 points
(c) 2 points
(d) 3 points
14. (a) 3 points
(b) 2 points
(c) 1 point
15. (a) 2 points
(b) 1 point
16. (a) 2 points
(b) 1 point
17. (a) 3 points
(b) 1 point
18. (a) 3 points if the answer to the previous question is no, or
1 point if the answer to the previous question is yes
(b) 1 point

Now add up your points to arrive at a total score.

Significance of score
If your total score is:

33-46 You have a background similar to that of many successful entrepreneurs elsewhere. For you, setting up and running your own business may seem quite natural and will certainly come as no great surprise.

25-32 Your background is a little similar to that of many entrepreneurs. However, to succeed you will need to be aware of and prepared for all the challenges and implications of setting up your own business.

17-24 The decision to set up and run your own business may not be an easy one for you to make. In any case, to succeed you will need to be highly motivated and determined, prepared to break with tradition and work hard at your idea. Do not be discouraged, though, for you can work on and develop the necessary competencies. You can also partner with people who can bring into the business some of the required attributes.

In the end open a discussion with the class on the issue of gender inequality, if prevailing, and its impact on the entrepreneurial decision.

References

Abereijo, I. (2011) Developing Entrepreneurial Mindset in Teaching and Research. A paper presented at the first phase of a workshop on Enterprise Education for Employability, organised by The Center for Industrial Research and Development (CIRD) in collaboration with the Carnegie Foundation of USA and Nigerian Enterprise Education Network (NEEN), held at The Learning Hall, Centre for Distance Learning, Obafemi Awolowo University, Ile-Ife, on Wednesday, 5th October, 2011.

Akinwumi, I. (2011) Strategies for Developing Entrepreneurial Competences In University Lecturers. A paper presented at the first phase of a workshop on Enterprise Education for Employability,organised by The Center for Industrial Research and Development (CIRD) in collaboration with the Carnegie Foundation of USA and Nigerian Enterprise Education Network (NEEN), held at The Learning Hall, Centre for Distance Learning, Obafemi Awolowo University, Ile-Ife, on Wednesday, 5th October, 2011.

Alarape, Aderemi. (2010) The Effects of Entrepreneurial Orientation on the Performance of Small Scale Enterprises in South-western Nigeria. An unpublished PhD Thesis submitted to the Department of Management and Accounting, Obafemi Awolowo University, Ile-Ife.

Aldrich, H. E. (1979) *Organizations and Environments.* Englewood Cliffs, NJ: Prentice-Hall.

Bruyat, C., and P.-A. Julien. (2001) Defining the field of research in entrepreneurship. *Journal of Business Venturing* 16(2): 165–180.

Covin, J. G., and M. P. Miles.(1999) Corporate entrepreneurship and the pursuit of competitive advantage. *Entrepreneurship: Theory and Practice* 23(4): 47–63.

Drucker, P. F. (1985) *Innovation and Entrepreneurship:Practice and Principles.* New York: Harper and Row.

Galbraith, J. K. (1970) *American Capitalism, The Theory of Countervailing Power.* London: Penguin Books.

Gartner, W. B. (1985) A conceptual framework for describing the phenomenon of new venture creation. *Academy of Management Review* 10(4): 696–706.

————. (1989) "Who is an entrepreneur?" is the wrong question. *Entrepreneurship: Theory and Practice* 13(4): 47–68.

————. (1990) What are we talking about when we talk about entrepreneurship? *Journal of Business Venturing* 5(1): 15–28.

Hornaday, J. A., and J. Aboud. (1971) Characteristics of successful entrepreneurs. *Personnel Psychology* 24(2): 141–153.

Hoy, F., and T. G. Verser. (1994) Emerging business, emerging field:entrepreneurship and the family firm. *Entrepreneurship: Theory and Practice* 19(1): 9–23.

Jegede, C. T. (2012a) Towards Understanding Enterprise, Entrepreneurship and Small Business Development: Obafemi Awolowo University's Position. A paper presented at the second phase of the workshop on Enterprise Education for Employability, organised by The Center for Industrial Research and Development (CIRD) in collaboration with the Carnegie Foundation of USA and Nigerian Enterprise Education Network (NEEN), held at The Learning Hall, Centre for Distance Learning, Obafemi Awolowo University, Ile-Ife, on Wednesday, 3rd May, 2012.

————. (2012b) Corporate Entrepreneurship and Organisation Performance in Manufacturing Industries in Nigeria. An unpublished PhD thesis submitted to the Department of Management and Accounting, Obafemi Awolowo University, Ile-Ife.

Kingon, Angus I., and Pedro Vilarinho. (2004) Issues in the Design of Entrepreneurship Education Programs. A paper published in the *Proceedings of the Workshop on Leading International Practices in Engineering Entrepreneurship Education*, Lisbon, Portugal, September 2004. Proceedings published by COTEC, Portugal.

Low, M. B. (2001) The adolescence of entrepreneurship research: specification of purpose. *Entrepreneurship: Theory and Practice*, 25(4): 17–25.

Maes, Johan. (2003) The search for corporate entrepreneurship: a clarification of the concept and its measures. A working paper presented at Policy Research Center on Enterprises, Entrepreneurship and Innovation, Katholieke Universiteit, Leuven, Belgium, September 5, 2003.

Manu, George, Robert Nelson, and John Thiongo (2005) *Know About Business: Entrepreneurship Education in Schools and Technical Vocational Training Institution.* Turin, Italy: International Training Centre of the International Labour Office.

Rothwell, R., and W. Zegveld. (1982) New ventures and large firms. The search for internal entrepreneurship. In: *Innovation and the Small and Medium Sized Firm: their role in employment and in economic change.* London: Pinter.

Rotter, J. B. (1966) Generalised expectancies for internal versus external control of reinforcement. *Psychological Monograph,* 80, 1–28.

Schumpeter, J. (1934) *Capitalism, Socialism, and Democracy.* New York: Harper and Row.

Shane, S., and S. Venkataraman. (2000) The promise of entrepreneurship as a field of research. *Academy of Management Review,* 25(1): 217–226.

Stevenson, H. H., and J. C. Jarillo. (1990) A paradigm of entrepreneurship: entrepreneurial management. *Strategic Management Journal,* Vol. 11, Special Issue: Corporate Entrepreneurship (Summer 1990), pp. 17–27.

Stopford, J. M., and C. W. F. Baden-Fuller. (1990) Corporate rejuvenation. *Journal of Management Studies*, 27(4): 399–415.

———. (1994) Creating corporate entrepreneurship. *Strategic Management Journal*, 15(7): 521–536.

Sykes, H. B. (1986) The anatomy of corporate venturing program. *Journal of Business Venturing*, 1(3): 275–293.

Zahra, S. A. (1993) A conceptual model of entrepreneurship as firm behavior: a critique and extension. *Entrepreneurship: Theory and Practice*, 17(4): 5–21.

Chapter 15

ENTREPRENEURS' ATTITUDES AND SKILLS

Longe, K.

Introduction

Entrepreneurs are just conventional people, not different from you and me. They are in every community and country and come from all sorts of background. But where they differ from the ordinary people are in the attitudes and skills which they possess and develop from their backgrounds. Thus, entrepreneurs are important people in societies, who search for change, who respond to change, and who exploit the change as an opportunity (Hisrich and Peters 2002). They perceive needs, conceive goods or services to satisfy the needs, organise factors of production, and originate business ventures in order to bring their ideas into fruition.

In essence, there are no rules on who can become an entrepreneur, and no one can be excluded from the group, because it is a self-recruiting and challenging career choice. Entrepreneurs are driven by will for power, and they are slightly ahead of their time because they get things done through sheer energy; they do not worry about social constraints, and they are present in all ethnic groups (Swayne and Turker 1973). Awe (2006) identifies the entrepreneur as a key element in capitalisation for undertaking activities in the expectation that they will yield gain in the future. In essence, entrepreneurs are seen as special figures in the organisational system endowed with a certain set of mental attitudes and skills, proactively unassuming in making other people to feel important and to get the best from them. As such, entrepreneurs, by their attitudes, raise their sights to see possibilities until they feel the exhilaration of achievements. This is further reinforced by their skills and intentions to look at the future with a certain degree of correctiveness by thinking right and making profitable investment within a time span.

Concept of Entrepreneurs' Attitude

Typical of most social science and management concepts, there is no consensus on the definition of entrepreneurs' attitudes, but most descriptions include willingness to think right, act right, and take risk in the pursuit of an opportunity. As such, being an effective entrepreneur is not about academic qualification and finance; although having them makes it easier to start a company, they do not guarantee a successful entrepreneur. Having a successful enterprise is all about having the right set of attitudes and skills.

According to Meredith, Nelson and Neck (1991) entrepreneurs have career attitudes, which they apply to a wide range of solutions. They observed that, while most people let conditions control their attitudes, entrepreneurs use their attitudes to control conditions. In this perspective, entrepreneurs' attitudes are the reflections of the real entrepreneurs, which make them aim for the highest, continually consistent, and project what they are, by acting out of choice and never as victims of fate.

Parks (2006) posits that entrepreneurs' attitudes are an enduring organisation of beliefs which guide them in the decisions of their businesses and keep them going. As such, attitudes are settled behaviours with drive-producing properties, which determine entrepreneurs' predisposition to respond in some preferential manner to challenges of business ventures. Ekpo-Ufort (1998) enunciated that entrepreneurs' attitudes determine entrepreneur's receptiveness to need for the change in behaviour and entrepreneurial innovativeness. The deduction from this is that they determine what businessmen can expect from enterprise ventures, confident in their abilities and the business concept. Entrepreneurial attitudes make effective corporate owners to profit from their mistakes and try again in a more intelligent manner and in a different way, using their future endeavours based on past experiences.

Meredith, Nelson and Neck (1991) noted that being entrepreneurial is a life style requiring strategy for being an entrepreneur. They listed a number of factors that could help people to develop entrepreneurial attitudes towards their career. These include:

- being action oriented,
- accepting change and using change as motivator,
- having sound understanding of one's personal strengths and weaknesses,
- accepting responsibility for ensuring that action will be successful,
- living in the present and not wasting time reliving the past,
- making effective decisions and acting on them,
- exhibiting confidence in self and others,
- combining the unique qualities of the individuals working for you to achieve optimum benefits, and
- following a routine in one's daily activities, which allows for more time to be entrepreneurial

Developing Entrepreneurial Attitudes

Entrepreneurs are open to learning from the past. They actively seek new ideas and information, and they build networks of contacts and mentors whom they can ask for advice and information. They are also happy to pass their experience along to colleagues, while believing that success is unlimited and that as many people that work for it can achieve it. Parks (2006) stated that entrepreneurs can develop two types of entrepreneurial attitudes as guiding beams from a light house, which their customers will pick up subconsciously and make use in their decision to buy from them and also make a repeat purchase. These are simple and complex entrepreneurs' attitudes.

Simple Entrepreneurs' Attitudes

The simple entrepreneurs' attitudes are simple golden rules for sustaining entrepreneurial capacity. Effective entrepreneurs must show particular strength in developing them, in order to show that they are classic and true business people. Thus, simple entrepreneurs' attitudes are being responsible, principled, open, passionate and resilient.

Responsible

With entrepreneurs, the focus is on taking responsibility for making things happen. This is how they change the world of business. They see problems and accept they could do some things about them, and if things prove to be otherwise, they don't shirk responsibility by blaming others. Senior managers in most big corporate organisations are always finding someone else to blame for their non-performance or ineptitude. By shirking the responsibility, these senior executives are giving away the power to avoid the same problem in the future. As such, real business leaders keep this power by knowing that it is expected of them and only them to have the responsibility to do what needs to be done. This does not imply that they do not delegate, but they retain the overall responsibility for what happens. Because, they have the power of responsibility, they can adjust, work out what they did wrong, remedy the fault and provide solutions by changing their approach. As such, real entrepreneurs believe that their success or failure depends on their own actions. This quality is known as *internal locus of control*, the belief that one controls one's own success. Effective entrepreneurs must be principled, having belief in what is right and wrong that is strong and overrides all temptations. Real entrepreneurs must sacrifice personal gain for what they think is the right thing to do and also show loyalty to employees, who help them in building the business. They have principles and they stick to them; when they hurt, some entrepreneurs do flout this golden rule.

Open

Successful entrepreneurs must practice openness and honesty. They must be open to the truth, open with it and tell it as it is. They must do business straightforwardly and ensure that they are learning from the past, without letting it consume too much of their time. Real entrepreneurs must realize that they need to be constantly receiving stimulus from the outside world in order to be the best they can be. The doors must be widely open to know the real views of both the internal and external customers and to ensure that new innovations are possible. They must love meeting new people and listen to what these people have to say about their organisation and personality. In their business, they must have ears close to the ground in order to spot early signs of trouble and not be caught off guard.

Passionate

Being passionate means that entrepreneurs must develop a spirit of affection. Their company's products and services must be of perfect quality, delivered perfectly on time to customers, and perfectly produced to budget. As such, passionate entrepreneurs don't settle for anything less than the best. This passion enables real entrepreneurs to prosper when others are stumbling and to keep going when otherwise they might think of giving up. Customers also tend to respond extremely well when they realise that the management of a business are passionate about their products or services, customers, and work-schedules. Business organisations face lots of challenges, which might make the business leader to become dispirited; it is only being passionate that can come to the rescue. Consequently, being passionate makes entrepreneurs to hold higher standards than the other competitors and to do what is necessary to deliver quality and perfect products or services by constantly improving the way they do things. As such, entrepreneurs must develop a burning passion for business and have more than a casual interest in order to overcome unexpected obstacles.

Versatile

The only thing constant in business is change. Plans derail, customers behave unexpectedly, suppliers give problems, and competitors present challenges. Inexperienced entrepreneurs start to panic when they discover that things are not in accordance with plan. Developing versatility to meet these challenges implies embracing established plans and taking corrective actions as and when necessary. Real entrepreneurs must develop subconscious systems to support this versatility by building up and maintaining professional contacts on who can assist, keeping up to date on industry news and information, and getting earlier signals of potential problems, so that corrective action and help could be offered.

Resilient

Accomplished entrepreneurs are those who are imbued with resilience, having the spirit of tenacity despite failure to "never, ever, give up". Entrepreneurs need resilience to ensure effectiveness and vibrancy in business organisations. It is about the day-to-day running of the business, and it is being resilient that keeps the motivation alive. Entrepreneurs need resilience to stay afloat and ensure competitiveness, and their resilience should not annoy other people but should impress them. Successful entrepreneurs don't have failures; they only have learning experiences. They know that difficulties are merely opportunities in work clothes (Lambing and Kuehl 2007).

COMPLEXENTREPRENEURS' ATTITUDES

According to Parks (2006), complex entrepreneurs' attitudes do not produce straightforward ways of behaving and managing in business. These are some of the attitudes that entrepreneurs display that seem to be opposite to each other. It's like the

Chinese concept of Yin and Yang—two opposing forces that are in balance. Some of these complex attitudes include:

Language

The language we use has a big impact on our business. It helps to create the right or wrong mind-set. We need to demonstrate the follow features in the use of language of business: clarifying, restating, reflecting, summarising and encouraging people to continue talking. The advancement of technology has given us all good reason to be concerned that our over-dependence on it can permanently damage the interpersonal skills demanded in the use of language. If care is not taken, e-mail wars will replace old-fashioned paper memo wars as the means by which some managers hide from accountability, blame others for their ineptitude, and cover their tracks at work. The use of language reflects the way we think and often determines our attitudes in business ventures.

Risk and Certainty

Risk is at the heart of running any business, and the ability to manage risk is one of the qualities of any successful entrepreneur. Real entrepreneurship is about assessing risk, then finding better ways to reduce it, until one can move nearer to certainty that the idea will work. Only when the balance between risk and certainty has been achieved do real entrepreneurs go with an idea. Contrary to general belief, successful business leaders do not take wild risks. Real entrepreneurs know the odds are long and that they cannot control anything to improve the odds. Thus, effective corporate business founders assess where the risks are and try to reduce them by hiring the right employees with the right skills and experience, investing in specialist equipment, commissioning detailed research, and doing careful planning in order to eliminate all risk and bring the conditionsof business nearer to certainty. All this must also still be balanced with separate certainties: one's entrepreneurial attitude needs to be that risk is fine when it is understood, minimised and balanced with certainty. Thus, to be a really successful entrepreneur when it comes to risk curtailment, one needs to:

- assess the risk;
- be open and honest about the potential risks within the business;
- plan and take action to minimise those risks in advance;
- assess any remaining risks;
- have an emergency plan in place in case those risks becomes reality;
- revisit the risk planning regularly, dutifully and politely, civilly, formally, complaisantly.

Respectful and Courteous

Respect is demonstrated in entrepreneurial attitude by being aware of employees' work and ideas, always willing to give them time and attention, and taking them seriously. Thus, successful entrepreneurs respect the people who work for them, respect their customers and shareholders, and even their competitors. Conversely, being arrogant creates only short-term success followed by failure in entrepreneurship. Effective entrepreneurs use respect to influence others and to get along with people. They are flexible, possess orientation towards clear goals, and are responsive to suggestions and criticism. Successful entrepreneurs rarely annoy people and use respect for breaking any barriers in their world of business.

Confidence

Entrepreneurs manage to achieve extra feats simply because they have the self-certitude to go where others fear failures. They have such assurance and confidence in their own ability, the strength of their team and their idea that it ignites their resilience. As a result of their cocksureness, they are constantly looking over their shoulders at what competitors are doing, what technology is developing, where the fashion trends are going, what social and political changes are taking place. More often than not, entrepreneurs believe that there are myriad forces working against them and still have the confidence and work extra hard to justify themselves and their belief in their ability. As such, effective entrepreneurs do not often fall into the comfortable trap of assuming their competitors are second-rate; they continuously search for problems that might occur in order to be ahead of their competitors. They respect their competitors and expect them to pose the most danger, which keeps the entrepreneurs prepared for the worst that could happen and therefore on top of any problem that might occur.

Prudence

Entrepreneurs are prudent with resources, most especially in financial matters. The money in the entrepreneurs' businesses is their money. The less that is spent, the more they can invest in making the business more secure for the future and achieving their lifestyle ambitions. As such, entrepreneurs are often very tight with cash. They know what a very valuable resource it is and that it should not be wasted or allowed to be frittered away. The prudent attitude affects all other resources. The balance of being rich and poor in the use of resources often affects the decisions being made by entrepreneurs, such as in the selection of business premises and the type of materials and things being used.

Luck

Entrepreneurs do believe in and thrive on luck, but their definition of it is often positive and always optimistic. They know they have the greatest gift: the ability to think to its full potential. Entrepreneurs work hard for luck to happen, because they believe that what you see is what you get. To them, destiny is not a matter of choice and not a thing to be waited for but a thing to be achieved. Luck to entrepreneurs is hard work and realising what is opportunity and what is not. They believe that the harder you work, the luckier you get. As such, success is not something you run into by accident; it takes a lot of preparation and character. These are what entrepreneurs call luck. Thus, entrepreneur-style luck can happen by directing your mind to what you are seeking and creating as many opportunities as possible for finding what you want. Opportunities are nectars for entrepreneur bees. As such, you need to react quickly and expertly to opportunities. Once an opportunity does reveal itself, you need to act before it is snapped up by someone else or simply passes by. Entrepreneurs are also persistent until the results are achieved. The key to success in entrepreneurship is to try and try again and just keep on going until it works.

Entrepreneurial Skills

Entrepreneurs' normal character shows extraordinary skill in organising work and people for goals achievement. In effect, most business organisations fail and are unable to succeed because of lack of entrepreneurial skill. This is the influencing ability and capacity to do expertly well and display confidence in enterprise venture activities. The skill acquisition has three aspects. Each entrepreneur needs the three skills: technical skill of the business, conceptual skill, and interpersonal skill. Result-oriented performance will be difficult or almost impossible to achieve in the absence of any of these fundamental skills. However, it is very rare for entrepreneurs to have problems because of the technical and conceptual skills.

In business, most problems are people problems. Successful entrepreneurs build and develop pleasing and magnetic personalities, which makes them charismatic. This helps them in getting friendly cooperation from others. Business problems are most often solved when people's problems are substantially resolved. As such, entrepreneurs use the interpersonal or social skills more than the technical and conceptual skills. Their achievement depends to a large extent on the application of the interpersonal or social skills to harmonise the individual aspirations and the business objectives. The social skills are both problem- and solution-centred, building and maintaining positive relationships and good performance.

Problem-centred skill

Problem-centred strategies are pacing, enquiring and diagnosis. Communicating and using of languages in business is a dynamic process, which constantly moves through the three.

Pacing

Pacing is the technique of varying one's communication to match that of other organisational members. Pacing establishes a rapport with the other person, enabling an open and honest dialogue to take place. The environment and behaviour of the entrepreneur often determine the pacing techniques, without which it would be impossible to bring the entrepreneurship idea into fruition.

Enquiry

Enquiry is listening carefully to what people are saying and asking to fill in the gaps. Knowing when to use the closed-ended enquiring or open-ended enquiring and when to focus on the facts or the feelings are the skills associated with this sector which the entrepreneurs must possess.

Diagnosis

A joint diagnosis of the root cause of a problem is essential before any discussion on solution is attempted. Many people implement a solution to the problem they think they have rather than to the problem they actually have. The use of problem-centred skills in entrepreneurship often reduce this faulty diagnosis.

Solution-Centred Skills

The solution-centred skill strategies are leading, proposing and directing.

Leading

Leading is one of the most critical situations-centred skills as it can focus the conversation on the important issue. It is a process of transmitting information in a way that leads entrepreneurs to talk about possible solutions rather than imposing their solutions. Leading can be done overtly (simple leading) or covertly (complex leading) and can involve advanced techniques. Entrepreneurs must lead their business organisations in order to achieve the desired results.

Proposing

Proposing involves presenting possible solutions as a choice of options. The number of choices will often depend upon the various roles and preferences of the entrepreneurs.

Directing

Directing is the technique that entrepreneurs use without thinking. It involves telling others what to do. Effective entrepreneurs believe that there is a time and place for directing which should be done only when:

- they know what the problem is;
- they know what the solution is; and
- they have good reasons to believe that the work-members will accept the direction when discussions are complex and long.

True entrepreneurs must sharpen their interpersonal skills to equip their businesses in a sensible manner by building the required resources. However, entrepreneurial social skillsa re not about being everybody's best friend in and outside the organisation. They are about being respected and rallying people around the company focus. The goal is to set the company focus and keep everyone focused in it.

- Set the standard for attitude and style of work mainly by example.
- Give recognition to those who meet or exceed these standards promptly and fairly.
- Discipline those who do not meet these standards promptly and firmly but fairly.

Conclusion

Venturing into business as an entrepreneur and ensuring good performance and progress require positive entrepreneurial attitudes, good relationship style and problem- and solution-centred skills. The entrepreneurial responsibilities entail knowing what you want out of the business, and discovering the area of your personal interest within your inherent abilities and potentials. The bottom-line of your requirements as real entrepreneurs, and which make the difference, are the attitudes you have, the way you identify opportunities, and a range of the key soft skills. Real entrepreneurs employ others to deal with the work, while their job is to build the team and systems that make the business, using their entrepreneurial attitudes and skills.

References

Awe, I. (2006) *Entrepreneurship Development*. Lagos: Gilgal Creation and Publications.

Ekpo-Ufort, A. (1981) How To Develop The Technologically Innovative Entrepreneur and His Planning Skill. Conference Paper, University of Lagos, Friedrich Ebert Foundation Workshop in Entrepreneurship Development in Nigeria.

Heller, R. (2006) Assessing Your Entrepreneurial Profile: Do You Have What It Takes In Business?*The Ultimate Resource TM.* London: Bloomsbury Reference Book Publishers.

Hisrich, R., and W. Peters (2002)*Entrepreneurship*, 5th edition. New York, USA: McGraw-Hill Publisher.

Lambing, P., and C. Kuehl. (2007) *Entrepreneurship*. Fourth Edition. Upper Saddle River, NJ: Prentice Hall.

Meredith, G., R. Nelson, and P. Neck. (1971) *The Practice of Entrepreneurship*. Lagos: University of Lagos Press.

Ogundele, O. (2007) Introduction to Entrepreneurship Development. *Corporate Governance and Small Business Management*. Lagos: Molofin Nominees.

Parks, S. (2006) *How to be an Entrepreneur.* Pearson Education Canada.

Swayne, C., and W. Turkes. (1973) *The Effective Entrepreneur*. Morristown, NJ: General Learning Press.

Chapter 16

PROBLEMS OR CONSTRAINTS OF ENTREPRENEURS

Kolawole, T. O. and Owonibi, E.

Introduction

SMEs, or small- and medium-sized enterprises, are companies whose headcount or turn-over falls below certain limits. The abbreviation *SME* occurs commonly in the European Union and in international organisations, such as the World Bank, the United Nations, and the World Trade Organisation (WTO). The terms *small and medium businesses* or SMBs are predominantly used in the USA. In most economies, smaller enterprises are much greater in number than large companies. SMEs are often said to be responsible for driving innovation and competition in many economic sectors.

Contribution of SMEs to the Economy

During the last decade, it has been increasingly recognised in policy-making bodies of developing countries that small-scale enterprises have potential for contributing meaningfully to the development process. The most important advantages are well known: a more equitable distribution of income through widely dispersed ownership and relatively labour-intensive production methods which are locally appropriate; they could therefore be a major source of employment, especially in areas where few alternative options exist. This recent upsurge of interest will lead to a host of supportive policy interventions aimed at promoting small business. A number of these, such as credit programmes, industrial estate programmes, marketing support and technological support, aim basically at strengthening enterprises through an improvement of the direct business environment. Second, there is a growing body of activities aimed at increasing the skills of the persons running such enterprises administratively and management-wise in order to properly manage both human and material resources adequately. Among these are vocational, management and entrepreneurship training.

Micro, small and medium enterprises (MSME) sector has been recognised as an engine of growth all over the world. The sector is characterised by low investment requirement, operational flexibility, location-wise mobility, and import substitution. In India, the Micro, Small and Medium Enterprises Development (MSMED) Act, 2006, is the first single comprehensive legislation covering all the three segments. In accordance with the Act, these enterprises are classified into two:

(i) Manufacturing enterprises engaged in the manufacture or production of goods pertaining to any industry specified in the first schedule to the Industries (Development and Regulation) Act, 1951. These are defined in terms of investment in plant and machinery;

(ii) Service enterprises engaged in providing or rendering of services and are defined in terms of investment.

In the US, small business (fewer than 500 employees) accounts for around half the GDP and more than half the employment. The most recent data shows that firms with fewer than 20 employees account for slightly more than 18% of the employment. It can be argued that a sole-proprietorship (an unincorporated business owned by a single person) is a type of family business, and there are 22 million small businesses (fewer than 500 employees) in the US and approximately 14,000 big businesses. It has also been found that small businesses created the most new jobs in communities. In 1979, David Birch published the first empirical evidence that small firms (fewer than 100 employees) created the most new jobs, and Edmiston claimed that perhaps the greatest generator of interest in entrepreneurship and small business is the widely held belief that small businesses in the United States create most new jobs. The evidence suggests that small businesses indeed create a substantial majority of net new jobs in an average year. Local businesses provide competition to each other and also challenge corporate giants. Of the 5,369,068 employer firms in 1995, 78.8% had fewer than 10 employees, and 99.7% had fewer than 500 employees.

Small businesses play a crucial role in any given economy. They are major job creators; in South Africa, it's estimated that 68% of workers are employed by businesses with 50 or fewer employees, and they tend to be efficient and innovative and thus to prod large businesses to improve their own operations, making the economy work better overall. And, of course, today's small businesses are tomorrow's corporate giants (think Facebook), so they offer a special set of opportunities for investors. Thus, the performance of the small, micro and medium enterprises (SMME) sector of an economy is a good indicator of its overall vitality and future prospects. A thriving SMME sector implies a healthy economy (especially in an emerging market like South Africa), while a struggling one implies that there is something wrong.

The Indian micro and small enterprises (MSEs) sector plays a pivotal role in the overall industrial economy of the country. It is estimated that in terms of value, the sector accounts for about 39% of the manufacturing output and around 33% of the total export of the country. Further, in recent years the MSE sector has consistently registered higher growth rate compared to the overall industrial sector. The major advantage of the sector is its employment potential at low capital cost. According to available statistics, this sector employs an estimated 31 million persons spread over 12.8 million enterprises, and the labour intensity in the MSE sector is estimated to be almost four times higher than that of the large enterprises.

India has a vibrant micro and small enterprise sector that plays an important role in sustaining the economic growth, by contributing around 39% to the manufacturing output and 34% to the exports in 2004–05. It is the second largest employer of human resources after agriculture, providing employment to around 29.5 million people (2005–06) in the rural and urban areas of the country. Their significance in terms of fostering new entrepreneurship is well recognised. This is because most entrepreneurs start their business from a small unit, which provides them an opportunity to harness their skills and talents, to experiment, to innovate and transform their ideas into goods and services and finally nurture it into a larger unit.

Over the years, the small-scale sector in India has progressed from the production of simple consumer goods to the manufacture of many sophisticated and precision products, like electronics control systems, microwave components, electro-medical equipment, etc. The process of economic liberalisation and market reforms has further exposed these enterprises to increasing levels of domestic and global competition. The formidable challenges so generated for them have led to a novel approach of cluster development for the sector. As a result, private and public sector institutions, both at the central and state levels are increasingly undertaking cluster development initiatives.

Clusters are defined as sectoral and geographical concentrations of enterprises, particularly small and medium enterprises, faced with common opportunities and threats, which give rise to external economies, favour the emergence of specialised technical, administrative and financial services,and create a conducive ground for the development of inter-firm cooperation to promote local production, innovation and collective learning. Clustering and networking has helped the small and medium enterprises in boosting their competitiveness. India has over 400 SME clusters and about 2000 artisan clusters.

It is estimated that these clusters contribute 60% of the manufactured exports from India. Almost the entire gems and jewelry exports are from the clusters of Surat and Mumbai. Some of the small-scale enterprise clusters are so big that they account for 90% of India's total production output in selected products. For example, the clusters of Chennai, Agra and Kolkata are well known for leather and leather products.

General Problems of Entrepreneurs

Although the contributions of SMEs to the economy of a nation cannot be overemphasized, entrepreneurship can provide wealth in different ways, mobilise people and other resources, and/or lead to innovative practices in businesses and in the ways we organise societies. The level of SMEs'problems differs from SME to SME and nation to nation. However, the attendant effects of SMEs cannot be overemphasized, especially in developing countries. Ogundele (2002) examined what he considered the "most important problems confronting indigenous entrepreneurs in Nigeria." The report of those that were sponsored by government and those who are self-sponsored was issued. All agreed that inadequate capital was a major problem for them. However, those assisted by government listed problem of capital as the most important, while the self-sponsored entrepreneurs listed it as second, along with acts of indiscipline. Balogun (2004) echoed the same concern when he stressed that the most important concern for most of potential or on-going entrepreneurs was that of finance. The focus of his paper was to examine the extent to which this claim is justified.

It is instructive that the issue of the problem of performance of small-scale businesses has long engaged the attention of researchers.Schatz (1964), in his studies of Federal Loans Board and Yaba Industrial Estate entrepreneurs, concluded that there appears to be a capital shortage illusion among them. Harris and Rowe (1966) found that capital shortage was not a serious problem due to availability of hire-purchase and overdraft facilities. Akeredolu Ale (1975), in his own study, reported that the problem confronting the indigenous entrepreneurs in Nigeria could only be partly explained by economic factors.

Contemporary writers and researchers like Izedonmi (2007) and Olumide (2007) confirm the position that arguments about inadequate sources of capital are unfounded. For example, Izedonmi (2007) says that "the place of capital in successful entrepreneurship has been over-exaggerated, so much so that many potential entrepreneurs are afraid to commence or pursue their dream business". In some cases it has resulted in the throwing-money-at-problems syndrome (capital injection solution). This requires that the problem be addressed urgently. In doing this, we shall address the inadequate capital problem by examining the implications and effects of government capital-injection solutions; the misconceptions of the components of business capital; the natural business capital accumulation processes; and the place of entrepreneurship education.

Small businesses often face a variety of problems related to their size. A frequent cause of bankruptcy is undercapitalisation. This is often a result of poor planning rather than economic conditions—it is a common rule-of-thumb that the entrepreneur should have access to a sum of money at least equal to the projected revenue for the first year of business in addition to his anticipated expenses. For example, if the prospective owner thinks that he will generate $100,000 in revenues in the first year with $150,000 in start-up expenses, then he should have not less than $250,000 available. Failure to provide this level of funding for the company could leave the owner liable for all of the company's debt should he end up in bankruptcy court, under the theory of under-capitalisation.

In addition to ensuring that the business has enough capital, the small business owner must also be mindful of contribution margin (sales minus variable costs). To break even, the business must be able to reach a level of sales where the contribution margin equals fixed costs. When they first start out, many small business owners underprice their products to a point where, even at their maximum capacity, it would be impossible to break even. Cost controls or price increases often resolve this problem.

In the United States, some of the largest concerns of small business owners are insurance costs (such as liability and health), rising energy costs, taxes and tax compliance. In the United Kingdom and Australia, small business owners tend to be more concerned with excessive governmental red tape.

Another problem for many small businesses is termed the 'Entrepreneurial Myth,' or E-Myth. The mythic assumption is that an expert in a given technical field will also be expert at running that kind of business. Additional business management skills are needed to keep a business running smoothly.

Another problem for many small businesses is the capacity of much larger businesses to influence or sometimes determine their chances for success. Data from an empirical survey showed that: "About 46% of members have seen sales decrease and 48% [report] that orders are down over the past six months. Worryingly, 63% of respondents don't expect to see any increases over the next six months. The vast majority of our members have reported that costs have risen over the past six months, with a further 76% expecting costs to rise further. This is having a massive impact on future investment plans." (CBI: The Voice of Business, 2011). The government across all tiers could be doing much more to help small and micro businesses with capital in the form of loans that will be well monitored for optimal use for the purpose they are meant for. Government, through the Ministry of Agriculture, could also come up with a policy that will help build and cement a good relationship between the SMEs so that they could work as a team. This will rapidly boost growth and development in all ramifications.

Finally, low adoption and use of relevant ICT facilities in SMEs, especially in developing nations and most especially in Nigeria, is a big problem that undermines the contribution and performance of SMEs. The majority of SMEs owners-managers fail to spend reasonable capital on ICT in order to compete with other SMEs globally. The use of ICT has its own constraints, but then there is an alternative to the use of ICT. Kolawole (2004) carried out a study on the adoption and use of ICT in four (4) medium entreprises in Ibadan, Oyo State, Nigeria. The level of ICT application and use stratified the four SMEs into two (2), that is, intensive and non-intensive ICT users. Findings of the study shows that the problems or challenges confronting SMEs in Nigeria include: lack of capital investment (61.3%); poor electricity (61.3%); high maintenance cost of ICT facilities (57.1%); and high cost of ICT (60.4%). The four problems highlighted above are peculiar to the Non-Networked ICT users (APL and NML). When observed critically, it should be noted that the problems are capital-oriented problems. It means that the Intensive ICT Users (SBC Quarterly 2003; FCD Bulletin 2000) are totally exempted from these problems because the level of ICT facilities currently available in these industries is high, indicating lots of capital investment. Extant literature continues to support the fact that ICT facilities are highly capital-intensive. (SBC Quarterly 2003; FCD Bulletin 2000). Another major problem confronting the adoption and use of ICT is the low level of education among production workers, such that they could not understand simple computer-based design instructions. Data from Botswana corroborates this finding. In Botswana, both small- and medium-scale enterprises are faced with problems of poor management skill, lack of access to improved management skill, inability to acquire and retain skilled workers, and lack of access to skill training (Duncombe and Heeks 2001).

Another area of concern is in the area of loss of job because of ICT adoption and use. In all the industries visited, none of them had concerns about the impact of ICT on employment status. This extract presents some opinions on this from a marketing manager. The extract supports the fact that ICT in these manufacturing industries has not negatively impacted on job security in general.

Extract: Interview with the Head of Marketing Unit, (SBC, Ibadan).
"I can understand the concern people have when they hear about computerization. When people heard that Navision would be implemented throughout the company, there were real concerns about job security. So far after the adoption of Navision in seven regions, I can confirm that there has not been one member of staff who has been retrenched because of ICT".

Table 1: Current Problems Encountered by Selected Manufacturing Industries after the Adoption and Use of ICT Facilities.

	YES		NO		TOTAL	
PROBLEMS OF ICT FACILITIES	**N**	**%**	**N**	**%**	**N**	**%**
Low capital investment	206	61.3	130	38.7	336	100.0
Lack of personnel trained in ICT use and development	256	76.2	80	23.8	336	100.0
Poor electricity	206	61.3	130	38.7	336	100.0
Cost of ICT facilities too high	203	60.4	133	39.6	336	100.0
Maintenance cost of ICT is too high	192	57.1	144	42.9	336	100.0
Poor telecommunication infrastructure	84	25.0	252	75.0	336	100.0
Employees' resistance to use of ICT facilities	58	17.3	278	82.7	336	100.0
No training opportunity for staff in the area of ICT technology	267	79.5	69	20.5	336	100.0
Employees display negative attitudes towards ICT adoption and use in their respective units.	56	16.7	280	83.3	336	100.0
Many employees are too old to change to ICT demand and standards	72	21.4	264	78.6	336	100.0

Source: Kolawole, T.O. 2004

It is noteworthy that most of the constraints or problems of SMEs identified in these studies in Africa (or Nigeria, as the case may be) are still in existence. For instance, the issues of capital: most business owners have no money to put their businesses on good footing in order to stand the test of time or compete with others globally. Those who have good business ideology and creativity have no money to put such ideas into reality. It is now that the government of President Jonathan established financial empowerment for those who have a flair for business in different capacities. The maiden batch was certificated with money ranging from 1 million to 10 million naira. Also, the issue of power: this has been a long-existing problem that those in SMEs have been battling with in Nigeria because, without power, there is absolutely nothing that can be processed manually. The absence of constant power greatly affects the performance of SMEs in Nigeria even though government at the federal level has spent many billions of naira on it, but there is nothing to show for it. Governments at state level try to alleviate the challenges their citizens are facing on their chosen businesses. Other identified and existing constraintson SMEs eight years after the study were the lack of personnel trained in ICT use and development and the lack of training opportunities for staff in the area of ICT technology. The rate of unemployment in Nigeria is very alarming; about 64 million graduates are jobless, but recently it was discovered that most of them are not adequately literate in computers. This goes beyond the ability to type to the ability to use some computer packages to do one or two things or to solve problems. No SMEs, no matter what, will want to employ someone who is not computer-literate. It is also important to note that those on the job were not given the exposure to modern-day computer programmes or packages that can help them on the job. So, you can see the status of SMEs in Africa, and in Nigeria most especially. No wonder a nation like Nigeria is still developing society after 52 years of giving birth to her. Nigeria cannot in anyway compare to nations like Ghana, South Africa, or Malaysia, to mention but a few.

There is need for SMEs in Nigeria to occupy their rightful status in order to contribute immensely to the economy of Nigeria via high performance so that life can be meaningful to all and sundry if all the afore-mentioned problems are reduced (Personal Discussion 2013).

Questions for Discussion

1. What is the contribution of entrepreneurs to the economy?
2. What is the classification of entrepreneurs?
3. Mention the global constraints of entrepreneurs.

References

Akeredolu, Ale E.O. (1975) *The Underdevelopment of Indigenous Entrepreneurship in Nigeria.* Ibadan: Ibadan University Press. http://sbaer.uca.edu/research/ sbi/2008/chalh1f.html.

CBI: The Voice of Business (2011).

Duncombe, Richard, and Richard Heeks. (2001) *Information and Communication Technologies and Small Enterprises in Africa.* Manchester, UK: Institute for Development Policy and Management of University of Manchester.

Friggoglass Company Division Bulletin. (2000) Quality: Our Priority Concern. *Quarterly Publication.* Lagos, Nigeria.

Harris, J. R., and M. P. Rowe. (1966) Entrepreneurship Pattern in Nigerian Saw Milling Industry. *Nigerian Journal of Social and Economic Studies* Vol. 8, No.1, pp. 67– 111.

Izedonmi, F. (2007) If you want to be poor, be an employee only. Lagos: Streams Communications. http://sbaer.uca.edu/research/sbi/2008/chalh1f.html.

Kolawole, T. O. (2005) Adoption and Use of Information and Communication Technology (ICT) in Selected Manufacturing Industries in Ibadan, Oyo State,

Nigeria. An unpublished Master's Thesis, Department of Sociology and Anthropology at Obafemi Awolowo University, Ile-Ife.

Ogundele, O. J. K. (2000) Determinants of Entrepreneurial Emergence, Behaviour and Performance in Nigeria. An unpublished PhD Thesis, University of Lagos.

Seven-Up Bottling Company Quarterly Bulletin. (2003) New Performance Management System Takes Off. Lagos.

Schatz, S. P. (1964) Aiding Nigerian Businesses: The Yaba Industrial Estate. *The Nigeria Journal of Social and Economic Studies* Vol. 6, No. 1, pp. 199–217.

Chapter 17

ENTREPRENEURSHIP AND FINANCE

Adesunkanmi, S. O.

Introduction

Entrepreneurship is a creative process of organizing and managing an enterprise and assuming the risk involved in the enterprise. Hisrich and Peters (2002) see entrepreneurship as a "process of creating something new and assuming the risks and rewards". This definition stresses four important aspects of entrepreneurship: creation process (creating something new for customers); entrepreneurship requires time and effort; financial, psychological and social concerns, and risk-taking; and the reward of an entrepreneur includes profit, personal satisfaction, and independence, etc.

Accordingly, Awodun (2005:118) adopts the same process approach to define entrepreneurship as an act of: recognizing opportunities in one's environment, mobilizing resources to take advantage of such opportunities, ensuring the provision of new or improved goods and services for customers, and obtaining profit in return for the risk to dare. Entrepreneurship is therefore "about learning the skills needed to assume the risk of establishing a business, developing the winning strategies, and executing them with all the vigour, persistence and passion needed to win any game" (Inegbenbor 2006:1).

In the same vein, Aruwa (2006) sees entrepreneurship as "the willingness and ability of an individual to seek for investment opportunities, to establish and run an enterprise successfully". Entrepreneurship serves as a linchpin between the invention, innovation, and introduction of new products and services in the market place and also enables the entrepreneurs to act as engines of growth in the economy (Ketchen 2003; Venkataraman 1997).

Entrepreneurship is, therefore, linked to entrepreneurial opportunities, the compelling forces enabling entrepreneurs to introduce or develop new products or services. Tunkella (2005) defines entrepreneurial opportunities as "a set of environmental conditions that lead to the introduction of one or more new products or services in the market place by an entrepreneur or by an entrepreneurial team through an existing venture or a newly created one". In a similar vein, Aina and Salao (2008) see entrepreneurship as comprising "any purposeful activity that initiates, maintains or develops a profit-oriented business interaction with internal situations of the business or with the economic, political and social circumstances surrounding the business".

Entrepreneur

Scholars rarely agree upon a universal definition of an entrepreneur. Rather, scholars want to see an entrepreneur from different perspectives and sometimes also reflecting a particular social milieu. The term "entrepreneur" is French in origin and literally translates to mean "one who takes between". Onuoha (1994) and Inyang (2004) are some important writers who expressed some views on the role of the entrepreneur. For Onuoha, an entrepreneur is one who bears uncertainty, buys labour and materials, and sells products at certain prices. He is one who takes risks and makes innovation on factors of production.

Inyang also makes a contribution, considering the entrepreneur as the pivot of the economy and a catalyst for economic change and development (Deakins 1996). On his part, Schumpeter (1934) sees the entrepreneur as an innovator. He does new things in a new way. He supplies new products, makes new techniques of production, discovers new markets, and develops new sources of raw materials. The modern use of the term "entrepreneur" is usually credited to the works of Schumpeter. Drucker (1985) opines that an entrepreneur always searches for change, responds to it and exploits it as an opportunity.

The American Heritage Dictionary defines an entrepreneur as a person who organizes, operates and assumes the risks that are connected with business ventures. In their own contribution, Meredith and Ojong (2005) posit that entrepreneurs are people who have the ability to see and evaluate business opportunities, to gather the necessary resources and to take advantage of them, and to initiate appropriate actions to ensure success.

Based on the above definitions, one can now conceptualize entrepreneur as a change agent, an innovator who is also a risk taker, who exploits business opportunities in the environment and utilizes resources effectively to develop new technologies, produces new products and services to maximize profits, and contributes significantly to society's development. This definition encompasses the desire of the entrepreneur to maximize profit and contribute to the economic and social well-being of the society. It shows the entrepreneur as one who is also imbued with the ability to organize a business venture with the desire to achieve valued goals or results. He is a catalyst of economic or business activities.

Ways to Own a Business

Franchises

Buying a franchise gives the right to sell a particular product or service to an entrepreneur. A portion of the business profits is retained and a portion is paid to the overall organization that sold the franchise. One of the easiest methods of becoming a sole proprietor and acquiring the needed capital at the same time is to purchase a franchise. It is possible to start some franchises with relatively little money and to obtain start-up financing directly from the company selling the franchise. If a direct loan is not possible, the seller of the franchise may be willing to co-sign a loan with another lender. The seller of the franchise supplies the materials, a recognized brand name, and sales and

204

marketing assistance. Some franchises are fairly inexpensive while others may cost hundreds of thousands of naira.

Purchasing an Existing Business

One path to becoming an entrepreneur is to buy an already operating business from its present owner. Especially with regard to financing, buying an existing business may have certain benefits over starting a business from scratch. In many cases, the current owner will finance the sale of the business (Statt 1999).

For example, it is advertised that a small restaurant is for sale in a good location. The owner is willing to sell his or her interest in the business for ₦150,000 if the buyer takes over existing business obligations, e.g., space rental, employee wages, etc. How can theinterested potential buyer pay for the business? Let's assume that the buyer does not have ₦150,000 but can only afford ₦30,000.

For such a buyer the alternatives are to: ask the owner to finance the ₦120,000; try to find a way to borrow the money; offer the owner less than the asking price, thereby reducing or eliminating the amount of cash needed. No matter which alternative is chosen, the buyer should note why the business is being sold. Learn why the owner is selling the business. Make certain that the reasons do not spell disaster. It is more advisable to purchase if the present owner is selling in order to retire; however, if he or she is selling because the business is not profitable due to few customers and/or poor location, attention should be focused on the ability to improve the situation. Otherwise the mistake might repeat itself.

Some Lingering Problems of an Entreprenuer

Constrained access to money and capital market

The banking sector tends to be lukewarm in meeting the credit requirements of small businesses. This can be attributed to poor project proposals as well as to the inability of the promoters of small business projects to raise the required equity contribution (Adesunkanmi 2012b).

High rate of enterprise mortality

Adesunkanmi (2012a) opines that the incidence of inadequate working capital, holding back the production capacities of the small business, as well as the absence of a succession plan in the event of the death of the entrepreneur lead in many cases to the frequent early demise of small businesses. Moreover, the persistence of an unstable macro-economic environment, arising mainly from fiscal policy excesses, has often smothered many small businesses.

Shortage of Skilled Manpower

According to Marsch (2007), inadequate financial resources as well as the desire to operate with limited openness on the part of proprietors contribute in no small way to the employment of semi-skilled labour by many entrepreneurs. This of course affects productivity, hampers expansion, and hinders competitiveness.

Financial Indiscipline

Some small business proprietors deliberately divert loans obtained for project support to ostentatious expenditure (Adesunkanmi 2012b). Others are unable to pay back the interest and principal as at when due, because of operational difficulties and macro-economic shocks.

Poor Implementation of Policies

Nurbani (2010) opines that the poor implementation of policies, including administration of incentives and measures aimed at facilitating the growth and development of small businesses, has had unintended effects on the subsection. This has resulted, for instance, in confusion and uncertainty in business decision and planning and has weakened the confidence the small businesses have regarding government's capacity to execute faithfully its programmes.

Poor Management Practices and Low Entrepreneurial Skill

Many small businesses do not keep proper accounts of transactions (Adesunkanmi 2012b). This hinders effective control and planning. Moreover, lack of relevant educational background and thorough business exposure fetters their ability to seize business opportunities that may lead to growth and expansion.

Restricted Market Access

Insufficient demand for the products of the small business also imposes constraints on its growth. Although many small businesses produce some inputs for larger industrial enterprises, the problem of quality assurance as well as weak purchasing power, arising from the customers' dwindling real incomes, effectively restrict their market access (Marsch 2007).

Overbearing Regulatory and Operational Environment

Factors like multiple taxes, cumbersome importation procedures, and high port charges have continued to encumber the operations of small businesses. Many of the entrepreneurs have had to deal with a myriad of agencies but at great costs (Kpelai 2009).

Why Financing is Important to your Business

Many businesses fold up because prospective business owners do not have access to sufficient funds to run and expand the businesses (Adesunkanmi 2012b). For many business owners, where and how to get the funds to start or expand their businesses can be confusing, frustrating and time consuming. The amount of financing may be as little as ₦100,000, based on the type of business, as many different businesses can be started with a relatively small amount of money.

This guide will explain how, when and where to secure the capital business needs to be a success. This guide also includes some step-by-step instructions on how to finance business in the most profitable ways possible. Finding money may be difficult at times, but the economy depends heavily on small businesses, so therefore it is necessary to get the money that business needs, and the first step to success is knowing how and where to look for it.

How Much Money Will Your Business Need?

Every business is different, but it is still possible to get a reasonable idea of how much cash a business is likely to need by considering a few key factors. Does the business produce a product or provide a service? Ordinarily, a service business will require less cash because it will not have high material and equipment costs. For a manufacturing business, the amount of direct materials and equipment needed and expenses incurred must be considered (Adesunkanmi 2012b).

Other factors include labour: Is it a one-man business or will the owner hire employees? For business owners to invest their own time in the business is one way to keep costs down. Later, when the business is firmly established, employees may be hired to take over many of the day-to-day operations.

Another thing to note is whether business owners have personal funds to invest in the business. This is usually preferred or required by the investors. This contribution of unborrowed funds is called equity. There is no fixed percentage for this equity contribution, but most lenders require at least 25 percent of the total amount needed to establish the business. The amount of equity required is also influenced by other credit factors, such as management experience and adequacy of collateral.

Estimating Business Expenses

There are certain expenses that virtually all businesses must incur. The following list includes the content of a typical expenses list. (This is not an all-inclusive list. It provides some of the more typical expenses.) (Statt 1999)

a) Office space rental
b) Office equipment
c) Office supplies
d) Insurance
e) Utilities (phone, electricity, heat, water)
f) Maintenance
g) Advertising
h) Labour
i) Business licenses

A manufacturing business will also have specific expenses that are related to production. Therefore, the following expenses should also be considered:

a) raw materials,
b) machinery and equipment rental,
c) warehouse or factory space rental,
d) total estimated costs.

Assessing Business Financial Needs

Once expenses have been determined, a business owner will need to estimate what percentage of the funds can be supplied as equity and what percentage must be found elsewhere. At this point, the figure may seem overwhelming, but determination is the key in this regard. It is always better to realistically assess the existing situation early than to rush into a new venture without planning adequately.

Almost all businesses need outside funds. Business owners should prepare a month-by-month cash-flow projection for the entire first year, perhaps with the help of an accountant or banker. If the projection is realistic, it will clearly show how much financing the business required.

Types of Funding

Debt Financing

Debt is a direct obligation to pay something (cash) to someone (an investor or lender). Most of these debts are paid back with interest while some are not. Obviously, debt with interest means that more money will be repaid than the amount borrowed. Therefore, an important feature of debt financing is the interest rate the borrower will be charged (Ojo 2003).

Interest Rate and Risk
The interest rate usually reflects the level of risk the investor is undertaking by lending out money. Investors will charge lower interest rates if they feel there is a low risk of the debt not being repaid. Investors will raise interest rates if they are concerned about the ability to repay the debt. It is important to realize that a new business is likely to be charged a higher interest rate than a well-established business because the lender will feel a new business represents a greater risk.

What Do Debt Lenders Look For? A debt lender will evaluate your loan request by considering answers to several key questions, such as: Can the borrower offer reasonable evidence of repayment ability either through established earnings (for an existing business) or income (profit and loss) projections (for a new business)? Does the entrepreneur have sufficient management experience to operate the business? Does the business owner have enough equity in the business? (Equity provides what lenders call a cushion for creditors.) Can the business owner provide a reasonable amount of collateral (assets to be acquired, residential property equity, etc.)? (Ojo 2003)

The biggest advantage of debt financing is that it allows the business owner to retain control of the business. This enables the entrepreneur to be entitled to all company profits and have ultimate decision-making authority. Since many entrepreneurs start a business for exactly these reasons, a critical advantage of debt financing is that it provides them with some financial freedom; debt is limited to the loan repayment period. The lender has no further claim on the business after the repayment (Ojo 2003).

The biggest disadvantage of debt financing is having to make monthly payments on a loan, because cash may be scarce and expenses may be higher than estimated during the early years of a new business. Despite these, the lender must be paid on time, and there are severe penalties for late or missed payments such as additional fees, a poor credit rating, and the possibility that the lender may call the loan due.

Another disadvantage of borrowing funds is the difficulty in obtaining them. In general, lenders prefer to invest in businesses of proven credibility.

Equity Financing

Equity financing involves no direct obligation to repay any funds. It does, however, involve selling a partial interest in the business. In effect, an equity investor becomes a partner in the business and will have a degree of control over how the business is run.

What Do Equity Investors Look For? Equity investors buy part of a business by supplying some of the capital the business requires. Because they will own a share of the business, equity investors are interested in the business' long-term success and future profitability. Equity investors can resell their interest in the business to other investors. If the business is doing well, they will be able to sell their stake at a higher price than they paid and make a profit. Legally, equity investors are more exposed to risk than are debt investors. This is because, if the business fails, equity investors stand to lose more money than debt investors, since creditors are typically paid before owners in the event of business failure. Since equity investors are taking the greater risk, they expect to earn more on their investment than do debt investors.

One of the advantages with equity financing is that entrepreneurs do not repay the money invested by others (unless a payoff agreement is made at the time of investment). This can be important when cash is at a premium. Also, the owner's ideas for making the business successful may carry more weight with a potential equity investor than with a debt investor since it is in an equity investor's best interest for the business to grow and expand. Many people who are interested in starting or expanding a business have more ideas than money; this can be an important factor in favour of equity financing. In addition, equity investors, with their genuine interest in the business' success, can be a good source of advice and contacts for the business.

The biggest drawback to equity financing is that business owners give up some control over the business. This may not be generally acceptable to all, but the entrepreneur should remember that, in accepting equity partners, he/she is selling part of the business. It may be very difficult to retain control in the future.

Also, the equity investors do not always agree with the entrepreneur's plans for the business. However, since they own part of the business, the entrepreneur will have to consider their point of view, even if it does not agree with his or her choices. Finally, equity financing tends to be very complicated and invariably will require the advice of attorneys and accountants.

Possible Sources of Financing

Most new small businesses start out by borrowing money rather than by selling stock. If the business does well, owners may combine both types of financing. Sources of finance fall into two basic categories: private sources, such as co-operatives, family and friends, Esusu, etc.; and public sources, such as the financial institutions.

Private Sources

Private sources of financing are either personal sources (savings or loans from friends and relatives) or external sources (debt lenders, equity lenders and arrangements that combine debt and equity).

Savings

Personal funds are the most likely, and the most typically used, source of funds for a new business. Most lenders require that a reasonable percentage of the owner's own funds be invested in business as an indication that the owner will work hard to make the business a success.

Friends and Relatives

Friends and relatives are often an important source of capital for business. One important advantage is that the terms of repayment are likely to be more flexible than those of strangers.

Even with the advantage, it is a good idea to prepare a formal agreement when a friend or relative is willing to invest money in a business. This will make the relationship professional and will help to avoid future misunderstandings about how much was borrowed or when it should be repaid. The investment can take the form of a direct loan or an equity investment.

Debt Financing

Banks

Banks are financial institutions that accept deposits and make loans. They fall into several categories, such as savings and loans, thrift institutions, and commercial banks. Knowing the category in which they include themselves can tell a lot about the kinds of loans these banks are interested in making. Savings banks are more experienced in dealing with consumer loans, such as home mortgages and automobile loans. Commercial banks have more experience and interest in business loans.

Banks may be one of the first financial sources when searching for additional business capital. Certainly, they have money available to lend. However, it may be difficult for a new business to borrow from a bank since lenders usually prefer to lend to established businesses. However, it should be noted that the first responsibility of a bank is to protect its depositors. As a result, bankers tend to be very cautious about lending money.

Banks come in all shapes and sizes, and there are some real differences among them. Small community banks with two or three branches may operate quite differently from large commercial banks with hundreds of loan offices. Each type offers certain advantages. A commercial bank may be more experienced and familiar with a business loan request, but a community bank may know business owners personally and have more confidence in the ability to repay debt.

However, it is extremely helpful to owners to approach a bank with which they already have a savings or checking account or a personal loan. For banks outside the area, business owners may need to consult a banking directory. Directories list the name, location, assets, liabilities and officers of banks.

Credit Unions

Credit unions are financial institutions developed by the members or employees of a company, labour union or other group. Their overall goal is service to their members, as opposed to profit making. As a result, their interest rates and other terms may be more favourable than those offered by a bank. Credit unions are regulated by the National Credit Union Administration.

Credit union interest rates are often lower than the rates charged by other lenders. Though the amount available to borrow from a credit union may not be large, this source of funds may be helpful in making initial purchases for the business. Also, a loan application through a credit union may be more likely to be approved because of the existing familiarity.

Consumer Finance Companies

Consumer finance companies make small personal loans secured by collateral. Unlike banks, they do not accept deposits and they lend under the jurisdiction of each state's small loan regulations. Consumer finance companies will often consider loans with 100 percent financing because the loans are secured by an asset. Consumer finance companies charge higher interest rates and processing fees than banks and credit unions but can be more flexible about approving requests. Loans from this source are more expensive because they are considered to be more risky.

Also, borrowers should keep in mind that if repayment is not met on time, the item purchased with the funds will be seized.

Commercial Finance Companies

The primary purpose of a commercial finance company is to provide loans to purchase inventory and equipment. This can be a useful resource, particularly if the business will manufacture a product or act as a wholesaler. Commercial finance companies are similar to consumer finance companies but concentrate on business loans rather than consumer purchases.

Like consumer finance companies, commercial finance companies charge higher rates of interest than banks do. They also may be more willing than banks to approve business loan requests. Commercial finance companies will require that debt be collateralized. This means if borrower purchases a computer with the funds borrowed, the finance company will have a direct claim on the computer, selling it to recover its investment when the borrower defaults.

Trade Credit

When a vendor allows purchase of a product and a delay in paying for it, this is known as trade or vendor credit. Vendors offer this service to help make their products more attractive and to induce buyers to buy from them rather than elsewhere. Offering easy credit terms encourages sales. Keep in mind that the vendor is in business to make money. There may be a hidden costs for flexible credit terms in the form of slightly higher prices.

Trade credit is one of the most readily available sources of financing for businesses. In many situations, business owners will be able to purchase supplies and equipment directly from a vendor and spread payments over several months or years. Often, it is possible to make no or a minimal down payment and to avoid interest charges as well. Even suppliers who will not extend credit initially may be very willing to do so after several orders have been placed.

Insurance Companies

Insurance companies are a possible source of financing for a business because they make commercial loans a means of investing unused portions of their income. Generally, insurance companies make term loans and mortgage loans. Terms and interest rates on money borrowed from an insurance company are similar to those available from a commercial bank. Insurance companies can provide businesses with a large amount of capital at market interest rates, but borrowers must have assets sufficient to cover the debt, plus 20–30 percent extra.

Factor Companies

A factor company can be a useful source of funds for an existing business. Factor companies purchase a business' accounts receivable at a discount, thereby freeing cash for the business sooner than expected. Business owners will transfer title of the business accounts receivable to the factor company in exchange for a cash payment.

Factor companies provide two types of financing alternatives: recourse factoring and non-recourse factoring. In recourse factoring, the business retains part of the risk for ultimately collecting its debts. The factor company assists by speeding up the process. For example, the factor company purchases business receivables and advances cash while the accounts are being collected. However, if customers do not pay, the business will be held responsible for repayment to the factor company.

In non-recourse factoring, all rights and obligations concerning business accounts receivable are sold. The factor company purchases business receivables and collects the debts owed. If a customer does not pay, the business will be under no obligation to the factor company. Factor companies can be a useful source of funds for a new or existing business. They are not appropriate as a means of seed capital to start a business because they require that you have accounts receivable to sell.

Leasing Companies

A leasing company is a business that rents various types of equipment to businesses and individuals. By renting rather than buying the equipment, the business will be able to avoid many capital expenditures associated with the purchase of equipment. Many leasing companies require a down payment or several months' prepaid rent. Some, however, may allow the business to lease equipment without requiring any pre-payment. This depends upon the relative size or worth of the asset leased.

An advantage provided by leasing, especially for a business that experiences rapid changes in technology, is that the business will need little or no cash to secure equipment and will be able to upgrade equipment more easily than by purchasing it. Also, for ongoing expenses, such as employee salaries, leasing can allow holding on to the cash that otherwise could have been spent on equipment.

Equity Financing

Venture Capital Firms

Basically, venture capital is an investment in an unproven business. Venture capital firms provide equity funds to new and young business. This immediately separates venture capital firms from investment firms, which prefer to invest in existing, financially secure businesses. Venture capital firms do not make outright loans. Instead, they buy an equity interest in the business that gives them the same advantages and disadvantages associated with equity arrangements.

Venture capitalists are looking for two basic things when considering whether to invest in a business: high return and easy exit. In general, venture capital firms are most interested in investing in new technology and can typically supply large sums of money. Venture capitalists are not passive investors. They play an active role in the strategic planning phase of business and seek continuing involvement. They will also expect to be fully informed about operations and problems and whether joint goals are being met (Statt 1999).

Closed-end Investment Companies

A closed-end investment company is similar to a venture capital firm but has smaller sums of money available to invest. Closed-end investment companies are most likely to invest in a proven business, but some specialize in new businesses. Like venture capital firms, closed-end investment companies are interested in purchasing the stock of a business (Statt 1999). Because closed-end investment companies have limited amounts of funds available to lend, they may or may not be looking for new investments. It depends upon whether they have cash available at a particular time.

Corporate Capital Sources

In order to generate additional profits, corporations sometimes establish corporate venture capital firms, which operate within the overall corporation. These firms differ substantially from traditional venture capital firms. One of the biggest differences is that they are not motivated purely by profit, at least not in the immediate sense. A corporate capitalist firm typically seeks access to new markets in addition to realizing a financial gain.

The corporation makes an investment in business in exchange for an ownership interest. In this way, the needs of both the corporate investor and the entrepreneur are met. The corporation benefits by accessing new markets; the business owner benefits by receiving additional capital (Statt 1999).

Investment Clubs

In many communities, groups of business people form organizations to invest in new and existing businesses, usually at the local level. These clubs are typically less formal than a professional organization might be. Private investors pool resources to make a business investment. Because members of the group invest together, small investors are able to make funds available to a business on a scale that would be difficult or impossible if they were operating independently. Investment conditions and standards vary from club to club. As with other equity arrangements, however, a percentage of the business will be given up in exchange for funds received from the investment club (Statt 1999).

Employee Stock Ownership Plans (ESOPs)

It is possible for a business that has employees to sell stock in the business directly to them. Like other equity arrangements, a degree of control over the business will be given up. But, with an ESOP, control will be shared with business employees rather than with outside investors. This can be beneficial because employees will have a vested interest in making the business successful, and employees can have a large impact on operations.

Employees purchase shares of stock and thereby gain an ownership interest in the business. Employees may also offer to take a reduction in salary or benefits in exchange for partial ownership in the company. This is a good point to consider if business owners anticipate problems in meeting a payroll but cannot reduce staff. One obvious drawback to an ESOP is that it is only possible in a business with employees (Statt 1999).

Private Investment Partnerships

A private investment partnership is an arrangement in which one or more individuals agree to provide funding for another individual's business. The role of the partner(s) providing the funding is limited to supplying capital. Partners are not responsible for any debts the business incurs and will typically not play a role in managing the day-to-day operations of the business.

Combining Debt and Equity Financing

Customers as a Source of Funds

In some industries, potential purchasers of a service may be interested in offering financial help as such a business starts or expands. They are interested because an additional supplier (business owner) provides them with another source for a product or service they need. The addition of the business to the market may also increase price competition, resulting in lower prices for the customer. Each of these aspects translates into important benefits for the customer, just as the customer's funds translate into important benefits for the business owner.

This can be made possible by both direct loans and equity. Again, a direct loan must be repaid, while an equity sale diminishes control of the business owner. It is a good idea to consider the advantages and disadvantages of each and prepare a tentative proposal.

Also, business owners may need to approach potential customers, or the customer may come directly with an offer. However, owners should be wary if the customer proposes that products or services be sold exclusively to him or her in exchange for financial help. This is because securing exclusive rights to the products will give the customer more control over business operations and pricing, and this may shrink the potential market tremendously. If the customer stops buying for any reason, the business may be in serious jeopardy.

Government Sources

In addition to the private sources we have discussed, there are a number of government financing sources that may be available to a business. A government agency may be interested in financing new businesses that will have a direct impact on the agency or the client population it serves. So any business that produces a product or service that would be of interest to a government agency can contact the agency directly and request information and applications for grants and other possible business development resources the agency may control. It may be helpful to investigate some or all of the following general sources of assistance available through the government.

Ten Rules of Negotiating for Financing

1. *Prepare a comprehensive business plan*, including an income (profit and loss) projection for one year and a cash-flow projection. An overview of competition, composition of management and staffing, marketing plans and pricing strategy are also important.
2. *Be prepared to explain uses and benefits of the proposed loan.* Summarise the information in the Sources and Funds Statement in your business plan, and provide specific examples and supporting data for uses of the funds (e.g., estimates, list prices for equipment, etc.).
3. *Speak to the appropriate person.* With banks, as well as with all other sources, find out who will make the ultimate decision about your financing request, and then deal with this person directly.
4. *Do not overstate your financial strength.* Be realistic! Guard your credibility like the very real asset it is. Remember, the investor will almost certainly verify everything you say.
5. *Give complete information about your business.* It is wise to present all the information the investor requests.
6. *Seek a lender with whom you feel comfortable.* There can be wide variations among investors. Be sure to settle on one who can give adequate attention to your account and who explains all aspects of the financing relationship clearly and thoroughly.
7. *Negotiate interest rates and fees.* A small difference in interest rates can have a big impact on loan payments. The length of the loan is also important. The shorter the term, the less total interest to pay.
8. *Give an impression of confidence and competence.* The investor needs to have a high degree of confidence in the ability to repay the debt or generate a profit.
9. *Carefully check all terms of the agreement.* Sign all documents after proper checking.
10. *Dress conservatively.* Dress carefully when meeting with an investor. Dress to fit the environment.

Some Final Points

No one ever said that starting a business would be easy. Without a doubt, finding the money to start or expand a business requires hard work and determination. It may be the largest obstacle faced when planning to own or expand a business. Perseverance makes all the difference. Most successful entrepreneurs have been turned down many times for financing. But a good entrepreneur will sell his/her ideas and pursue every possible means of securing capital.

References

Adesunkanmi, S. O. (2012a) The Impact of Micro Financing on the Survival and Growth of Sole Proprietorship Business in Ife Central Local Government Area of Osun State. A paper accepted for publication in the *Journal of Management and Accounting*, Obafemi Awolowo University, Ile-Ife, Nigeria.

————. (2012b). Banks Consolidation and Small Business Lending in Nigeria. Unpublished Master of Philosophy Thesis of the Department of Management and Accounting, Obafemi Awolowo University, Ile-Ife, Nigeria.

Aina, S. A., and B. A. Salao.(2008) The role of three tiers of government in entrepreneurial national development. *International Business Management* 2(4):122–125.

Aruwa, S. A. S. (2006) *Entrepreneurial Development, Small and Medium Enterprises*. Kaduna: Entrepreneurship Academy Publishing.

Awodun, M. (2005) A process approach towards defining entrepreneurship. *Lagos Organisation Review* 1 (1) (June–August): 118–120.

Deakins, D. (1996) *Entrepreneurship and Small Firms*. London: McGraw-Hill Companies.

Drucker, P. F. (1985)*Innovation and Entrepreneurship*. London: William Heinemann.

Hisrich, R. D., and M. P. Peters. (2002) *Entrepreneurship* (5th ed.). New York: McGraw-Hill.

Inegbenebor, A. U. (2006) You can be an entrepreneur. In Inegbenebor, A. U. (ed.), *The Fundamentals of Entrepreneurship* (1st ed.). Lagos: Malt House Press Limited, pp. 1–14.

Inyang, B. J. (2004) *Management Theory: Principles and Practice* (2nd ed.). Calabar, Nigeria: Merb Publishers.

Ketchen, D. J. Jr. (2003) From the special issue editor: Entrepreneurship: past accomplishments and future challenges. *Journal of Management* 29(3): 281–283.

Kpelai, S. T. (2009) *Entrepreneurship Development in Nigeria*. Makurdi: Aboki Publishers.

Ojo, A. T. (2003) Partnership and Strategic Alliance Effective SME Development. *Small and Medium Enterprises Development and SMIEIS: Effective Implementation Strategies*. Lagos: CIBN Press Ltd, pp. 185–212.

Marsch, K., C. Schmieder, and K. F. Aerssen. (2007) Banking consolidation and small business finance: empirical evidence for Germany. Discussion Papers Series 2: Banking and Financial Studies, No. 09/2007, Deutsche Bundesbank Euro System, Frankfurt.

Nurbani *et al.* (2010) Survival Through Entrepreneurship: Determinants of Successful Micro-enterprises in Balik Pulau, Penang Island, Malaysia. *British Journal of Arts and Social Sciences.*

Ojong, C. M. (2005) Starting a new business. In Udo, S. N. (ed.), *Entrepreneurial Development: Principles and Practice.* Calabar: Wusen Press, pp. 43–45.

Onuoha, B. C. (1994) *Entrepreneurial Development in Nigeria.* Okigwe: Avan Global Publications.

Schumpeter, J. A. (1934) *The Theory of Economic Development.* Cambridge, MA: Harvard University Press.

Statt, D. A. (1999) *Concise Dictionary of Business Management.* London: Routledge.

Tumkella, K. (2003) The Challenge of Globalisation and SME Sector in Nigeria: Repositioning through Technology and Innovation. Paper presented at the National Summit on SMIEIS organised by the Bankers' Committee and Lagos Chambers of Commerce and Industry (LCCI), Lagos, 10th June, 2003.

Venkataraman, J. D. (1997) The distinctive domain of entrepreneurship research. *Advances in Entrepreneurship, Firm Emergence and Growth* 3: 119-138. JAI Press.

Chapter 18

CREATING AND STARTING A VENTURE

Akinbami, C. A. O.

Introduction

This chapter deals with entrepreneurship as the formation of a new venture. It contains the descriptions of and the practice and techniques of venture creation. It is based on resource-based theory that provides the understanding of new venture creation as to how entrepreneurs themselves develop and grow their businesses from the resources and abilities they possess or can acquire (Dollinger 1999). This theory argues that the choice of which business to do is not alone a criterion for success but that one must also consider the nature and quality of the resources, abilities and knowledge the entrepreneur possesses that can sustain and lead the business to success. Dollinger (1999) stated that using resources that are rare, valuable, hard to copy, and without good substitutes in favourable business conditions provides sustainable competitive advantage. He also said that choosing the appropriate resources matched with appropriate capabilities is ultimately a matter of entrepreneurial vision, which depends on the creative act/mind of the entrepreneur. Therefore, for an entrepreneur to create (found and originate) a new venture, he must take his psychological, sociological and demographical abilities into consideration. These characteristics are what the entrepreneur (founder) brings to the new business. The environment in which the needed resources lie is also a major factor to be considered before the formation of a new venture, because the environment possesses both the opportunities and threats that have great effects on the venture.

A business venture can,therefore, be defined as a business that is pursuing opportunities, characterized by innovative practices, and has profitability and growth as its main goals (Coulter 2001). However, it is important to note that a small business is different from a business venture. It is not all small businesses that are entrepreneurial in nature because the elements of innovation and opportunity-seeking are lacking. A venture may start small and also remain small either by choice or default; the experience of venture founders may be different due to different situations and circumstances, but there are some processes or factors that are common in creating and starting a venture.

- ○ **Generating Business Ideas**

The idea-generating stage is very crucial to the formation of ventures. Ventures would be borne out of the opportunities/ideas generated. According to Holt (2008), idea-generating is the conscious identification of a product idea that logically addresses an opportunity, which is the identification of a gap that is based on both wants and needs of people in a particular environment. Markets arise for new venture from wants and needs of consumers. Ideas can be generated through the desire to improve an existing product or service, newspaper advertisement, shopping trip, observing the environment to ask questions on how to resolve familiar problems, research, etc. Ideas must be money-makers and not necessarily fantastic ideas. A business idea is therefore a short description of the step-by-step involvement in an intended business. An entrepreneur must have a clear idea of the business he/she wants to run, since a good business starts with a good business idea. An entrepreneur must have a creative mind to develop likely areas of product or services that are related to his/her business interest, since ideas are everywhere, and this is done through brainstorming. It is best to keep your mind open to everything around you and make a list of all business opportunities you can think of. The brain-storming exercise is based on the local needs, environment, local activities, interest and hobbies. Holt (2008) called this process *mind-mapping exercise*, which must be developed to be able to determine what are involved in each idea, and this will assist in taking the right decision on appropriate business ideas. This can be done by exploring the external environmental changes and trends that can provide distinct opportunities for innovative and creative ideas through the following:

- ❖ Experiences: Your personal experience as a customer can help you to generate a business idea. If you have ever been in search of a particular product in the market, it can be a good opportunity to think about the product or service as a marketable idea. Other people's market experience can also help you to generate a good idea by interacting with different groups of people (elders, teenagers, and people from different ethnicities, opposite sex, etc.) in your area to know their needs that can be turned into a business outfit.
- ❖ Visit to business areas and environment: Look around your business area(s) to know the existing businesses and industries in the locality. This will give you the chance of identifying any gap that you can work on to satisfy the needs of members of your community. Thinking about the natural resources that are abundant in your area which could be turned into products or services is a unique way of generating business ideas.
- ❖ Waste product: ILO (2002) stated that there is always something that is left from anything that we make. This may come from household wastes that can be used to make animal feeds, papers, nylons, and iron pieces, etc., that can be recycled into other useful products. Take a look at the environment to locate such things that are classified as wastes; you may find something interesting that can metamorphose into a lucrative business outfit. At the end of the brainstorming exercise, you will have been able to generate some ideas which you can further break down into activities. Identify the requirements and the business ventures that can emerge from the ideas as illustrated in Figure 1 below.

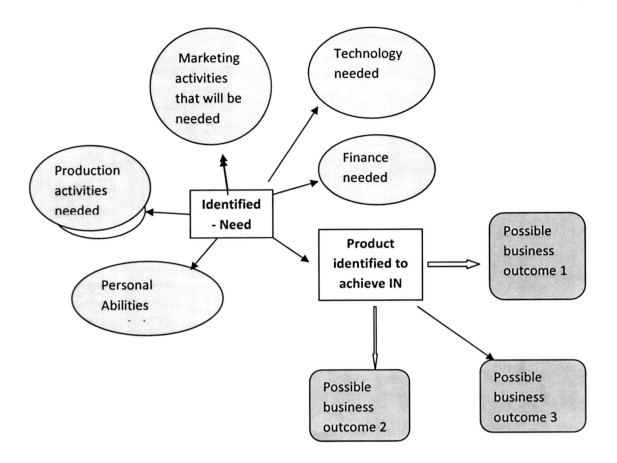

Figure 18.1: Mind-Mapping Exercise Diagram

Source: Adapted from *Entrepreneurship: New Venture Creation*, by David H. Holt

o **Screening The Ideas**

Once entrepreneurs have explored the external environment and generated ideas, they must now look at issues surrounding and involving each idea generated in order to bring the actual venture to reality. This is the screening stage of all ideas listed. The screening stage is the subjective evaluation which relies on the knowledge, interests, strength, experience and training of the entrepreneur to rate each idea and go for the one most suitable and commercially viable. This exercise is important to the entrepreneur because there is a lot he does not know about the listed ideas and this will help to answer certain questions that will clarify and aid his decision/choice. It is not wise to go into a business because a friend is doing well in a particular venture or it is the reigning business without subjecting it to thorough evaluation. You, therefore, evaluate your ideas by asking the following questions:

➢ Which: It is important that an entrepreneur identify the need(s) of the future customers that he wants to satisfy and identify the need(s) of the product or services that will satisfy the customers. In order to satisfy any need, an entrepreneur must identify his customers. Is it that your customers are not satisfied with the taste or quality of the existing product or that they need a new product entirely? Another useful tip is to ask which type of business you are best suited for. Is it at the . . .

- Retailing level, or
- Wholesaling level, or
- Manufacturing or service level?

➢ What: You need to first identify what product or services your future customers want and then research into the market size. An entrepreneur must be able to ascertain the sustainability of the market before starting production. If it is a product or service whose demand has a short lifespan and small market (Will there be enough customers?), an entrepreneur must not go into it no matter how lucrative it may be. He will soon be out of business. In order to remain in business, he must take decisions on the quality of the products or services the customers want so that he will be able to sustain the interest of the customers. A question that is desirable: "What information do you know about the product?" It is of great importance for the entrepreneur to know the current competition trend and pinpoint the possible competition advantage.

➢ Who: Who are you, what are your areas of interest, your hobbies? Does running the business suit your character? The success or failure of new ventures depends on the character of the founder, because even an exceptional product in the best market has no life style of its own without a skilled and interested founder. The abilities, interests and strengths of the entrepreneur breathe life into the product or service (Holt 2008). A founder must, therefore, do a personal assessment to identify and understand his own skills and limitations. He should ask himself if he is the right person to actualize the business idea. Doing a SWOT analysis will help to answer the questions above. SWOT stands for . . .

- S – Strengths,
- W – Weaknesses,
- O – Opportunities, and
- T – Threats.

For example, your strengths may be in the area of marketing skills and work experience in areas that are related to the business, while the weaknesses could be that there are no funds to carry out the venture. The opportunity could be that the alternate product is too expensive or of lesser quality, and the threat is that the needed technology is expensive and not locally available. If the areas of strength and opportunities are more than the identified weaknesses and threats, then it may be a good business, especially if the entrepreneur has ways of overcoming the areas of threats and weaknesses. Else, he should go for another business.

➤ How: There are so many 'how' questions the founder of a venture must provide answers to before arriving at a suitable idea for commercial purpose, questions such as:
- How will you source for funds?
- How will you sell and get the product or service to the customers?
- How will you strengthen your weak areas?
- How does running this sort of business suit your personal characteristics and abilities?
- How will you source for the needed materials and technology to start the business?

Starting a Venture

o **Marketing Research**

Marketing research is defined as the systematic and objective process of gathering, recording, and analysing data that will serve as aids in making market decisions (Zikmund *et al.* 2007). The main reason for marketing research is to provide needed information that will aid decision-making concerning the new venture. In any venture creation, the satisfaction of customers is a fundamental principle that will lead to the success of a venture. Therefore, research and findings should take place before starting the new venture in order to give value in products and services that are needed to the customers. The entrepreneur should create a good reputation with his customers by ensuring that the quality of such products and services will satisfy them, and this can be done through research. By doing this, he will empathize with the prospective customers, thereby obtaining a great deal of useful information about the reasons why they purchase the products, their purchasing patterns, and the intended products or services. An entrepreneur must not assume that the product or service will automatically sell. He should not expect people to have the same or equal passion as he has for the product or service.

The marketing research will encourage entrepreneurs to understand customers' needs, and to make decisions based on those needs rather than rely on perceived notions (Holt 2008). Also, it will help him to know and ascertain certain factors: (a) if a market exists for the new product or service; (b) who the primary customers will be; (c) how to position the new product in the market, especially if there is a high level of competition; (d) pricing, promotion and distribution strategies. This is important for the entrepreneur so that he will know how he can focus on long-term profitability and encourage the new products. There are phases that are involved in market research which an entrepreneur should be cognizant of when he is about starting a venture. They are:

- Who is the customer?
  Identifying the potential customers plays a key role in starting a venture rightly. Customers may be young or old, married or single, depending on the identified group that will be interested in the business idea you have created. However, whatever the target group is, you need to study the customers' characteristics that contribute to their buying pattern, such as:

- Gender and age

  The gender of the potential business is very important in marketing so that the entrepreneur will know the strategies to adopt in attracting a targeted gender category for the products and where they are usually concentrated. Age may not be easily classified, but the entrepreneur can find out the age group that may likely be involved in the use of such products or services. This information will aid decision making in starting the venture and satisfying the taste, colour and size preferences of the customers.

- Education and occupation

  These factors will significantly influence an entrepreneur's decisions on staffing, shop location, and stock. For example, a bookshop located near a university environment will require books that are different from those in a shop which is located in a rural area.

- Income status

  The ability of customers to buy and the amount they can part with will influence product concept, price and method of distribution. There are some customers for whom price is not an object because of the level of their income. For them, higher prices may be a sign of prestige. But for some, money is an object and they will go for a product that is moderately priced. An entrepreneur should be guided by this information and stock the shop accordingly so that the groups within the targeted category will be satisfied.

- Where is the market?

  An entrepreneur must be able to determine and secure the market for current and future sales. As a result, the entrepreneur must assess the local market where he intends to sell the product. Local markets differ from each other because of certain factors like culture, prevailing ethnic group, weather, etc., and this explains why a particular product may sell better in one area than in another. This can help the entrepreneur to segment the market based on the characteristics of the customers and location. He will also be able to project the sales volume in each area.

- Who are the main or major market competitors?

  An entrepreneur must be aware and conscious of competition. He should remember that he is not the only one with such an idea within the venture and he should keep this in mind as long as the business exists. Competitors are those ventures that satisfy the same customers' needs. Competition exists everywhere, so he should lunch out to gather information on the existing competitors from all available sources in order to be well informed about what they are doing and how their activities will affect his business. He should also find answers about the product substitutes that exist and key into the untouched opportunities presented by even the most common product. That is, the entrepreneur should find out what already exists, key in this information into the location and the customers already identified, find out what is offered with the product in markets, and see if there is still a certain area or opportunity that does not exist within the venture or product. This information can be gathered through an informal market survey, information from distributors, etc.

- How will customers be reached?
  This is the process of getting the product from the factory to the market, where the customers can assess the product or service. The success of the venture depends on the imagination of the entrepreneur to define channels of distributing the product or service to its final destination (customers). The chosen channel of distribution must reflect the appropriate quality and image of the product or service. The entrepreneur should decide the best strategy to employ, whether he will take the product to a particular location or market in a van on market days or have distributors in different locations or rent a shop in which to display the product. This has made people equate the ability to sell with entrepreneurial success (Hills and LaForge 1992).

o **Finance**
Financial resources are very essential to starting an entrepreneurial venture. Getting the amount needed at the time when it is needed is important to the entrepreneur. Getting money is considered to be difficult for some entrepreneurs, especially the beginners, because they are taken to be more risky than the established ones. So, a would-be entrepreneur must think of how and where he would get the needed funds from. It is pertinent to state that financing a venture means more than obtaining funds; it also involves the process of managing assets wisely in order to use capital efficiently (Holt 1992). It is also important to state that you do not need to have access to millions of naira in order to be successful as an entrepreneur. Starting small and growing with your business is one of the beauties and achievements of entrepreneurship. Having money makes things easier, but it is not required to make it big as an entrepreneur. Some of the most successful businesses in the world started out on a shoestring budget. Many businesses can be started with minimal investments, because it is not every business model that requires money from one's own pocket to get started. If the business idea is good enough, you may be able to get some investments from other sources to help you get things started. This will provide you with the money you need without forcing you to come up with it on your own. Basically, there are two ways of getting funding for the venture, which are (a) from personal resources (equity) and (b) from funds provided by others (debt). Figure 2 shows some of the various options available to fund the venture, and each shall be discussed.

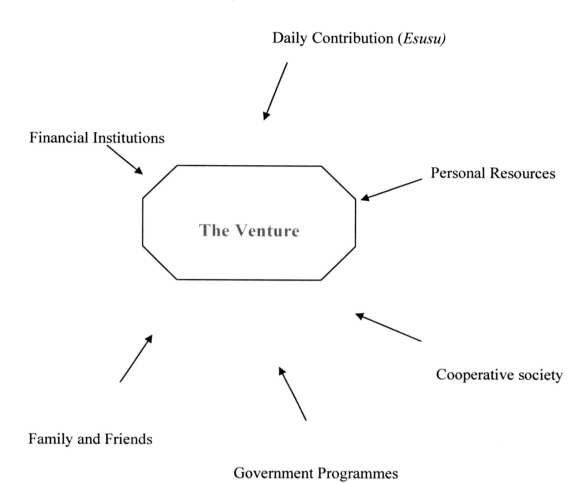

Daily Contribution (*Esusu*)

Financial Institutions

Personal Resources

The Venture

Cooperative society

Family and Friends

Government Programmes

Figure 18.2: Sources of funding

- Entrepreneur's personal resources (*equity*): This is the capital that the owner is ready to invest in the business. It can be a good source of funding for him because he must first look into what he has as start-up capital and it does not put pressure on him, even if the business fails. It can involve the following:
  - personal savings,
  - proceeds from the sale of personal assets,
  - credit cards (*where available*),
  - personal assets converted to business use (*e.g., computers, furniture, car, etc.*).
- Financial Institutions: Approaching financial institutions is another possible way of financing the venture. Financial institutions provide loans over a period of time to the entrepreneur, which is funding that is paid back by the entrepreneur with interest to the financial institution. This can be sourced from financial institutions such as microfinance houses or commercial banks. However, getting a loan can be a bit difficult for new start-ups because the

financial institutions see new ventures as uncertain and they (financial institutions) deal with certainty. So it may not be the best source of financing for a new business, because the repayment puts pressure on the entrepreneur and the business. Any venture that approaches the financial institution must have collateral, which may be difficult for a new entrepreneur to provide. However, the new entrepreneur can access funds from the financial institution if he comes up with a convincing business plan or feasibility plan. This is a comprehensive, detailed document that will show the viability of the project for which the loan is being sourced. The document will show, among other things:

i. the profile of the entrepreneur,
ii. a description of the product or services being rendered,
iii. a technical profile of the business,
iv. a marketing profile,
v. the manpower structure,
vi. the accounting/profitability index.

The loan given out by the financial institutions to a prospective borrower can take any of the following forms:

1. *Short-term loan*: This is the type of loan with a repayment period of less than six calendar months. This is the popular type offered by microbanks and venture capitalists ata high rate ofinterest.

2. *Medium-term loan*: The duration of payment for this facility does not exceed twelve months. Both commercial banks and microfinance institutions are reluctant most times to grant this type of facility because they need funding to run their own businesses. They avoid anything that will tie down their money.

3. *Long-term loan*: An entrepreneur can enjoy this type of facility for about two years or more. It is sourced for capital projects; it is usually provided by specialised banks such as Bank of Industry. But small-scale business entrepreneurs may not be able to access this type of loan because of stringent conditions attached to it.

4. *Overdraft*: This is a facility that allows an entrepreneur to withdraw more than what he/she has in his/her account. It is an arrangement between the bank and its customers to withdraw above the balance in the account. It is approved from the appropriate authority in the bank. It is usually for few days or weeks. Microfinance and commercial banks offer this type of facility, which is subject to renewal.

Esusu
This is one of the informal financial systems in Nigeria, formed on the basis of affiliation, which can be described as a credit union. It is a fund to which a group of individuals contributes daily and the total amount contributed is assigned to each of the members in rotation. *Esusu* has become a major avenue for low-income earners in Nigeria, which enables them to do

something worthwhile, especially where a large sum of money is required. These credit unions are growing fast, not only among market women but also among office workers. If properly managed, it could be part of the solution to the social crisis in the country. The entrepreneur can make use of this means to fund a new venture.

- Cooperative society

A cooperative society is a voluntary association of persons who work together to promote their economic interest. It works on the principle of self-help as well as mutual help. The main objective is to provide support, mainly financial, to the members. People come forward as a group, pool their individual resources together, utilise them in the best possible manner, and derive some common benefit out of it. Through this joint effort, an entrepreneur could achieve greater success by accessing more funding than what he alone could gather singlehandedly. There are different types of cooperative societies, and they differ with regard to the nature of activities they perform. Here are some types of cooperative societies in Nigeria that an entrepreneur can avail himself of:

1. Consumers' Co-operative Society: These societies are formed to protect the interests of general consumers by making consumer goods available at a reasonable price. They buy goods directly from the producers or manufacturers and thereby eliminate the middlemen in the process of distribution.

2. Producers' Co-operative Society: These societies are formed to protect the interests of small producers by making available items they need for production like raw materials, tools and equipment, machinery, etc.

3. Co-operative Credit Society: These societies are formed to provide financial support to the members. The society accepts deposits from members and grants them loans at reasonable rates of interest in times of need. This is commonly found in organisations, and it is well-structured.

- Government Programmes

Government has identified the need for the development of Small andMedium-Scale Enterprises (SME) in Nigeria. As a result, there are various financing options for SMEs so as to encourage and strengthen their growth in Nigeria. The government provides finance to companies in the form of cash grants and other forms of direct assistance as part of its policy of helping to develop the national economy to reduce the high unemployment rate. Various governments have different financial interventions for different groups, for example, rural women, the youth, etc. It is now the duty of any entrepreneur to find out such an opportunity within his environment and do what is required to access it.

Factors that lead to success for new ventures
Since most of the new ventures are advised to start small, it becomes imperative to identify factors affecting the success of the entrepreneurs in this category, as this will

help increase the role and success of small-scale entrepreneurs in boosting the economy. These include:

o **Human resources**

The success of the new venture depends more on the business owner than on the product or service because no product has a life of its own, no matter how well-positioned it may be in the market. The combination of determination, hard work, inspiration and sense of direction of the entrepreneur creates and sustains the venture. So, he must be ready to play various roles at once, such as leading, managing, and administering the new venture. In addition to his roles, Holt (1992) stated that the entrepreneur must have the foresight to hire people with the complementary skills needed to guide the enterprise towards success. In doing this, the entrepreneur must identify his area(s) of strength and limitation(s) before inviting others who have the needed skills that will lead to the management and growth of the new venture. This will also help to have the needed number of people and the right people in the right place and at the right time. Merit should come first and not relationship if the venture must grow. In addition to the above, an entrepreneur must possess certain traits that will aid his success. According to Kirby (2003), there is no uniform definition of the entrepreneur, but all entrepreneurs must display certain common traits such as:

- total commitment, determination and perseverance;
- drive to achieve and grow the business in the face of all difficulties (being persistent in problem-solving);
- creativity and innovativeness not to do what all other people are doing in the business line and being original in their thinking (ability to add value even to an existing product);
- integrity and reliability;
- team building;
- hard work and emotional stability;
- decisiveness, urgency and patience;
- flexibility; and
- calculated risk-taking and risk-sharing.

o **Experience**

This has been considered to be the best predictor of business success (Staw 1991). Experience is the means of being equipped with the necessary technical skills and managerial acumen. The entrepreneur's willingness to acquire the needed skills is very important, as entrepreneurs with vast experiences in managing business are more capable of finding ways to sustain such businesses compared to employees with different career pathways who see a business start-up as a means to be out of poverty. The importance of experience for small-scale business success is also underscored by other experts, such as Haswell *et al.* (in Zimmerer and Scarborough 1998), who note that prominent reasons behind business failures are managerial and experiential incapabilities.

o **Good business philosophy**

For the new venture to succeed, the owner's priorities must not get in the way of his business activities and practices. The new venture requires the whole attention of the entrepreneur, especially at the early stage, when he/she needs to spend long hours and sacrifice a lot to make things work. The entrepreneur must be ready to give the business what it takes. Part of the good philosophy the entrepreneur must imbibe is not to disregard the customers, as this (to satisfy the customers) is a key factor leading to success. The entrepreneur should aim at being of good value to the society by providing a needed, useful, and safe product or service (Drucker 1977). An entrepreneur must not exploit the customers, because he/she will feel the customers' reactions faster than the large and public organizations will.

o **Case Studies**

These are life experiences of people put together for one to learn from. An upcoming entrepreneur should study to identify the processes involved, challenge(s) and how they were overcome. An existing entrepreneur should equally study to know how to improve his business. These were adopted from different sources.

Case 1

A woman in a transportation business knows how difficult being a successful entrepreneur is. As a former civil servant, she was aware of the transportation problems faced by individuals who are trying to move off from public assistance to self-sufficiency. She herself faced this situation as she struggled during her lunch break to get her son from morning kindergarten class to his afternoon day care setting. With no alternative transportation available, she had no choice but to go on welfare. However, during the time she was on welfare, she inquired on phone from the day care centres and elementary schools, asking if other people faced the same dilemma. The response: a resounding yes! So she has made it her business to get children and people where they need to be. Every week, her buses deliver adults and children to jobs and day care centres around the city. She has worked hard to get her successful business up and running.

Source: A. Walmac, 'Reality Clicks,' Working Woman July–August, 1998, p. 32, cited in Coulter, Entrepreneurship in Action.

Case 2

This is Sir Richard Branson's experience, as recorded in the *Guiness Book of Records*, as the first man to cross the Atlantic in a hot air balloon and possessing a reported personal wealth of €2.4 billion from his 150 business ventures. He is perceived as a typical entrepreneur, and he demonstrates many of the traits and patterns of behavior traditionally associated with the entrepreneur.

He was born in 1950 and had a somewhat unusual but privileged upbringing. For example, his mother determined to develop his self-reliance. She was reported to have pushed her four year-old son from the car one day, asking him to find his way home. Some distance away from home, he got himself completely lost and had to knock on the door of strangers to ask the way. Again, while other parents banned their children from climbing the tree where he was brought up, his mother made him climb right to the top. Such experiences developed his self-confidence and self-belief. Although he suffered and did not excel in school, he grew up confident in his own ability. Through his mother's method of upbringing, he emerged as a doer rather than an observer. In spite of his academic failure, he developed an interest in journalism and the possibility of publishing a magazine for sixth-formers. The magazine was focused on students and would carry features written by well-known personalities, including rock stars, movie stars, etc. So he began writing to celebrities, requesting interviews. Surprisingly, he received replies, many of them positive. He had to persuade his lawyer-father to let him leave school to start publishing at age 16. This he started with a friend. On the eve of his departure from school, his head teacher predicted that Richard would either become a millionaire or go to prison.

To launch his business, his mother gave him the start-up capital. He equally approached and persuaded a respected magazine designer to work for no fee and some of his friends to work for a token weekly.

The venture was not a success because it had cash-flow problems. So in 1970, together with two other friends, he started another venture, selling records by mail order, and it was highly successful. Though he also encountered some problems which he was not slow to overcome, those problems helped him to recognise how easy it was to get around some regulations, and he thereafter looked for how to cut down on the overhead cost. Later, this act landed him in the court, but he pleaded that he did not know he had acted illegally and realized that rules were to be obeyed and not to be broken.

Source: D.A. Kirby, Entrepreneurship *(New York: McGraw-Hill Education, 2003).*

Case 3

Dorcas Dada, a hairdresser, had a dream of being a self-employed hair dresser. Her dream was almost derailed when, upon graduation, she did not have the money to set up a hair salon. She approached a bank for a loan. The bank demanded a landed property and two guarantors as security. She had none to offer.

Dorcas narrated her story to a friend, who introduced her to an informal financial institution called *Esusu,* or credit union. She was able to raise a N30,000 interest-free loan from the weekly contribution of N50 from other members. With this, she was able to realize her desired venture.

Source: Adapted from "Bank Closed, Esusu Closes."
http:www.newswatchngr.com/editorial/prime/2002/25032002/biz10324222106.htm

Summary

The Nigeria environment is full of entrepreneurial opportunities and new venture creation. These are having positive effects on the world's business and economy. Therefore, new venture creation is the key to Nigeria's economic development and progress. Entrepreneurship is giving people the opportunity to live better and rewarding lives since it creates value for both the customers and the founders.

For the entrepreneur to be successful, he should realise that operating a new business involves considerable risks and efforts which are needed to overcome the inertia that stands against creating new ventures. Entrepreneurs here will take the responsibility of business development and so take the risk of survival and enjoy the benefits and rewards from business outcome.

All he needs to create and start new venture is a unique idea and the concept which fulfills the needs of society as a whole in some particular way. He needs to find sources of new ideas and analyse and study in detail each of the sources from which he can come up with the unique idea to build his business enterprise. Starting a new venture does not just end there. It will also take the entrepreneur through long journeys of growth and development. Formal education and previous business experience also give an additional potential to the entrepreneur in acquiring the skills needed to form and manage a new enterprise.

References

Coulter, M. (2001) *Entrepreneurship in Action.* Upper Saddle River, NJ: Prentice-Hall.

Dollinger, M. J. (1999) *Entrepreneurship: Strategies and Resources.* Upper Saddle River, NJ: Prentice-Hall.

Drucker, P. F. (1977) *People and Performance: The Best of Peter Drucker on Management.* New York: Harper and Row.

Hills, G., and R. LaForge. (1992) Research at the Marketing Interface to Advance Entrepreneurship Theory. *Entrepreneurship: Theory and Practice* 16 (1992): 33–59.

Holt, D. H. (1992) *Entrepreneurship: New Venture Creation.* New York: Prentice-Hall Professional Technical Reference. Reprinted, New Delhi: Prentice Hall of India, 2008.

Kirby, D. (2003) *Entrepreneurship.* London: McGraw-Hill Education.

International Labour Office. (2002) *Generate Your Business Idea.* A workbook for potential entrepreneurs. Geneva: ILO Publications.

Zikmund, W. G., S. Ward, B. Lowe, and H. Winzar. (2007) *Marketing Research: Asia Pacific Edition.* Victoria: Nelson Australia Pty Ltd.

Zimmerer, T. W., and N. M. Scarborough. (1998)*Essentials of Entrepreneurship and Small Business Management* (2nd ed.). Upper Saddle River, NJ: Prentice Hall.

Chapter 19

PREPARATION AND PRESENTATION OF A BUSINESS PLAN

Akinola, G. O.

Introduction

There are numerous people who are eager to start a small business but have only a vague notion of what they want to do. An entrepreneur needs a realistic business plan at the point at which he/she comes up with an idea for a business and begins discussing the idea with consultants, friends and other business people. What is a Business Plan? A business plan is a detailed written document that describes the nature of the business, the objectives, the strategies, the target market, the advantages the business will have in relation to competition, the financial forecasts, and the resources and qualifications of the owner(s). It sets out the basic idea underlying a business and related startup considerations. It demonstrates persuasively that enough products or services can be sold at a profit to become a viable business. It is a living document that helps in monitoring business' performance and makes it stay on track; it therefore needs updating and changing as business grows.

For the entrepreneur starting a new venture, a business plan has four basic objectives. First, it identifies the nature and the context of business opportunity—why does such an opportunity exist? Second, it presents the approach the entrepreneur plans to take to exploit the opportunity. Third, it identifies the factors that will most likely determine whether the venture will be successful. Finally, it serves as a tool for raising financial capital. It forces potential owners of small businesses to be specific about the products or services they intend to offer. It is also regarded as a roadmap detailing how an entrepreneur will move a business from its current status to the intended status. It details the current status of the business (*finance, manpower and other resources*), the goals of the business, reasons why the entrepreneur is convinced that those goals are achievable, and strategies to be employed for making the goals a reality. It is an attempt to predict future opportunities and put in place financial, operational and marketing strategies that will enable the entrepreneur achieve his or her goals.

Simply put, a business plan is a map showing where you are now, where you intend to get to and how to get there. It gives the reader the **what, when, where, why** and **how** his/her business will accomplish its objectives and it tells **who** will be involved in running it. When planning, you need to define the goals of your business, determine the actions that need to be taken to accomplish them, gather and commit the resources needed, and aim for well-defined targets. A business plan is the difference between running a business proactively or reactively. The owners of businesses must analyze the competition, calculate how much money they need to start, and cover other details of operation. Thus, a business plan has many functions, from securing external funding, as it is mandatory for talking with bankers and other investors, to measuring success within the business. Above all, the business plan should explain the key variables for success or failure, thereby helping the entrepreneur prepare for different situations that may occur by thinking about what could go right and what could go wrong.

There are many benefits to creating and managing a realistic business plan. Even if it is just in-house, it can help in spotting potential pitfalls before they happen, structure the financial side of the business efficiently, focus owner's efforts on developing the business, and work as a measure of the business' success. Many people regard a business plan as a document used to secure external funding to enable potential investors, including banks, to invest in an entrepreneur's idea, work with the entrepreneur or lend him money as a result of the strength of the entrepreneur's plan. The people who may request to see the business plan at some stage, therefore, are banks; external investors—a friend, a venture capitalist firm, or a business angel, grant providers, anyone interested in buying the business as well as potential partners. It provides a structure for communicating the entrepreneur's mission to current and prospective employees of the firm.

Guidelines for Writing a Business Pan

The quality of a completed business plan depends greatly on the quality of the underlying business concept. It should be noted that the plan is not the business. A poorly conceived new venture idea cannot be rescued by good writing. A good concept may be destroyed, however, by writing that fails to effectively communicate. Clear writing gives credibility to the ideas presented in a business plan. Factual support must be supplied for any claims or promises made. When promising to provide superior service or explaining the attractiveness of the market, for example, the entrepreneur must include strong supporting evidence; i.e., the plan must be believable. Plans are unique to each business situation; there is no rigid formula for writing business plans that would fit every new business. Still, there are general guidelines to be followed:

1 **Consider your Audience.** You need to show the benefit of your business to your reader. Investors want their money to go into market-driven businesses, which satisfy wants and needs of customers, rather than technology-driven ones, which focus more on the product or service being made than on what people want.

2 **Keep it Brief.** Your business plan should be long enough to cover all major issues facing the business yet should not look like a copy of *War and Peace*. Your final plan should be complete, yet concise. Your plan should be less than 40 pages long, with financial projections and appendices inclusive. Your first draft could be longer, which could be edited to 40 pages or less.

3 **Point of View.** Try to write your business plan in the third person (do not use "I" or "we"). This helps maintain objectivity by removing your personal emotions from the writing process.

4 **Create a Professional Image.** The overall appearance should be professional and attractive but not extravagant. Having your document laser printed on white paper, with coloured stock cover, dividers and spiral binding is fine. Think of the message your business plan will send to

bankers and investors: having it bound in leather with gold leaf trimmed pages is not a good sign. It should show that you really need the money and will spend it wisely. Let it look like you were really serious about your business. As you write the first draft of your plan, have several people who are not involved in your business read your work to get their initial reactions. Do they quickly grasp the essence of your proposal? Are they excited about your idea? Do they exclaim "Wow!"? Getting feedback while you are still writing the plan can help you refine your work and get the reader to say "Wow!"

5   **Where to Get Help**. You should write the business plan for your proposed venture. This is because the person who is best qualified and who receives the most benefit from the planning process is the person who is going to implement the plan. It is your business and it needs to be your plan, though you can get aid in writing the plan if you need it. You can get assistance in writing your plan from one of the many guides written on business plan, Small Business Administration pamphlets, your area Small Business Development Center, your local Chamber of Commerce, and a college or university near you. You need to emphasize your competitive advantage and show your objectives in order to distinguish your business from others.

Business Plan Contents

One of the most difficult tasks in writing a business plan is knowing where to start. A good business plan takes a long time to write, but it is required that your reader be convinced not to throw the plan away in not more than five minutes. As there is no perfect business plan, prospective entrepreneurs should think out the smallest details in writing their business plans. It should provide details of how the business should be developed, when it should be developed, who is going to play a part, and how the finances would be managed. According to Nickels, McHugh and McHugh (2008), a good business plan is between 25 and 50 pages long and takes at least six months to write; but Hatten (1997) believes that the plan should present your strengths clearly and in a logical order in 40 pages or less.

Four interdependent factors should be given thorough consideration in deciding on the content of a business plan for a startup company:

- *The people*. A description of the men and women starting and running the venture as well as any outside parties, such as lawyers, accountants and suppliers providing key services or important resources.
- *The opportunity*. A profile of the business itself: what it will sell and to whom, how much and how rapidly it can grow, what its financial outlook is, and who and what may stand in the way of its success.
- *The context*. The big picture: the regulatory environment, interest rates, demographic trends, inflation and other factors that inevitably change but cannot be controlled by the entrepreneur.

- *Risk and reward.* An assessment of everything that can go wrong or right, with a discussion of how the entrepreneurial team can respond to the various challenges. Keep these general factors in mind as you compose the specific content of your business plan. While a plan's contents vary from business to business, its structure is fairly standardized; no single format or formula can guarantee success. Your plan should contain as many of the following sections as appropriate for your type of venture.

1   **Cover Letter**: A business plan could be used to source for funds, and so when writing any business plan, write it as if you are using it to source for funds. You should therefore remember that you are not the only one applying for money to start a business; you need to make the funders be interested in reading your business plan instead of the other hundreds on their desks. The cover letter is the first thing they will read about your business plan and so you have to be tactical in writing it. This should summarize the most attractive points of your project in as few words as possible. Be sure to address the letter to the potential investor by name. You should avoid "To whom it may concern" or "Dear Sir"; it is not the best way to win an investor's support.

2   **Cover Page**: This is also referred to as the title page. It is the first page of the business plan and should include the name of the business, its address and phone number, fax number and Web address, and company logo (if available); names, titles, addresses and phone numbers of the owners and key executives; the date on which the plan was issued; number of the copy (to help keep track of how many copies are outstanding); and name of the preparer, if other than the owners and key executives. If this information is overlooked, you will have a problem if a potential investor tries to reach you to ask additional questions (or send a cheque).

3   **Table of Contents**: For the business plan to be as easy to read as possible, an orderly table of contents will allow the reader to turn directly to the sections desired.

4   **Executive Summary**: This is crucial for getting the attention of the one-minute investor. Begin this with a two- or three-page management summary of the proposed venture. This is the most important section of the plan because readers do not want to wade through 35 to 40 pages to get the essential facts. It must convey a clear and concise picture of the proposed venture and at the same time create a sense of excitement regarding its prospects. This means that it must be written—and, if necessary, rewritten—to achieve clarity and create interest. If you do not capture the reader's attention here, s/he is certainly not likely to read the rest of the plan. Include a short description of the business and discuss major goals and objectives, mission and keys to success. The executive summary should include:

Company Information. What product or service you provide, your competitive advantage, when the company was formed, your company objectives, the background of you and your management team.

.

Market Opportunity. The expected size and growth rate of your market, your expected market share and any relevant industry trends.

Financial data. Include financial forecasts for the first three years of operations, equity investment desired and long term loans that will be needed.

This is a lot to condense to two pages. Although the executive summary is the first section of the plan, it should be written last. A hint for writing the executive summary is: As you compose all the other sections of the plan, highlight a few key sentences that are important enough to include in your executive summary.

5   **Vision and Mission Statement:** An organization's mission is the purpose or reason for the organization's existence. It tells what the company is providing to society—either a service or a product. A well-conceived mission statement defines the fundamental, unique purpose that sets a company apart from other firms of its type and identifies the scope of the company's operations in terms of products (including services) offered and markets served. It may also include the firm's philosophy about how it does business and treats its employees. It puts into words not only what the company is now, but what it wants to become—management's strategic vision of the firm's future. A mission statement describes what the organization is now; a vision statement describes what the organization would like to become.

6   **Company and Industry:** Describes company operations to date (if any), potential legal considerations and areas of risk and opportunity. Summarizes the firm's financial condition and includes past and current balance sheets, income and cash flow statements and other relevant financial records. It is also wise to include a description of insurance coverage. Here, investors want to be assured that death or other mishaps do not pose major threats to the company. Give company history by going into some detail describing what your business does and how it satisfies customers' needs. How did you choose and develop your products or services to be sold? Do not be afraid to describe any setbacks or missteps you have taken along the way in forming your business. They represent reality and leaving them out could make your plan and projections look "too good to be true" to lenders or investors.

You should also describe the industry you operate within. One helpful way to draw the line between what and who to include in your industry is to consider possible substitutes that your customers have for your product. You should consider businesses that sell these substitutes as part of your industry. What competitive reactions and industry-wide trends can you identify? Who are the major players in your industry? Have any businesses recently entered or exited? Why did they leave? In other words, things to be included are company ownership, start-up summary, company locations and facilities and government regulations. In writing this section, the entrepreneur should answer the following questions:

When and where was this business started?
What changes have been made in structure and/or ownership?

In what stage of development is the firm—for example, seed stage or full product line?

What has been achieved to date?

What is the firm's distinctive competence?

What are the basic nature and activity of the business?

What is its primary product or service?

What customers will be served?

What are the firm's objectives?

What is the firm's form of organization—sole proprietorship, partnership or corporation?

What are the current and projected economic states of the industry?

Does the firm intend to become a publicly traded company or an acquisition candidate?

7   **Products and Services:** List and describe the products or services to be offered to the firm's customers. For each business offering, cover the main points, including what the product or service is, how much it costs, what sorts of customers make purchases, and why. What customers need does each product or service line fill? You might not want or need to include every product or service in the list, but at least consider the main sales lines. Focus on customer benefits. It is always a good idea to think in terms of customer needs and customer benefits as you define your product offerings, rather than thinking of your side of the equation—how much the product or service costs, and how you deliver it to the customer. Things to be included here are: product and service description, competitive comparison, sales literature, technology, and future products and services. If a new or unique physical product is to be offered and a working model or prototype is available, a photograph of it should be included in this section of the business plan. Investors will naturally show the greatest interest in products that have been developed, tested and found to be functional. Any innovative features should be identified and any patent protection explained. If the product or service is similar to those offered by competitors, any special features should be clearly identified.

8   **Market Analysis Summary/ Marketing Research and Evaluation:** You need to know what constitutes your market: customer needs, where they are, how to reach them, etc. Evidence that a market exists for your business is much more convincing than an unsubstantiated claim or guesswork. Present the facts you have gathered on the size and nature of your markets. An investor will want to know if a large enough market exists and if you can be competitive in that market. State market size in naira and units. Give your sales forecast by estimating from your marketing research how many units and naira-worth of your product you expect to sell in a given period. That sales forecast becomes the basis for projecting many of your financial statements. Indicate your primary and secondary sources of data and the methods you used to estimate total market size and your market share.

Market Needs/ Target Market Segment Strategy. Marketing is the process of creating and delivering goods and services to customers and involves all of the activities associated with winning and retaining loyal customers. The "secret" to successful marketing is to understand the company's target customers' needs, demands and wants before competition can; to offer them the products and services that will satisfy those needs, demands and wants; and to provide those customers with quality, service, convenience and value so that they will keep coming back. The marketing function cuts across and affects every aspect of a company's operations, such as finance, production, hiring and purchasing. You must identify your target markets and then concentrate your marketing efforts on these key areas. These markets must have some commonly identifiable need that you can satisfy. What do people who buy your product have in common with each other? There could be a demographic variable, a geographic variable, a psychographic variable or other variable used to segment your markets. Describe actual customers who have expressed a desire to buy your product. What trends do you expect to affect your markets?

Market Trends. Markets and consumer tastes change, so you will need to explain how you will assess your customers' needs over time. A danger of segmentation and target marketing is the belief that those segments and markets will stay the same. Identify how you will continue to evaluate consumer needs so you can improve your market lines and aid new product development.

Market Growth. Among three or four primary competitors, identify the price leader, the quality leader and the service leader. Realistically discuss the strengths and weaknesses of each. Compare your products or services with those of competitors on the basis of price, product performance and other attributes. This section offers a good opportunity to include the SWOT analysis. Identify the strengths and weaknesses of your business and the opportunities and threats that exist outside your business. Since you have identified the size of your market and your competitors, you can estimate the market share you intend to gain. *Market share* refers to your sales in relation to the total industry sales expressed as a percentage. It can effectively be shown and explained using a pie chart.
Other things to be included under this section are: a service business analysis, which includes distributing a service; competition and buying patterns; main competitors and business participants. Your job in writing the marketing research section of your business plan is to convince the reader that a large enough market exists for your product for you to achieve your projected sales forecasts.

9   **Marketing Plan/ Strategy and Implementation Summary:** On several occasions, entrepreneurs create business plans that describe in great detail what the entrepreneur intends to accomplish (e.g., "the financials") and pay little, if any, attention to the strategies to achieve those targets. Other entrepreneurs fail miserably because they are not willing to invest the time and energy to identify and research their target markets or to assemble any business plan at all. These entrepreneurs squander enormous efforts pulling together capital, staff, products and services because they neglect to determine what it will take to attract and retain a profitable customer base. To be effective, a business plan must contain both a financial plan and a marketing plan. Like the financial plan, an effective marketing plan projects numbers and analyzes them, but from a different

perspective. Rather than focus on cash flow, net profits and owner's equity, the marketing plan concentrates on the customer. This section is on how to create an effective marketing plan, which is an integral part of a total business plan. Before producing reams of computer-generated spreadsheets of financial projections, an entrepreneur must determine what to sell, to whom and how often, on what terms and at what price, and how to get the product or service to the customer. Your marketing plan shows how you intend to reach your sales forecast. The marketing plan must identify user benefits and the type of market that exists. You should start by explaining your overall marketing strategy by identifying your potential markets and deciding the best ways to reach them. Include your marketing objectives (what you want to achieve) and the strategies you will use to accomplish these objectives. In short, a marketing plan identifies a company's target customers and describes how that business will attract and keep them. Be specific. Include management responsibilities with dates and budgets. Make sure you can track results.

Value Proposition: The value proposition conveys the benefit(s) to be offered or offered by the brand of your product. These benefits may be functional, emotional or self-expressive. The intent is to consider the benefits that distinguish a brand from its competition. The value proposition expresses the underlying logic of the relationship between the brand and the customer.

Competitive Edge: What are your competitors doing? How many competitors do you have? What is your advantage over your competitors? Is the market large enough to support you and your competitors? Compare the features, benefits and advantages of your product or services over your competitors' offerings of the same, similar or substitute products. This is where you explain the uniqueness of your product or service, why there is a need or demand for it, and what benefits it offers the customer. This is also where you compare the offerings of your competitors and what makes your product different or better. Many people include a SWOT analysis as part of this section, which is a method by which to examine the strengths, weaknesses, opportunities and threats in relation to your business. It's usually done in a grid or table format with bullet points listed in each section.

Marketing Strategy: Small business owners must understand the importance of developing relevant marketing strategies that will work in today's turbulent global business environment, noting that these marketing strategies are not just for mega-corporations competing in international markets. Though they may have small marketing budgets, small businesses are not powerless in developing effective marketing strategies. Small businesses have a lot of strategies at their disposal, which may include: frontal assault, flank defense or flanking maneuver, pre-emptive defense, bypass attack, encirclement and guerrilla warfare. To develop a winning marketing strategy requires a business to master three vital resources: people, information, and technology. People are the most important ingredient in formulating a successful marketing strategy. Hiring and retaining creative, talented, well-trained people to develop and implement a marketing strategy is the first step; implementing a successful marketing strategy relies on an entrepreneur's ability to recruit people with the talent to do the job and to teach them to work together as a team. Information is the fuel that feeds the marketing engine, without which a marketing strategy soon sputters and stops. Successful marketing relies on a company's ability to collect more data than competitors, put them into a meaningful form faster and disseminate the information to everyone in business, especially those who deal with customers, in order to give the company a competitive edge. Technology has proved to be a powerful marketing weapon, but technology alone is not the key to marketing success. Competitors may duplicate or exceed the investment of a small business in technology, but this does not guarantee their marketing success. However, the way a company integrates the use of technology into its overall marketing strategy is what matters most.

Promotion Strategy: How will you attract the attention of and communicate with your potential customers? For industrial products you might use trade shows and advertise in trade magazines, direct mail, or promotional campaigns. You should also give the advertising schedule and costs involved. Examples of advertising or brochures may be included in the appendix of the business plan.

Positioning Strategy: This is the combination of product, value-chain, price and promotion strategies that a firm uses to position itself against its key competitors in meeting the needs and wants of the market target. It seeks to position the brand in the eyes and mind of the buyer and distinguish the product from competition.

Pricing Strategy: Your pricing policy is one of the most important decisions you will have to make. The price must be "right" to penetrate the market, to maintain your market position, and especially to make profits. Compare your pricing policies with the competitors you identified earlier. Explain how your gross margin will allow you to make a profit after covering all expenses. Many people go into business with the intent of charging lower prices than the competition. If this is your goal, explain how you can do this and still make a profit: through greater efficiency in manufacturing or distributing the product, through lower labor costs, lower overhead, or whatever allows you to undercut the competition's price. You should discuss the relationship between your price, your market share, and your profits. For example, by charging a higher price than the competition you may reduce your sales volume, but hold a higher gross margin and increase the bottom line.

Sales Strategy: Describe how you intend to sell and distribute your products. Will you use your own sales force or independent sales representatives or distributors? If you will hire your own sales force, describe how it will be structured, the sales expected per salesperson per year, and the pay structure. Your own sales force will concentrate more on your products by selling them exclusively. If you will use sales representatives, describe how they will be selected, the territories they will cover, and rates they will charge. Independent sales representatives will also be handling other products and lines than just your own, but they are much less expensive for you since they are not your employees. Your place strategy describes the level of coverage (local, regional, or national) you will use initially and as your business grows. It includes the channels of distribution you will use to get and to sell products.

Sales Forecast: Forecasting is usually easier when you break your forecast down into components. As an example, consider a forecast that simply projects ₦10,000 in sales for the month, compared to one that projects 100 units at ₦100 each for the month. In the second case, when the forecast is price x units, as soon as you know the price is going up, you know that the resulting sales should also increase. Thinking of the forecast in components is easier. Developing your sales forecast is not as hard as most people think. Think of your sales forecast as an educated guess. Forecasting takes good working knowledge of your business, which is much more important than advanced degrees or complex mathematics. It is much more art than science. Whether you have business training or not, do not think you are not qualified to forecast. If you can run a business, then you can forecast its sales. Most people can guess their own business' sales better than any expert device, statistical analysis, or mathematical routine. Experience counts more than any other factor. Break your sales down into manageable parts, and then forecast the parts. Guess your sales by line of sales, month by month, then add up the sales lines and add up the months.

Service Policies: If you sell a product that may require service, such as cameras, copy machines, or bicycles, describe your service and warranty policies. These policies can be important in the customer's decision-making process. How will you handle customer service problems? Describe the terms and types of warranties offered. Explain whether you will provide service via your own service department, subcontract out the service work, or return products to the factory. Also state whether service is intended to be a profit center or a break-even operation.

The marketing plan focuses the company's attention on the customer and recognizes that satisfying the customer is the foundation of every business. Its purpose is to build a strategy of success for a business, but from the customer's point of view. Therefore, a marketing plan should accomplish four objectives which are: determine customer needs and wants through market research, pinpoint the specific target markets that the small company will serve, analyze the firm's competitive advantages and build a marketing strategy around them, and help create a marketing mix that meets customer needs and wants.

10   **Web Plan Summary**: For e-commerce, include discussion of website, development costs, operations, sales and marketing strategies. If your business has or will have a Web site, describe how your Web site fits into your advertising and promotion plan.

11   **Management Summary:** Describe the organization and the key management team members.
Management Team: A good management team is the key to transforming your vision into a successful business. Show how your team is balanced in technical skills (possessing the knowledge that is specific to your type of business), business skills (the ability to successfully run a business), and experience. As in building any team, the skills and talents of your management team need to

complement one another. Include a job description for each management position, and specify the key people who will fill these slots. Can you show how their skills complement each other? Have these individuals worked together before? An organizational chart can be included in the appendix of your plan to graphically show how these positions fit together. Résumés for each key manager should also be included in the appendix. State how your key managers will be compensated. Your chances of obtaining financing are very slim unless the managers are willing to accept substantially less than their market value for salary while the business is getting started. Managers must be committed to putting as many proceeds as possible back into the business. Discuss the management training your key people have had and may still need. Be as specific as possible on the cost, type, and availability of this management or technical training. Like your managers, you may need professional assistance at times. Identify other people with whom you will work, including a lawyer, a certified public accountant, an insurance agent, and a banker. Identify contacts you have supporting you in these areas.

Management Team Gaps/Personnel Gap: If you plan to employ staff, now or in the future, you need to specify the type of employment arrangement you are going to use, the number of staff you intend to employ, the positions they will hold, and the duties they will perform. Include the positions filled by owners and family, even if they are not paid a commercial wage or salary for their contribution. The laws that govern employment conditions differ according to the type of arrangement—i.e., full-time, part-time, casual or contract—and whether your employees come under the state or federal industrial relations system. The fines and penalties for mistakes in relation to employee benefits such as superannuation, workers' compensation, holiday pay and sick leave can be costly, so it is important to consult the relevant experts to ensure you get it right from the outset. Provide the name of any award or industrial agreement covering your employees and once you have checked that you are complying with all the legal requirements of an employer, including having in place workers' compensation insurance, making superannuation contributions and providing a safe work place, you will be able to make a statement to this effect in the business plan. Other issues to consider include office space and furniture requirements, company vehicles, communication networks (computers and mobile phones), payroll tax and the extra administration costs in relation to managing all of this. Given the importance of a good team in achieving business success, it is worth taking some time to formulate policies in relation to recruitment and retention, performance management, remuneration structures and any opportunities for career advancement and training. This section of your plan can prove to be a valuable tool in both attracting and retaining good staff. Depending on the size of your business, you may also wish to outline its organisational structure which should clearly demonstrate who reports to whom and the different levels of accountability and responsibility within the business. There are alternatives to employing staff, such as outsourcing, engaging sub-contractors or using the services of a labour hire firm (often referred to as a temp agency).

12   **Financial Plan**: Your financial plan will be highly scrutinized by your business plan reader. All the ideas, concepts and strategies discussed throughout your

entire business plan form the basis for, and should flow into, your financial statements and projections in some manner. When it gets down to it, your reader wants to know if and when you will make money and become profitable. Financial statements and projections should follow generally accepted accounting standards and must (at a minimum) include properly prepared balance sheets, income statements, and cash-flow statements. Bankers and investors are familiar with the correct content, organization and presentation of financial statements and expect to see them in your business plan. Don't cut corners or attempt to devise your own method of financial and pro forma statement presentation. In most cases, capital sources expect financial projections for a three- to five-year period, and historical statements for the past three years (or since inception if operating period is less than three years).

Your financial plan is where you demonstrate that all the information from previous sections like marketing, operations, sales, and strategies can all come together to form a viable, profitable business. Potential investors will closely scrutinize the financial section of your plan to ensure it is feasible before they become involved. Projections should be your best estimates of future operations. Your financial plan should include the following statements (existing businesses will need historical statements and pro forma projections, while start-ups will only have projections):

- sources and uses of capital (initial and projected),
- cash-flow projections for three years,
- balance sheets for three years,
- profit and loss statements for three years, and
- break-even analysis.
  With the financial statements, you need to show conclusions and important points, such as how much equity and how much debt are included, the highest amount of cash needed, and how long the payback period for loans is expected to be.

Sources and Uses of Funds: This section explains to your reader which sources you expect to secure capital from, and what you specifically plan to spend it on.

Cash Flow: This is the most important financial statement for a small business because if you run out of cash, you are out of business. A cash flow statement shows you that from your opening cash balance you add all the money that comes into your business for a given time period (week, month, quarter), then you subtract all the money you spend for the same time period. The result is your closing cash balance, which becomes your opening balance for the next time period. A cash flow statement should be projected by month for the first year of operation and by quarter for the second and third years. Cash flow shows what the highest amount of working capital will be; this can be critical if your sales are seasonal in nature or cyclical.

Break-even Analysis: These figures demonstrate the volume of sales, in units and dollars, that must be generated to cover fixed and variable expenses. At the break-even point, you start becoming profitable. Normally this data is presented in a graph format with sales on the X-axis and units sold on the Y-axis. Your break-even point is that point at which income from sales covers all costs, including overheads. At this point the business will make neither a profit nor loss. Sales volume below this point will result in a loss, while sales above this point will render a profit. How many units (or naira worth) of your products or service will have to be sold to cover your costs? A break-even analysis will give you a sales projection of how many units or naira need to be sold to reach your break-even point, that is, the point at which you are neither making nor losing money. To reinforce your financial projections, you may want to compare them to industry averages for your chosen industry. Compare your projected financial ratios with industry averages to give the reader an established benchmark.

Projected Profit and Loss: This is a financial document that shows sales revenues, expenses, and net profit or loss. Don't expect your profit and loss statement to be a finely honed, 100-percent-accurate projection of the future. Your objective is to come up with as close an approximation as possible to what your sales revenues and expenses will be.

In making your projections, it is helpful to break sales down by product line (or services) and to determine a best-case scenario, a worst-case scenario, and a most likely scenario somewhere between the two extremes. Start with the left column to show what your sales and expenses would be under the worst of conditions. Assume that you have difficulty getting products, that the weather is terrible, that your sales people are out spending all their time playing golf instead of selling, that the state highway department closes the road that runs in front of your only location for repairs. Imagine that anything bad that can happen will. Now, in the right column, make projections as if everything goes exactly your way. What would your sales and expenses be if customers with cash in their hands are waiting in line outside your door every morning at opening time, if suppliers rearrange their schedules so you never run out of stock, and if competitors all close their doors for a month of vacation just as you are beginning operations. This is a lot more fun, but not any more likely to happen than the first scenario, although either could happen. Your most realistic estimate will fall between the two in the center column. Question and test your projections. Is there enough demand for you to reach your sales goal? Do you have enough space, equipment and employees to reach your sales goal? Break your sales down into number of units, then the number of units bought per customer, and then the number of units sold per day. When viewed this way, you may find that every person in town would have to buy eight cartons of bottled water per day, 365 days per year, for you to achieve your sales projections for your proposed bottled water shop. Obviously, you would need to revise your goal, expand your menu, do more to control your expenses, or convince people to drink more water than is humanly possible for your business to succeed.

Balance sheet: The balance sheet shows all the assets owned by your business and the liabilities, or what is owed against those assets. The difference between the two is what the company has earned, or the net worth of the business, which is also called capital. From the balance sheet, bankers and investors will calculate some key ratios, such as debt to equity and current ratio, to help determine the financial health of your business. You need to prepare balance sheets ending each of the first three years of operation.

Business/Financial Ratios: Providing standard financial ratios helps your business plan reader to analyze how well your company will perform compared to other companies within your industry. For existing companies, show the trends over the last 3 to 5 years to outline any improvements in your performance.

Capital Required: Indicates the amount of capital needed to commence or continue operations and describes how these funds are to be used. Make sure the totals are the same as the ones on the cash-flow statement. This area will receive a great deal of review from potential investors, so it must be clear and concise.

13   **Manufacturing and Operations Plan:** The manufacturing and operations plan will stress elements related to your business's production. It will outline your needs in terms of facilities, location, space requirements, capital equipment, labor force, inventory control, and purchasing. Stress the areas most relevant to your type of business. For instance, if you are starting a manufacturing business, outline the production processes and your control systems for inventory, purchasing, and production. The business plan for a service business should focus on your location, overhead, and labor force productivity.

Geographic Location: Describe your planned location and its advantages and disadvantages in terms of wage rates, unionization, labour pool, proximity to customers and suppliers, types of transportation available, tax rates, utility costs, and zoning. Again you should stress the features most relevant to your business. Proximity to customers is especially important to a service business, while access to transportation will be of greater concern to a manufacturing business.

Facilities: What kind of facilities does your business need? Discuss your requirements for floor space (including offices, sales room, manufacturing plant space, and storage areas), parking, loading areas, and special equipment. Will you rent, lease, or purchase these facilities? How long will they remain adequate: One year? Is expansion possible?

Make or Buy Policy: In a manufacturing business, you must decide what you will produce and what you will purchase as components to be assembled into the finished product; this is called the make-or-buy decision. Many factors go into this decision. In your business plan, you should justify the advantages of your policy. Describe potential subcontractors and suppliers.

Control Systems: What is your approach to controlling quality, inventory, and production? How will you measure your progress toward the goals you have set for your business?

Labor Force: At the location you have selected, is there a sufficient quantity of adequately skilled people in the local labor force to meet your needs? What kinds of training will you need to provide? Can you afford to offer this training and still remain competitive? Training can be one of those hidden costs that can turn a profit into a loss.

14 **Critical Risks and Assumptions**: All business plans contain implicit assumptions, such as how your business will operate, what economic conditions will be, and how you will react in different situations. Identification and discussion of any potentially major trends, problems, or risks you think you may encounter will show the reader that you are in touch with reality. These risks and assumptions could relate to your industry, markets, company, or personnel. This section gives you a place to establish alternate plans in case the unexpected happens. If potential investors discover unstated negative factors after the fact, they can quickly question the credibility of you and the business. Too many businesses are started with only a Plan A and no thought to what if X, Y, or Z happens. Possible contingencies you should anticipate are:

❖ Unreliable sales forecasts. What will you do if your market does not develop as quickly as you predicted or, conversely, if your market develops too quickly? Each situation creates problems. Sales that are too low cause serious financial problems; sales that are too high can cause bottlenecks in production, difficulties in purchasing enough products from vendors or suppliers, trouble hiring and scheduling employees, or dissatisfied customers who must wait longer than they expected for your product or service.
❖ Competitors' ability to underprice or to make your product obsolete.
❖ Unfavourable industry-wide trends.
❖ Appropriately trained workers not as available as predicted.
❖ Erratic supply of products or raw material, and
❖ Any one of the 10,000 other things you didn't expect.

15   **Location Analysis:** The location of the business is one of the most important factors in retailing and some peculiar businesses. A comprehensive demographic analysis of consumers in the area of the proposed business as well as a traffic-pattern analysis and vehicular and pedestrian counts should be provided.

16   **Benefits to Community**: Your new business will have an impact on many other people beside yourself. Describe the potential benefits to the community that the formation of your business could provide.

> *Economic development*: Number of jobs (to be) created (total and skilled), purchase of supplies from local businesses, the multiplier effect (which shows the number of hands that new dollars brought into the community pass through before exiting).
>
> *Community development*: Providing needed goods or services, improving physical assets or the appearance of the community, contributing to a community's standard of living.
>
> *Human development*: Providing new technical skills or other training, opportunities for career advancement, developing management or leadership skills, offering attractive wages, other types of individual growth.

17   **Appendix:** Supplemental information and documents not crucial to the plan, but of potential interest to the reader, are gathered in the appendix. Résumés of owners and principal managers, advertising samples, brochures, or any related information can be included. Different types of information such as résumés, advertising samples, organization chart, and floor plan should each be given a separate appendix labeled with successive letters of the alphabet (Appendix A, Appendix B, and so on). Be sure to identify each appendix in your table of contents (for example, "Appendix A: Advertising Samples"). It also includes all marketing research on the product or service (off-the-shelf reports, article reprints, etc.) and other information about the product concept or market size. It also provides a bibliography of all the reference materials you consulted; and it should demonstrate that the proposed company would not be entering a declining industry or market segment. Start each appendix on a new page.

Review Process: Writing a business plan is a project that involves a long series of interrelated steps. Beginning with your idea for a business, you want to determine its feasibility through the creation of your business plan. The technique illustrated in Figure I will allow you to identify the steps you need to take in writing your plan. Steps connected by lines show that lower-numbered steps need to be completed before moving on to higher-numbered ones. Steps that are parallel show that these take place simultaneously. For example, Steps 6 through 10 can be completed at the same time, and all must be accomplished before you can estimate how much capital you need in Step 11. As with any project involving a number of complex steps and calculations, your business plan should be carefully reviewed and revised before you present it to potential investors. After you have written your plan, rate it yourself as lenders and investors will evaluate it.

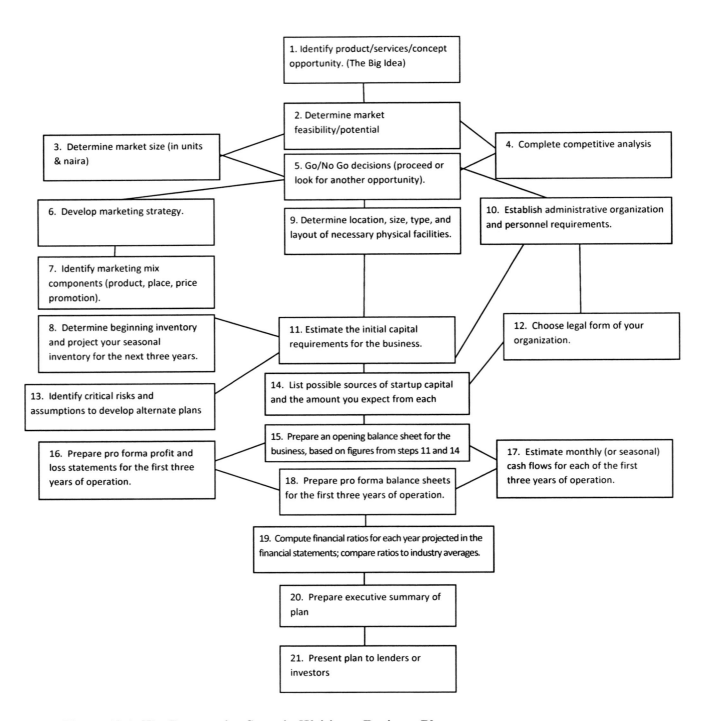

Figure 19.1: The Progressive Steps in Writing a Business Plan
Source: Adapted from Hatten 1997

Features of a Successful Business Plan

In order to raise capital from outside investors, the business plan must be the "right" plan, that is, it must speak the investors' language. It should hardly exceed 40 pages in length, as investors generally will look at brief reports and avoid those that take too long to read. Also, the overall appearance of the report should be attractive and the report should be well organized, with numbered pages and a table of contents. Investors are also more market-oriented than product-oriented, realizing that most patented inventions never earn a dime for the inventors. Other features that interest investors include:

➢ evidence of customer acceptance of the venture's product or service;
➢ an appreciation of investors' needs, through recognition of their particular financial goals, as evidenced in their required rates of return;
➢ evidence of focus, through concentration on a limited number of products or services; and
➢ proprietary position, as represented by patents, copyrights and trademarks.

According to Rich and Gumpert (1985), as cited by Longenecker, Moore and Petty (2004), a successful business plan must:

- be arranged appropriately, with an executive summary, a table of contents, and chapters in the right order;
- be the right length and have the right appearance—not too long and not too short, not too fancy and not too plain;
- give a sense of what the founders and the company expect to accomplish three to seven years into the future;
- explain in quantitative and qualitative terms the benefits to the user of the company's products or services;
- present hard evidence of the marketability of the products or services;
- justify financially the means chosen to sell the products or services;
- explain and justify the level of product development which has been achieved and describe in appropriate detail the manufacturing process and associated costs;
- portray the partners as a team of experienced managers with complementary business skills;
- suggest as high an overall "rating" as possible of the venture's product development and team sophistication;
- contain believable financial projections, with the key data explained and documented;
- show how investors can cash out in three to seven years, with appropriate capital appreciation;
- be presented to the most potentially receptive financiers possible to avoid wasting precious time as company funds dwindle; and
- be easily and concisely explainable in a well-orchestrated oral presentation.

References

Abrams, R. M. (1993) *The Successful Business Plan: Secrets and Strategies*, 2nd ed. Grants Pass, OR: Oasis Press.

Cravens, D. W., and N. F. Piercy. (2006) *Strategic Marketing*, 8thed. New York: McGraw-Hill/Irwin.

Fraser, J. A. (1999) Who Can Help Out With a Business Plan? *Inc.* 21(8): June: 115–117.

Hatten, T. S. (1997) *Small Business—Entrepreneurship and Beyond.* Upper Saddle River, NJ: Prentice-Hall, Inc.

Longenecker, J. G., C. W. Moore, and J. W. Petty. (2004) *Small Business Management—An Entrepreneurial Emphasis.* Mason, OH: Thompson South-Western.

Lussier, R. N. (1999) *Management Fundamentals.* Mason, OH: South-Western College Publishing.

Nickels, W. G., J. M. McHugh, and S. M. McHugh. (2008) *Understanding Business*, 8th ed. New York: McGraw-Hill/Irwin.

Rich, S. R., and D. E. Gumpert. (1985) *Business Plans that Win $$$: Lessons from the MIT Enterprise Forum.* New York: Harper and Row.

Scarborough, N. M., and T. W. Zimmerer. (1999) *Effective Small Business Management—An Entrepreneurial Approach.* Upper Saddle River, NJ: Prentice-Hall, Inc.

Sahlman, W. (1997) How to Write a Great Business Plan. *Harvard Business Review*, 75(4); July–August: 98–108.

Stevens, M. (1995) Seven Steps to a Well-Prepared Business Plan. *Executive Female*, 18(2); March: 30

Wheelen, T. L., and J. D. Hunger. (1998) *Strategic Management and Business Policy.* Reading, MA: Addison Wesley Longman.

Chapter 20

ENTREPRENEURSHIP DEVELOPMENT

Osezua, O. C.

Introduction

In an emerging economy like Nigeria's, the term *entrepreneur* means different things to different people. A simplified definition of an entrepreneur is one that has the ability to envision opportunities or avenues, one who can multiply value inherent in a thing or place, in what others have discountenanced and considered previously as less valuable or of no value. An entrepreneur has the uncanny tenacity to turn challenges of what people generally perceive as obstacles or difficulties into rewarding ventures by creating wealth from such endeavours or giving value to it. The entrepreneur simply makes business ideas happen deliberately, by self-effort or by galvanising the efforts of others. The entrepreneur has the ability to envision ideas and create them into concrete realities and thereby cause a positive change.

Many scholars of entrepreneurial research have identified sets of commonalties in the attributes of successful entrepreneurs. Many of these scholars (McClelland 1961; Stewart and Roth 2001; Bates 1995) maintained that psychological traits are imperative for the development of entrepreneurship by individuals. They argued that these traits are intrinsic in the individual. Other theorists (Lee and Peterson 2002; Wilken 1979) have disagreed with this school of thought, maintaining that the environment can adversely affect the development of the entrepreneur. Environmental factors can therefore accelerate or discourage entrepreneurial activities in any geographic location. Abimbola and Agboola (2011) stated that the environment encompasses factors such as infrastructure, culture, economics, and social and political environments. However, there appears to be a consensus among these scholars that entrepreneurs have distinctive characteristics. These include:

a) *Ability to take calculated risks:* A successful entrepreneur weighs potential reward against perceived risks.
b) *Business environment:* Every good entrepreneur must have adequate information and understanding of the "context" that is popularly referred to as the business environment. A good understanding of the context or business environment distinguishes a successful entrepreneur.
c) *Passion:* A strong insistence and desire to succeed against all odds has been identified as a critical possession of any successful entrepreneur. This has to do with being self-motivated and having a genuine conviction and persuasion about his business idea.
d) *Persuasive ability:* An effective communication ability that sounds convincing is an important quality that distinguishes and entrepreneur as one who is able to establish the rationale for his new products or services in a compelling manner so that the potential consumers can appreciate the indispensability of his novel business idea.

Evidently, these attributes identified are distinctive features of the person who qualifies to be described as an entrepreneur. In other words, entrepreneurs must do the following to remain vitally relevant in the business world:

- launch new or novel ideas (Vision);
- convert those ideas to business idea (Resourceful);
- convert those ideas to concrete realities (Create);
- make these concrete realities in a problem-solving product, service or venture, (Innovative);
- engage this business idea to bring about a positive change that is beneficial to humanity (Development).

Just as in any other field of endeavour where concepts are used to provide information to a specific audience, entrepreneurial studies have basic concepts that are unique to the discipline. Some of these concepts are discussed in the next section of this chapter.

Definition of Terms

Enterprise
This is a combination of skill and attitude that enables an individual, who is usually an entrepreneur, to turn ideas into concrete or visible entities.

Entrepreneur
An entrepreneur can be defined as one who has the uncommon capacity of converting new ideas into problem-solving outfits, products or services, which can yield financial rewards. Carland *et al.* (1984:358) defined *entrepreneur* as an individual "who establishes and manages a business for the principal purposes of profit and growth," while Pickle and Abrahamson (1990:5) introduced a more elaborate definition of an entrepreneur which took cognisance of the salient feature that characterises an entrepreneur. The authors stated that

> "an entrepreneur is one who organizes and manages a business undertaking, assuming the risk, for the sake of profit. The entrepreneur evaluates perceived opportunities and strives to make the decisions that will enable the firm to realize sustained growth."

Entrepreneurial Activities

Activities which have been found to be capable of making a positive impact on the economy of a nation and the quality of the lives people lead are categorized *entrepreneurial activities* (Schumpeter 1934; Adejumo 2001). Entrepreneurial activities are often linked to socio-economic development; hence, they are vitally relevant in accelerating the rate of economic development. Many scholars have argued that the development of the Western world was as a result of the emergence of entrepreneurial activities by a group of people. This attitude or the spirit of the entrepreneur has been described as responsible for the development of many societies in the global North today (Weber 1904).

Business Environment

In a broad sense, the business environment includes the infrastructures and the cultural, social, and economic environment in which the entrepreneur incubates and initiates his or her business idea into an enterprise. Literally, it is inclusive of the infrastructure available within a context (locale, region or state). It includes infrastructures like transportation, electricity supply, and water, and physical resources as well as the non-physical environment, which includes prevailing regulatory policies, education, available credit facilities, and so on. Countries in the global North enjoyed a good business environment for a long time. In Nigeria, a country characterised by poor infrastructure,much of which is reminiscent of the colonial era, many young entrepreneurs have had to contend with incessant power outages, a poor road network, and an unreliable communications network.

Entrepreneurship

Entrepreneurship involves the application of energy and passion towards the implementation of new ideas and generating creative solutions. It involves a dynamic process of vision, creation and change. It is often defined as new venture creation (Gartner 1988; Parker and Gartner 2004). Kuratko and Hodgetts (2004) described entrepreneurship as the ability to formulate effective venture, the creative skills to marshal needed resources, and the fundamental skills of building a solid plan, with an ability to recognize opportunities where others see chaos and contradictions. Stevenson, Robert and Grousbeck (1985) described the concept of entrepreneurship as the process of innovation to create value by bringing together a unique bundle of resources to explicit opportunity, while Ronstadt (1988: 28) defined entrepreneurship by taking into account the incremental wealth associated with its development as well as the traits of the entrepreneur.

> Entrepreneurship is the dynamic process of creating incremental wealth. The wealth is created by individuals who assume the major risks in terms of equity, time and/or career commitment or provide value for some product or service. The product or service may or may not be new or unique but value must somehow be infused by the entrepreneur by receiving and allocating the necessary skills and resources.

The utility of Ronstadt's definition in relation to this chapter lies in its emphasis on creation of wealth based on a concomitant value that has been provided in the form of goods or services.

Opportunities

Opportunities are what the entrepreneur actually seizes to create a novel idea. Opportunities have been described as a product of change. These changes, according Schumpeter (1934), are essentially of three kinds: technological, political and regulatory, or social-demographic. The discovery of entrepreneurship opportunities constitutes the core of theorising on the development of entrepreneurship. The reasons why some persons discover opportunity more than others have also continued to generate debates along the lines of biology and social/ cultural as well as economic reasons.

Entrepreneurship Development in the Western World

The study of contemporary entrepreneurship is traceable to the works of the renowned economist, Joseph Schumpeter, a prominent young economist in the early 1930s. Joseph Schumpeter perceived entrepreneurs as those who were innovatively creative in driving positive economic changes within their societies.

Recently, some scholars from Europe and America in the United Kingdom conducted a groundbreaking research to determine why people engaged in entrepreneurial activities. Just like the nature-versus-nurture debate that has raged over the years, there has been contentious posture about why some individuals are more entrepreneurial than others are, or why some people in a particular region have a greater predisposition to engaging in entrepreneurial activities than do those elsewhere. The disposition by individuals to be entrepreneurial has a direct effect on the economic systems of the location where such entrepreneurial activities are carried out. This is because wealth creation, increase in profit, and improvement in the value of services or goods provided by the entrepreneur positively affect the economic systems. For instance, Kuratko and Hodgetts (2004) observe that the United States achieved its highest economic performance during the last ten years by fostering and promoting entrepreneurial activities. This success in the growth of entrepreneural activities was linked to what they described as three entrepreneural components.

First, large firms that existed in mature industries adapted, downsized, restructured, and reinvented themselves during the 1990s and began to thrive. A good example cited by Kuratko and Hodgetts (2004) was how General Electric cut its work force by 40 percent, from more than 400,000 twenty years before to fewer than 240,000 workers in 1996, while sales increased fourfold, from less than $20 billion to nearly $80 billion over the same period. This goal was accomplished in many cases by returning to the firm's areas where the company had a relative competitive advantage, and then contracting out functions, formerly done in-house, to smaller firms.

Secondly, even as the previous companies were undergoing transfomation and thriving, the new entrepreneurial ones that emerged were also blossoming.Kuratko and Hodgetts (2004) provided another example of how entrepreneurial engagement can stimulate the economic activities positively. Nucor Steel was a small steel manufacturer with a few hundred employees. It embraced a new technology called thin slab casting, allowing it to thrive while other steel companies were stumbling. Nucor Steel grew to 59,000 employees, with sales of $3.4 billion and a net income of $274 million. Newer entrepreneurial companies, some of which did not exist previously, have collectively created 1.4 million new jobs during the past two decades.

Thirdly, thousands of smaller firms have been founded, including many established by women, minorities, and immigrants. These new companies have come from every sector of the economy and every part of the country. Together, these small firms make a formidable contribution to the economy, as many firms, some hiring only one or two employees, together created more than 1 million net new jobs during the decade of the 1990s. These entrepreneurial components as identified by Kuratko and Hodgetts (2004) had a direct impact on the marketing economies of the United States by propelling major technological innovations in the country as well as providing several opportunities for immigrants to access the main stream of the American economy, thereby living their American dream.

Scholars have continued to explore the various factors asscociated with the development of entrepreneurial perpective or inclinations by certain people. For instance, among the Nigerians, a higher level of entrepreneurial spirit or inclination is more pervasive among the Igbo people of South Eastern Nigeria. Young men of South Eastern Nigeria origin are made to stay with relatives to learn a trade, and then eventually such people start their own businesses, usually surpassing their previous trainers in terms of growth and expansion.

Nicolaou, Shane, Cherkas, Hunkin and Spector (2008) have affirmed that the engagement and predisposition of people to entrepreneurial activities are not randomly determined. A variety of factors are associated with the tendency of people to engage in entrepreneurial activities. Those factors identified by Nicalaou *et al.* include psychological attributes, such as the need for achievement, overconfidence, locus of control, optimism, and risk-taking propensity; and demographic factors, such as education, employment status, age, marital status, income, career experience, social ties, and social skills.

However, Nicolaou *et al.* (2008:173) discovered that genetics significantly influenced the predisposition of an individual towards engagement in entrepreneurial activities but does not determine entrepreneurial engagement:

> We found qualitatively similar heritability estimates across different operationalizations of entrepreneurship, which were of similar magnitude to that obtained in many studies of other social outcomes (MacGregor 2000). Moreover, our estimates of heritability remained high even after we adjusted the model for potential confounders such as gender, age, income, education, marital status, race, and immigrant status. In short, our results indicate that genetic factors influence the tendency to become an entrepreneur.

While these authors have added a caveat to their findings by also identifying the relevance of environmental factors in shaping an individual's inclination to entrepreneurial engagements, the model proposed by White *et al.* (2007),which had a bio-social component, provides an apt synergy of both biological and sociological factors, which, in my opinion, is critically relevant in the development of entrepreneurship disposition or perspectives. This has become imperative, based on the close affinity increase in entrepreneurial activities with economic development and a more bouyant lifestyle by citizens of such state.

Entrepreneurship Development in Nigeria

Nigeria, the most populous black nation in the world, can best be described as having a transitional economy, as typical of most countries in the global South. Former President Olusegun Obasanjo can be credited for bringing entrepreneurial studies to the fore in the Nigerian educational curriculum. The former president's persuasion was that economic development in a global world was only achievable through the sustained growth of entrepreneurship, which is best driven by innovative technology and communications, hence his aggressive support for the telecommunication industry in Nigeria.

The Federal government of Nigeria had continued to sustain efforts to stimulate entrepreneurial development based on the overwelming evidence in other developed economies, especially in the global North and recently among the Asian Tigers, that it is a major bedrock for economic development. Hence, several agencies have been established by the government to sustain this drive towards competent and responsible entrepreneurship. The Central Bank of Nigeria in June 2001 established a Small and Medium Entreprise Equity Investment Scheme in order to liberalize access to funds through commercial banks and provide a veritable pool for small- and medium-scale enterprises (Inyang and Enuoh 2009). Others included the Bank of Industry, the Micro Finance Banks, Nigerian Agricultural Rural Development Bank and a federal government-funded agency known as SMEDAN (Small and Medium Size Enterprise in Nigeria).

Since a significant percentage of Nigerian youths are unemployed, the aggressive commitment by the government is understandable in the light of ameliorating the debilitating scourge of massive unemployment among youths in the country. Invariably, Anyanwu *et al.* (2003) in a survey found that the beneficiaries in SMEEIS scheme disclosed that there was a significant increase in employment in their enterprises, following the injection of SMEEIS funds. In Nigeria, small and medium enterprises are known to have contributed significantly to economic development, job creation and sustainable livelihood (Abimbola and Agbola 2011).

Furthermore, these small firms have been found to contribute meaningfully to social and economic transformation, culminating into national development. For instance, Owualah (1999) affirmed the imperativeness of small firms in stimulating social and economic growth. Many indigenous industries are being translated into global agencies through very innovative entrepreneurs. This is very visible in the fashion industries in Nigeria, where local tie and dye, ankara materials are being used to make corporate outfits, dinner wear and tuxedos by young entrepreneurs. Also clutch bags and designers' shoes showcasing our local fabrics are known, popularly engaged in wedding ceremonies and other important events. Traditional bead making has also undergone a significant transformation, as the accessories are competing favourably with other designers' outfits in the Western world. Consequently, a new entrepreneurial way of life is being birthed, which one can actually refer to as an entrepreneurial culture. Hence, Inyang and Enuoh

(2009) maintained that economic benefits arising from stimulated entrepreneurial engagements involve the utilization of local resources, the dispersal and diversification of economic activities, and the mobilization of savings. Entrepreneurs constitute a veritable force in the promotion of an entrepreneurial culture. The role of entrepreneurs in stimulating economic growth and promoting the engagement of indigenous technology, while providing meaningful employment for the teeming youth population in Nigeria, has made entrepreneurial education a front-burner issue for successive administrations in Nigeria. A report by the Central Bank of Nigeria, as cited in Aruwa (2006), revealed that small and medium enterprises contributed 90 percent to industrial development and provided 70 percent of industrial employment, with a contribution of 10–15 percent of industrial production. It is on this note that one would want to consider factors that initiate or stimulate entrepreneurial development.

Theories which Account for Entrepreneurial Development

Several scholars have attempted to explain the development of entrepreneurship in different ways. Initially, this chapter had identified the bio-social model. This aspect of the chapter attempts to examine the various theories that constitute the bio-social model which this chapter considers an aggregate of several theories. It is on these bases we will examine the psychological theories, the sociological theories and cultural / environmental theories which explain the development of entrepreneurs.

Psychological Theories:
These theories are generally associated with the works of McClelland's discourse on the individual and his need for achievement, which serves as an impetus for entrepreneurial engagement. Psychological theories such as those developed by McClelland (1971) pay attention to the personal traits, motives and incentives of an individual and conclude that entrepreneurs have a strong drive towards self-actualization.

A similar focus on locus of control as psychological motivation was also examined by Low and MacMillan (1988), which emphasized the fact that entrepreneurs usually believe in their capabilities to commence and complete things and events through their own action and need for achievement. Psychological theories therefore consider the possession of certain psychological traits as a basis of the involvement in entrepreneurial activities as well as ability to sustain the entrepreneurial spirit, especially in the face of a seemingly contrary situation. Hence, these theorists attribute success in entrepreneurship to achievement motivation.

Sociological Theories
The sociological theories emphasize the context or the environment in which the entrepreneur operates. The entrepreneur's role as the *highly visible hand* depends on the environmental (social) context. Johnson's (1990) study refers to the sociological perspective of entrepreneurship by proposing that a detailed description of the environmental context is required before achievement motivation research will make further progress. The sociological theories are very similar to that of the anthropological theories, which, however, concentrate on the social-cultural processes.

In addition to sociological entrepreneurship theories, opportunity recognition could be described by anthropological theories. Reynolds (1991) identified four social contexts in relation to entrepreneurial opportunity: (1) social networks, (2) life-course stage, (3) ethnic identification, and (4) population ecology stage. In explaining the context in which the entrepreneur operates, the theory of social change posits how a traditional society (context) becomes one in which continuing technical progress takes place. In addition, the theory added that the entrepreneur's creativity constitutes a key element of social transformation and economic growth. The model or theory emphasizes the context and takes into cognizance interrelationships among physical environment, social structure, personality and culture. Similarly, in identifying the context or environment as being critical to the development of entrepreneurship, Max Weber's theory of entrepreneurial growth in the spirit of capitalism linked entrepreneurial activities with the religious beliefs system which is endogenous.

Economic Theories

This theory links entrepreneurship to economic development as interdependent in nature. Schumpeter's 1934 theory of innovation is a pioneering work of economic development that illustrated this relationship very succinctly. According to Schumpeter (1934), an entrepreneur is one who perceives the opportunities to innovate, i.e., to carry out new combinations or enterprises. In his view, the concept of new combination leading this innovation covers the following five cases:

- the introduction of new goods, that is, the ones with which consumers are not yet familiar, of a new quality;
- the introduction of a new method of production;
- the opening of new market(s);
- the conquest of a new source of supply of raw material;
- the carrying out of new organization.

Schumpeter gave emphasis to the role of entrepreneurial functions in economic development. In his view, development means basic transformation of the economy that is brought about by entrepreneurial functions.

Cultural Theories

Cultural theories explain entrepreneurship development, or entrepreneurship is the product of culture. Entrepreneurial talents come from cultural values and the cultural system embedded into the cultural environment. Cultural theorists posit that the supply of entrepreneurship is governed by cultural factors, and culturally minority groups are the critical agents of entrepreneurial and economic development. This theory associated the development of entrepreneurship along cultural lines. The theory argues that, in many countries of the world, entrepreneurs are usually from particular cultural groups or a particular socio-economic class. For instance, culturally marginal groups like the Jews and the Greeks in medieval Europe, the Chinese in South Africa, and the Indians in East Africa have been associated with high entrepreneurial engagement, thereby promoting economic development.

Conclusion

Entrepreneur development is a function of a combination of factors, which are both intrinsic and exterior to individuals. Therefore, a combination of the psycho-social factors basically accounts for the flourishing of entrepreneurship. Furthermore, entrepreneurs share basic commonalities that distinguish them from others, as they have the uncanny ability to turn obstacles to opportunities that can add value to humanity and at the same time culminate in the creation of wealth. Entrepreneurship can be stimulated, with the right form of education and the right business environment with good regulatory policy, which give opportunities to small-scale entrepreneurs to grow and boost entrepreneurial activities, thereby leading to economic growth and prosperity. Finally, this chapter holds the truism that entrepreneur development is a veritable tool for growth and development in an emerging economy like Nigeria's.

Questions

1) Define the following concepts:
   a) Entrepreneurship
   b) Business Environment
   c) Opportunity
2) Can everyone be an entrepreneur? What are the factors that predispose an individual to being a successful entrepreneur?
3) Explain the theoretical standpoints of various views, which explain the development of entrepreneurial activities in a place.
4) Highlight the various efforts by the Nigerian government toward stimulating entrepreneurship in recent times.
5) Give some examples of how entrepreneur development has led to economic buoyancy of any developed country.

References

Adejumo, G. (2001) Indigenous entrepreneurship development in Nigeria: characteristics, problems and prospects. *Advances in Management: Journal of Department of Business Administration,* University of Ilorin, Ilorin, Nigeria, 2(1): 112–122.

Anyanwu, C. M., B. S. Adebusuyi, and B. O. N. Okafor. (2003) The slow pace of disbursement of Small and Medium Industries Equity Investment Scheme (SMIEIS) fund and the need for remedial measures. Occasional Paper No. 30, Central Bank of Nigeria, Research Department.

Aruwa, S. A. S. (2006) *Entrepreneurial development, small and medium enterprises.* Kaduna: Entrepreneurship Academy Publishing.

Bates, T. (1995) Self employment entry across industry groups. *Journal of Business Venturing* 12, 109–124.

Carland, J. W., F. Hoy, W. R. Boulton, and J. C. Carland. (1984) Differentiating entrepreneurs from small business owners: A conceptualization. *Academy of Management Review*, 9 (2), 354–359.

Drucker, P. F. (1985) *Innovation and entrepreneurship.* London: William Heinemann.

Gartner, W. (1988) "Who is an entrepreneur?" is the wrong question. *American Journal of Small Business* 12(4), 11–32.

Inyang E., and B. Enuoh. (2009) Entrepreneurial competencies: The missing links to successful entrepreneurship in Nigeria. *International Business Review*, Vol. 2. No. 2.

Johnson, B. R. (1990) Toward a multidimensional model of entrepreneurship: the case of achievement motivation and the entrepreneur. *Entrepreneurship, Theory and Practice*, Vol. 14: 3, 39–54.

Kuratko, D. F., and R. M. Hodgetts. (2004) *Entrepreneurship: Theory, Process, Practice.* Mason,OH: South-Western Publishers.

Low, M. B., and I. C. MacMillan. (1988) Entrepreneurship: Past Research and Future Challenges. *Journal of Management*, Vol. 14, No. 2, 139–161.

Lee, S. M., and S. J. Peterson. (2000) Culture, entrepreneurship orientation and global competitiveness. *Journal of World Business* 34 (4), 401–416.

MacGregor, A. (2000) Practical approaches to account for bias and confounding in twin data. In Spector, T., H. Sneider, and A. MacGregor (eds.), *Advances in Twin and Sib-Pair Analysis*. London: Greenwich Medical Media, pp. 35–52.

McClelland, D. C., and D. G. Winter. (1971) *Motivating economic achievement.* New York: The Free Press.

Nicalaou, N., S. Shane, L.Cherkas, J. Hunkin, and T. D. Spector. (2008) Is the Tendency to Engage in Entrepreneurship Genetic? *Management Science* 54(1), pp. 167–179.

Owualah, S. I. (1999) *Entrepreneurship in Small Business Firms*,1st ed. Lagos: G-MAG Investment, Ltd. (Educational Publishers).

Pickle, H. B., and R. L. Abrahamson. (1990) *Small Business Management.* Hoboken, NJ: John Wiley & Sons, Inc.

Reynolds, P. D. (1991) Sociology and entrepreneurship: concepts and contributions. *Entrepreneurship: Theory and Practice* Vol. 16, No. 2, 47–67.

Ronstadt, R. (1988) The corridor principle. *Journal of Business Venturing* 3:31–40.

Schumpeter, J. A. (1934) *The Theory of Economic Development.* Cambridge, MA: Harvard University Press.

Stevenson, H. H., M. J. Roberts, and H. I. Grousbeck. (1985) *New Business Ventures and the Entrepreneur.* Homewood, IL: Irwin.

Stewart, W., and P. Roth. (2001) Risk taking propensity differences between entrepreneurs and managers: A meta-analytic review. *Journal of Applied Psychology* 86(1), 145–153.

Weber, M. (1904) *The Protestant Ethic and the Spirit of Capitalism.* New York: Routledge.

White, R., S. Thornhill, and E. Hampson. (2007) A biosocial model of entrepreneurship: The combined effects of nurture and nature. *J. Organ. Behav.* 28, 451–466.

Wilken, P. (1979) *Entrepreneurship: A Comparative and Historical Study.* Norwood, NJ: Ablex Publishing Corp.

Chapter 21

ENTREPRENEURSHIP DEVELOPMENT IN NIGERIA: THE GENDER DIMENSIONS

Aderemi, H. O. and Kehinde, O. O.

Introduction

Discussions on industrial development and stiff competition amongst nations have made the concept of entrepreneurship prominent. Entrepreneurship encompasses the conception, perception and realization of business opportunities (Aderemi 2010). Entrepreneurship can also be defined as the act of using initiative to transform a business concept into a new venture or to grow and diversify an existing business with high growth potential, taking calculated risk. It is considered as a viable option to solving the problem of unemployment in many developing countries of the world. It has also been associated with wealth creation and innovation. The interest in entrepreneurship in a developed economy is kindled by its contribution towards innovation and technological change, thus serving as a significant impetus for gaining technological advantage in firms and economic growth of nations. Notably, entrepreneurship has been recognised as a viable strategy for economic growth and development in all nations of the world, particularly in respect to technological capability and innovation. Aside this, Small and Medium Enterprises (SMEs), which are usually the offshoot of entrepreneurship, have been fully recognised by government and development experts as the main engine of economic growth and a major factor in promoting private sector development and partnership. Thus, entrepreneurship development is synonymous with the development of SMEs and the promotion of a country's economic growth. It is worthy of note that in the developed economies of Germany, the USA and even South Korea, SMEs account for as much as 64% of industrial employment, while in Nigeria, SMEs contribute about 31% to industrial growth (Onugu 2005). Percentage Gross Domestic Product (GDP) contribution by sectors of the economy as at 2012 by the *World Factbook*[1] are: Agriculture 31.1%, Industry 43% and Service 26%. Meanwhile, business enterprises account for about 58% of global working population.

Entrepreneurship development, according to Alonge (2008), involves more than mere increase in per capita output and income. It involves initiating, implementing and constituting a positive change in the structure of businesses and society at large for socio-economic and technological development. Enterprises and nations at large cannot continue to do business as usual in this age of globalisation, knowledge economy and business competition. There is a need for a strategic approach involving all stakeholders and elements geared towards promoting entrepreneurship and encouraging innovation

---

[1]This entry gives the percentage contribution of *agriculture, industry,* and *services* to total GDP. Agriculture includes farming, fishing, and forestry. Industry includes mining, manufacturing, energy production, and construction. Services cover government activities, communications, transportation, finance, and all other private economic activities that do not produce material goods.

and its commercialisation. A very prominent issue that bears relevance to the purpose of entrepreneurship development is the eight (8) international development goals commonly referred to as the Millenium Development Goals (MDGs). The goals, which were formulated at the United Nations (UN) Summit in 2000 and were to be achieved by 2015, include eradicating extreme poverty and hunger; achieving universal primary education; promoting gender equality and empowerment; reducing child mortality rates; improving maternal health; combating HIV/AIDS, malaria and other diseases; ensuring environmental sustainability; and developing global partnerships for development. These goals were intended to address three basic areas: human capability development, infrastructural improvement, and socio-economic rights and development. In any effort geared towards entrepreneurship development, these issues are directly or indirectly addressed.

It should be noted that the first five (5) goals of MDGs have the female gender more in focus. Gender differences come into play in many aspects of life, including social, economic, cultural, political, and technological aspects, amongst others. Furthermore, literature has established the gender differences in poverty level, education, and employment with females at the marginal end. For instance, Aderemi (2010) and Africa Competitiveness Report (ACR) 2011 mentioned the marginalisation of women entrepreneurs both by the industrial sector and in the nature of business involvement. This can be said to have implications for development. In the first instance, the prominence of women entrepreneurship in informal sector businesses prevents the inclusion of their contribution to value addition in national accounts, and, second, their involvement in non-technological businesses suggests a view that female entrepreneurs have little or no contribution to innovation, technological change and technological competitiveness of their economies. This conclusion is unacceptable, and, hence, it is important that, as efforts are being made to achieve the MDGs and promote entrepreneurship, the gender differences that may advance or inhibit this process are also made clear. Thus, the main thrust of this chapter is to discuss the gender dimensions of the various interventions for promoting and fostering entrepreneurship in Nigeria. In doing this, the chapter attempts to answer the following questions: How does Nigeria's current population by gender analysis hold implications for entrepreneurship? Is there any existing gender gap in entrepreneurship? What is the gender dimension of institutional, legal and regulatory framework that favours entrepreneurship development? What should be the focus of a gender-inclusive human resource development for entrepreneurship?How can technology, research and development (R and D) be directed towards entrepreneurship development? How can we achieve gender-inclusive entrepreneurship development using extension and support services? How can gender perspectives bring flavour to marketing in such a way as to promote entrepreneurship? Are there gender-specific considerations in terms of infrastructure and finance for entrepreneurship development? The discussions and answers to the questions are aimed towards the design of appropriate gender-inclusive interventions for entrepreneurship development.

Nigeria's Economy: Gender Differences and Implications for Entrepreneurship
The demographic profile of Nigeria, using 2011 estimates, revealed that 40.9% of the country's population were between 0 and 14 years, with males totalling 32,476,681 and

females 31,064,539. Those between 15-64 years were55.9% (males 44,296,228 and females 42,534,542), while those 65 years and overwere 3.1% (males 2,341,228 and females 2,502,355). These statistics clearly show that about 50% of the country's population are women, and they constitute a critical mass of unharnessed potential that could bring speedy contribution to national development. Moreover, greater efficiency can be achieved if women participate in the production of technologies.

A close examination of the labour force statistics (CBN, NBS, 2010) revealed that the unemployment rate has been increasing from 12.3% in 2006 to 21.1% in 2010. Further analysis of unemployment through gender evaluation (Figure 2) revealed that unemployment of females, particularly from age 25, is much higher than that of their male counterparts.

Table 21.1: Labour Force Statistics 2006 – 2010 (CBN, NBS, 2010)

	2006	2007	2008	2009	2010
Total Population	140,003,542	144,483,655	149,107,132	153,878,560	158,802,674
Total Labour Force	58,933,891	61,249,485	62,946,096	64,960,371	67,039,103
Total Employment	50,886,826	52,326,923	53,807,775	55,529,624	57,306,572
Total Unemployment	8,047,065	8,922,562	9,204,515	9,499,059	9,803,029
Unemployment Rate (%)	12.3	12.7	14.9	19.7	21.1

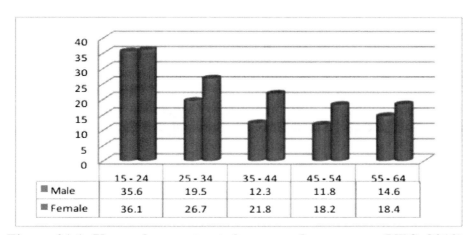

	15 - 24	25 - 34	35 - 44	45 - 54	55 - 64
Male	35.6	19.5	12.3	11.8	14.6
Female	36.1	26.7	21.8	18.2	18.4

Figure 21.1: Unemployment rate by sex and age group (NBS, 2010)

There is no gainsaying the fact, therefore, that entrepreneurship could help to reduce the rate of unemployment. Today, 61% of Nigerians are living in poverty, 100 million of them live on less than $1/day (NBS 2010). Meanwhile, the nation possesses quality human capital, booming economic activities, and good eyes for business, and its people have been voted the happiest in the world. Perhaps an entrepreneurial mindset from the very outset of pre-secondary school days will go places in the quest to reduce unemployment and poverty.

The Gender Gap in Entrepreneurship

Literature (Insight 2005; Paton 2006) supports the existence of a global gender gap in entrepreneurship. Reports have it that the gap is greatest in poor and middle-income countries. That is, fewer women than men participate in entrepreneurial activities. In Nigeria, a recent study (Siyanbola *et al.* 2012) revealed a negative correlation of entrepreneurial interest to gender, that is, male students were more likely to be entrepreneurial. Notably, the gender factor was one of the most significant of the nine background factors tested in the study (Siyanbola *et al.* 2012). Other studies that confirm a higher male propensity and sustainability of interest towards entrepreneurship include de Wit and van Winden (1989), Lerner and Yeoshua (1996), Kourilsky and Walstad (1998), and Matthews and Moser (1996). This gender imbalance in entrepreneurship calls for specific interventions not only to develop entrepreneurship in the country but also to increase the entrepreneurial interest and participation level of the female gender. This is of particular interest considering the reproductive and family roles of women in the society and also because participation in entrepreneurship has been associated with productivity and economic development of nations.

Approaches to Entrepreneurship Development and Gender Dimensions

In this section, the authors share the view of Awasthi (2011) that entrepreneurship development is not just interventions directed solely to start-ups but also to the other processes of promoting entrepreneurship, which include pre-start-up—otherwise referred to as 'rationale' by Aderemi (2010)—survival and growth. In this regard, the National Policy on SMEs identified seven key areas of creating support, fostering and developing entrepreneurship in Nigeria. These include: Institutional, Legal and Regulatory Framework; Human Resource Development; Technology, Research and Development; Extension and Support Service; Marketing; Infrastructure; and Finance. Each of these areas, using a holistic entrepreneurial development programme (EDP), can be grouped into three categories. These include (a) Entrepreneurship Orientation and Sensitization; (ii) New Enterprise Creation; and (iii) Small Business Survival and Growth for Existing Firms.

Institutional, Legal and Regulatory Framework

The first port of call is to address an important issue: the setting up of institution(s) that would be guided by a legal and regulatory framework in the form of policy instruments to guide, direct, coordinate and monitor activities in the subject area. These areas include business registration, land use planning, land and property rights, contract enforcement and dispute resolution, labour laws and regulations, tax administration, standards and quality regulations. We discuss these issues with their gender aspects:

i)   Business Registration

The issue of business registration in entrepreneurship is crucial, most especially because it is a means through which the contribution of entrepreneurship to national accounts can be determined. Also, it serves as a convenient avenue for the implementation or dispatch of intervention to the entrepreneurs. In this regard, laws promoting, protecting and facilitating business creation must be in place before entrepreneurship can become a reality. The bureaucratic procedures in getting a company registered and obtaining a business licence vary from one business to another. On the global front, Nigeria ranked 116th of 183 economies as regards the ease of starting a business (DB 2012). This ranking gives one an idea of how easy it is for Nigerian entrepreneurs to start businesses when compared with other African countries such as Senegal and Ghana, which ranked 93rd and 104th respectively.

Aderemi (2010) found that entry requirement is one of the perceived variables that determine the type of business choice as women were more likely to operate in activities with lower entry barriers, that is, activities that require little capital investment and those that do not require a unique business premise. To this end, more women than men were found to be prominent in informal businesses that require, more or less, no registration. Also, the same scenario was observed with regard to type of business choice as more women than men were engaged in non-technological businesses that require little or low skill and contribute minimally to economic development.

It should be noted that when regulations are strict, levels of informality tend to be higher, as people seek to have their needs met by personally making contacts with those who they feel may expedite business actions. For the females, these may expose them to unpleasant and unfavourable abuse or harassment. However, Doing Business Database (DB) 2010 noted that informality is not without a cost, as firms in the informal sector usually grow at a lesser speed, receive less access to credit, have fewer staff. The greatest concern is that most activities in the informal sector are not being protected by labour laws.

For a government trying to create opportunities to curb rising unemployment and income loss, the first priority should be to create flexible regulations and effective institutions, where both men and women can easily exploit their ideas, irrespective of their gender or ethnic origin. Also, established businesses and existing firms can invest, grow and create more jobs. When regulations are flexible and institutions are effective, with efficient processes for start-ups, it can help to reduce the risk of entrepreneurship in terms of bankruptcy; it can create accessibility to funds; it will open up more opportunities for the poor; and it encourages closure of the success gap between formal and informal businesses. Government should also note that the dynamic and growing economies of the world are known for their continual reform, review and update of regulations and strategies for implementation to favour private sector investments, unlike poor economies.

ii)   Land: Usage and Property Rights

Nigeria, as of 2010, when compared with the rest of the world, ranked 167th and 101st of 183 economies (Table 21.2) in terms of days and number of procedures to get through construction permits respectively; the best performing state, Jigawa, ranked 6th and 9th of the 183 economies on the said indicators. This good performance in Jigawa is noteworthy and should be a benchmark for other states. Meanwhile, on cost and procedures to register properties, Nigeria ranked between 177th and 178th, while the best performing states, Yobe and Kwara, ranked 104th and 136th respectively. These are clear indications that the process of getting through land use and property registration could be a bottleneck for most entrepreneurs, especially if they are micro- or small-scale businesses. Reforms have, however, proved useful because, as of 2012, Nigeria now ranks 84th of the 183 economies as it relates to the ease of dealing with construction permits (DB 2012). Nevertheless, on cost and procedures to register properties, Nigeria now ranks 180th of the 183 economies (DB 2012). It is noteworthy that government interventions could help to cushion the effects of the initial difficulties that start-ups might encounter with respect to business registration, land usage and property rights.

Nigeria is notably a patriarchal society, where men dominate all spheres of work and endeavour except in a few cases, such as nursing and teaching (primary and secondary). Thus, the social relations and activities of Nigerian women and men are governed by patriarchal systems of socialization and cultural practices which favour the interests of men to the detriment of those of women. For instance, though Section 43 of Nigeria's constitution permits both male and female Nigerians to own and acquire movable and immovable property, a large proportion of women in Nigeria are barred from owning land by customary laws of inheritance. Consequently, men are usually the owners of land and the issues of land usage and property rights are usually male concerns. In modern times, this role has not changed much as very few women own and use land. Most women have joint ownership of land with their husbands. This scenario has implications for entrepreneurship development in the sense that women entrepreneurs are discouraged and do not really entertain thoughts of obtaining a permanent business premises. To make progress, anti-gender customary laws and norms on gender roles should be frowned at and completely eliminated from the society.

iii)   Contract Enforcement and Dispute Resolution

Entrepreneurial justice matters to businesses. This is because it serves as a mechanism by which contractual obligations are enforced towards positive economic activities (DB 2010). Anderson *et al.* 2005 noted that judicial systems in transition economies set the rules by which markets function. Also, they provide a means through which disputes are resolved and economic and social rights protected. Along this direction, Ogundele *et. al.*(2010) noted that Nigeria, like every other country on the globe that emphasizes excellence and competitiveness, has customs and moral values that could be used as building blocks in developing business ethical values. However, Nigeria has had political and economic instability and leadership problems, which have disrupted the application of these values in entrepreneurship development (Ogundele *et al.* 2010). It should be noted that lack of entrepreneurial ethics and justice could lead to the failure and collapse of multi-million-dollar public corporations, enterprises and contracts.

In terms of days and cost to enforce a contract, Nigeria ranked 101st and 120th respectively among 183 economies (Table 21.2). The best performing states, Jigawa and Katsina, ranked 10th and 86th respectively. These are states that others could benchmark.

There has, however, been an improvement in 2012, as Nigeria ranked 97th with regard to ease of enforcing contracts (DB 2012).

A report (DB 2010) states that it takes an average of 511 days (about 1½ years) and costs 36.3% of the claim value to resolve a commercial dispute through the courts. While this figure is better than the sub-Saharan average of 644 days and 49.3%, it is not as good as that of Ghana, where it takes 487 days and costs 23% of the claim value.

On the gender implications of dispute resolution in business, a study by Shadare *et al.* (2011) found a significant difference between female and male managers' conflict resolution effectiveness. This vividly reveals the influence of gender on conflict resolution effectiveness. The dimensions of this in business are that, first, women-owned businesses could experience little or better dispute management in terms of cost and number of days; second, involvement of the female gender in leadership position, particularly in the judiciary, could lead to better conflict management.

Table 21.2: Comparing Best Practice of Doing Business in Nigeria with Global Ranking

Indicator	Nigeria in DB 2010 (represented by Lagos)		Nigeria best practice		
	Performance	Global rank (183 economies)	Best performing state within Nigeria	Performance	Global rank (183 economies) How Nigerian states would compare globally
Days to deal with construction permits	350 days	167	Jigawa	47 days	6
Number of procedures to deal with construction permits	18 procedures	101	Jigawa	10 procedures	9
Days to enforce contract	457 days	64	Jigawa	261 days	10
Number of procedures to start a business	8 procedures	94	Abuja, FCT	5 procedures	25
Days to register property	82 days	140	Borno	14 days	26
Cost to deal with construction permits	580.3% of income per capita[1]	143	Kano	94.6% of income per capita	67
Cost to enforce a contract	32% of the claim value	120	Katsina	26% of the claim value	86
Days to start a business	31 days	117	Abuja, FCT	22 DAYS	92
Cost to register property	20.9% of the property value	178	Yobe	5.2% of the property value	104
Number of procedures to register property	13 procedures	177	Borno, Gombe, Kwara	8 procedures	136
Cost to start a business	77% of income per capita[2]	153	Abuja, FCT	58.5% of income per capita	148

1 At the time of publication of Doing Business 2010: Reforming through difficult times, the cost was 573.4% of income per capita.

2 At the time of publication of Doing Business 2010: Reforming through difficult times, the cost was 76.7% of income per capita.

Source: Doing Business Database, 2010

iv)   Labour Laws and Regulations

Entrepreneurship plays an important role in economic growth, therefore improving the investment climate and market access for both men and women through appropriate labour laws and regulations eases the entrepreneurs' ability to do business and enhances that growth (World Bank 2007). Entrepreneurship development requires an understanding of the different challenges often faced by Nigerian entrepreneurs in this sphere. Most entrepreneurs usually encounter a lot of bottlenecks with the regulatory authorities in the process of growing their businesses. As of 2012, Nigeria ranked 65th of 183 economies on the strength of investor-protection index (DB 2012). However, there are discriminatory labour practices based on gender considerations. Specifically, several practices are held against the female gender as regards their suitability for starting and managing certain businesses; that is why it is extremely difficult in some societies for women to go into some particular careers and trade (Nwakeze 2011). This view was also shared by Aaron and Egwu's (2003) findings that 75 percent of male entrepreneurs would rather employ males than females. The study further suggested that the males are preferred to their female counterparts because the former are presumed more likely to ensure maximum productivity and efficiency, probably because of their strength and abilities. For an effective entrepreneurship development in Nigeria, government has to create conducive and better gender-friendly labour laws and regulations to encourage entrepreneurs' ease of starting and managing their businesses.

v)   Tax Administration

Taxation has been a viable option for raising revenue for the state, and funds realised from it are usually employed for developmental projects. Taxes are usually in forms of corporate income tax, turnover tax, labour taxes and contributions paid by public and private organisations. In Nigeria, taxation is enforced by the three tiers of government, i.e., federal, state, and local governments, with each having its sphere clearly spelt out in the Taxes and Levies (approved list for collection) Decree, 1998. Favourable tax policy is one of the most pressing needs of the Nigerian entrepreneurial environment. Eboh (2007) quoted that "the tax burden on Nigerian entrepreneurs and businesses is internationally competitive, but the mode of collection is one of the worst in the world. Multiple taxes levied by the three tiers of government have resulted in a proliferation of taxes, some of which are illegal". Most entrepreneurs also complain of multiple taxation, which could adversely affect profitability and return on investment, and consequently prevent potential entrepreneurs/investors from penetrating the market. Moreover, proceeds from taxation are not usually remitted to the states. In cases where they are remitted, they are not utilised in the provision of adequate infrastructural development, which is critical to entrepreneurship development in Nigeria. With respect to gender considerations, the female entrepreneur is subject to some sort of discrimination in wage and tax policies. This was illustrated in the report of CIDA Nig. GSAA 2006 and Nwakeze 2011, where the assumption is that males are mainly responsible for their families' financial and material obligations and thus are given tax benefits unlike those given to females, irrespective of their status. This is a form of gender discrimination and cannot promote entrepreneurship development. Entrepreneurs should be given tax rebates in order to encourage local participation and exports. On the other hand, imported goods should be heavily taxed so as to promote development of indigenous competences. To further ensure entrepreneurship development in Nigeria, federal, state, and local governments must be disciplined to embrace the entrepreneurship option of increasing the internally generated revenue through other means than over-reliance on tax, especially company tax. This is fast becoming a global practice (Moyassar 2010). Tax holidays should be given to existing entrepreneurs to serve as incentive for growth.

vi)   Standards and Quality Regulations

Regulations are fundamental for effective management of entrepreneurial activities in an economy. A more efficient and less costly standard and quality regulatory system is necessary for entrepreneurship development in order to compete favourably in the global market. This system can be in the form of new rules, improved existing regulations and more. Indeed, improving standards and quality regulations is one of the viable ways that government can leverage upon to promote entrepreneurship development. In furtherance of this, the Nigerian government set up a number of agencies, such as Standard Organisation of Nigeria (SON), National Food and Drug Administration and Control (NAFDAC), among others, whose responsibilities are to ensure standard and quality control of both the processes and products of entrepreneurship. However, the bureaucracy involved in compliance by businesses could be cumbersome and could lead entrepreneurs to give up and go in a different direction. Also, important standardization and quality testing equipment are lacking in the country; government and public-private partnership could help to provide them. Furthermore, it usually costs businesses time and money to fill out forms and to gather and report information required by government regulations (OECD 2008). Hence, cutting red-tape through the simplification of administrative processes is important in reducing the regulatory burden, improving the quality of regulations, and encouraging greater entrepreneurial engagements in the country. Efforts should be directed at removing unnecessary paperwork, reducing delays and streamlining application and licensing processes. Administrative simplification programmes reduce the costs of compliance by entrepreneurs, thereby removing impediments to innovation and facilitating entrepreneurship and business development. The challenge for the years to come will be to improve the implementation of better regulation policies and tools, and to continue to introduce innovations in regulatory reform to respond to emerging challenges (OECD 2009).

Human Resource Development

Entrepreneurship education is a virile tool for developing entrepreneurship against the backdrop of rising unemployment and business failures. Sharing this viewpoint, the National University Commission (NUC) and National Board for Technical Education (NBTE) introduced entrepreneurship education into higher institutions' curricula in 2006. Apart from this initiative, several other government and private agencies had devised innovative ways of building capacity and capabilities of incumbent and future entrepreneurs. Amongst these initiatives are the National Directorate of Employment, National Poverty Eradication Programme, and Central Bank of Nigeria Entrepreneurial Training for members of the National Youth Service Corps. While these have yielded their dividends, linking R and D and innovation to the real sector and improving capacity to manage technological changes are the main challenges of technological entrepreneurship development. This is because technological entrepreneurship, which exploits existing scientific and technological knowledge to meet market needs, is what brings about the national productivity and competitiveness that entrepreneurship is said to provide (Siyanbola *et al.* 2011). Hence, there is need to develop technological competencies through a reformed higher education that accentuates a virile and coordinated research and development (R and D) and innovation system, at the very minimum.

While the need to get more people into entrepreneurship is valid, understanding that the educational empowerment of females, beginning from post-basic level to tertiary level, is the springboard to other forms of empowerment in the country should also be noted. This education, when combined with entrepreneurship, brings about creativity, innovation, self-employment, job creation, wealth generation and socio-economic development. Government policy for SMEs has the intention to create a critical mass of entrepreneurial, managerial and technological skills for the growth and competitiveness of Nigeria's industrial sector (UNDP/SMEDAN 2007).There is a need to look within and outside the school walls to be able to achieve this. Apprenticeship in the informal economy is the major route for most young people in developing countries to acquire the technical skills of a craft or trade and the entrepreneurial competences to start their own business. Moreover, the current conventional education does not suffice because learning is too theoretical and memorization-based. Furthermore, the content, delivery system, and adequate reward system that will attract and retain students' interest in entrepreneurship should not be overlooked. In addition, teachers need to get and deliver high quality education, with skills development and mentoring. Educational regulators need a curriculum restructuring, both at the secondary and university levels, to include entrepreneurial extension and support services.

Technology, Research and Development

One of the main pillars of the routes to entrepreneurship development is a dynamic and strong infrastructure in education, science, and technology that is adequately responding to the rapidly evolving human resource and R and D needs of businesses. In the absence of such infrastructure, the innovative capacities of Nigeria's enterprises and the capability of its human resource base to absorb, adapt and develop new technologies will not materialize.

An important approach, often overlooked, that can be used to address the technology, research and development needs of businesses is to deploy technology need assessment (TNA). The concept of needs is a universal one, and needs may be perceived, imagined, desired or thought to be important or real. Therefore, it is generally necessary to carefully assess situations so as to determine what real needs are. The CME Primer defined needs assessment as "any systematic approach to collecting and analyzing information about the needs of individuals or organizations." Needs assessment can also be identified as a gap, the difference or distance between what is occurring in practice and what is expected (the desired outcome), or the difference between what is and what should be. Usually, needs assessment is attached to a particular domain such as education, health, agriculture, environment or technology; and it can be carried out at various levels, ranging from individuals to nations and even regions. Within the context of entrepreneurial development in the specific domain of technology and R and D, Technology Needs Assessment is a tool for the entrepreneurs and other stakeholders to define a portfolio of capacity-building actions and problem-solving approaches to be undertaken to facilitate, and possibly accelerate, the development, adoption and implementation of environmentally benign solutions in the form of R and D efforts and technologies.

More specifically, technology assessment studies the social, ethical and economic implications of development, diffusion, and the use of certain technologies, strategies, organisations or structures and informs policy decisions. Its aim is to improve the quality and cost-effectiveness of technology applications and R and D efforts. TNA prioritizes technologies, best practices and policy reforms that can be implemented in different sectors of an entity/state/country, and it is the first step in planning technology acquisitions.

An ILO 2008 report noted the reality of the technological challenge and the gender divide, as almost everywhere women lag behind men either in access to training or in the application of technology. In order to meet the technological challenge, the ILO 2008 report identified the need for the adoption of development strategies that combine new technological capacity with investments in a broad variety of traditional and non-traditional economic sectors. These strategies need to be supported by improvements in education, skills development, and vocational training and research. Furthermore, training in the use of technology is essential and a key step in taking advantage of emerging economic opportunities; technological knowledge and techniques are constantly evolving and bridging geographical distances (for example with e-learning and e-commerce). Practical advances often lead to broad usage, which in turn lowers the costs of products for the end-users and makes technologies more accessible (ILO 2008). Innovation and certain technologies may also have unwanted effects, such as pollution and environmental degradation, which a TNA or environmental impact assessment (EIA) could alleviate.

Extension and Support Service

Indigenous enterprises, especially those of female entrepreneurs, find it difficult to compete in both local and international markets. Many of them lack technical, managerial and marketing skills. Also, access to information and the ability to adequately utilize information available to them has continued to be a challenge. Some businesses are battling with obsolete technologies due to lack of information, technical know-how or financial incapability. For instance, with the wave of e-commerce, many international businesses have been able to upgrade and globalize their operations. However, this is not the case with most of the indigenous enterprises in developing economies.Consequent to this, the gains of globalisation and technological developments have continued to be an illusion. In Nigeria, there are quite some number of public and private business development and extension services (Aderemi 2010). Some of the public ones include Ministries of Industry and Women Affairs at the state levels; the National Association of Small and Medium Enterprises (NASME); commercial, development and micro-finance banks; the Small and Medium Enterprise Development Agency (SMEDAN) and their Industrial Development Centres in major cities of the country. There are local business development service (BDS) providers in the private sector, which include specialized consulting firms, educational institutions, business membership organizations, NGOs and supply-chain firms. However, as earlier mentioned, most entrepreneurs either do not know of the existence of such services or are unprepared to pay for them.

For a government that is committed to developing entrepreneurship, conscious efforts should be made to reach out to these enterprises, whether they are registered with the organised private sector or not. With respect to governments in cooperation with non-governmental organizations and the private sector, specific interventions in this regard, as recommended by ILO 2001, are as follows: (a) provision of public infrastructure to ensure equal market access for women and men entrepreneurs; (b) development of programmes that provide training and retraining, particularly in new technologies, and affordable services to women in business management, product development, financing, production and quality control, marketing and the legal aspects of business; (c) providing outreach programmes to inform low-income and poor women, particularly in rural and remote areas, of opportunities for market and technology access, and provide assistance in taking advantage of such opportunities; (d) creating non-discriminatory support services, including investment funds for women's businesses, and targeting women, particularly low-income women, in trade promotion programmes; (e) disseminating information about successful women entrepreneurs in both traditional and non-traditional economic activities and the skills necessary to achieve success, and facilitating networking and the exchange of information; (f) increasing incentives to enterprises to expand the number of vocational and training centres that provide training for women in non-traditional areas; (g) providing affordable support services, such as high-quality flexible and affordable child-care services, that take into account the needs of working men and women.

With respect to local, national, regional and international business organizations and non-governmental organizations that are concerned with women's issues, recommendations include advocating, at all levels, for the promotion and support of women's businesses and enterprises, including those in the informal sector, and the equal access of men and women to productive resources.

Marketing

Marketing is a term used in business to define activities that relate to the exploitation and promotion of a venture. It is often considered as an effective means of reaching or expanding a new business enterprise. It is also one of the business strategies employed by entrepreneurs to grow their businesses. Marketing is said to comprise issues such as identifying the customer, defining the right product and service to meet customers' needs and expectations, product pricing, distribution, promotion and so on (Adaramola 2008). Entrepreneurs are to anticipate these marketing issues in the short or long run and consequently develop and prepare a marketing plan. Many business failures are attributed to these marketing issues rather than to lack of finance or poor management (Adaramola 2008).

Gender perspective is viewed as significant to achieving effective marketing goals in entrepreneurship (Momodu *et al.* 2011). Pritchard and Morgan (2000) also identified different ways in which gender inequalities are embedded within the promotion and marketing strategies of an economy, e.g., tourism. Entrepreneurs should realize that men's and women's needs are different, and as such they should design products and adopt appropriate marketing/advertising styles to meet such identified needs. Men demand clear structures and symbols of status, while women are more likely to emphasize interpersonal relationships. Therefore, men are more likely to support a product which is improving their status in society, while women want to intensify, improve or express relationships (Wolf 2007). Moreover, men, unlike women, also tend less to engage in actively providing information to other consumers; they are less likely to be impulsive as well as compulsive buyers and more likely to engage in variety-seeking purchasing. All these are important decisive factors for entrepreneurship development. The main objective of the entrepreneur should be how to implement different marketing strategies, for both men and women, that would lead to effective communication of his or her products and services and subsequent growth of the business. For example, in multinational marketing, the product is targeted to the business environment of the host countries. So there is a need to strengthen the marketing approaches to capture both men and women's needs for greater business exploits and competitiveness.

Infrastructure

Infrastructure development is one of the prerequisites for business growth and expansion in any economy. Okpukpara (2009) attributed the slow growth of entrepreneurship and SMEs in developing economies to the bad state of infrastructure. Moreover, Ode-Ojowu *et al.*(2007) concluded that one of the reasons for poor quality and low productivity among Nigerian entrepreneurs, especially agricultural entrepreneurs, was inadequate infrastructure. This problem is compounded for women by the gender inequalities in access to land, good road and rail networks, technology, ICTs and other infrastructural facilities, which constitute a bottleneck to entrepreneurship development. In Nigeria, more men utilize public infrastructural facilities such as the computers, internet services, communication networks, technologies, etc., than women do (Obayelu and Ogunlade 2006). Usually, the technological environment is a core element of the investment climate and is also critical for the competitiveness and dynamism of entrepreneurs. This environment to a greater extent favours men to women in most African countries. For example, women may be less able than men to afford the capital outlay required to acquire the sophisticated infrastructures and equipment required for business operations. All these and other factors contribute to reducing women's ability to participate and compete favourably and effectively in business (Bardasi *et al.* 2009). Government should, therefore, partner with the private sector to facilitate infrastructural development in the country, as this is the nucleus of any entrepreneurship development.

Finance

Access to finance is identified as one of the most important factors in the development of entrepreneurship. Finance is essential for the establishment of small-scale industries for increased production and employment generation (Ajani 2008). It provides a means through which an entrepreneur can facilitate business transactions. However, inaccessibility sometimes constitutes a major obstacle to the growth of businesses of entrepreneurs, especially women entrepreneurs. Bardasi *et al.* (2009) opined that access to finance is usually one of the major constraints recognized as more critical for women entrepreneurs than men. Another major issue is the weak financial system in Nigeria. This considerably affects the growth of women's businesses. Robb and Coleman (2009) found out that women entrepreneurs have less access to capital than men do; yet on the contrary, a study by Cohoon *et al.* (2010) revealed that there were no differences in the types of funding sources for both male and female entrepreneurs, with one exception: women were almost twice as likely as men to secure their main funding from business partners. In view of the above, there is need to strike a balance in the access to funds by both men and women entrepreneurs for the establishment and management of businesses for entrepreneurship development.

Conclusion

Entrepreneurship is considered as a viable option to solving the problem of unemployment in many developing countries of the world. In Nigeria, the female gender unemployment rate, particularly from age 25, is much higher than that of their male counterpart, and entrepreneurship development holds huge potential concerning redressing the situation. About 50% of the country's population are women, and they constitute a critical mass of unharnessed potential that could bring speedy contribution to national development. This chapter noted the gender divide in entrepreneurship and called for specific interventions not only to develop entrepreneurship in the country but also to increase the entrepreneurial interest and participation level of the female gender. The approach to entrepreneurship development as given in the National Policy on SMEs was proposed; this consists of seven key areas including: Institutional, Legal and Regulatory Framework; Human Resource Development; Technology, Research and Development; Extension and Support Service; Marketing; Infrastructure; and Finance. This chapter discussed the issues related to these seven key areas with their gender implications. Some of the conclusions made, amongst others, were that flexible regulation and effective institutions, where both men and women could easily exploit their ideas, irrespective of their gender or ethnic origin, were of paramount concern; anti-gender customary laws and norms on gender roles should be frowned at and completely eliminated from the society; tax rebates to local entrepreneurs will help to encourage indigenous participation and exports; important standardization, quality testing equipment and other infrastructures are inadequate in the country, which government and public-private partnership could help provide; linking R and D and innovation to the real sector and improving capacity to manage technological changes are some of the main challenges of technological entrepreneurship development of which a reformed entrepreneurship education could help address.

References

Adaramola, A. O. (2008) The Product Marketing Plan of an Entrepreneur. In Alonge, M. F., F. Omotoso, G. Adaramola, T. K. O. Aluko, and O. I. Wale-Awe (eds.), *Entrepreneurship Development in Nigeria*. Ado Ekiti, Nigeria: University of Ado-Ekiti Press.

Aderemi, H. O. (2010). *Women in Technological and Non-technological Enterprises: Divergent or Convergent Paths?* Saarbrücken, Germany: LAP Lambert Academic Publishing AG.

Ajani, Olubunmi, and Idowu Yetunde. (2008) Gender Dimensions of Agriculture, Poverty, Nutrition and Food Security in Nigeria. Background Paper of Nigeria Strategy Support Program (NSSP), No. NSSP 005, International Food Policy Research Institute.

Anderson, James H., David S. Berstein, and Cheryl W. Gray. (2005) Judicial Systems in Transition Economies: Assessing the Past, Looking to the Future. Washington, DC: World Bank.
http://siteresources.worldbank.org/INTECA/Resources/complete.pdf.

Awasthi, Dinesh. (2011) Approaches to Entrepreneurship Development: The Indian Experience. *Journal of Global Entrepreneurship Research*, Winter and Spring, Vol. 1, No. 1, pp.107–124.
ent.ut.ac.ir/Jger/Images/UserFiles/1/file/pdf/dinesh%208.pdf

Bardasi, Elena, C. Mark Blackden, and Juan Carlos Guzman. (2007) Gender, Entrepreneurship, and Competitiveness in Africa. Washington, D.C.: World Bank.

Central Bank of Nigeria. (2010). Central Bank of Nigeria 2010 Annual Report.

Canadian International Development Agency. (2006) Nigeria: Gender Situation Assessment and Analysis. In National Gender Policy (2007) ed., Federal Republic of Nigeria. Abuja: Federal Ministry of Women Affairs and Social Development.

Cohoon, J. McGrath, Vivek Wadhwa, and Lesa Mitchell. (2010)The Anatomy of an Entrepreneur. Are Successful Women Entrepreneurs Different From Men?.
www.4dinternationaljournal.com/journal/pdf/11.pdf.**P,**

DB. (2010). Doing Business in Nigeria 2010 Report.

DB. (2012). Doing Business in Nigeria 2012 Report.

De Wit, G., and F. A. Van Winden. (1989) An empirical analysis of self employment in the Netherlands. *Small Business Economics* 1 (4), 263–272.

Eboh, M. (2007) World Bank, UNDP blame multiple taxation, corruption for investors apathy. *Vanguard* September 25.
http://www.allafrica.com/stories/200709250594.html. Accessed June 28, 2008.

Gana, Aaron Tsado, and Samuel G. Egwu (eds.). (2003) *Federalism in Africa: The imperative of democratic development*, Volume 2. Trenton, NJ: Africa World Press.

International Labour Organisation. (2008) Skills for improved productivity, employment growth and development. Report V, International Labour Conference, 97th Session, Geneva, p. xiii.

Insights. (2005) The Entrepreneurship Gender Gap in Global Perspective: Implications for Effective Policy Making to Support Female Entrepreneurship. Briefing Note Number 22. http://www.simmons.edu/som/docs/insights_22.pdf. Accessed June 2012.

Kourilsky, M. L., and W. B. Walstad. (1998) Entrepreneurship and female youth: knowledge, attitudes, gender differences and educational practices. *Journal of Business Venturing* Vol. 13, No. 1, pp.77–78.

Lerner, M., and H. Yeoshua. (1996) New entrepreneurs and entrepreneurial aspiration among immigrants from the former USSR in Israel. *Journal of Business Research*, Vol. 36, No. 1, pp.59–65.

Majoux, L. (2001) Jobs, Gender and Small Enterprises: Getting the Policy Environment Right. International Labour Organisation Series on Women's Entrepreneurship Development and Gender in Enterprise (WEDGE). Geneva: ILO Press.

Matthews, C. H., and S. B. Moser. (1996) A longitudinal investigation of the impact of family background and gender on interest in small firm ownership. *Journal of Small Business Management* Vol. 34, No. 2, pp.29–43.

Momodu, A. S., C. A. O. Akinbami, and J. F. Obisanya. (2011).Achieving food security and climate change mitigation through entrepreneurship development in rural Nigeria: Gender perspective. *African Journal of Environmental Science and Technology* Vol. 5(10), pp. 834-854.

Moyassar, I. A. (2010) Using Entrepreneurship Opportunity in Optimizing Organizational Excellence: A Case Study. *Advances in Business Related Scientific Research Journal (ABSRJ)* Vol. 1, No. 1.

National Bureau of Statistics. (2010) National Manpower Stock and Employment Generation Survey Report. Nigeria.

Nwakeze, Ngozi M. (2011) Gender and Labour Force Participation in Nigeria: Issues and Prospects. Society for Research and Academic Excellence. http://www.academicexcellencesociety.com/gender%C2%AD_and_labour_force_participation_in_nigeria_issues_and_prospects.html.

Obayelu, A. E., and I. Ogunlade. (2006) Analysis of the uses of information and communication technology for gender empowerment and sustainable poverty alleviation in Nigeria. *International Journal of Education and Development Using Information and Communication Technology (IJEDICT)* Vol. 2, Issue 3, pp. 45–69.U

Ode-Ojowu, H. Bulus, and B. T. Omonona. (2007) Nigeria Poverty Assessment (Harmonized). Post-seminar draft. July 1, submitted to the World Bank Office, Abuja, Nigeria, forthcoming.

Ogundele, O. J. K., A. R. Hassan, A. A. Idris, M. A. Adebakin, and P. I. Iyiegbuniwe. (2010) Challenges of Ethics in Nigeria within the Context of Global Ethical Practice. Conference Paper, National Conference of the Academy of Management, Nigeria, 2010.

Okpukpara, Benjamin. (2009) Strategies for effective loan delivery to small scale enterprises in rural Nigeria. *Journal of Development and Agricultural Economics* Vol. 1(2), pp. 041–048.

Onugu, Basil Anthony Ngwu. (2005) Small And Medium Enterprises (SMEs) in Nigeria: Problems and Prospects. A dissertation submitted to the St. Clements University in partial fulfillment of the requirements for the award of the degree of Doctor of Philosophy in Management, St. Clements University.

Organization for Economic Cooperation and Development. (2008). Policy Brief on Measuring Regulatory Quality.
www.oecd.org/gov/regulatory-policy/44124554.pdf.

Paton, Nic. (2006) Global Gender Gap for Entrepreneurship. *Management Issues: Entrepreneurship, Women and Work.*
http://www.management-issues.com/2006/8/24/research/global-gender-gap-for-entrepreneurs.asp.

Pritchard, Annette, and Nigel J. Morgan. (2000) Privileging the Male Gaze: Gendered Tourism Landscapes. *Annals of Tourism Research* 27(4): 88-95.

Robb, Alicia, and Susan Coleman. (2009) *Characteristics of New Firms: A comparison by gender.* Kansas City, MO: Ewing Marion Kauffman Foundation.

Shadare, A. Oluseyi, O. Christopher Chidi, and Oluwakemi Ayodeji Owoyemi. (2011) Gender Influences on Managerial Style and Conflict Resolution Effectiveness in Work Organisations in South-Western, Nigeria. *International Journal of Business Administration* Vol. 2, No. 1, February 2011.

Siyanbola, W. O., O. O. Afolabi, O. A. Jesuleye, A. A. Egbetokun, A. D. Dada, H. O. Aderemi, Maruf Sanni, and M. A. Rasaq. (2012) Determinants of entrepreneurial propensity of Nigerian undergraduates: an empirical assessment. *International Journal of Business Environment* 5(1), pp. 1–29.

———, Helen Aderemi, Abiodun Egbetokun, and Maruf Sanni. (2011) Framework for Technological Entrepreneurship Development: Key Issues and Policy Directions. *American Journal of Industrial and Business Management* 1, October 2011, 10-19. http://www.SciRP.org/journal/ajibm.

United Nations Development Programme/Small and Medium Enterprises Development Agency of Nigeria (2007) (Draft) Small and Medium Enterprise Policy.

Wolf, Tobias. (2007) Effect of Gender Marketing on Consumer Behaviour. Term Paper in GRA 2418 Understanding the Consumer. E-book Publisher: GRIN Verlag GmbH.

World Bank. (2007) Private Sector Development and Gender. Gender and Development Briefing Notes. Gender and Development Group, the World Bank.

World Economic Forum. (2011) The Africa Competitiveness Report 2011. World Economic Forum, the World Bank and the African Development Bank. http://www.afdb.org/fileadmin/uploads/afdb/Documents/Publications/Africa_Competitiveness_Report_2011-1.pdf.

Chapter 22

ENTREPRENEURSHIP EDUCATION AND ENTREPRENEURIAL SKILLS

Akanmu, O. E.

Introduction

Entrepreneurship is a dynamic process of vision, change, and creation. It requires an application of energy and passion towards the creation and implementation of new ideas and creative solutions. Entrepreneurship has been generally explained in many ways, such as:

- a theory of evolution of economic activities;
- a continuous process of economic development;
- an ingredient to economic development;
- essentially a creative activity or an innovative function;
- a risk-taking factor which is responsible for an end result;
- usually understood with reference to individual business;
- the name given to the factor of production which performs the functions of enterprise;
- creates awareness among people about economic activity;
- generates self-employment and additional employment.

Entrepreneurship can be defined as the process of using private initiative to transform a business concept into a new venture or to grow and diversify an existing venture or enterprise with high growth potential. Entrepreneurs identify an innovation to seize an opportunity, mobilize money and management skills, and take calculated risks to open markets for new products, processes and services (UNDP Evaluation office 1999).

Entrepreneurship is a vibrant assertion of the facts that individuals can be developed, their outlook can be changed and their ideas can be converted into action through an organized and systematic programme for entrepreneurs. Systematic training can be given a better output and attracting people for taking up a business venture can change the economic scenario.

The basic objective in developing entrepreneurship and multiplying it in the society has been to enable the society to generate productive human resources and mobilize and sustain the same in subsequent process of development. The spontaneity and continuity of the process would depend on the kind of people that can be prompted and groomed in the entrepreneurial career.

Entrepreneurship is an employment strategy that can lead to economic self-sufficiency for people with disabilities. Self-employment provides people with disabilities and their families with the potential to create and manage businesses in which they function as the employer or boss, rather than merely being an employee. Oftentimes, people with disabilities are eligible and receive supplemental support (technical and financial), which can serve as a safety net that may decrease the risk involved with pursuing self-employment opportunities.

Who is an Entrepreneur?

The term 'entrepreneur' stems from French, meaning *between-taker* or *go-between*. According to Hisrich (1986), the term *entrepreneur* has evolved through history:

Middle Ages: an entrepreneur is an actor and person in charge of large-scale production projects.

17th century: an entrepreneur is a person bearing risks of profit (loss) in a fixed-price contract with government.

1725 Richard Cantillon: an entrepreneur is "a person who pays a certain price for a product to resell it at an uncertain price, thereby making decisions about obtaining and using the resources while consequently admitting the risk of enterprise". That is, a person bearing risks is different from one supplying capital.

1803 Jean Baptiste Say: an entrepreneur is an economic agent who unites all means of production—land of one, the labour of another and the capital of yet another—and thus produces a product. By selling the product in the market he pays rent of land, wages to labour, and interest on capital, and what remains is his profit. That is, he separates profits of the entrepreneur from profits of capital.

1876 Francis Walker: distinguished between those who supplied funds and received interest and those who received profit from managerial capabilities.

1934 Joseph Schumpeter: entrepreneurs are innovators who use a process of shattering the status quo of the existing products and services to set up new products through new technology and new services.

1961 David McClelland: an entrepreneur is a person with a high need for achievement (N-Ach). He is energetic and a moderate risk taker.

1964 Peter Drucker: an entrepreneur is one that searches for change, responds to it, and maximizes opportunities.

1975 Albert Shapero: entrepreneurs take initiative, organize some social and economic mechanisms, accept risk of failure, and have an internal locus of control.

1983 Gifford Pinchot: 'Intrapreneur' is an entrepreneur within an already established organization.

1985 Robert Hisrich: an entrepreneur is one who creates something different with value by devoting the necessary time and effort, assuming the accompanying financial, psychological, and social risks, and receiving the resulting rewards of monetary and personal satisfaction.

In the contemporary period, sociologists, psychologists and economists have also attempted to give a clear picture of an entrepreneur. Sociologists analyze the characteristics of entrepreneurs in terms of caste, family, social value and migration. Psychologists, on the other hand, attempt to isolate entrepreneurs from the general population on various personality traits, such as need for achievement, creativity, propensity to take risk, and independent leadership, among others. Economists highlight situational characteristics such as occupational backgrounds, access to capital, business and technological experience, and managerial skills, with economic gains considered as characteristic of the entrepreneur.

Summarily, an entrepreneur is an enterprising individual who builds capital through risk and/or initiative. An entrepreneur by implication is one who ventures out, who prefers change as a means of growth, and in the process is prepared to take calculated risks. While taking risks, he is aware of the possibilities—success as well as the consequence of failure.

Requirements to Becoming a Successful Entrepreneur

If one's goal is success in business, then there are certain musts that have to be fully developed, implemented and managed for one's business to succeed. James Stephenson suggested twenty-five steps that are required of a successful entrepreneur as follows: do what you enjoy; take what you do seriously; plan everything; manage money wisely; ask for the sale; remember, it's all about the customer; become a shameless self-promoter (without becoming obnoxious); project a positive business image; get to know your customers; level the playing field with technology; build a top-notch business team; become known as an expert; create a competitive advantage; invest in yourself; be accessible; build a rock-solid reputation; sell benefits; get involved; grab attention; master the art of negotiations; design your workspace for success; get and stay organized; take time off; limit the number of hats you wear; limit your number of tasks; and finally, follow-up constantly.

Qualities of a Successful Entrepreneur

Successful business people have many traits in common with one another. They are confident and optimistic. They are disciplined self-starters. They are open to any new ideas which cross their paths. James Adams highlighted ten traits of the successful entrepreneur as thus:

1. *Disciplined*: Successful entrepreneurs focus on making their businesses work and eliminate any hindrance of their goals. They take steps toward the achievement of their objectives.
2. *Confidence*: Successful entrepreneurs do not ask questions about whether they are worthy of success. They are confident with the knowledge that they will make their businesses succeed.
3. *Open-mindedness*: Entrepreneurs realize that every event and situation creates a business opportunity. They have the ability to look at everything around them and focus it toward their goals.
4. *Self-starter*: They set the parameters and make sure that projects follow that path.
5. *Competitive*: Entrepreneurs need to win at the businesses that they create.
6. *Creativity*: Entrepreneurs often come up with solutions which are the synthesis of other items.

7. *Determination*: Successful entrepreneurs do not believe that something cannot be done. They are determined to make all of their endeavours succeed, so they will try and try again until they succeed.
8. *Strong Communication Skills*: The entrepreneur has strong communication skills to sell the product and motivate employees. Most successful entrepreneurs know how to motivate their employees so the business grows overall.
9. *Strong Work Ethic*: The successful entrepreneur will often be the first person to arrive at the office and the last one to leave. He/She will come in on the days he/she is to be off duties to make sure that an outcome meets their expectations.
10. *Passion*: Passion is the most important trait of the successful entrepreneur. Entrepreneurs genuinely love their work. They are willing to put in those extra hours to make the business succeed because there is a joy their business gives which goes beyond the money.

Successful entrepreneurs want to see what the view is like at the top of the business mountain. Once they see it, they want to go further. They know how to talk to their employees, and their businesses soar as a result.

Brief History of Entrepreneurship in Nigeria

It was revealed from an article submitted by Nicks (2008) in Bizcovering Online Magazine that there was early (traditional) and modern entrepreneurship. Early entrepreneurship started with trade by barter even before the advent of any form of money, when people produced more products than they needed; as such, they had to exchange these surpluses. In this way, producers came to realize that they could concentrate in their areas of production to produce more and then exchange for what they needed. Early entrepreneurship is characterized by production or manufacturing, in which case the producer most often started with a small capital, most of it from his own savings.

Modern entrepreneurship in Nigeria started with the coming of the colonial masters, who brought in their wares and made Nigerians their middle-men. Most of the modern entrepreneurs were engaged in retail trade or sole proprietorship. One of the major factors that has in many ways disrupted this flow of entrepreneurship development in Nigeria is the value system brought about by formal education. For many decades, formal education has been the preserve of the privileged, and with formal education people had the opportunity of being employed in the civil service. In those periods, the economy was large and good enough to absorb all Nigerians into prestigious occupations; as such, the system made Nigerians to be dependent on the colonial masters.

Furthermore, the contrast between Nigerian and foreign entrepreneurs during the colonial era was very detrimental, and the competitive business strategy of the foreign entrepreneurs was ruinous and against moral standards established by society. They did not adhere to the theory of "live and let live". For instance, the United African Company (UAC), which was responsible for a substantial percentage of the import and export trade in Nigeria, had the policy of dealing directly with producers and refused to make use of the services of Nigerian entrepreneurs. The refusal of the expatriates to utilize the services of local businessmen inhibited their expansion and acquisition of necessary skills and attitude. Because of this, many eventually folded up. Those that folded up built up resentment against business, which became very demoralizing to other prospective entrepreneurs. As a result, the flow of entrepreneurship in the country was slowed down. But, with more people being educated and the fact that government could no longer employ most school leavers, economic programs to encourage individuals to go into private business and be self-reliant were initiated (Nicks 2008). Therefore, from all the stated definitions and explanations of entrepreneurship, it could be categorized as the process of doing small- and medium-scale business, since it is more of individual activity.

Entrepreneurship Education

Defining Entrepreneurship Education

Entrepreneurship education seeks to prepare people, especially the youth, to be responsible, enterprising individuals who become entrepreneurs or entrepreneurial thinkers and who contribute to economic development and sustainable communities. It is not based on a textbook course. Instead, students are immersed in real-life learning experiences, in which they have an opportunity to take risks, manage the results, and learn from the outcomes. Entrepreneurship education is not just about teaching someone to run a business; it is also about encouraging creative thinking and promoting a strong sense of self-worth and accountability (Familoni 2012).

Kourilsky (1995) defines entrepreneurship education as opportunity recognition, marshalling of resources in the presence of risk, and building a business venture. Entrepreneurship education has also been defined in terms of creativity and innovation applied to social, governmental, and business arenas (Gottleib and Ross 1997). It is explained by Bechard and Toulouse (1998) as a collection of formalized teachings that informs, trains, and educates anyone interested in business creation or small business development. They point out that entrepreneurial education focuses on combining and carrying out a new combination of business elements, while education for small business ownership focuses on the skills needed to reproduce or acquire an existing business.

Advantages of Entrepreneurship Education

According to a report from the Office of Disability Employment Policy of the United States Department of Labour (2009), entrepreneurship education offers a solution. It seeks to prepare people; particularly the youth, to be responsible, enterprising individuals who become entrepreneurs or entrepreneurial thinkers by immersing them in real life learning experiences where they can take risks, manage the results, and learn from the outcomes.

Through entrepreneurship education, young people, including those with disabilities, learn organizational skills, including time management, leadership development and interpersonal skills, all of which are highly transferable skills sought by employers. According to Logic Models and Outcomes for Youth Entrepreneurship Programs (2001), a report by the D.C. Children and Youth Investment Corporation, other positive outcomes include:

- improved academic performance, school attendance, and educational attainment;
- increased problem-solving and decision-making abilities;
- improved interpersonal relationships, teamwork, money management, and public speaking skills;
- job readiness;
- enhanced social-psychological development (self-esteem, ego development, self-efficacy); and
- perceived improved health status.

Advantages of entrepreneurship cannot be highlighted without mentioning its benefits to individual persons and the nation as a whole, which is discussed next.

Benefits of Entrepreneurship Education

Hull University Business School, University of Hull (2009), highlighted the importance of entrepreneurship education as a key driver of a nation's economy and as a lifelong learning process that would become an advantage to individuals as well.

Entrepreneurship is a key driver of a nation's economy. Wealth and a high majority of jobs are created by small businesses started by entrepreneurially-minded individuals, many of whom go on to create big businesses. People exposed to entrepreneurship frequently express that they have more opportunity to exercise creative freedoms, higher self-esteem, and an overall greater sense of control over their own lives. As a result, many experienced business people, political leaders, economists, and educators believe that fostering a robust entrepreneurial culture will maximize individual and collective economic and social success on a local, national, and global scale. It is with this in mind that the National Standards for Entrepreneurship Education were developed to prepare youth and adults to succeed in an entrepreneurial economy.

Entrepreneurship education is a lifelong learning process. Starting as early as elementary school and progressing through all levels of education, including adult education, the Standards and their supporting Performance Indicators are frameworks for teachers to use in building appropriate objectives, learning activities, and assessments for their target audience. Using this framework, students will have progressively more challenging educational activities, experiences that will enable them to develop the insight needed to discover and create entrepreneurial opportunities, and the expertise to successfully start and manage their own businesses to take advantage of these opportunities.

Also, a research study by the Office of Disability Employment Policy of the United States Department of Labour (2009) regarding the impact of entrepreneurship education on youth with disabilities shows the following benefits:

(1) *Opportunity for Work-Based Experiences*: Work experiences for youth with disabilities during high school, both paid and unpaid, help them acquire jobs at higher wages after they graduate. Also, students who participate in occupational education and special education in integrated settings are more likely to be competitively employed than students who have not participated in such activities.

(2) *Opportunity to Exercise Leadership and Develop Interpersonal Skills*: By launching a small business or school-based enterprise, youth with disabilities can lead and experience different roles. In addition, they learn to communicate their ideas and influence others effectively through the development of self-advocacy and conflict resolution skills. Moreover, they learn how to become team players and to engage in problem-solving and critical thinking—skills valued highly by employers in the competitive workplace of the 21st century. Mentors, including peer mentors both with and without disabilities, can assist the youth in developing these competencies.

(3) *Opportunity to Develop Planning, Financial Literacy, and Money Management Skills:* The ability to set goals and to manage time, money and other resources are important entrepreneurship skills which are useful in any workplace. For youth with disabilities, learning about financial planning, including knowledge about available work incentives, is critical for budding entrepreneurs with disabilities who are currently receiving cash benefits from the Supplemental Security Income Program (SSI).

What are the factors to put into consideration to have an effective entrepreneurial education? Entrepreneurship education can be provided in many different settings. There is no particular right program or set of activities. Rather, it is a matter of identifying and considering what works for the young people served in a program. For effective entrepreneurship education, the following issues are to be considered:

- the age of the young people;
- their interests and abilities;
- the time they have to devote to entrepreneurial activities;
- the available fiscal and human resources (i.e., community support, business support);
- the expertise of staff and what kind of training and support staff might need;
- the effect program participation may have on youth support and benefits;
- the availability of existing entrepreneurial programs in the area;
- the availability of well-drawn curriculum;
- the support of the program from organization's leadership; and
- the intended outcomes of the program/activities.

The importance of entrepreneurship to any economy is like that of entrepreneurship in any community. Entrepreneurial activity and the resultant financial gain are always of benefit to a country. If one has entrepreneurial skills then one will recognise a genuine opportunity when it comes.

Contemporary Approach to Entrepreneurship Education in Nigeria

Over the last decade, Nigeria has implemented far-reaching economic reforms aimed at improving macroeconomic management and liberalizing markets, trade, and the business environment. The recent developments on the Niger Delta agenda are a sign of the commitment and determination of the government to address its seven-point reform agenda, which covers critical reform priorities, notably, essential infrastructure, Niger Delta regional development, food security, land tenure reforms and home ownership, national security and wealth creation. Likewise, in the area of entrepreneurship, the nation's development has been recorded. In recognition of this progress, the United Nations Development Program (UNDP) indicated that recent improvements in development policy and performance mean that the country now benefits from a positive medium-term economic outlook.

In the not too distant past, business schools paid little attention in the direction of entrepreneurship education by offering it as an elective. Students today are demanding integrated programs that teach practical skills for starting and expanding business enterprises (Farrell 1994). Traditional business education programs, though well attended, have come under criticism for failing to be relevant to the needs of the changing business environment. For example, entrepreneurial education emphasizes imagination, creativity, and risk-taking in business, whereas traditional business schools tend to over-emphasize quantitative and corporate techniques at the expense of more creative skills (Porter 1994). Traditional business school programs emphasize the large established corporation over the small or startup venture and nurture the follower and steward over the leader, creator and risk taker (Chia 1996). However, entrepreneurial education has firmly established a beachhead in academia as a result of a shift in academic thinking about the value of this field.

In a bid to arrest the disturbing trend of massive graduate unemployment and the social menace which it represents, the Federal Government has resolved to promote entrepreneurial education in Nigeria's tertiary educational institutions as a means of equipping graduates to function as job and wealth creators rather than job seekers. As a first step in addressing this problem, some Nigerian universities have introduced courses in entrepreneurship as an entry point into making graduates think and act as entrepreneurs. As a further step to concretize entrepreneurial education in the universities, the Federal Government has directed the establishment of Entrepreneurship Study Centres in universities.

It is now recognised that entrepreneurship is an important educational innovation that provides the impetus to learn about learning (Charney and Libecap 2003). Interest in entrepreneurship as a field of research and teaching has been fuelled by the growing demand for entrepreneurship courses by business students, probably because entrepreneurial education is an opportunity to address some of the contemporary needs of business education in ways that the traditional system does not (Mitra 2002).

Entrepreneurship education can be viewed broadly in terms of the skills that can be taught and the characteristics that can be engendered in individuals that will enable them to develop new innovative plans. It focuses on the expertise that is used to conceive of and commercialize a business opportunity.

Entrepreneurship Education and Entrepreneurial Skills

In order to understand the correlation entrepreneurship education has with entrepreneurial skills very well, one has to understand the meaning of entrepreneurial skills. In a layman's language, entrepreneurial skills are the skills or basic qualities that one needs to build a great business. Meanwhile, the United Kingdom Centre for

Bioscience, Higher Education Academy, has listed a wide range of both personal traits and skills that are seen as useful to entrepreneurs as follows:

- management skills: the ability to manage time and people (both oneself and others) successfully;
- communication skills: the ability to sell ideas and persuade others;
- ability to work both as part of a team and independently;
- ability to plan, coordinate and organise effectively;
- financial literacy: having financial skills, such as book-keeping and calculating tax;
- ability to research effectively: inquire more about available markets, suppliers, customers and competition;
- awareness of intellectual property and possibly patent law;
- self-motivation and self-discipline;
- ability to market and sell new products or ideas;
- adaptability: ability and willingness to change in order to suit various conditions;
- acquisition of innovative and creative thought, for example, being able to draw up a business plan for a new venture;
- ability to multi-task—being able to work as a manager, accountant, marketer, among others;
- ability to take responsibility and make decisions;
- ability to work under pressure;
- perseverance: continued effort and determination;
- competitiveness: willingness to win or be more successful than other people;
- willingness to take risks;
- ability to network and make contacts.

What traits and skills really make Richard Branson, Bill Gates, Donald Trump, and countless other entrepreneurs so successful? According to Lavinsky (2009), key ingredients that lead to success have been identified, which have been observed, both in celebrity entrepreneurs and in the most successful clients, over the past decade. He made it clear that, when it is all said and done, they have all of the following critical skills, which are essential to entrepreneurial success:

1. *Vision and Leadership:* Entrepreneurs have a vision of where the company will be in the future. In addition, they are able to communicate their vision to motivate employees, investors, and partners, who will help them achieve that vision. They are able to identify staffing needs, expertly fill them, and lead their teams to success.

2. *Focus and Execution***:** Entrepreneurs with good skills focus to make sure that goals are achieved, customers are satisfied, and employees are motivated. They are careful not to be seduced by the next exciting opportunity without executing on the priorities at hand. They do not let perfectionism prevent them from taking action, either; at the end of the day, a product on the market is better than a product shelved due to lack of focus, execution, or perfectionism. They get to market and get feedback from their customers as soon as possible.

3. *Persistence and Passion:* Entrepreneurs with professional skills are passionate about what they are trying to accomplish. They are always willing to commit whatever is needed of them (time, energy, money, or other resources). They persist through trying times and fight as much as needed to achieve the goals they have set for themselves and their teams.

4. *Technical skills:* Good entrepreneurs, as the owners of their firms, may not need to be the most skilled technicians on their teams. But they need to have the necessary foundational knowledge to be able to lead their technical teams and make informed decisions.

5. *Flexibility:* Successful entrepreneurs understand that the world and the environment in which they operate are constantly changing. While they focus on the end game, they also adapt their strategies and offerings to meet changing market conditions.

Entrepreneurship education focuses on developing understanding and capacity for pursuit of entrepreneurial behaviours, skills and attributes in widely different contexts. It can be portrayed as open to all and not exclusively the domain of the high-flying growth-seeking business person. The propensity to behave entrepreneurially is not exclusive to certain individuals. Different individuals will have a different mix of capabilities for demonstrating and acquiring entrepreneurial behaviours, skills and attributes. These behaviours can be practised, developed and learned; hence, it is important to expose all students to entrepreneurship education. Entrepreneurial skills and attitudes provide benefits to society, even beyond their application to business activity. Obviously, personal qualities that are relevant to entrepreneurship, such as creativity and a spirit of initiative, can be useful to everyone, in their working responsibilities and in their daily existence. Also relevant is that the needed technical and business skills be provided to those who choose to be self-employed and/or to start their own venture—now or in the future.

Conclusion

In recent times, Nigerian government has come to recognise the importance of entrepreneurship education in institutions in that it will stimulate the interest of students to explore the potential and opportunities of entrepreneurship when graduated so that they become self-employed and job creators rather than job seekers.

Since research has shown that entrepreneurship in terms of small- and medium-scale enterprises are crucial to the development of any economy, it should be seriously engraved into students before they graduate. In order to break away from the shackles of unemployment, students in the universities, polytechnics, monotechnics, and colleges of education should see entrepreneurship education as mandatory so as to be equipped with some skills that will form the basis of sustaining them outside the field of paid employment after graduating.

However, since proper utilization of entrepreneurship skills leads to economic development, government should always see it as a plus and create friendly environments for it to succeed. Economists have noted the assumption that, once business opportunities exist in an economy, people who are enterprising will emerge to take advantage of them, provided there are no major impediments on their way. The World Bank also emphasized the need for governments in developing countries to create enabling environments that are business-friendly so that entrepreneurship can flourish.

In all, graduates should emulate Nigeria's great entrepreneurs, who have made a mark in their respective enterprises in recent years and have succeeded impressively in self-employment,in spite of the constraints arising from a difficult socio-economic environment, the poor state of infrastructural development, and poor employment opportunities.

Review Questions

1.   What is entrepreneurship?
2.   "Successful entrepreneurs have many traits in common with one another." Discuss.
3.   What is entrepreneurship education? Explain the contemporary approach to entrepreneurship education in Nigeria.
4.   How is entrepreneurship relevant with entrepreneurial skills?

References

Adams, J. (2007) Ten Qualities of a Successful Entrepreneur. http://under30ceo.com/10-qualities-of-a-successful-entrepreneur/. Accessed on September 27, 2010.

Bechard, J. P., and J. M. Toulouse. (1998) Validation of a Didactic Model for the Analysis of Training Objectives in Entrepreneurship. *Journal of Business Venturing* Vol. 13, No. 4, pp. 317–332.

Bronte-Tinkew, Jacinta, and Zakia Redd. (2001) Logic Models and Outcomes for Youth Entrepreneurship Programs. Report to the D.C. Children and Youth Investment Trust Corporation. http://www.cyitc.org/cyitc/outcomes/LogicModels_YouthEnt.pdf.

Charney, A. H., and G. D. Libecap. (2003) The Contribution of Entrepreneurship Education: An Analysis of the Berger Program. *International Journal of Entrepreneurship Education*, Vol. 1, No. 3, pp. 385–417.

Chia, R. (1996) Teaching paradigm shifting in management education: University business schools and the entrepreneurial imagination. *Journal of Management Studies* Vol. 33, No. 4, pp. 409–428.

Familoni, J. (2012) Need for Entrepreneurial Education. *Nigeria BusinessDay Online.* http://www.businessdayonline.com/NG/index.php/entrepreneur/entrepreneur-news/40788-need-for-entrepreneurial-education.htm.Accessed on July 09, 2012.

Farrell, K. (1994). Why B-Schools Embrace Entrepreneurs. *Venture*, Vol. l6, No. 4, pp. 60–63.

Gottleib, E., and J. A. Ross. (1997) Made not born: HBS courses and entrepreneurial management. *Harvard Business School Bulletin* Vol. 73, pp. 41–45.

Hisrich, R. D. (1986) Entrepreneurship and Intrapreneurship: Methods for Creating New Companies That Have an Impact on the Economic Renaissance of an Area. In Hisrich, Robert D. (ed.), *Entrepreneurship, Intrapreneurship, and Venture Capital*. Lexington, MA: Lexington Books.

Kourilsky, M. L. (1995) *Entrepreneurship education: Opportunity in search of curriculum*. Kansas City, MO: Center for Entrepreneurial Leadership, Ewing Marion Kauffman Foundation.

Lavinsky, D. (2009) Entrepreneurial Skills and Traits: Are you the Next Richard Branson? *Online Growthink Blog*. www.growthink.com/content/entrepreneurial-skills-and-traits-are-you-the-next-richard-branson/. Accessed on January 13, 2009.

Mitra, J. (2002) Consider Velasquez: Reflections on the Development of Entrepreneurship Programmes. *Industry and Higher Education* Vol. 16, No. 3, pp. 191–202.

Nicks. (2008) The History of Entrepreneurship in Nigeria. *Bizcovering Online Magazine*. http://bizcovering.com/history/the-history-of-entrepreneurship-in-nigeria/#ixzz21uCMgHDV.Accessed on May 24, 2008.

Office of Disability Employment Policy of the United States Department of Labor. (2009) Encouraging Future Innovation: Youth Entrepreneurship Education. http://www.dol.gov/odep/pubs/fact/entrepreneurship.htm.

Porter, L. (1994) The Relation of Entrepreneurship Education to Business Education. *Simulation and Gaming* Vol. 25, No. 3, pp. 416–419.

Stephenson, J. (2007) *Entrepreneur Magazine's Ultimate Small Business Marketing Guide: Over 1500 Great Marketing Tricks That Will Drive Your Business Through the Roof* (Second Edition). Toronto, Canada: Entrepreneur Press.

UK Centre for Bioscience, The Higher Education Academy. (2009) What are Regarded as Entrepreneurial Skills? http://www.bioscience.heacademy.ac.uk/resources/entrepreneurship/skills.aspx. Accessed on June 30, 2009.

Chapter 23

ENTREPRENEURSHIP EDUCATIONAL PROMOTION: A TOOL FOR NATIONAL SELF-RELIANCE

Adekeye, D. S.

Introduction

There is a big challenge for Nigerian youths. Not only the youths, even the adults face a lot of challenges. The pathetic situation in Nigeria today is that after struggling to graduate at the 'normal' or 'abnormal' time, you go out to serve the nation only to experience irregularity in the payment of your stipends. Upon the completion of service, you get back home to join the unemployment market—and this can go on for only God knows how long. Your aged parents find it difficult to get their gratuities and equally find it more difficult to access their pensions. We are all familiar with what is currently being referred to as the 'Pension scam' in Nigeria.

Haftendorn and Salzano (2003) submit that "66 million young people are unemployed and even higher numbers are underemployed. Overall, the unemployment rate of young people is two to three times higher than for adults." They argue further that "a generation without the hope of a stable job is a burden for the whole society" and that "the economic investment of governments in education and trading will be wasted if young people do not move into productive jobs that enable them to pay taxes and support public services".

Although the fight against youth unemployment is part of the Millennium Goals set by the heads of state and federal governments,the question that should readily come to mind is: "Which of the MDGs has been achieved in Nigeria?" Not to waste time, the answer is: None.

It should be noted from the outset that different countries are integrating entrepreneurship and enterprise education into different levels of education through a variety of modalities and at different speeds, depending on the availability of expertise and resources. There is no single pathway or approach and no single intervention that can be expected to deal with the whole range of problems facing young people. Though not all the students will eventually move to self-employment, such projects will be effective in providing a better understanding of enterprise culture, in supplying students with skills for use in companies, and in improving their knowledge of enterprise and entrepreneurship through practice.

Consequently, youth entrepreneurship programmes are promoted in schools and communities across the world and on the Internet.

At Secondary Level

In many developed nations, at secondary level, many interventions are designed to impart a spirit of entrepreneurship and teach business concepts through team-based, experiential learning. Entrepreneurship and enterprise can be integrated throughout the curriculum, as an optional subject or as an after-school activity. Activities in the classroom are based on managing a project and are often presented through the simulation of how an entrepreneur operates when setting up and running a small business, as distinct from operating in a large company, where individual roles and responsibilities are clearly designated.

At Technical and Vocational Education

In the area of enterprise education, students obtain direct experience in applying their technical knowledge in a commercial environment, or participate in creating and developing a real company that markets its own products.

At University Level

It is an established reality that universities around the world supply highly skilled manpower to the public sector, commerce and industry. For instance, several universities in Nigeria, like their counterparts in Western Europe, now offer entrepreneurship courses at undergraduate and graduate levels. Many have established Centres for Entrepreneurship toengage in training, research and development, consultancy and information dissemination andprovide follow-up services for students. At the Obafemi Awolowo University, this unit is being run under the Center for Industrial Research Development (CIRD).

Common Features

In spite of the broad differences in economic, social and cultural contexts for entrepreneurship and enterprise education across regions and countries, there are nevertheless some similarities in the way that these programmes at different levels of education have been conceived and are delivered. The key to promoting entrepreneurial initiative is in engaging the imagination of students, that is, in assisting them to think of developing their own business ideas, by showing them, at least in part, what it could be like to establish and run their own businesses.

A common theme running through entrepreneurship and enterprise education programmes, irrespective of socio-economic context, is that they are often delivered within the framework of partnership arrangements and coalitions at both national and international levels.

Socio-Economic Context Affecting Youth Entrepreneurship

Cultural Influence on Entrepreneurship

It is not an overstatement that the national cultural attitude influences the entrepreneurial activities of the population of a country or a region.
Entrepreneurship involves life attitudes, including the readiness and the courage to act in the social, cultural and economic context.
Entrepreneurial qualities or behaviour include:

i. creativity and curiosity;
ii. motivation by success;
iii. willingness to take risks;
iv. ability to cooperate;
v. identification of opportunities;
vi. ability to be innovative and tolerate uncertainty.

Cultures that value and reward such behaviour promote a propensity to develop and introduce radical innovations, whereas cultures that reinforce conformity, group interests, and control over the future are not likely to show risk-taking and entrepreneurial behaviour (P. A. Herbig and J. C. Miller 1992). In Nigeria, for instance, the issue of patriarchy greatly affects the participation of women in certain enterprises.
However, the cultural difference is not the only reason that people become entrepreneurs. There are two types of entrepreneurs: those voluntarily pursuing an attractive business opportunity and those who are engaged in entrepreneurship out of necessity, because they can find no other suitable work. Young people seeking work, particularly in the developing world, fall mainly into this "necessity" group.

Entrepreneurial education has to be an integrated part of national curricula in primary, secondary, vocational and higher education. Focusing on awareness-raising programmes at education institutions and start-up programmes for youth allows governments to influence the cultural attitudes towards a positive perception of entrepreneurial activities. The ILO Recommendation No. 18910 indicates how these cultural attitudes could be influenced.

Nigeria, like all other ILO member states, should adopt measures, drawn up in consultation with the most representative organizations of employers and workers, to create and strengthen an enterprise culture which favours initiatives, enterprise creation, productivity, environmental consciousness, quality, good labour and industrial relations, and adequate social practices which are equitable. The following should be considered:

1) pursuing the development of entrepreneurial attitudes, through the system and programmes of education, entrepreneurship and training linked to job needs and the attainment of economic growth and development, with particular emphasis being given to the importance of good labour relations and multiple vocational and managerial skills needed by small and medium-sized enterprises;

2) seeking, through appropriate means, to encourage a more positive attitude towards risk-taking and business failure by recognizing their value as a learning experience, while at the same time recognizing their impact on both entrepreneurs and workers;

3) encouraging a process of lifelong learning for all categories of workers and entrepreneurs;

4) designing and implementing, with full involvement of the organizations of employers and workers concerned, awareness campaigns to promote respect for
a) the rule of law and workers' rights, better working conditions, higher productivity and improved quality of goods and services; b) entrepreneurial role models, and award schemes, taking due account of the specific needs of women and disadvantaged and marginalized groups.

The main characteristics that influence the labour market and the entrepreneurship situation in a country are:

• enterprise culture,
• institutional context,
• policy framework,
• outreach of the social network,
• education and skills level,
• enterprise promotion,
• strength of the economy and its sectors

Socio-Economic Context by Category of Countries

Industrialized Countries

The policy of industrialized countries favoured in general market economy and private sector development:
These countries are characterized by the following nine features: (1) a high-tech, (2) export-oriented production sector, and (3) a large service sector—both dominated by private enterprises of medium and small size. Agriculture in terms of employment is insignificant.
(4) The social protection and labour market measures are well developed. (5) Reduction of unemployment has highest political priority. (6) Unemployed persons can obtain financial support, benefit from retraining measures, and apply for support and loans for start-ups, etc. (7) Active labour market interventions facilitate the re-integration of unemployed into the labour market. Social transfer payments can even be higher than minimum wages. (8) Education and skills level is high due to compulsory school attendance, a large high school and university system, and a modern vocational training system. (9) Entrepreneurship development and enterprise creation is facilitated in many ways. There is buying power for goods and services and a variety of promotion programmes and training facilities through Chambers of Commerce, Chambers of Crafters, business associations, government-subsidized programmes, start-up financing

and many others. There is also tough competition that prevents many potential starters from taking the risk of becoming an entrepreneur.

Developing Countries

On the other hand, developing countries are characterized by the following five features: (1) extreme poverty, (2) high demographic pressure, (3) dominant agriculture sector and (4) little integration in the global economy, and (5) corruption.

Schooling is not generalized and vocational training centres are insufficient in numbers and quality. In most countries like Nigeria, youth unemployment can be classified into two groups: primary school leavers not selected for secondary school education and secondary school leavers who are unable to gain employment in the formal sector.

Importance of Entrepreneurship Education

Entrepreneurship education stimulates young people to think about entrepreneurship and the role of the business community in economic and social development. Students also get an opportunity to analyse the changes taking place in their countries and are encouraged to consider self-employment as a career choice.

National Government Policy

Nigeria has not really created clear and comprehensive policy frameworks to promote youth entrepreneurship and self-employment. Instead, we find elements of education and training policy at different levels as they relate to the world of work and the world of business. Increasingly, the concern of governments is to foster a spirit of enterprise and promote self-employment as an important part of their efforts to reduce youth unemployment.

Government should design awareness-raising programmes at primary- and secondary-school level designed to familiarize pupils with the philosophy of entrepreneurship by developing beliefs, behaviours and motivation that will have a long-term effect; they are expected to exert a positive influence on enterprise culture. Such programmes integrated in vocational training curricula and university courses will prepare the ground for entrepreneurship as a career option.

Enterprise education refers to the learning directed towards developing in young people those skills, competencies, understandings, and attributes which equip them to be innovative and to identify, create, initiate, and successfully manage personal, community, business and work opportunities, including working for themselves.

The University of Durham (United Kingdom) suggests that there are a number of different objectives and outcomes that can be achieved.

- Firstly, and most universally, enterprise education can be a path towards developing enterprising skills, behaviours and attitudes through any curriculum subject at every phase of education to provide a wider preparation for autonomy in life, including work, family or leisure.

- Secondly, it can provide insight into and help young people understand *about* the entrepreneurial and business development processes through business education in secondary schools and in further and higher education, allowing young people to work more effectively in a flexible labour market economy or working in a small business.
- Finally, it can develop awareness of, and capability for, setting up a business now or sometime in the future. This approach can be used in vocational and professional education.

An important part of stimulating the imagination in this way is the process of "learning-by-doing", or experiential learning, which nurtures the personal qualities, characteristics and attitudes of successful entrepreneurs. The learner reflects on personal experience and relates it to the theoretical aspects, creating a dynamic relationship. Repeated cycles of learning from classroom experiences are the essence of the entrepreneurial way of learning.

Developing countries

Entrepreneurship courses at university level are much less widespread in developing countries. While the content of the courses which do exist is usually similar to that on offer in Western countries, the sophistication of the tools varies according to the resources available.

Youth Programmes for Specific Target Groups

At-risk and Marginalized Youth

The Youth Outreach Programme (YOP) in Australia, for instance, recruits and trains local mentors to work intensively on a one-on-one basis with young people to help them identify their own potential, build personal and career goals, and develop links to support services. Special consultants work with young people on individual problems when needed, providing drug and alcohol counseling.

In Azerbaijan, the Center for Youth Starting Business was established in February 2001. The main goal is to bring young people together and assist them in acquiring a basic knowledge of business before actually launching their own venture. In South Africa, the Centre for Education and Enterprise Development (CEED) is a not-for-profit organization established in response to the problems faced by black youth in the communities south of Durban, which have minimal resources for young people. Programmes initially focused on life skills and vocational guidance. However, as the needs of youth in both the community and the broader environment changed, CEED shifted its focus to unemployment issues in urban areas. In an attempt to increase young people's access to training and the SME sector, CEED has established branches in the Durban Metro Region, in the Ugu Region and Uthungulu Region.

In Nigeria, the National Directorate was established by the National Directorate of Employment Act 1989. Its organs are the Director-general (Sections 6 to 8), the Board (Section 3), the National Advisory Council (Section 4) and the State Advisory

Committees (Section 5). The objectives of the Directorate are not directly aimed at women, but can serve women's interests. According to Section 2, they must:

a. design and implement programmes to combat mass unemployment;
b. articulate policies aimed at developing work programmes with labour intensive potential;
c. obtain and maintain a data bank on employment and vacancies in the country, with a view to acting as a clearing house to link job seekers with vacancies in collaboration with other government agencies; and
d. implement any other policy as may be laid down, from time to time, by the Board.

Know about Business (KAB)

Entrepreneurship Education in Vocational and Technical Training
The specific objectives of any entrepreneurship education in vocational and technical training package are to:

- create awareness of enterprise and self-employment as a career option for beneficiaries in vocational and technical training institutions;
- develop positive attitudes towards enterprise and self-employment;
- provide knowledge and practice of the required attributes and challenges for starting and operating a successful enterprise, particularly a small business;
- prepare beneficiaries to work productively in small- and medium-sized enterprises and more generally for an environment in which formal, full-time wage employment may be scarce or unavailable.

Experience from the Philippines on introducing entrepreneurship education at university level revealed the following difficulties:

a) *Motivating students to enroll in the course:* The students perceived that faculty members do not themselves have the entrepreneurial spirit and that they are talking only from the books. Also, students had a negative attitude towards entrepreneurship education. They stated that entrepreneurship is not a profession; therefore, it should not be taken as a course in college/university.

b) *Lack of entrepreneurship faculty:* Faculty members know the subject matter of entrepreneurship and some of the techniques, but their techniques are also limited because they have repeatedly used the same techniques over the years. There is a lack of creativity and innovation on the part of the faculty.

c) *Lack of support from the faculty:* Entrepreneurship faculty members were full-time faculty members and were handling other subjects. They had no time to devote to the practical aspect of the entrepreneurship courses, such as developing materials. There was very strong dependence on textbooks, which were patterned after the American style of teaching.

d) *Lack of commitment of faculty:* Few faculty members volunteer to undergo training-of-trainers courses.

e)   *Sequencing of entrepreneurship curriculum:* There was a need to look at the totality of subjects in order to determine the required prior skills and knowledge. For example, it was found that natural science subjects were offered when students were already in their third or fourth years. Students should have already followed their natural science courses before business planning and environmental scanning sessions, which consider environmental factors.

f)   *Contents of the subjects were not clearly designed:* Model syllabi were copied from textbooks and reference books.

g)   *Lack of teaching materials.*

h)   *Lack of capital to assist the students in starting a small business.*

In Nigeria, while these problems are present, a much bigger problem, "corruption" (*fardunism*), has negatively affected entrepreneurship education.

Recommendations

Wider Policy Environment for Youth Entrepreneurship and Enterprise Creation

There is no single pathway or approach and no single intervention that can be expected to deal with the whole range of problems facing young people. Though not all the students will eventually move to self-employment, the projects are effective in providing a better understanding of enterprise culture, in supplying students with skills for use in companies, and in improving their knowledge of enterprise and entrepreneurship through practice.

Creating favourable conditions for small enterprise development among young people begins with assessing the incentives and disincentives that economic policies may create, perhaps unintentionally, for smaller businesses. Small enterprises must be able to make a profit and be competitive. Education and training programmes should also be reformed in a way that creates a system of incentives to encourage the private sector to provide mentoring for young entrepreneurs as well as training and skills acquisition opportunities for young people.

Incentives might include tax breaks or tax holidays, wage subsidies, preferential purchase agreements, etc. Entrepreneurs and others from the business community (including university alumni) should be encouraged to have a broad involvement in teaching, as guest lecturers, subjects for case studies, mentors, and even entrepreneurs-in-residence.

Finally, in some countries, an area-based approach to youth entrepreneurship has been receiving particular attention from policy makers. In this context, entrepreneurship programmes at different levels of education would be more closely integrated into broader development frameworks and training strategies. For example, in transition countries, links can be established between vocational education reforms and the PHARE and TACIS Programmes.

Secondary level: Although not everybody can be an entrepreneur, certainly teachers, school administrators, staff and students can be trained to display the characteristics of successful entrepreneurs, so that the ultimate result is an enterprising school environment.

University level: Within universities, there are possibilities for developing entrepreneurship courses for graduate and postgraduate students in the science, engineering and medical faculties. However, moving towards a more entrepreneurial focus within conventional business school structures can encounter some obstacles, particularly the lack of lecturers with real experience of working as businesspeople in the commercial sector.

References

Haftendorn, Klaus, and Carmela Salzano. (2003) *Facilitating Youth Entrepreneurship.* Geneva: International Labour Office.

Herbig, P. A., and J. C. Miller. (1992) Culture and Technology: Does the traffic move in both directions? *Journal of Global Marketing,* 6(3), 75–104.

Chapter 24

THE RELEVANCE OF SKILLS AND KNOWLEDGE TO SUCCESSFUL ENTREPRENEURS IN NIGERIA

Oluwale, B. A.

Introduction

Entrepreneurship has been acclaimed by scholars as a veritable tool for economic growth and development. It is also a tested tool for creation of wealth and taming the dragon of unemployment in a developing country like Nigeria.

Statt (2004) defines skill as a learned response, often as the result of specific training, which affords someone the ability to perform a particular task and achieve a particular goal. Skill can be acquired through formal education or on-the-job experience (Onwualu 2010). While skill is an important ingredient to any entrepreneurial endeavour, it has been observed (Onwualu and Obasi 2008; Bassi *et al.* 2008) that most entrepreneurs within the small and medium enterprise (SME) subgroup consider acquisition of skills through formal training as a waste of time. However, entrepreneurship skills are business skills which individuals acquire to enable them to function effectively in the turbulent business environment (Ademiluyi 2007; Folahan and Omoriyi 2006), and they are often acquired through learning and practice (Erhurun 2007).

Knowledge is of tremendous importance to the growth of any firm. Day-to-day knowledge is derived from insights that individuals gain from their occupation, job routines, networks, and life experiences, and this is a resource that entrepreneurs exploit to their own advantage (Hayek 1945; Venkataraman 1997; Alvarez and Barney 2000).

The dichotomy of thought with respect to entrepreneurship education often arose because of the notion that entrepreneurs are born (McClelland 1961; Brockhaus 1982), whereas others believe that entrepreneurship can be learnt. Coulson-Thomas (2003) observes that knowledge can exist and be expressed in many forms, such as facts, attitudes, opinions, issues, values, theories, reasons, processes, policies, priorities, rules, cases, approaches, models, tools, methodologies, relationships, risks and probabilities. Coulson-Thomas (2003) submits that different people may vary in their perceptions of what constitutes or represents knowledge. Professionals, for example, tend to value practical know-how that can be used in client relationships, and stress the sensitivity, awareness and familiarity that often arise from experience. Academics, on the other hand, may focus on theoretical understanding, and value acceptable addition to what a peer group regards as being known about a particular topic.

Required Skills for Entrepreneurship

Many scholars have proposed several skills that are necessary for successful entrepreneurship. McClure (2001) notes that many skills (at least 50) are required and posits that first-time entrepreneurs are often unfamiliar with most of them (see Table 1).

He asserts that the most important "prime movers" for the entrepreneur are organizational growth, market creation and product development.

Table 1

Accounting	Management skills
Accounting controls	Manufacturing resources planning
Administrative skills	Manufacturing system layout
Assertiveness	Marketing skills
Communication skills	Leadership skills
Computer network management	Motivation and image-building
Corporate governances	Multimedia techniques
Crises planning and disaster recovery	Negotiating skills
Customer service	Office management
Dealing with lawyers	Operational planning
Distribution management	Organizational skills
Engineering design	Procurement and supplier management
Environmental risk management	Productive meetings
Facilities management	Project management
Financial management	Quality control methods
Group doctrine leadership	Research and development management
Human resources management	Sales force management
Information systems deployment	Selling
Insurance and risk management	Shop floor execution and control
Intellectual property	Strategic planning
International relations	Taxes
Internet access and use	Team building
Inventory management	Training
Investor relations	Treasury management
Languages	Valuation of companies

It has been stressed that an entrepreneur requires at least three management skills (Aluko *et al.* 2007; Ugokwe and Itua 2006). These are technical skill, human skill and conceptual skill. Two others attributed to Iyayi (2006) are negotiation and time management skills. These are expanded further below.

(a) Technical Skill

Technical skill refers to the ability to use specialized knowledge and to requirements and techniques necessary to carry out a task, process or procedure. This can be acquired through education, apprenticeship, training and experience. Two major sources of technical skill are explicit and tacit knowledge. Polanyi (1966) describes tacit knowledge as what individuals know but cannot or have not yet expressed as knowledge that is shared and diffused. Geisler (2007) defines tacit knowledge as the set of cognitive skills that the individual possesses, while Mehra (2003) describes it as unmodified knowledge, which is passed from generation to generation. Thus, tacit knowledge is subjective and experience-based (Nonaka *et al.* 2003). It is highly personal and is deeply rooted in action and in an individual's commitment to a specific context (Nonaka 1991).

Brandon (2002) notes in respect of Henry Ford, the man who revolutionized mass production of automobile in America:

> Although he had no formal engineering training, he knew intuitively, though without being able to explain it precisely or mathematically, why this thickness of metal, that distribution of weight or tensile strength would work.

It is pertinent to note here that Ford had a background of familiarity with farm equipment and also had experience at the Edison Company before starting his own business.

(b) Human Skill

Human skill is very important for successful entrepreneurship in Nigeria. The entrepreneur has to work with and through people; therefore, he must demonstrate effective leadership, build interpersonal relationships, and establish good rapport with both workers and customers. He must be able to motivate workers to achieve set goals within the spectrum of available resources and available time limits. In essence, the entrepreneur must be able to bring the best out of his workers at all times.

(c) Conceptual Skill

Conceptual skill refers to the analytical, creative and intuitive talents of the entrepreneur (Higgings 1994; Ugokwe and Itua 2006). It is the ability to understand the complexities of the overall organization (Aluko *et al.* 2007). Thus the entrepreneur must have the "big picture" of the entire organization, knowing where he fits in and where others do too.

(d) Negotiation Skill

The importance of negotiation skills for the Nigerian entrepreneur cannot be overemphasized. This is so because prices of goods and services are not strictly fixed even in the same industry. The entrepreneur must therefore be adept at haggling to obtain good value for his money. Iyayi (2006) gives four reasons why negotiation skills are important to the entrepreneur:

i. The business owner experiences a sense of personnel satisfaction in the agreement that he or she strikes with others. Thus the business owner is spared the agony of "feeling like a fool".
ii. The business owner is able to gain access to resources and facilities that would otherwise not have been available.
iii. The business is able to operate at lower costs than would otherwise have been the case.
iv. The business owner is better able to plan for contingencies and uncertainty.

In addition to the above, since resources are usually scarce (especially financial resources), negotiation helps to plug unnecessary wastes and leads to an optimum deployment of financial resources.

Types of Negotiation

Two types of negotiations are proposed by Iyayi (2006). These are (i) win-lose negotiation and (ii) win-win negotiation.

(i)   Win-lose negotiation

According to Iyayi (2006), in a win-lose negotiation, each party attempts to maximize his/her gain at the expense of the other party. The resultant effect is that one party goes home satisfied while the other goes home disgruntled. The win-lose negotiation is characterized by mutual distrust as each party tries to exploit the other's weakness. This kind of scenario is not healthy for a green entrepreneur who is still trying to find his/her footing in his/her new venture. Whether he wins or loses, he may not be able to do business with the other party in the future as a result of distrust.

(ii)   Win-win Negotiation

In a win-win negotiation, both parties reach a solution that benefits both of them. The gains of one party do not translate to the loss of the other (Iyayi 2006). Since there is no aggrieved party, the two sides build trust and can become partners in business for a long time after. This is healthy for an up-and-coming entrepreneur who thereby gradually builds up his network.

(e) Time Management Skill

Time is the only resource that both the rich and the poor, the wise and the foolish have equally. The difference, however, is the way and manner each utilizes his/her time. While one person may sit down to watch movies six hours daily, another may spend the same time creating a new product, process or concept. For the former, if he/she spends 60 years watching movies, he/she has succeeded in spending 15 years of his/her lifetime on that alone. In a nation such as Nigeria, where tradition permits visitors to come and go anytime, the budding entrepreneur must act wisely. Wisdom demands that the entrepreneur gets his priorities right. Iyayi (2006) identifies four sets of activities from which the entrepreneur must choose: (i) urgent and important; (ii) urgent but not important; (iii) not urgent but important; (iv) not urgent, not important.

He suggests that priority be given to numbers (i) and (ii), which represent crisis situations and planning/relationship-building respectively. This is moreso because a new entrepreneur may find that he/she has a lot of time on his/her hands at the beginning of the business since the business is still tender. But such time should be reinvested into creating a solid base for the business through strategic network building and establishment of a strong market.

(f)   Industry and Customer Knowledge

The entrepreneur needs to demonstrate a good knowledge of practical issues that pertain to the particular industry in which he/she operates and the customers he/she serves. According to Stokes, Wilson and Mador (2010), an in-depth knowledge of an industry can provide an entrepreneur with many opportunities for innovation. Similarly, they argue that a good knowledge of customers can serve as a source of opportunity to meet unfulfilled needs, trigger new ideas and even create new products. If an entrepreneur is aware of his/her customers' needs, then he/she can package the products or service to specifically meet that need, thus creating a niche in the market.

(g)   Networking

Networking is a veritable tool that every entrepreneur must exploit. The aim of networking is to establish linkages with people, firms and institutions for mutual benefits. Through this, entrepreneurs meet prospective partners, employees, customers and sponsors (Stokes, Wilson and Mador 2010). This leads to prompt location of resources which the entrepreneur can attract to his own enterprise.

Stokes, Wilson and Mador (2010) identify five characteristics that entrepreneurs who network successfully possess:

i.   They have something to say about themselves, their roles and their venture. People want to hear about personal details.

ii.   They think about what they are looking for, whether it is partners, help, finances, information or customers.

iii.   They network with an open mind—they never know what will happen, who they will meet, or what they will discover.

iv.   They stay interested in other people—those are the source of ideas, money, resources and help of all sorts.

v.   They think about what they have to offer—networking is a reciprocal activity, and people they help give information to or otherwise support will be likely to help them in return.

(h)   Recognition of Opportunity

An opportunity is a recognized need in the market place, to which an entrepreneur has a response or solution (Stokes, Wilson and Mador 2010). It is the starting point for entrepreneurial activity (Politis 2005). Recognizing the need, understanding it, and coming up with a feasible means of dealing with it implies a certain kind of knowledge. This kind of knowledge is likely to come from theoretical learning, but for entrepreneurs it often has its roots in the experience of accessing and evaluating previous opportunities (Stokes, Wilson and Mador 2010).

(i)   Accepting and Handling Challenges

A new venture or product may come with a myriad of problems or liabilities. The entrepreneur must accept and deal with these challenges as they come to the fore. Some of these challenges, as noted by Stokes, Wilson and Mador (2010), include finding customers, establishing positive cash-flow, and developing lasting competitive advantage. These may be informed by theoretical learning, but the experience of actually undertaking these activities provides the substantive lessons on which entrepreneurs build their knowledge base.

(j)   Listening Skills

The entrepreneur needs to develop effective listening skills. He or she must be able to discern and understand what people (customers, employees, suppliers, etc.) are saying or are not saying, thereby taking prompt action. While reports, e-mails and other sources of official information are important, the most crucial information may not come through these channels but by direct contact with people—from their comments, complaints, suggestions, and even commendations.

(k) Communication Skills

Communication skills are a crucial factor to the success of the entrepreneur. Communicating well requires the entrepreneur to have a very clear idea of his/her concept or product. This is important because people cannot buy into an idea, concept or product that is foggy to the entrepreneur. The entrepreneur may be required to present his/her idea in oral and/or written form. Whatever the case, the end result should be to sell his/her ideas and persuade others to buy into them. These may be potential financiers, bankers, friends, or even family members, who can provide the much-needed help for the business take-off or expansion.

(l) Ability to Access Capital

One of the most difficult problems in the new venture creation is obtaining finances, especially in a country like Nigeria. For the entrepreneur, available financing needs to be considered from the perspective of debt *versus* equity and using internal *versus* external funds (Hisrich, Peters and Shepherd 2008). There are various sources from which capital can be accessed. Some of these are personal savings, family and friends, commercial banks, private investors, bank of industry, etc. However, the entrepreneur must be able to develop a good business proposal with convincing cash-flows that can serve as an attraction to financiers.

References

Ademiluyi, F. L. (2007) Business Competencies needed for effective entrepreneurship as perceived by fresh graduates. *Business Education Journal* 69 (1), 18–28.

Aluko, M., O. Odugbesan, G. Gbadamosi, L. Osuagwu. (2007) *Business Policy Strategy.* Lagos: Longman Nigeria Plc.

Alvarez, S., and J. Barney. (2000) Entrepreneurial capabilities: A Resource-based View. In Meyer, G. D., and K. A. Heppard, (eds.), *Entrepreneurship as Strategy: Competing on the Entrepreneurial Edge.* Thousand Oaks, CA: Sage Publishing.

Bassai, S. Y., P. A. Onwualu, S. C. Obasi, and S. Suleiman. (2008) The Role of Clustering in Fostering Innovation and Competitiveness in Industries: A case study of Jabi Metal Fabrication Cluster in Abuja, Nigeria.

Brandon, R. (2002) *Automobile: How the car changed life.* London: Macmillan.

Brockhaus, R. H. (1982) The Psychology of the entrepreneur. In Kent, C. A., D. L. Sexton, and K. H. Vesper (eds.), *Encyclopedia of Entrepreneurship.* Englewood Cliffs, NJ: Prentice Hall, pp. 39–71.

Coulson-Thomas, C. (2003) *The Knowledge Entrepreneur: how your business can create, manage and profit from intellectual capital.* London: Kogan Page Limited.

Erhurun, H. E. O. (2007) Skills acquisition: A tool for Youth Empowerment for economic growth and development. *Journal of Business and Management Studies* 1 (2), 116–125.

Folahan, S. A., and J. O. Omoriyi. (2006) Entrepreneurial Development Prospects for the Modern Society. *Business Education Journal* 5(2), 59–71.

Geisler, E. (2007) *Knowledge and Knowledge Systems: Learning from the Wonders of the Mind.* Hershey, PA: IGI Global.

Hayek, F. A. (1945) The use of knowledge in society. *American Economic Review* 35, 519–530.

Higgins, J. (1994) *The Management Challenge* (2nd ed.). New York: Macmillan.

Hisrich, D. H., M. P. Peters, and D. A. Shepherd. (2008) *Entrepreneurship* (7th Ed.). Boston: McGraw Hill/Irwin.

Iyayi, F. (2006) Negotiation and time management skills for the small business owner. In Inegbenebor, A. U. (ed.), *The Fundamentals of Entrepreneurship.* Lagos: Malthouse Press Limited.

McClelland, D. C. (1961) *The Achieving Society.* Princeton, NJ: Van Nostrand.

McClure, P. F. (2001) *New Entrepreneur's Guidebook: Leading Your Venture to Business Success.* Canterbury, Kent: Financial World Publishing.

Mehra, K. (2003) Regional Innovations and the Economic Competitiveness in India. In Shavinina, L. V. (ed.), *The International Handbook on Innovation.* Oxford: Elsevier Science, pp. 904–914.

Nonaka, I. (1991) The knowledge-creating company. *Harvard Business Review* 69: 96–104.

———, K. Sasaki, and M. Ahmed. (2003): Continuous Innovation in Japan: The Power of Tacit Knowledge. In Shavinina, L. V. (ed.), *The International Handbook on Innovation.* Oxford: Elsevier Science, pp. 882–889.

Onwualu. P. A., and S. C. Obasi. (2008) A Raw Materials Processing Cluster Programme for Nigeria: Concept, Structures and Implementation Strategies. A paper presented at the Global Competitiveness Conference, Cape Town, South Africa, October.

———. (2010) Cluster Development as a Strategy for Promoting Entrepreneurship and Technological Skills for Socio-Economic Development. A Keynote Address presented at The South-East Zone Investors' Forum/ 1st Abia Technology Entrepreneurship Fair, Umuahia, Nigeria, August 15–17. In *Promoting Entrepreneurship and Technological Skills for Socio-Economic Development.* Proceedings of the 1st Abia Technology Fair/Raw Materials Research and Development Council South-East Zonal Investors' Forum, pp. 58–71.

Polanyi, M. (1966) *The Tacit Dimension.* London: Routledge and Paul Kegan.

Politis, D. (2005) The Process of Entrepreneurial Learning: A conceptual framework. *Entrepreneurship: Theory and Practice* 29(4): 399-424.

Statt, D. A. (2004) *The Routledge Dictionary of Business Management.* London: Routledge.

Stokes, D., N. Wilson, and M. Mador. (2010) *Entrepreneurship.* Andover, Hampshire, UK: Cengage Learning EMEA.

Ugokwe, F. N., and G. E. Itua. (2006) Negotiation and time management skills for small business owners. In Inegbenebor, A. U. (ed.), *The Fundamentals of Entrepreneurship.* Lagos: Malthouse Press Limited.

Venkataraman, S. (1997) The distinctive domain of entrepreneurship research. In Katz, J. A. (ed.), *Advances in Entrepreneurship Firm Emergence and Growth*. Greenwich, CT: JAI, pp. 119–138.

Chapter 25

GLOBALIZATION, ENTREPRENEURSHIP AND THE NIGERIAN ECONOMIC GROWTH

Egbuwalo, M. O.

Introduction

This paper endeavours to explain the concepts of globalization, entrepreneurship and economic growth. It establishes the nexuses between globalization and entrepreneurship, and between entrepreneurship and economic growth. It highlights some of the challenges and prospects of globalization and of entrepreneurship in the Nigerian economy.

The paper is structured as follows:
Section 2 deals with conceptual issues, while Section 3 deals with the entrepreneurship / globalization/growth relationships. Section 4 concerns itself with recommendations and conclusions.

Conceptual Issues

For a thorough understanding of this study, certain concepts as contained in the literature must be brought to the fore here for explanation.

Economic Growth

Economic growth is very essential in the life of any nation. Dwivedi (2009) asserted that economic growth means a sustained increase in per capita national output or net national output over a long period of time. It implies that the rate of increase in total output must be greater than the rate of population growth. If population and output grow at the same rate, there will be no increase in per-capita income, and there will be no improvement in the general standard of living despite increase in output. Such a growth is considered to be as good as stagnation in the economy. On the other hand, increase in per capita income as a result of a decrease in population faster than the decrease in output amounts to general decay in the economy; there is no growth despite increase in per capita income. Thus, economic growth implies a considerable and sustained increase in per capita income with or without increase in population. It is a prerequisite for economic development, which Husted and Melvin (1993) defined as the achievement of a quality of life for the average citizen of a country that is comparable to that enjoyed by the average citizen of a country with a modern economy.

Globalization

Globalization is not a new word in economic literature. International contacts and exchanges are not new. Since the beginning of history, inter-country movements, travels, trade and migration have been taking place. Even in the ancient and medieval world, international trading companies were formed, promoted, and financed by states, governments, and groups of individuals to explore, and at times pillage and conquer, distant and less privileged communities and countries for the benefit of the more privilege ones (Aluko 2003) .

The genesis of globalization is traceable to Marco Polo in the 13th century. The differences between the "old" and the "new" globalization are in the rate, depth, and intensity with which global markets are being penetrated and integrated, while the hands of finance capital seem to reign supreme more than before. The expansion of trade, the diffusion of technology, extensive migration, and the cross-fertilization of diverse cultures and ideas are common characteristics of the two periods (Ndiyo and Ebong 2003).

The word "globalization" is a victim of multitudinous definition. It does not have a unique definition that enjoys universal acceptance. Many scholars have defined the word in various ways.

It is firmly believed by Carbaugh (2006) that globalization is the process of greater interdependence among countries and their citizens. It consists of increased integration of products and resource markets across nations via trade, immigration and foreign investment, i.e., via international flows of goods and services, of people, and of investments such as equipment, factories, stocks and bonds. It also includes non-economic elements such as culture, and the environment.

Simply put, globalization is political, technological, and cultural as well as economic.

Achoja and Ayaefe (2010) believed globalization to be a process of increasing integration of nation states into the world civilization. Globalization encourages the weakening of territorial boundaries and barriers of nations in various areas of human endeavours, via political, ideological, socio-economic and cultural spheres. But it does not permit the break-down of international borders.

Globalization promotes the liberalization and identification of international linkages in agriculture, trade, finance, market, production, research, transportation, energy, medicine, education, politics, and culture (Babangida 1992)..

In a similar vein, Osuji (2003) believes that globalization is the revolution in communication and information technology, trade liberalization, formation of regional organizations, such as the Economic Community of West African States (ECOWAS), etc., and high mobility of capital and labour. All these have contributed to reduce the whole world to a global village, wherein what happens in one part of the globe is immediately transmitted to other parts of the globe.

Nexus Between Globalization and Economic Growth

The nexus between globalization and economic growth can be examined by looking at two major channels of globalization: trade and capital flows.

Trade-Growth Relationship

Economic theory is replete with the ways by which international trade can catalyse economic growth of a country. Husted and Melvin (1993), Krugman and Obstfeld (2001), Bhatia (2006), and Jhingan (2008) were unanimous in saying that the classical economists argued in favour of international trade as a catalyst to economic growth. Division of labour and specialization, both at the domestic and international levels, results in greater productivity and output.

Access to a larger market, as a result of international trade, allows countries to specilize in their areas of comparative advantages, which results in increased productivity, as countries take advantage of economies of scale in production.

International trade can also promote growth by allowing countries access to better technologies,for instance,through the importation of capital goods (World Bank 2002). Increased competition arising from trade liberalization may spur innovation and growth as firms strive to retain or possibly increase their market shares. This is likely to be more important for developed countries that are already using the latest technologies rather than for less developed countries that are still trying to catch up. Technology spill-overs, arising from the importation of capital goods or the greater diffusion of knowledge occasioned by trade openness, may, however, provide developing countries with the opportunities for rapid catch-up growth (Grossman and Helpman 1994; Alonso-Gamo *et al*. 1997). In view of the wide technological gaps existing between the developed and developing countries, Obioman and Osanyintuyi (2003) submitted that the potential for technological catch-up is great.

However, many factors affect the ability of less developed countries to benefit from trade in the ways aforementioned. One of such factors is a country's geographic characteristics, such as its population density and whether or not it is land-locked. A land-locked state and low population density usually impose high transport and communication costs on a country, making its products less competitive in the world market (Ajayi 2001). Poor and inadequate infrastructure also result in high transport and communication costs, making a country less competitive in the world market (World Bank 2000).

Also the nature of the product in which a country has comparative advantages, depending mostly on its factor endowments, contributes to the competitiveness or otherwise of a country's product in the world market. Not all products have the potential for promoting economic growth. For example, primary products have less growth potential than manufactured products. There is less scope for innovation, product diversification and economies of scale in production of agricultural products and in natural resources extraction than there is in manufactured goods. Thus, for countries or regions whose comparative advantage lies in primary products, specialization may fail to promote the growth, especially in the long-run. This is the kind of dilemma facing most developing nations (Grossman and Helpman 1994).

The use of better technologies and reaping the benefit of technology spill-overs often require the existence of a skilled and educated workforce. Where these are lacking, as they are in most African countries, international trade may fail to provide the expected growth benefits. However, globalization has become an engine of economic growth in countries that globalize their economies wisely.

Capital Flows, Foreign Direct Investment and Economic Growth.

Substantial capital flows can promote economic growth in three major ways. In the first place, capital flows provide resources for investment in developing countries. In developing countries, which are known for low and inadequate savings rates, the inflow of capital would complement domestic savings, permitting higher levels of investment and raising growth rates.

Apart from providing capital for investment in less developed countries (LDCs), foreign direct investment (FDI) promotes increased productivity and economic growth through the transfer of technology as well as management and organization skills (Ajayi 2001).

In addition, increased capital flow into LDCs can promote financial sector development, which is beneficial to growth in many ways. Savings provided by financial intermediaries like savings mobilization, projects evaluation, risks management, monitoring managers, and facilitating transactions, and others, are important for technological innovation and economic development (King and Levine 1993).

Several factors affect the ability of a country to successfully attract capital and FDI flows. Usually, capital flows to places with the highest returns, which in turn is determined by a country's growth process. Ajayi (2001) pointed out that other important requirements include a stable and predictable economic and political environment, sound macroeconomic policies, well-developed financial markets, transparent laws, good governance, fair competition, and a reliable legal system. Where these factors are lacking, capital flows are unlikely to accrue to such a region, even though it may have high rates of returns on investments.

The ability and desirability of capital inflows to promote economic growth is, however, affected by the volatility associated with such flows. As the East Asian financial crisis has shown (Frank and Bernanke 2001), capital can flow out as easily as it can flow in. The process of financial sector liberalization is usually accompanied by increased volatility in financial markets. Financial integration exposes a country to risk of financial markets bubbles, irrational behaviour, speculative attacks and crashes. Such a situation hampers growth.

The foregoing suggests that there is a need for developing countries to exercise caution with respect to financial markets integration. In this regard, Bhatia (2006) stressed that globalization can give rise to a massive boost in the economic growth of countries, but it carries with it some harmful spill-over effects. Countries all over the world, whether developed or less developed, have come to realize that it is expedient to eschew isolation and become more "open," "globalized," and "integrated" with the rest of the world, while at the same time protecting themselves against potential ill-effects of the process.

To say that FDI promotes economic growth is no longer in doubt. This submission is attested to by Table 1.

Table 25.1: FDI and the Growth in the Nigerian Real GDP: 1968-2008

Year	(1) Total FDI (#Million)	(2) % Increase	(3) Real GDP (#Million)	(4) % Increase
1968	1,021.4		2,543.8	
1978	2,863.2	180.3	29,212.4	1,048.4
1988	11,339.2	296.0	219,875.6	652.7
1998	152,409.6	1,244.1	310,860.1	41.4
2008	397,395.2	160.7	674,889.0	117.1

SOURCES: Central Bank of Nigeria, *Statistical Bulletin*, various issues

Table 25.1 takes a telegraphic view of FDI in Nigeria from 1968 to 2008 by dividing the 40-year period into intervals of 10 years each and calculating the percentage increase in FDI vis-à-vis the corresponding increases in the real GDP. Between 1968 and 1978, FDI recorded an increase of 180.3%, while the corresponding increase in real GDP was 1,048.4%. By 1988, FDI increased by 296.0%, while the corresponding increase in real GDP was 652.7%. By 1998, the increase in FDI was 1,244.1%, while the corresponding increase in real GDP within the period was 41.4%. Between 1998 and 2008, FDI experienced an increase of 160.7%, while the corresponding increase in real GDP was 117.1%. It should be noted that Column 2 was calculated from Column 1, while Column 4 was calculated from Column 3 by the author of this paper.

Globalization and the Nigerian Economy

Globalization in Nigeria has come with its challenges and prospects as highlighted here.

Challenges

The experience of most African countries, particularly Nigeria, is the dumping into their markets of goods and services from the developed economies and the raping of Africa's environment. The use of African countries, Nigeria inclusive, as dustbins for second-hand and inferior goods and for untouchable rubbish, such as radioactive waste, which richer and industrial countries are increasingly unwilling to keep in their countries, is a particularly destructive aspect of globalization. The developed and rich countries are increasingly taking advantage of the economic weakness of African countries by producing and dumping toxic or dangerous goods in Africa. Toxic waste had been occasionally deposited on the Nigerian soil (Aluko 2003).

Globalization tends to encourage policy interdependence while reducing national policy sovereignty, especially for developing countries, to which Nigeria is no exception. It makes the pursuit of independent monetary policy difficult. Coupled with these is the rapid spread of shocks and disturbances that is transmitted from one market to the other as a result of globalization.

The degree of adjustment to absorb such shocks and achieve macro-economic stability in developing countries is, however, less than that of developed nations. Globalization is also accompanied by production and consumption methods which are damaging to the environment; high unemployment, which is a source of diverse migration; as well as violence, which is damaging to the social sector (Annan-Yao 1996).

Globalization further constrains the ability of government to control domestic monetary and fiscal policies. When there is speculation against a currency like the Naira, the central bank of such a country—the central Bank of Nigeria (CBN) in this case—becomes helpless to curb the speculation because of international dependence occasioned by globalization. As economic power shifts from government to the hands of private operators in the face of globalization, fiscal resources of government are threatened, as government can neither tamper with any of its taxes indiscriminately nor spend it recklessly. Perceived or imagined excesses on the part of government can lead to tremendous capital flight, which will not be in the best interest of a nation like Nigeria.

Apart from the foregoing, the fact remains that there is no lender of the last resort at the international level. This makes international financial crisis very difficult to manage. Such a crisis cannot only submerge a whole nation like Nigeria, it can also submerge her trading partners.

At any time, there could be some internal domestic problems in a developing nation like Nigeria; the economy of such a country becomes weak during such a time. Again, this could be another cause of massive capital flight from the weak/developing country (Nigeria) to strong developed economies, leading to what has been dubbed "social Darwinism". Such capital flight is usually accompanied by the flight of other resources like human capital, thereby festering the problem of the weak and less developed country, and widening the yawning gap between the rich and poor countries (Pally 2002).

Prospects
The challenges of globalization not withstanding, it still brings some prospects to developing nations, Nigeria inclusive. Some of such prospects are hereby highlighted, as the literature is replete with such prospects.

Globalization promotes division of labor, specialization, trade and exchange (Edwards 1998). As far back as the 18th century, Adam Smith (1770) had demonstrated that specialization leads to increased output, *ceteris paribus*, and equitable distribution translates into improved standard of living.

Globalization reduces the cost of capital. Two factors are said to be responsible for the cost of capital. The first factor, information asymmetry (a situation where a firm's management has more information than the share holders), is removed. A share holder buying up the shares of a firm in another country will not be an ignoramus (and certainly the pension funds, mutual funds, insurance companies, and so on that buy on behalf of their clients are not ignorant). Such a share holder will be likely to have sufficient skill and information that enables him to monitor the firm in ways that local investors probably cannot (Adegbite 2003).

Apart from the removal of information asymmetry, under globalization the menology/ monophony power in the hands of few local providers of funds, who would have demanded a high premium for parting with their funds, is removed as well.

Thus, the cost of capital to the user is reduced as the rent that accrues to domestic suppliers of capital is reduced. With increased globalization and increased level of economic growth and development, a country will be able to steer capital into the most useful projects (Stulz 1999).

Globalization of capital is supposed to allow capital to move freely to places where it can get the maximum returns (Stulz 1999). Such free movement of capital provides relief to investors, who can now have access to funds beyond the frontiers of their countries of domicile and, hence, do not have to be constrained by the size of the investment.

There is also the prospect of free flow of essential technology that accompanies globalization, from which a country like Nigeria has benefited and will continue to benefit. This makes it possible for countries that would have remained developing to move out of the developing syndrome. With globalization of capital and technology, a country can develop financial market architecture, as firms have access to financial technology that enables them to raise funds using new securities and also allows them to manage their risks more effectively (Adegbite 2003).

Mobility of capital under globalization permits new knowledge and new technologies to yield new commodities and new services.

Long-term value is thus created and retrained for the world economy as a whole.

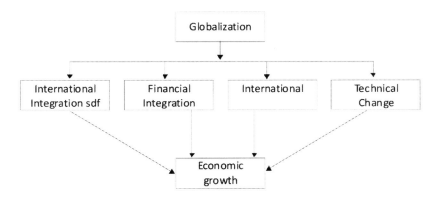

Fig: 25.1

Source: Husain Ishrat (2000) "Impact of Globalization on Poverty in Pakistan," Mahbubal Haque Human Development Centre, Islamabad, July 15

(a) The "hyperglobalists," who see globalization as a new epoch in human history that celebrates the rise of a single market and competition as the pillars of future human progress.
(b) The skeptics, for whom globalization is no new thing but has precedents in the last century, and as such is just another stage in the evolution of the capitalist system.
(c) The transformers, who assert that the processes of globalization are novel in their present form and are generating new patterns of exclusive and inclusion in global economic policies, and therefore governments will have to adapt to a world in which no clear distinction can be drawn between internal and external affairs.

They conclude with the conviction that the present globalization is a re-engineering of the power, functions and authority of national governments, and from that standpoint they reject both hyperglobalism and skepticism.

Entrepreneurship

Like the concept of "globalization", the concept of "entrepreneurship" is yet to have a concise and universally accepted definition. However, some operational definitions of the concept have emerged.

Hisrich and Peters (2002) defined entrepreneurship as the process of creating something new with value by devoting the necessary time and efforts, assuming the accompanying financial, psychic, and social risks, and receiving the resulting rewards of monetary and personal satisfaction and independence.

Entrepreneurship refers to the innovating, organizational, and risk-taking activities of individuals and firms that create new products and markets (Henderson and Poole 1991). It is sometimes considered a productive input, but it cannot be quantified the way labour and capital can. Entrepreneurship involves more than inventions; inventions do not bring themselves to markets. It takes the drive, business sense, and marketing skills of entrepreneurs to turn good inventions into good products and good ideas into good business practices. Entrepreneurial activities almost always involve risk; it is rarely clear ahead of time whether a new product will really work and whether consumers will accept it if it does work.

Lindaver (1977) conceived of entrepreneurs as the enterprising people who change economies by introducing new products and new ways of doing things. They are the ultimate sense of growth; for changes must occur if an economy is to have better product and increased production capabilities.

Schumpeter (1912) has drawn people's attention to the importance of entrepreneurs and made them the central figures in his explanation of economic development. He saw them as the special people who use the innovation and money of others to introduce the changes that make growth possible. If the innovations they introduce are successful, the economy grows and they make profit and capital gains. This lasts until their innovations are imitated by others so that their gains are competed away. According to him, their motivation is money, their legacy is growth, and their future is dim.

Jhingan (2002) espoused the view that an entrepreneur is an economic leader who possesses the ability to recognise opportunities for successful introduction of new commodities, new techniques, and new sources of supply; to assemble the necessary plant and equipment, management, and labour force; and organize them into a running concern. Whatever be the form of economic and political set-up of a country, entrepreneurship is essential for economic growth and development. The entrepreneur is the kingpin of any business enterprise, for without him, the wheels of the industry cannot move in the economy. The private entrepreneurship is an indispensable ingredient in economic development over the long period. The entrepreneur may be a highly educated, trained and skilled person or he may be an illiterate person, possessing high business acumen which others might be lacking.

Entrepreneurs (Frank and Bernanke 2001) are people who create new economic enterprises. Because of the new products, services, technological processes, and production methods they introduce, entrepreneurs are critical to a dynamic and healthy economy. In the late 19th and early 20th centuries, individuals like Henry Ford and Alfred Sloan (automobiles), Andrew Carnegie (steel), John D.Rockefeller (oil) and J. P. Morgan (finance) played central roles in the development of American industry. In Nigeria, somebody like Alico Dangote, a business mogul who has invested and diversified into the various sectors of the economy, is worthy of note. His like, such as Mike Adenuga (telecommunications), Femi Otedola (oil), and others, are doing a lot in the Nigerian economy by providing jobs for many Nigerians, and thereby contributing to the growth and development of the Nigerian economy.

This paper conceptualizes entrepreneurship as the conversion of intellectual resources of a person into production currency (money) without waiting for government jobs. The government must encourage this in Nigeria by providing the enabling environment for entrepreneurship to thrive and reduce poverty to the minimal level.

Challenges Facing Entrepreneurship Development in Nigeria

Suffice it to say that entrepreneurship development in Nigeria is faced with numerous challenges, some of which are mentioned here.

One of such challenges is political instability. For many years, the political environment of Nigeria has been unstable. There had been military coups and counter-coups, which did not encourage the development of entrepreneurship.

Similarly, even after Nigeria returned to democratic rule in 1999, the country has not enjoyed much peace as there have been ethnic militia threatening the government of the nation, like the MASOP in the Niger Delta, Buko Haram in the northern part of Nigeria, and others. This kind of situation does not encourage entrepreneurship development.

There is also the challenge of finance to fund entrepreneurship development. Nigeria is a poor nation, where the savings rate is very low; hence, capital formation is low. This hampers entrepreneurship development.

The dearth of plants and equipment also constitutes a challenge. No meaningful entrepreneurship development can take place if the necessary plants and equipment are not on the ground. These are very scarce in Nigeria as a result of financial constraints and the required logistics.

Inadequate technical knowledge to operate and maintain the necessary equipment when they are available hampers entrepreneurship development in Nigeria.

Competition in the world market is not in favour of Nigeria, since Nigerian industrial products may not meet international standards and as such cannot bring home much profit to sustain and boost the industries.

Prospects of Entrepreneurship Development in Nigeria

Nigerian governments have a lot to do in order to brighten the prospects of entrepreneurship development in Nigeria.

In the first place, the Nigerian legal system must be made to be investment friendly so as to encourage entrepreneurship development.

The financial institutions in Nigeria must bring down their interest rates so as to become investment friendly. This would encourage prospective entrepreneurs to seek financial accommodation from the commercial and micro-financial banks.

Islamic Banking, which has yet to find its feet in Nigeria, must be embraced because of its interest-free policy. If Nigerian entrepreneurs can take advantage of that, it will go a long way to encourage entrepreneurship development in Nigeria.

Tax holiday must be given to Nigerian entrepreneurs for the first five years of their existence. This will allow them to find their feet before they begin to carry the burden of tax payment; otherwise some of the young industries can become still-born industries.

Entrepreneurship/Globalization/Growth Nexuses

Relationships exist between entrepreneurship and globalization and economic growth. Entrepreneurship products result in the output of goods and services that are of value to human beings. Division of labour, which is cardinal to entrepreneurship production, gives room for specialization and greater output beyond local and domestic needs and, hence, exchange across international borders (international trade) which opens the way for globalization driven by information and communication technology (ICT).

The machinery and equipment required by the entrepreneurs for production are products of globalization, without which the Nigerian entrepreneur will not be able to produce anything. With machinery and equipment at the disposal of Nigerian entrepreneurs, they are able to produce something of value, thereby contributing to the growth and development of the Nigerian economy.

It is clear that symbiotic (bi-directional) relationships exist between entrepreneurship and globalization. Both of them contribute to the growth of an economy like Nigeria's—if they are well managed.

Recommendations and Concluding Remarks

Recommendations
In the light of the foregoing discussions, the following recommendations are presented.

(i)   Nigeria needs to be more cautious in her trade relations with the developed countries and ensure that Nigeria is not used as a dumping ground for products that are no more needed by the developed world.

(ii)   Nigeria is a monocultural economy, relying mainly on crude oil. Any negative shock experienced in the world oil market will have adverse effects on the Nigerian economy, so Nigeria should diversify her economy and no longer pay just lip-service to economic diversification.

(iii)   The political environment in Nigeria should be made more stable. No nation can benefit maximally from globalization without a stable political environment.

(iv)   Internal security in Nigeria must be strengthened for any investment to take place and be successful in Nigeria. The Boko Haram insurgency must be tackled head-on to ensure that peace reigns again in Nigeria.

(v)   Entrepreneurship development in the form of micro-, small-, and medium-scale enterprises (SMES) must be encouraged by providing an investment-friendly environment in the country.

(vi)   Financial support in form of soft loans should be placed at the disposal of Nigerian entrepreneurs.

(vii)   Efforts should be made by the government to ensure that Nigerian entrepreneurs are patronized so as to broaden the markets for their products.

(viii) The Federal Government of Nigeria has taken the right step in the right direction by introducing entrepreneurship education in our institutions of learning. This should be intensified and carefully monitored so that it can achieve the desired results.

Conclusion

Nigeria can benefit from globalization subject to the following conditions: ensuring a stable and secured political environment, fighting corruption with sincerity and reducing it to its lowest ebb, diversifying the economy away from oil, and creating job opportunities through entrepreneurship development. Globalization promotes entrepreneurship and both assist in growing the Nigerian economy. Financial infrastructure is very essential for the success of entrepreneurship in Nigeria. This should be made easy for entrepreneurs to access.

References

Achoja, F. O., and J. A. Eyaefe. (2010) Repositioning Women Entrepreneurs in a Depressed Global Economy: The Nigerian Experience. *Journal of Research in National Development* Vol. 8, No. 1, June, pp. 1–4.

Adegbite, E. O. (2003) Consolidating the Development of the Nigerian Financial Services Sector for Beneficial Globalization. *Nigerian Economic Society Selected Conference Papers*.

Ajyi, S. I. (2001) What Africa Needs to Do to Benefit from Globalization. *Finance and Development* 38 (4) December.

Alonso-Gamo, P., A. Fedlino, and S. Paris Horvitz. (1997) Globalization and Growth Prospects in Arab Countries. IMF Working Paper WP/97/125, September.

Aluko, Sam. (2003) Background to Globalization and Africa's Economic Development. *Nigerian Economic Society Selected Conference Papers*.

Annan-Yao, E. (1996) Economic Migration: Poverty, Unemployment, Income Differentials and Population. In Adepoju, A., and T. Hammar (eds.), *International Migration in and from Africa: Dimensions, Challenges and Prospects*. Dakar, Senegal: Population, Human Resources and Development in Africa; Stockholm: Centre for Research in International Migration and Ethnic Relations (CEIFO).

Babangida, I. B. (1992) Challenges of Democracy. A Lecture Delivered on 11th April, 1992 at the Institute of Governance and Social Research, Jos, Plateau State, Nigeria.

Bhatia, H. L. (2006) *International Economics*. New Delhi: Vikas Publishing House Pvt Ltd.

Carbaugh, R. J. (2006) *International Economics.* Mason, OH: Thomson South-Western Publishing.

Dwivedi, N. D. (2006) *Managerial Economics*. New Delhi: Vikas Publishing House Pvt Ltd.

Edwards, S. (1998) Openness, Productivity and Growth: What Do We Really Know? *Economic Journal* 108.

Frank, R., and M. Bernanke. (2001) *Principles of Economics*. New York: McGraw-Hill Higher Education.

Grossman, G., and E. Helpman. (1994) Endogenous Innovation in the Theory of Growth. *Journal of Economic Perspective* 8(1) Winter:23-44.

Henderson, J. V., and W. Poole. (1991) *Principles of Economics*. Lexington, MA: D.C. Heath and Company.

Hisrich, R. D., and M. P. Peters. (2002) *Entrepreneurship*. New York: McGraw-Hill Education.

Husain, I. (2000) Impact of globalization on poverty in Pakistan. A paper read by Ishrat Husain, Governor, Bank of Pakistan, at Mahbubal Haque Memorial Seminar, held at Mahbubal Haque Human Development Center, Islamabad, 15 July.

Husted, S., and M. Melvin. (1993) *International Economics*. New York: Harper Collins College Publisher.

Jhingan, M. L. (2002) *The Economics of Development and Planning*. New Delhi: Vrinda Publication Ltd.

———. (2008) *International Economics*. New Delhi: Vrinda Publication Ltd.

Keat, P. G., and P. K. Y. Young. (2006) *Managerial Economics*. Upper Saddle River, NJ: Pearson Education, Inc.

Krugman, P. R., and M. Obstfeld. (2006) *International Economics*. New York: Pearson Addison-Wesley.

Lindauer, J. (1977) *Economics: A Modern View*. Philadelphia, PA: W.B. Saunders Company.

Ndiyo, N. A., and F. S. Ebong. (2003) The Challenges of openness in developing economies: some empirical lessons from Nigeria. Nigerian Economic Society Selected Conference Papers.

Obioma, E. C., and T. A. Osanyintunyi. (2003) Globalization and Economic Growth. In *Globalization and Africa's Economic Development*. Nigerian Economic Society Selected Conference Papers.

Osuyi, A. (2003) Globalization and the Nigerian Economy. *The Sun*, Monday, 25 August, p. 17.

Palley, T. I. (2002) Soros on International Capital Markets and Developing Economies: Multiple Equilibra and the Role of Policy. Paper prepared for the Conference on Reforming the Reforms at the Brazil Center for Policy Studies, Rio de Janeiro, Brazil, November.

Schumpeter, J. A. (1912) *Theory of Economic Development*. Oxford, UK: Oxford University Press.

Smith, Adam. (1770) *The Wealth of Nations*. Reprinted London: Penguin Books, 1992.

Stulz, R. M. (1999) Globalization of Equity Markets and the Cost of Capital. Paper prepared for the SBF /NYSC Conference on Global Equity Market, Paris, France, October 20–22.

World Bank. (2000) Globalization, Growth and Poverty: Building an Inclusive World Economy. A World Bank Policy Research Report. New York: Oxford University Press.

Chapter 26

ENTREPRENEURSHIP: A TOOL FOR POVERTY REDUCTION IN NIGERIA

Makinde, T.

Introduction

Poverty appears to be one of the major problems confronting Nigeria despite the various strategies adopted for its reduction over the years. Some of these strategies include the introduction of some programmes such as the Operation Feed the Nation (OFN:1979), Directorate of Food, Roads and Rural Infrastructure (DFRRI:1986), the National Directorate of Employment (NDE:1986), the Better Life Programme (BLP:1987), People's Bank (1989), and Community Bank (1990) since independence in 1960. The incidence of poverty is even compounded by the level of unemployment which seems to be on the increase among the youth in the age bracket of 19 and 29 years old (Oteje 2012). This is also in spite of the existence of the National Directorate of Employment (NDE) since 1986. According to Franklin Sonn, as quoted in Oteje (2010), poverty is the single greatest social burden in the world today. It is a timeless matter which has defied all redemptive economic and social systems. The proliferation of tertiary institutions in Nigeria, leading to the turnout of many university and polytechnic graduates, has contributed also to the level of poverty in the country because not only are these graduates, most of whom are jobless, unable to provide for their parents as expected, but the little that these parents have is also shared with these unemployed youths. Most of these graduates fall back on their parents for their upkeep simply because they fail to get white-collar jobs that no longer exist in large numbers. Unfortunately, most of the tertiary institutions do not prepare these students for self-sufficiency through education in entrepreneurship. The resultant effect is that graduates of five to ten years are still found roaming the streets in search of employment. The question that comes to mind is: "Should citizens depend on government alone to provide jobs?" The answer will be in the negative since even the developed world cannot boast of such a luxury. However, the developed world provides a conducive environment to make employment generation by individuals or groups of individuals possible, thus reducing the incidence of poverty in their communities. This chapter will not only look at the possibility of entrepreneurship being a tool for poverty reduction in Nigeria, it will also discuss the concept of entrepreneurship, that of the entrepreneur, the concept of poverty and the poor, the role of government as regards entrepreneurship, and the relationship between entrepreneurship and poverty reduction.

Concept of Entrepreneurship:

According to Oghojhafor *et al.* (2011), entrepreneurship has increasingly been helping out as an alternative to traditional economic development strategies and policies. Entrepreneurship may be described as the process of value creation through the identification and exploitation of opportunities, which may be through the development of new products, seeking new markets, or both. Entrepreneurial practices abound in many countries, developed and developing. They are found in the United States of America, where entrepreneurial practices have created businesses like Kentucky Fried Chicken (KFC) and McDonald's, thereby providing employment opportunities for many people. Even in Nigeria, such entrepreneurial practices have created fast food joints and home delivery laundry service, among others. It will be quite in place if one argues that there may be no economic growth without entrepreneurship, which means that there may be no serious business development in any economy without entrepreneurship. This shows the importance of entrepreneurship. Who, then, is an entrepreneur?

The Merriam-Webster dictionary defines an entrepreneur as "one who organizes and assumes the risks of a business or enterprise", while dictionary.com defines it as "a person who organizes and manages any enterprise, especially a business, usually with considerable initiative and risk." The difference between the two definitions is that word "any". The word "any" shows that there is no limit to the type of business an entrepreneur can engage in. It could be big or small; it could be local or international. Dictionary.com further defines the entrepreneur as one who identifies a need—any need—and fills it. It is a primordial urge, independent of product, service, industry or market. From the above definitions of an entrepreneur, entrepreneurship can be referred to as "the capacity and willingness to undertake conception, organization and management of a productive venture with all attendant risks, while seeking profit as a reward" (BusinessDictionary.com).

An empirical study was carried out on the campus of Obafemi Awolowo University, Ile-Ife, using an entrepreneur popularly known as "Iya Rasaki" as a case study. Personal observations and interviews were employed for the study. Iya Rasaki is a middle-aged woman, about 55 years old. She has a mini-market, which is well located on the campus. According to her, she started the business in 1973, i.e., 39 years ago. She depends on this business for her livelihood, and from all observations she can be considered as being comfortable. Her responses to interview revealed that she has very little education (Primary Six, to be precise). However, she was able to identify the need of the community where she lives. This led her into going into a small-scale business which enables her to supply daily needs such as toiletries, bread, biscuits, pure water and bottled water, etc., to the community. With time, she started to make *moinmoin*—a special food made from beans and usually eaten along with *ogi* (corn pap) in the morning to supplement breakfast for those who can make *ogi* in their homes but have no time to make *moinmoin*. Because her shop is close to a big primary school (The University Staff School), she introduced the preparation and sale of *puff-puff*, *chin-chin*, donuts, and egg rolls, which are delicacies for school children. By this singular act of entrepreneurship, she succeeded in providing jobs for herself and some three other people. This was in addition to supplying the needs of the people. She has thus conquered poverty around her, thereby using entrepreneurship as a tool to fight poverty in her and her family's life. She is a very good example of an entrepreneur. Iya Rasaki has succeeded thus far because she operates in an environment where security is in place, where there are good roads, and there is adequate provision of electricity and water. Under such a conducive atmosphere, it is not surprising that her business booms every day. She not only takes care of her financial needs, she also takes care of the needs of those in the environment. In fact, she is so famous that a bus stop is named after her mini-market for the campus shuttle bus, known as "Iya Rasaki bus stop".

Concept of Poverty

Poverty can be conceptualized in both "relative" and "absolute" terms. According to Oghojafor *et al.* (2011), "the relative conceptualization of poverty is largely income-based". Absolute poverty refers to the lack of basic requirements to sustain physically healthy existence. This is different from relative poverty, which is the relative deprivation that people suffer from when, or because, they are unable to enjoy things that the majority of the people in a particular society enjoy, and which corroborates the conceptualization of relative poverty by Oghojafor as largely income-based. In such a situation, a millionaire may feel poor in the midst of billionaires (Makinde 2008).

Poverty, which has no geographical boundary, is felt in all parts of the world, rural and urban areas inclusive. At the start of the 21st century, poverty remains a global problem of huge proportions. According to the World Development Report (2000/2001), out of the world's 6 billion people, 2.8bn live on less than $2 a day and 1.2 billion on less than $1 a day. According to Kankwenda *et al.* (2000:62-63), poverty is recognized as a multidimensional phenomenon, influenced by a wide range of factors. These include people's lack of access to income-earning and productive activities and to essential social services. Poverty is evident in poor people's lack of political power and voice and in their extreme vulnerability to ill health, economic dislocation, personal violence and natural disasters. Poverty has many faces, changing from place to place and across time, and has been described in many ways. Poverty is hunger. Poverty is lack of shelter. Poverty is being sick and not having access to a doctor. Poverty is not being able to go to school and not knowing how to read. Poverty is not having a job; it is fear for the future, living one day at a time. Poverty is losing a child to illness brought about by unclean water. Poverty is powerlessness, lack of representation and freedom (World Bank 2003). In a Resource Paper on poverty reduction in Bangladesh, development was viewed as freedom. It was also argued that poverty is lack of development, and, by implication, poverty is lack of freedom (CPD Dialogue Report No. 31, 2000:8) as claimed by the World Bank above.

The causes of poverty are multifarious. They include unemployment, low wages and salaries, and laziness (Ogwumike 2001). Other causes include armed conflicts, illiteracy, political instability, lack of good governance, violence, and poorly designed policies as well as insufficient or unrealistic attention paid to the implementation and monitoring of the policies set out in national plans. This last cause shows that government action or inaction can result in poverty.

The consequences of poverty cannot be over-emphasized. They include armed robbery, death, corruption, under-development, oil bunkering (which sometimes leads to death through fire outbreak), drug trafficking, kidnapping, and other terrible crimes. Kidnapping seems to be the order of the day in Nigeria today. There is hardly a day without a newspaper report on one form of kidnapping or another. (Actually, is it really kidnapping or "adult-napping"? The word "adult-napping" should find its way into the Nigerian dictionary since adults are the targets of these criminals rather than kids.) In the *Vanguard* of Friday, October 12, 2012, page 11, kidnappers (or "adult-nappers") were demanding a ransom of N100,000m for the abducted Delta State Commissioner. Also in the *Sunday Sun* of October 14, 2012, page 13, the report was given on "How Osun Speaker's wife was kidnapped". The above incidents show that there is no limit to what poverty can drive people to do. To make it worse, the editorial of the *Punch* newspaper of October 19, 2012, page 18, was titled "Nigeria as Kidnap Capital". Below is an excerpt from the write-up:

> Nigeria's rising profile as a haven for kidnapping was the focus of attention at a recent meeting of the African Insurance Organisation in Balaclava, Mauritius. Unsurprisingly, Nigeria was designated, in a statement at the African Reinsurance Forum, as the **"global capital of kidnapping"**.

What a title!

Since unemployment has been seen as one of the major causes of poverty, it means that the provision of meaningful employment represents one of the essential components of poverty alleviation. It is said that "the devil finds jobs for idle hands", hence, the need for employment generation, especially among the youths. However, some youths with employment are not happy with what they have. Most of them are underemployed. For example, a university graduate taking up a job as a clerk or working as an *okada* rider cannot be said to be happily employed. Therefore, it is not only the quantity of employment that matters but also the quality of work.

In some developed countries, monthly stipends are given to unemployed people or the poor. This practice cannot be said to be reducing the incidence of poverty and, therefore, would not be advocated in Nigeria. As a matter of fact, it can encourage or promote poverty since man generally enjoys free food. Everything that is rewarded grows. If, therefore, poverty is rewarded through the payment of stipends to the poor, poverty will increase. A Chinese proverb says: "Give a man a fish and you feed him for a day. Teach a man how to fish and you feed him for a lifetime". When one talks about poverty, it is important that one knows who the poor really are, i.e., one should be able to define the poor.

Who are the Poor?

The identification of who the poor are has attracted a lot of scholarly attention over the years. Olusi (2001:176), in identifying "the poor", makes reference to different countries for different definitions of who the poor are. In the United States, for example, the poor consist of the aged (over 65 years), minority, racial and ethnic groups living in urban slums. The poor in the U.S. also include youths, especially black youths in places like New York, New Jersey, Dallas, etc. Also, in the United States, many Native Americans experience high rates of joblessness and alcoholism. By implication, many Aboriginal people in Australia, who live in similar conditions as described in the United States, are poor (Poverty:MSN Encarta, 2008). In Nigeria, who are the poor? They include young unemployed people and those workers who earn wages which cannot take them through the month. In their own contribution, Amaghioyeodiwe and Osinubi (2004) identify the poor as the rural landless, the small farmers, the urban under-employed and the unemployed. For the purpose of this topic, the poor will be defined as the unemployed youths and adults and those who earn incomes which cannot sustain their healthy living, be it in the rural or urban areas. Having identified the poor and having established what entrepreneurship is all about, it will not be out of place to look into how government can encourage entrepreneurship.

The Role of Government in Entrepreneurship

The case study of Iya Rasaki discussed earlier has shown that entrepreneurship is a strategy towards poverty reduction. Already the definition of entrepreneurship has shown that it entails someone having to identify a need which he/she is ready to satisfy by taking a risk, especially financial risk. People talk about America as a country which is doing well economically through entrepreneurship. Why, we may ask, is this so? Some people who have lived in America testify to the fact that America is a country where things work. There is no power outage, water flows freely from the taps, there is security and there is attention paid to the provision of health facilities as well as education. With all these in place, the level of risk to an entrepreneur is highly reduced, unlike in an environment devoid of such facilities. In Nigeria, how can the government be involved in minimizing the risk to entrepreneurs? That is where administration/government comes in as regards entrepreneurship.

Administration, public administration to be precise, is "centrally concerned with the organization of government policies and programmes as well as the behaviour of officials..." (Wikipedia). Administration involves planning and organizing, among other things. Where government plans adequately for its people, things will work. From observation, one cannot say that there is no planning in Nigeria. After all, part of planning is budgeting and policy development. One of the challenges of these two (budgeting and policy development) is the problem of implementation, which, most of the time, is characterized by corruption. Other challenges are lack of necessary tools for planning and budgeting. One of such tools is adequate information. Planning for the people requires correct and adequate information on the population in the country. This will involve having correct statistics, showing the number of adults as well as the number of youths with or without employment. Such information will enable a projection to be made as to the way out of unemployment. As in the policy-making process, the problem of unemployment must be identified and defined. This will be followed by setting objectives as regards the identified problem. Various alternatives will emerge as to how to achieve the set objectives, one of which may be entrepreneurship. With the adoption of entrepreneurship, appropriate infrastructures will be put in place. These will include funding, which can come through micro-financing or some other forms of loans. However, funding alone cannot achieve the purpose. There should be provision of electricity, water, security and other facilities that will assist the entrepreneur to operate with minimum of discomfort and risk. Another important role which administration can play is to come up with a policy that will ensure that entrepreneurship becomes part of the curriculum in both secondary and tertiary institutions. For example, the 6-3-3-4 system of education was intended to help students to develop some skills which could be useful to them in future in order to be able to make a living without necessarily looking for a white collar job. However, things do not appear to be going in that direction. Besides, most of the schools do not have adequate facilities for the acquisition of skills. In addition, the mentality of the people is such that does not encourage skill acquisition in schools. Everyone wants his/her child to go to the university, even when such a child does not possess such capability. There is, therefore, the need for orientation programmes to be organized for both the young and the old to enlighten them on the need to rely less on white collar jobs. Rather, they should think of how to be an employer of people, like Iya Rasaki, instead of being an employee.

At the moment, the Nigerian government has tried to provide loans to individuals through one of the programmes under NAPEP – Micro Credit (Makinde 2008), and there is also the provision of credit facilities through the micro-finance banks to low income earners like artisans, to start their own businesses (Oteje 2010). In a study carried out by Makinde and Fayomi (2010), it was revealed that market women in Ile-Ife were empowered through facilities provided by the micro-finance banks. However, the provision of funds alone cannot encourage entrepreneurship. Other incentives that can encourage the entrepreneur to risk attempting new ventures are the provision of laws that will enforce property rights and encourage a competitive market system. Apart from the provision of funds and other facilities, Oteje (2010) argued that "the best thing you can do to reduce poverty is make the poor people believe that there were others in their situation that rose above poverty, worked hard and are rich today". By this, it means that there should be enlightenment programmes, where the poor can be encouraged by giving them information on those who had been in their situation before but whose stories have changed for the better. Oteje (2010) stated thus:

> Give the poor people heroes they can look up to. And they will model
> after these heroes and change their lives.

> Tell them rags-to-riches stories. And they will surprise you by rising out of
> poverty in record time.

> Give just one autobiographical rags-to-riches book to just one poor
> person to read and see how his life changes.

In the midst of all these, there must be adequate provision of infrastructures so as to ensure that the loans collected by the entrepreneur are not used to service those things which should have been provided by government. After all, almost all Nigerians have become local governments, since they provide everything, including roads and security for themselves (Makinde, Popoola, and Ologunde 2010). Other ways by which government can assist entrepreneurship is by providing low rent and accessible industrial and office premises as well as subsidized use of office equipment. Government can also offer professional advice and consultancy (United Nations 1999).

Lastly, what is the relationship between entrepreneurship and poverty reduction? With entrepreneurship, the entrepreneur not only provides a job for himself, but he also provides for others, thereby reducing the incidence of poverty. The case of Iya Rasaki, which was discussed earlier, is very relevant. Drucker, as quoted in Oteje (2010), describes the entrepreneur as someone who actually searches for change, responds to it, and exploits change as an opportunity. Such opportunity is what leads him or her out of poverty.

The relationship between entrepreneurship and poverty reduction cannot be overemphasized because successful small businesses, as in the case of Iya Rasaki, are the primary engines of job creation, income growth and poverty reduction.

Conclusion

This chapter has tried to look at entrepreneurship from the administrative perspective by examining the role of administration in the encouragement and sustenance of entrepreneurship. There is no doubt, based on the empirical study discussed earlier, that entrepreneurship is one of the tools for poverty reduction in Nigeria. Other tools include good governance through good planning and provision of social services. However, entrepreneurship can only thrive in a conducive environment where infrastructural facilities such as water, electricity, and security are provided, and where enabling laws are provided by government.

References

Amaghionyeodiwe, L. A., and Osinubi, T. S. (2004) *Poverty Reduction Policies and Pro-Poor Growth in Nigeria*. Ibadan: University of Ibadan.

Centre for Policy Dialogue (CPD). Report No. 31, 2000:8.

How Osun Speaker's wife was kidnapped. *Sunday Sun*, October 14, 2012:13.

Kankwenda, M., L. Gregoire, H. Legros, and H. Ouedraogo. (2000) *Poverty Eradication: Where Stands Africa?* A UNDP Publication, London: Economica Ltd.

Kidnapped Delta Commissioner: Gunmen increase ransom to N100m. *Vanguard*, October 12, 2012:11.

Lumpkin, G. T., R. Shrader, and G. E. Hills. (1998) Does formal business planning enhance the performance of new ventures? *Frontiers of Entrepreneurship Research*, pp. 180–199.

Makinde, Taiwo. (2008) An Appraisal of the National Poverty Eradication Programme (NAPEP) in Selected States of Southwestern Nigeria. A PhD Thesis in the

Department of Public Administration, Obafemi Awolowo University, Ile-Ife, Nigeria.

———, Femi Popoola, Olusola Ologunde. (2008) Corruption and Its Implications for Social Service Delivery in Nigeria. *Ife Social Sciences Review* No. 1, Vol. 23, pp. 160–175.

———, and Ike Fayomi. (2008) Gender-based Poverty and Micro-financing in Parts of South-Western Nigeria. *African Journal of Public Administration and Management (AAPAM)*, Vol. XIX, No. 2, July 2008, pp. 48–58.

Nigeria as kidnap capital. *Punch* (editorial), October 19, 2012:18.

Oghojafor, Ben Emukufia Akpoyomare, Olufemi Olabode Olayemi, Patrick Sunday Okonji, and Peter O. Olayiwola. (2011) Entrepreneurship as an Intervention Strategy to Poverty Alleviation in Developing Economy. A paper presented at the 10th International Entrepreneurship Forum, Tamkeen, Bahrain, 9–19 January, p.1–10.

Ogwumike, F. O. (2001) Current State of Knowledge on Poverty in Nigeria. In Afonja, S., D. Adelekan, F. Soetan, T. Alimi, and B. Ayanwale (eds.), *Research and Policy Directions on Poverty in Nigeria.* Ile-Ife: Anchor Print.

Olusi, J. O. (2001) Poverty Alleviation in the Nigerian Economy: Policy Issues and Prospects. In Afonja, S., D. Adelekan, F. Soetan, T. Alimi, and B. Ayanwale (eds.), op. cit., pp. 173-185.

Oteje, Kehinde M. J. (2010) Entrepreneurship, Job Creation, Income Empowerment and Poverty Reduction in Nigeria. A Seminar Paper.

MSN Encarta. Poverty. http://encarta.msn.com/encyclopedia_761577020_5/Poverty.html. Accessed 1/18/2008.

Schumpeter, J. A. (1942) *The Theory of Economic Development.* Cambridge, MA: Harvard University Press.

Sonn, Franklin A. (as quoted in Oteje, Kehinde M. J. (2010), op.cit.)

The Role of Entrepreneurship in Economic Development. http://www.mouan.edu.ng/handbook/eloquent-testimony-purposeful-le..

United Nations. (1999) The Development of Entrepreneurship and Small Business in Transitional Economies. A working paper.

World Bank. (2000) World Development Report 2000/2001. Washington D.C.

World Bank Poverty Net. (2003) Understanding and Responding to Poverty. http://www.worldbank.org/poverty/mission/upl.htm.

Chapter 27

ENTREPRENEURSHIP TRAINING AMONG YOUTH AS A PANACEA TO MASS EMIGRATION OF YOUTH IN NIGERIA

Ikuteyijo, L.

Introduction

The global trend in people desperate to leave their country of origin to find security, work and a new way of life is now widespread (Lee 2005). Nigeria in particular faces demographic challenges as the population of her youth increases while access to jobs and other necessities of life continue to be a mirage. With a population of over 160 million, more than half of which is made up of youth, Nigeria falls within the category of a nation that could be described as a "demographic giant" in Africa. Ironically, this giant has often been described as the "sleeping giant," blessed with a myriad of resources yet accommodating some of the poorest people in the world. The bulk of migration stock in Nigeria is among the youth, and this is largely due to economic motives. Unemployment rate continues to rise with rising cost of living. This in part drives the determination of the youth to want to migrate out of the country, even to unpredictable and bleak chances in other parts of the world. The promulgation and enforcement of strict migration laws by advanced countries notwithstanding, the poor economic situation in many developing countries, including Nigeria, continues to sustain desperation among the youth to move.

Various forms of irregular migration have been documented and some of these include: forgery of passports, visas and other travelling documents; false marriage; bogus claims for asylum; human smuggling and trafficking—the list is endless. The United Nations estimated that four million people are trafficked globally each year (Arlacchi 2000; Raymond 2002), whilst the International Organization for Migration (IOM) (2001) suggested that between 700,000 and 2,000,000 women and children are trafficked within and across international borders annually. The Nigerian case makes for an interesting record, as the country was noted as one of the suppliers of the largest cache of prostitutes to the trafficking network (Carling 2006; UNODC2009). Nigeria, as a major demographic force in sub-Saharan Africa is expected to take the lead in the fight against irregular migration in the sub-region. A number of policies and institutions have been established to stem the tide of mass emigration among various classes of Nigerians, especially among the youth. However, most of these policies have been short-lived or at best failed to achieve their laudable aims. This chapter examines the promotion of entrepreneurial skills among the youth as a possible panacea to the problem of mass emigration of this category of Nigerians, both internally and internationally. The chapter also examines past efforts by both the state and federal governments to create employment opportunities for the teeming Nigerian youth and x-raying the challenges to the success of these initiatives. The chapter ends by proffering solutions to the identified problem.

The Youth and Migration in Sub-Saharan Africa

A majority of those who migrate out of their regions, either within or outside their country, are usually motivated by economic needs and in most cases are in search of greener pastures. This is, however, exacerbated in a closely connected, globalised world, with increasing interdependence among nations, new infrastructures of transportation, increasing income differentials and demographic inequalities. Furthermore, the economic situation of the world today is deplorable and in crisis; most developed economies of the world are facing some of the greatest challenges of all time. This in turn has telling effects in terms of youth employment. The ILO (2012) noted that young people are three times more likely to be unemployed than adults and over 75 million youth worldwide are looking for work.

The case is worse in most countries in sub-Saharan Africa, where the majority of the youth are seeking white collar jobs, which are nonexistent in most cases. More often than not, the youth are more likely to resort to migration in response to unemployment since they are active and young, with other enabling characteristics like energy, less commitment at the family level and love for adventure. This is what makes migration a selective phenomenon (Afolayan *et al*. 2008).

All over the world, the percentage of youth migration often outnumbers that of older people. In most countries in sub-Saharan Africa, the acquisition of additional skills and qualifications often serves as impetus for youth to migrate from rural areas to the urban centres in search of greener pastures. This is due to the fact that most of the rural areas lack the necessary infrastructure to retain the youth. One of the immediate effects of this is usually felt in the agricultural sector, which has been abandoned for the older folks. There is, however, another twist to this issue as those who migrate to the urban centers mostly find it problematic to adapt, as the increasing rate of urban unemployment often forces some of the youth to attempt leaving the country in search of the "golden fleece." This has been described as step migration by migration scholars.

The Global Employment Trend (GET 2008) reported that youth in sub-Saharan Africa were among the most disadvantaged in the world as far as securing decent and productive employment is concerned. The nature of the problem is not different from the overall labour market problems that afflict the region (ILO 2008). Also, because working poverty is widespread, more than half of those who had secured one form of employment or another were unable to lift themselves and their families out of poverty, and vulnerable employment accountsfor more than two-thirds of workers.

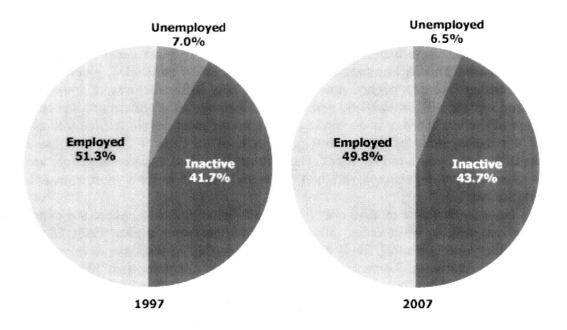

Figure 27.1: Youth Population by Economic Activity Status in Sub-Saharan Africa, 1997 and 2007

Source: International Labour Office, Global Employment Trend, 2008

The Nigerian Scenario

The case of migration informed by youth unemployment in Nigeria is assuming a more worrisome dimension. This is moreso when the rate of industrialisation in the country is dwindling and hitherto existing companies are folding due to a myriad of problems. The youth are often the most hit as they constitute the bulk of the working population of the country. There are two categories of the unemployed in Nigeria: those who had never worked and those who were laid off due to the processes of retrenchment, redundancy and bankruptcy. The latter group add to the army of unemployed youth in the country and the consequences are better imagined than experienced. Available statistics show that Nigeria's youth population constitutes 60% of the total population in the country, 80% of which are unemployed and 2% underemployed (Awogbenle and Iwuamadi 2010; Okafor 2011).

Table 27.1: Percentage of unemployed persons in Nigeria by year

S/N	Year	% of people unemployed
1	2000	31.1
2	2001	13.6
3	2002	12.6
4	2003	14.8
5	2004	13.4
6	2005	11.9
7	2006	13.7
8	2007	14.6
9	2008	14.9
10	2009	19.7

Source: Nigerian Bureau of Statistics, 2009; 2010

Some drivers of irregular migration generally and mostly among the youth have been identified by various scholars. These include: "demographic pressures of a rapidly growing young but unemployed labour force" (Adepoju 2011); proliferation of human trafficking and organised criminal gangs (Asis 2005); insecurity (Nwajiuba 2005); high income differentials in both sending and receiving countries; the porous nature of Nigerian borders (Ikuteyijo 2010); the "imagined West" (Fujita 2009) phenomenon, whereby the youth tend to have a misrepresented and often over-bloated imagination about living conditions in the Western world, among other factors. The issue of youth unemployment has, however, enjoyed the most attention among the listed factors. In Nigeria today, there is an increasing "army" of graduates without corresponding efforts at providing gainful employment for them. Therefore, many of the youth often opt for the "traveling out" option as they are often misinformed about the labour market conditions of destination countries as well as the migration norms of those countries. But the strict migration regimes of most of these destination countries (especially in Europe and North America), make the youth to detour to alternative means of leaving the country. Some of these avenues include hiding beneath ship decks or in luggage compartments of aircraft or enlisting the services of fake agents (Adepoju 2011).

Over the years, successive regimes in Nigeria have attempted to tackle the problem of youth employment headlong, and these efforts have culminated in the establishment of various employment and capacity development schemes, but most of these schemes hit the rocks not too long from their dates of establishment. However, little attention has been paid by scholars to the possibility of using the entrepreneurial model as an antidote for regulating irregular migration among the youth in Nigeria.

Entrepreneurship as Social Security Package and Panacea to Youth Emigration

In Nigeria, there is a trend among some state governments to introduce various programmes to engage the teeming youth in their respective states. These programmes, which have been christened differently, going by various nomenclatures, have often fallen short of the expectations of the people in terms of ability to dissuade youth from migrating in search of better life, either in urban areas or outside the country. Unfortunately, these programs fail more because the promoters of the programmes often attempt to "provide fish to the youth rather than teaching them to catch fish." Most of the programmes come in form of employment generation and not the inculcation of entrepreneurial skills to the youth. Entrepreneurship would enable the youth to develop the capacity and willingness to undertake conception, organisation and management of a productive venture with all attendant risks, while seeking profit as a reward. This is irrespective of the location of the youth, whether rural or urban, as the skills will entail the identification of the opportunities available in these areas through a viable Strength, Weaknesses, Opportunities and Threats (SWOT) analysis of the business environment. Youth need to be prepared to take advantage of potential opportunities and to create opportunities on their own through self-employment and entrepreneurial activities. Preparation for employment starts with basic good-quality education, which provides the foundation for future human capital accumulation and the later acquisition of vocational skills in schools, training institutes, and the workplace (World Bank 2006).

In an interview, Mr. Femi Aminu, a seasoned entrepreneurship expert based in Lagos State, Nigeria, observed that entrepreneurship is a panacea to the problem of massive youth emigration in search of greener pastures abroad. According to him, small businesses have always been at the forefront in many advanced countries in Europe and Asia and, of course, the United States of America. In these countries, more people are employed by private firms, which in most cases are family businesses and enterprises. Femi Aminu explained further that:

> Governments in advanced countries provide funding, good climate, introduce entrepreneurship in the school curriculum early enough and follow it through. In fact, in Germany at the age of 13, you either go to a grammar school if academically inclined or a vocational school (US equivalent of polytechnic). There are also junior community colleges that provide courses suited to the local industry so as to supply a ready pool of skilled labour.

A very good example of how entrepreneurial skills could be harnessed by the youth is what has been demonstrated by some youth in the ICT sector in the global West. For example, the quintessential Google search engine was founded by Larry Page and Sergey Brin, both students at Stanford University. The company, which was incorporated in 1998 with a start-up capital of about $1.1 million, now has total assets of over $31 billion and is employing over 19,000 fulltime employees as of March 31, 2009 (Oteh 2009).

Likewise, Facebook, a social network site, was founded by Mark Zuckerberg with the help of Andrew McCollum, both computer science students at Harvard University. The success of the project on their university campus made them enlist the support of their roommates to spread the system, first to other US Ivy League universities. Facebook has now become a worldwide social networking site and youth movement (Oteh 2009). Meanwhile, these examples were made possible largely because the governments of the respective countries provided the enabling environment.

Furthermore, Nigerian youth stand the best chances of experiencing entrepreneurial excellence through the platform of the ICT, given the demographic composition of the country. The government can actually ensure that all youth are computer literate, and computer appreciation should be inculcated at the early stages, not only in theoretical but practical terms. The rural schools should be well supported/funded to realise this feat.

Another area where entrepreneurial skills could be harnessed is the agricultural sector. In Nigeria, agricultural production is still carried out using physical strength, which declines with age. In fact, available evidence suggests an ageing farming population in Nigeria (Akpan 2010). This has, therefore, been observed as one of the major constraints to agricultural production in Nigeria (Okeowo *et al.* 1999). Though youths have desirable qualities that can promote agriculture, most of them have strong apathy toward it (Jibowo 1998; Adedoyin 2005; Adewale *et al.* 2005).With the large expanse of arable lands in Nigeria, it is actually an irony that the country still imports a huge percentage of the food Nigerians eat. The neglect of agriculture, especially by the youth, is mostly accountable for the rural–urban migration in Nigeria. The interest of the youth can be sustained in agriculture, and this will be a very important structure for land and agrarian reform, which will go a long way towards promoting the interest of the youth in the agricultural sector of the economy.Surveys have revealed that over 90% of the youth in urban areas in Nigeria are involved in non-agriculture-based activities (Adekunle *et al.* 2009).

Merits of Entrepreneurship

Entrepreneurship has a number of merits if well incorporated at the individual and societal levels. At the societal level, entrepreneurship serves as a catalyst to economic growth and development in the following ways:

- Entrepreneurship helps in developing very early one's knowledge of the business world as well as improving better understanding of the role of entrepreneurs in the community.
- Entrepreneurship also fosters the creation of employment opportunities, as businesses are set up on both small and large scales, thereby reducing the problem of unemployment, which has assumed the dimension of a social problem in most developing countries like Nigeria.
- Entrepreneurship promotes balanced development and reduces the unequal level of development between regions, especially the disparity between the rural and urban areas, in terms of development. This is facilitated by the establishment of businesses in areas of less development, with the concomitant development of social infrastructure. This can help reduce the ubiquitous rural–urban drift, which is the bane of development in most developing countries.
- Entrepreneurship has the potential to improve the standards of living of the people. This is facilitated by the adoption of the latest innovations in the production of a wide variety of goods and services on a large scale, which also comes at a lower cost. This will allow the people to have access to quality goods at lower prices, and it will ultimately lead to an improvement in their standard of living.

However at the level of the individual, entrepreneurship has the following benefits:

- People exposed to entrepreneurship frequently express the opinion that they have more opportunity to exercise creative freedoms, higher self-esteem, and an overall greater sense of control over their lives (National Consortium 2004).
- Entrepreneurship also allows people to be independent and be their own bosses, making very crucial decisions and being responsible for their actions.
- Entrepreneurship facilitates originality, whereby people offer new products and services that no one has offered before.
- Entrepreneurship facilitates flexibility and freedom, as entrepreneurs can schedule their work hours to spend quality time with families, or for any other reason, as well as work whenever they want, wherever they want, and however they want.

Challenges to Entrepreneurship in Nigeria

There are a number of challenges facing entrepreneurship in Nigeria and these challenges are individual as well as institutional. At the individual level, most Nigerian youth are desirous of white collar jobs, with little or no interest for self-employment. Also, the educational curricula in Nigeria are devoid of entrepreneurial skills, and many of the young graduates always consider seeking employment in government institutions or in the petroleum industry, which are the greatest employers of labour in the country. Moreover, the motivation to acquire entrepreneurial skills by the youth is grossly lacking, as many would rather prefer a shortcut to success rather than the patience and endurance which entrepreneurship entails. Besides these individual challenges, there are institutional factors which serve as bottlenecks for entrepreneurship in Nigeria. Some of these institutional features include the crisis in the energy sector, most visibly seen in the power sector. The promise of successive regimes to guarantee regular and uninterrupted power supply in Nigeria has made it appear as if the problem facing the energy and power sector is insurmountable. Billions of Naira have been expended on the perennial problem, but no solution seems to be in sight. Apart from the huge financial resources, a number of policies in form of reforms have also been suggested, but all to no avail. One of such was the Electricity Power Sector Reform Act which was promulgated in March 2005. This reform was made in line with the understanding that liberalisation of the sector would bring about the much-needed change in the industry, but the result so far is an epileptic energy and power sector. This serves as a huge barrier to entrepreneurship, as most people have to rely on self-help alternatives to power generation. Another institutional barrier to entrepreneurship is lack of adequate infrastructure. Facilities such as roads and good transportation system are lacking, and the railway system has been moribund for years.

At the political level, there is a general lack of political will for the development of entrepreneurial skills in Nigeria. The government has not put adequate laws in place to protect local businesses, and this affects their chances of competing with their foreign counterparts. The problem of piracy is a point in reference as local manufacturers are ostensibly lame in the fight against pirates, which serve as their major constraints. Furthermore, the general lack of security in the country has made entrepreneurship to dwindle in Nigeria. All over the country, there are regular occurrences of civil unrest, most especially with ethnic and religious undertones. A number of young, up-and-coming entrepreneurs have lost quite a fortune in some of these skirmishes. This serves as a disincentive for entrepreneurship in Nigeria.

The Way Forward

The use of entrepreneurship to stem the tide of youth migration in Nigeria is a feat that is achievable only if the following recommendations are followed:

- incorporation of entrepreneurial skills in school curricula;
- synergy between government parastatals/ministries to tackle youth unemployment;

- synergy between NGOs/individuals and government agencies at training the youth;
- social/value re-orientation towards made-in-Nigeria products and services;
- mass mobilisation of the youth on the need for self sufficiency;
- establishment of research institutes on youth entrepreneurship;
- partnership between government agencies responsible for employment generation and academia; and
- the use of ICT to drive entrepreneurial skills among the youth.

Conclusion

In conclusion, the need for all stakeholders to engage the youth in Nigeria in entrepreneurial training and dissuade them from seeing emigration to the West as a panacea to unemployment is quite essential and cannot be over-emphasised. Entrepreneurship will not only address the issue of unemployment in the country but equally will bring out the best in the teeming youth population of the country. All over the world, the private sector is at the forefront of wealth creation and employment generation.This is at variance with what obtains in Nigeria, where the government attempts to do everything by itself, including the trend among both state and federal government to create more jobs. Apparently, this jobs creation, apart from being politically motivated, with no genuine intention, equally has negative effects on entrepreneurship and innovation. The focus of the government and other stakeholders should, therefore, be on how to nurture the spirit of enterprise and creativity among the youth by encouraging the introduction and implementation of entrepreneurial skills in the curricula of schools at very early stages. It is obvious that, when the youth see that there is the enabling environment with opportunities for economic advancement, they stay back in the country to contribute their own quota to its development and not to migrate to the developed countries, where they are often treated as second-class citizens. Likewise, Nigerians in the diaspora will be willing to return home to start industries and companies, building on the knowledge they have garnered during their stay abroad. This is what is applicable in other developing countries, which are fast thriving in terms of economic development and growth.

References

Adedoyin, S. F. (2005) Youth and Children Programme in Nigeria. In Adedoyin, S. F. (ed.), *Agricultural Extension in Nigeria.* Agricultural Extension Society of Nigeria (AESON). Ilorin: AESON Publications, pp. 251.

Adewale, J. G., J. A. Oladejo, and L. T. Ogunniyi. (2005) Economic Contribution of Farm Children to Agricultural Production in Nigeria: A case study of Ekiti State. *Journal of Social Science* 10(2): 149–152.

Adekunle, O. A., L. L. Adefalu, F. O. Oladipo, R. S. Adisa, and A. D. Fatoye. (2009) Constraints to youth's involvement in agricultural production in Kwara State, Nigeria. *Journal of Agricultural Extension* Vol. 13(1), pp. 102–108.

Adepoju, A. (2010) Rethinking the Dynamics of Migration Within, From and To Africa. In Adepoju, Aderanti (ed.), *International Migration Within, To and From Africa in a Globalised World*. Accra, Ghana: Sub-Saharan Publishers, pp. 9–45.

Afolayan, A. A., G. O. Ikwuyatum, and O. Abejide. (2008) Dynamics of International Migration in Nigeria. Paper prepared as part of the African Perspectives on Human Mobility Programme, funded by the MacArthur Foundation.

Akpan, S. B. (2010) Encouraging Youth's Involvement in Agricultural Production and Processing. International Food Policy Research Institute. Available at http://www.ifpri.org/sites/default/files/publications/nssppn29.pdf.

Arlacchi, P. (2000) Against all the Godfathers: The Revolt of the Decent People. *The World against Crime*, Special Issue of *Giornale di Silica*, p. 7.

Awogbenle, A. C.,and K. C. Iwuamadi. (2010) Youth Unemployment: Entrepreneurship Development Programme as an Intervention Mechanism. *African Journal of Business Management* 4(6), 831–835.

Carling, J. (2006) Migration, Human Smuggling and trafficking from Nigeria to Europe. A Report Prepared for the International Organization for Migration (IOM), Geneva.

Fujita, Y. (2009). *Youth, Media, and Migration in New York and London*. New York: Lexington Books.

Ikuteyijo, L. O. (2010) Criminalization of Harmful Environmental Practices as a Panacea to Environmental Crimes in Nigeria. In Adebooye, O. C. (ed.), *Biotechnology Development and Threat of Climate Change in Africa: The Linkage in the Future of Human Livelihood*. Göttingen: Cuvillier Verlag, pp. 256–264.

International Organisation on Migration. (2001) Victims of Trafficking in the Balkans: A Study of Trafficking in Women and Children for Sexual Exploitation to, through and from the Balkan Region. IOM, Geneva.

Jibowo, A. A. (1998) Agrological Transmission: The Secret of National Food Surplus. An Inaugural Lecture delivered on July 11 at the Obafemi Awolowo University, Ile-Ife.

Lee, M. (2007) *Human Trafficking*. Devon, UK: Willan Publishing.

National Content Standards for Entrepreneurship Education. (2004) Preparing Youth and Adults to Succeed in an Entrepreneurial Economy. Available at http://www.entre-ed.org/Standards_Toolkit/.

Nwajiuba, C. (2005) International migration and livelihoods in southeastern Nigeria. Global Migration Perspectives. Available at http://www.gcim.org.

Okeowo, T. A., J. B. Agunbiade, and L. A. Odeyemi. (1999) An Assessment of the Level of Involvement of Farm-Children in Farming Decisions in Ikorodu Area of Lagos State. In Stella, B. W., F. O. Oginni, and J. F.Akinloye (eds.), *Farm Children and Agricultural Productivity in the 21st Century*, proceedings of the Second Annual Conference of Children-In-Agricultural Programme (CIAP) held at the Conference Centre, O. A. U., Ile-Ife, May, pp. 275–282.

Okafor, E. E. (2011) Youth Unemployment and Implications for Stability of Democracy in Nigeria. *Journal of Sustainable Development in Africa* Vol. 13, No. 1, Clarion University of Pennsylvania, pp. 358–373.

Oteh, A. (2009) The Role of Entrepreneurship in Transforming the Nigerian Economy. A paper delivered at the 7th Convocation Lecture of Igbinedion University, Okada, Edo State, 4 December.

Raymond, J. (2002) The New UN Trafficking Protocol. *Women's Studies International Forum* Vol. 25, No. 5, pp. 491–502.

Chapter 28

PROSPECTS AND CHALLENGES OF UTILIZING ENTREPRENEURSHIP AND SOCIAL ENTREPRENEURSHIP IN IMPROVING PRISON CONDITIONS IN NIGERIA

Agunbiade, O. M.

Introduction

The unwavering reliance on the existing penal system in addressing crime and criminally labelled behaviours in Nigeria can only take a few criminals off the streets for a limited period (Chiemeka 2002). In the long run, events could likely repeat themselves, except there are changes in the existing methodologies and efforts aimed at resuscitating existing entrepreneurship programmes within and outside the penal system. There are structural and attitudinal constraints in adopting and implementing strategies for sustainable reformation of the penal system and prison conditions in Nigeria (Amnesty International 2008; Jefferson 2007). These constraints are dynamic and complex. Thus, resolving them for meaningful transformation demands approaches that are somewhat different from the conventional entrepreneurship model. With cues from Smith (2009), this chapter pitches its tent with the position that calls for functional prison-based entrepreneurship and social entrepreneurship as frameworks to achieving sustainable diversion from pathways that lead to imprisonment.

The diversionary roles of entrepreneurship from pathways to crime occupy a central position in criminological discourse (Smith 2009). Nigeria, like other countries, has inconsistently relied on this approach in prison reformation and creating pathways from crime. However, inadequate political will, diminishing public funds, and other structural constraints have restricted the desired reformation within the penal system. With the lingering challenges of recidivism and facilitating humane prisons in Nigeria, there is a need to consider potential approaches. Social entrepreneurship is an emerging area of research and a framework with promising alternatives to providing options in filling the gaps created by diminishing public funding as well as dealing with complex social needs (Johnson 2000:1). Appropriate contextualization of social entrepreneurship models could enhance the achievements of humane prisons and the general well-being of the populace. Against this backdrop, this chapter examines the plausibility of adopting and contextualising prison-based entrepreneurship and social entrepreneurship programmes within and outside the penal system as useful in creating pathways for healthy prison conditions and the general well-being of the inmates. In addition, it focuses on constraints to moving in this direction within the Nigerian society.

The chapter starts with an overview of the ideology of punishment and its focal position in the penal system. Next, focus is on entrepreneurship and its potentials for reformation and diversionary roles from recidivism. Under this aspect, the chapter argues for a reinvigoration of existing entrepreneurship practices in the Nigerian prison system. Also examined are the existing constraints in building a sustainable entrepreneurship culture within the Nigerian prison system.

In the final analysis, the chapter decries the absence of social entrepreneurship in the Nigerian society and makes a call for plausible adoption and contextualisation of some tested models within the Nigerian prison system as a sub-system of the larger Nigerian society. It concludes with a focus on social entrepreneurship, prevailing models, and their potentials in improving the general well-being of the populace and invariable access to essential services.

The Ideology of Punishment: An Overview

The evolution of the penal institution and its modern form is traceable to the influence of two political and philosophical positions (Murphy 1995). One position is that inflicting pain as punishment is fundamentally different from inflicting pain on innocents and thus is not inherently wrong. The other is the belief that punishment is a wrong that can be justified only if it results in a "greater good" (Murphy 1995). These two views consist of the retributive and utilitarian approaches. While what qualifies as the ideal type of punishment is problematic among philosophers and across cultures, punishment has remained the underlying basis for the continuous existence of prisons in modern society.

Historically, imprisonment as a mode of punishment is traceable to the 16th century but became widely spread only in the 19th century (Foucault 1977). Before then, the few prisons that existed housed those destined for some punishments, like those people marked for execution or those with inabilities to pay their debts (Foucault 1977). In terms of influence, conservatism and liberalism as philosophical positions have remained dominant in the wide acceptance of prison as a system of social control (Durham 1994). The conservatism paradigm views human beings as agents with free will and the ability to make rational choices and expects logical results from their choices. In contrast, the liberal ideology holds that upbringing, affluence or poverty, education and life experiences in general influence human behaviour. The former perspective emphasises deterrence and incapacitation as conditions to discourage individuals from indulging in deviant acts and motivates conformity to socially acceptable forms of behaviour. In contrast, the liberal philosophy encourages rehabilitation and reform. A major assumption guiding this is that imprisonment could change the individual rather than causing destruction.

Since its inception, the prison has been a social agent of the criminal justice administration. The prison has two basic roles: incarcerating convicts and providing custodial care for those under trial and in detention (Durham 1994). The radical movement, which views prisons as instruments of the powerful to enslave the powerless, has criticised prison's functionality. In its own position, the abolishment of prison and the reformation of law and equitable access to social means of achieving socially approved goals would yield more fruits than the prison system (Durham 1994). Ironically, a middle position between the conservative and liberal philosophies of imprisonment is dominant in the existing reforms and operation of the modern penal system. The situation in Nigeria is similar to the mid-point as shown in the reformation activities that have taken place in the penal system. It is noteworthy to emphasise the colonial origin of the penal system in Nigeria (Rotimi 1982; Ikuteyijo and Agunbiade 2009) and questions about its probable role in achieving the desired reformation in the Nigerian prison system. Thus, a penal system built on the ideas of the conservatism philosophy of punishment and unwilling political dispositions to the adoption of context-based reform would not have produced a better result than the prevailing poor conditions of a number of prisons in Africa and some other developing nations (African Prisons Project 2012; Amnesty International 2008). While prisons have changed in several dimensions, especially in some developed nations, the apathy towards prison conditions and the health of the inmates in Africa only reflects what is obtainable in the larger society (Sarkin 2008).

A number of scholars have enumerated social and psychological conditions that could precipitate criminal behaviour in any society (Marsh 2006). While some have emphasised structural factors, some have considered psychological factors to be of more importance, and others considered bio-psychosocial factors. Among these various schools of thought consensus does not exist (Akers and Sellers 2008). Irrespective of the perspectives or the assumptions, criminal behaviour is a multi-causal phenomenon and thus cannot be pinned to a singular factor (Akers and Sellers, 2008; Marsh, 2006). However, a presumption in this chapter is that social factors play crucial roles in creating, encouraging, and sustaining criminal behaviours among humans. The same factors can also be a stimulus to how individuals could also be discouraged from indulging in criminal behaviours.

Prison Conditions in Nigeria

The prison conditions in Nigeria assessed in terms of physical condition reflect congestion and unending emotional and psychological strains on the inmates in particular and the prisons' staffs to an extent. The congestion in many Nigerian prisons has caused both imagined and unimagined consequences for many inmates. Critics have argued the dysfunctional nature of prisons as a social institution that attacks the soul and acts on the thoughts, the will, and the inclinations of the prisoners (Howe 1994). There are observable consequences, psychological as well as remote consequences, that may often be difficult to trace. In a number of Nigerian prisons, an average inmate appears mentally, physically and psychologically worse off than he or shewas before incarceration (Amnesty International 2008; 1983; Chiemeka 2002). As a product of the conservatism philosophy of punishment and prison, the conditions of Nigerian prisons and the working conditions of staff qualify as an objective reflection of the Nigerian state towards a reformative penal system. At this point, a cursory look at the conditions of two prisons in Nigeria may become more concrete through a summary of a recent Amnesty International (2008) report on five prisons in Nigeria.

Case 1: Wudil prison

> *The Wudil prison, located in a rural area, Kano State, has a capacity to accommodate only 160 inmates. At the moment, it contains fewer than 60 per cent of its official maximum capacity of inmates. In reality, it is doubtful if it could hold more than its present capacity. For instance, many of the 91 inmates sleep on bare floors, with no mattresses or bedding; new beds are sometimes left in the prison storeroom because the prison had not received any mattresses for them. The ceiling in one cell had collapsed. One of the beds in another cell jutted into the toilet area. Inmates spent their time outside their cells in a small, empty courtyard, with no space for any exercise and apparently nothing to do. The tailoring workshop in the prison is dusty and disused due to abandonment. Some inmates worked in the kitchen area, a roofless alcove where they prepared food in large pans over wood fires.*
>
> (Amnesty International 2008)

Oftentimes, discussions on prison conditions in Nigeria are focused on the weaknesses associated with the penal system and its reformation. Alternative measures that could lead to prison decongestion and fair trials of those awaiting trial are on the margin. The high level of congestion in Nigerian prisons may influence this. Available statistics have placed the proportion of Awaiting Trial Persons at 30,000 persons, representing over 65 per cent of the estimated prisoner population of 46,000 in Nigeria. The situation is similar across all the various categories of prisons in Nigeria (*ThisDay*, May 2012). The prison system is not alone in terms of neglect, poor physical conditions, and work environment. A number of other sub-systems within the Nigerian society are faced with similar challenges. Despite the similarities, the prison system has received the least form of concrete support in both finance and infrastructure that could transform the prisons into reformation centres. A possible explanation may be found in the erroneous view that those in incarceration deserve to be punished by denying them of all forms of privileges. Such views are enshrined in positions that offenders or inmates should be made to suffer since they have consciously taken a route that they should otherwise not have.

Case 2: Ikoyi Prison

> *The Ikoyi prison is one of the maximum prisons in Nigeria located in Lagos State. Twenty to thirty new inmates arrive at Ikoyi prison every day. The prison is extremely overcrowded as the initial capacity was for 800 inmates but now contains 1,933 men, of whom 1,820 (94 per cent) were awaiting trial. There are not enough spaces for the inmates, and the buildings are crying for reconstruction. Most cells are large dormitories meant for 50 inmates, but now up to 100 men share a single toilet. Only half of the inmates sleep in beds. Disease is widespread with unclean cells and little ventilation. Convicted prisoners and a few other inmates are allowed outside their cells to exercise or for outdoor recreation, but most inmates only go outside once a week. There is no running water inside the cells, so those who are locked up are dependent for water on those who are able to leave the cells.*
> *Ikoyi prison offers its inmates several daytime programmes: there are workshops in carpeting, tailoring, electronics and shoemaking. The school operates from an old building without a roof and offers an education programme up to tertiary level. However, only 6 per cent of inmates were registered for these activities: fewer than 50 were employed in a workshop and 75 attended school. Inmates awaiting trial are allowed neither to work nor go to school.*
> (Amnesty International, 2008)

In the social sequence of events, prisoners are most times from the poorest sectors of the society and suffer more from inequitable access to essential social services. This experience also exacerbates existing health problems of inmates (de Viggiani 2007). Yet to an extent, both the 'incarcerated' and the 'free' are created by the society. Beyond the discrimination of inmates in form of neglect, the poor prison conditions in Nigeria also portray an act of hypocrisy to the well-being of the prison staff. The temptation to focus on the inmates and their present and observable or imagined consequences of poor prison conditions is understandable since handling the present most times might be easier than the unimagined or future effects of poor prison conditions. It often escapes the mind in such instances that prison staff are only workers within the prison system and do interact often with the inmates and the public concomitantly. By virtue of their work environment, the average prison staff person is exposed to physical assault and health hazards. With this kind of neglect by the society in general and the government in particular, prison staff and inmates are encouraged to struggle for their survival. This has also created challenges for both inmates and prison staff alike. Some prison staff have vented out their frustrations on inmates by physical assault, maltreatment, and denial of rights, including availability and access to the acquisition of relevant entrepreneurship skills while in prison.

Entrepreneurship and Constraints in the Nigerian Prison System

Entrepreneurship in criminology literature has been portrayed in diverse ways, such as portraying crime as a career, e.g., the professional thief, and the viewpoint that crime or stealing is an art or profession that requires specialised skills and experience (Smith 2009:163). The emphasis on entrepreneurship in criminological discourse may have fuelled the proportion of entrepreneurship programmes across prisons (Smith 2009). While it is not novel that criminality may be viewed as entrepreneurial, the quest for rehabilitation of inmates, and crime prevention to an extent, has furthered the argument on the functionality and addressing entrepreneur constraints in development initiatives.

As a social phenomenon, entrepreneurship consists of economic as well as behavioral dimensions. From a managerial position, entrepreneurship entails the pursuit of opportunity without regard to resources currently available (Stevenson 1999:10). An implicit assumption in this position is the readiness of social actors to engage in creating or identifying opportunities and their utilization for personal and general benefits. While the ability of inmates to reconstruct their realities may not be doubted, based on available evidence (Smith 2009), there is limitation imposed by the internal and external environments of the prison. Prominent among such external influences include structural, economic, organizational, and behavioural barriers.

Structural and economic constraints often appear in the form of processes and procedures that influence everyday practices and outcomes within a social setting. At any form or level, structural and economic constraints are core in the factors that have influenced prison congestion in Nigeria (Amnesty International 2008). This makes their roles fundamental in the search for sustainable decongestion of prisons as well as health promotion within the prisons. Structural influence can be observed on what, when, how, and by whom entrepreneurship is accessed. At different levels and historical epochs, the Nigerian government has introduced a number of measures in scaling up entrepreneurship development. At the national level, the National Economic Empowerment and Development Strategy (NEEDS) was one of such recent initiatives aimed at empowering and developing the average Nigerian. More than five years after its introduction, the achievements of the NEEDS objectives are still at the margin (CBN 2004). While this programme is aimed at the larger society, the prison system has been at the margin of the strategy. While a skeletal prison-based entrepreneurship programme has been imitated from the developed nations, the sustainability of such programmes is questionable, as prison entrepreneurship in Nigeria has grown worse over the years (Amnesty International 2008). It is agreed that no perfect prison entrepreneurship exists anywhere; however, commendable efforts at functional prison-based entrepreneurship programmes have been recorded in a number of developed countries in Europe and North America (Smith 2009). With the present social arrangement of things in the Nigerian penal system, the possibility of operating culturally relevant prison-based entrepreneurship appears far off. This submission hinges on the existing constraints and structural impediments that are spanners in the wheel of achieving meaningful prison reforms in Nigeria.

The prison as an open system receives input as well as influences its environment. Within the prison system, the what, when, and how questions of entrepreneurship are further influenced by internal factors, among which include the availability of relevant current knowledge and skills among the prison staff, poor prison conditions, and the disposition of inmates and prison staff towards entrepreneurship, among other factors. Besides the influence from prison staff, access and utilization of entrepreneurship programmes could become gender-biased. A recent assessment on African prisons shows that, despite the existing inadequacies, skills programmes are often withheld from women prisoners entirely, as their stay in prison is usually shorter than men's and they are seen in this context as a waste of resources. Men enjoy trade-related skills programmes, where available, whereas women are taught how to scrub floors, sew, knit, and grow vegetables, contributing to gender inequalities in the region (McLean 2012). The poor conditions and inadequacy or absence of prison entrepreneurship programmes did not just emerge over night. Despite the existing constraints, there are emerging signs of progress that prison conditions could be improved by leveraging on the social entrepreneurship framework.

Social Entrepreneurship: An Emerging Framework

There is a wide variation in understanding what it means to be a social entrepreneur (Martin and Osberg 2007). A somewhat dominant way of conceptualizing social entrepreneur is in Dees (2001). In Dees' position, social entrepreneurs occupy active positions in effecting desirable change in the social sector. This entails adopting a mission to create and sustain social value (not just private value); recognizing and relentlessly pursuing new opportunities to serve that mission; engaging in a process of continuous innovation, adaptation, and learning; acting boldly without being limited by resources currently in hand; and exhibiting heightened accountability to the constituencies served and for the outcomes created. Clearly, Dees' (2001) conception of entrepreneur places strong emphasis on leadership skills, on being a problem solver and on the ability to take initiative and to think laterally.

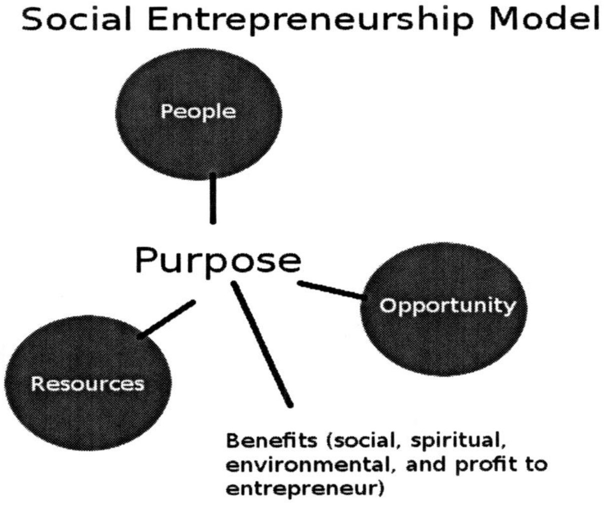

Figure 28.1: Social Entrepreneurship Model

(Source: Venture Pragmatist 2010)

Whereas a business entrepreneur typically measures performance in profit and return, a social entrepreneur focuses on creating social capital. Thus, the main aim of social entrepreneurship is to further social and environmental goals. However, whilst social entrepreneurs are most commonly associated with the voluntary and not-for-profit sectors, this need not necessarily be incompatible with making a profit.

With the diminishing public funding, social entrepreneurship as an innovative way of dealing with complex social needs is more prominent (Johnson 2000:1). Without denying the difficulties associated with the operationalisation and the contextual variations in the existing models and their strengths in achieving the core focus of social entrepreneurship, the prevailing challenges in a number of prisons in Nigeria and other African countries have re-enacted the need for alternatives that could support the drive towards humane prisons. One of such alternatives is the utilization of social entrepreneurship framework at all levels of the society, with the prison in particular. In a recent assessment, Smith (2009) opined that social entrepreneurship and prison-based entrepreneurs have strong potential for reducing recidivism as well as empowering inmates for positive change in the society. With overcrowding already a problem in Nigerian prisons, accessibility to programmes aimed at reforming prisoners for successful reintegration remains problematic. Against this backdrop, the next section of the chapter emphasises the plausibility of improving prison conditions in Nigeria by taking a cue from workable models within the framework of social entrepreneurship.

Different models of social entrepreneurship have been tested and found useful in effecting desirable social change. There are social entrepreneur models on capital provision as a means of empowerment. Social entrepreneurial organizations or individuals that believe in capital provision as a way out of poverty employ capital provision in form of small loans that will enable poor or marginalized groups in the society access to wealth creation. A prominent organization that has successfully demonstrated the value associated with this model is the Nobel Prize winner Mohammad Yunus (Bloom 2009).

Similar to the capital provision model is the business development assistance. The focus here is on the need for technical competence as a measure of creating expertise for the poor and marginalized in the society. This is built on participatory philosophy as a way of ensuring a sense of belonging in the drive towards social change. Another prominent model is the focus on improving access to quality and quantitative education. The presumption is that the right education is a form of empowerment to break out from poverty and marginalization. A number of organizations have remained at the forefront of ensuring access to quality education among the poor. The early Christian missionary in Nigeria and other parts of Africa could qualify as a model of social entrepreneur in this direction. In Nigeria, a majority of the schools that have withstood the test of time in terms of quality at both primary and secondary levels are those established by the early Christian missionaries (*The Nigerian Tribune* 2011). Despite the limited quantity and quality of such efforts in Nigerian prisons, religious bodies and non-governmental organizations have contributed minimally in providing educational materials to support skills acquisition within the prison system.

Resource matching in form of providing a link between resources and person in effecting a desirable change are common among some organizations. This form of linkages creates a platform for individuals and organizations to form alliances without necessarily encountering bureaucratic constraints. Organizations that operate with this model employ micro-lending and exchange of technical knowledge between suppliers and those in need. Such platforms have led to appreciable outcomes. A major organization in this direction is Kiva (see Bloom 2009 for details). Provision of products and services for those in need is also similar to resource matching. Organizations within this model focus their attention on providing products or services at prices that are affordable and not available in the open market system; such products and services could range from new technologies that are useful in the household, agriculture, health, education, and the legal fields.

The provision of relevantinformation and advocacy in creating better opportunities for the poor and marginalised is also common. The rationale of organisations operating with this model is to ensure that quality information is available to the needy. This could be in form of advocacy and political lobbying in the interest of the marginalised or poor. With a vibrant prison-based entrepreneurship programme, organisations can come in this direction and solicit necessary technical knowledge and information that will enhance skills acquisition among willing inmates. Despite the lofty goals and achievements associated with social entrepreneurship models, the workability of a model may differ from one cultural context and setting to the other. While there is limited information on the constraints and failures of some social entrepreneurship models, promising benefits are accruable from such programmes when focused on the prisons (African Prison Project 2012).

In Nigeria, entrepreneurship is an old cultural practice, but negatively affected by several factors. Among these factors are colonialism, a get-rich-culture, paid employment, an educational system built along colonial interest, unwillingness for internally and culturally motivated change, absence of policies originating in our cultural values, corruption, high life and ostentatious living by our political leaders, and our inability to learn from our mistakes and take bold steps (Adelola 1994; Chiemeka 2002; Enuku 2001). There are several examples one can cite in support of these factors. For instance, it is no longer new that the educational curriculum predominant in our educational system differs remarkably from the present socio-economic challenges confronting us as a nation.

Trying to make prison more humane should not be at the expense of the larger public interest. As stated earlier, a culture of entrepreneurship should not only be enshrined in the prison walls alone. Steps are on-going in this direction by non-governmental agencies and religious bodies taking entrepreneurship beyond this level, however, and its sustainability will require its incorporation into the culture outside the prison world. For instance, the National Economic Empowerment and Development Strategy started by the Obasanjo administration could be extended to those in prisons, especially the youths and the women in incarceration. If properly done, quite a number of the prisoners, who are mostly from poor economic backgrounds, will be better after leaving the prison. However, introducing such programmes will require a reorientation of the prison staff from previous work ethics to new ones. Recruitment of additional qualified hands is needed in the Nigerian prison service, especially in the drive towards professionalism and maintenance of social order. This will affect the quality of staff and interaction outcomes, as they relate more often with the prisoners than any other government agency. In the final analysis, alternatives to prison, such as the parole system and community service, may be better options than imprisonment. Alternative measures such as the ones mentioned here might be more cost-effective and functional than the present system with proper designs and sensitive implementation within the socio-cultural context of the Nigerian society.

Conclusion

Prisons are fast losing their relevance in Nigeria, as the four fundamental objectives for their existence are questionable (Adelola 1994; Civil Liberties Organisation 1995). The purpose of contemporary prison is ill-defined or neglected in the Prison Act, also known as *CAP 366, Laws of the Federal Republic of Nigeria 1990* (Jefferson 2007). Nevertheless, some of the problems bedevilling Nigerian correctional institutions are economic, social, and psychological in nature. These factors have also made Nigerian prisons unfavourable for the realisation of reformative and rehabilitative goals of prison (Amnesty International 2008; *ThisDay* 2012).The current state of affairs of Nigerian prisons can only take criminals off the streets for a while; in the end, events will likely repeat themselves (Chiemeka 2002). Much can be achieved if there is a general reorientation of the populace on wealth creation through cultivating entrepreneurship in and outside the prison wall. Work itself has health benefits, and these benefits, if properly harnessed outside and within the prison wall, will likely increase and encourage profitable activities among Nigerian youths, outside the prison and those within the prison especially, in the drive towards the rehabilitative ideology of modern-day prisons.

References

Adelola, I. O. (1994). Living and Health Conditions in Nigerian Prisons. A study of Inmates in Ado-Ekiti Prison in Nigeria. *Journal of Social Science and Humanities*, 11,122-139.

African Prisons Project. http://www.africanprisons.org/

Akers, R. L., and C. S. Sellers. (2008). *Criminological Theories: Introduction, Evaluation, and Application*, 5th Edition. Los Angeles: Roxbury.

Amnesty International. (2008) Nigeria: Prison conditions 'appalling'—New findings. Retrieved August 2, 2010, from http://www.amnesty.org.uk/uploads/documents/doc_18750.pdf

Bloom, P. N. (2009) Overcoming Consumption Constraints through Social Entrepreneurship. *Journal of Public Policy and Marketing* 28 (1): 128–134.

Central Bank of Nigeria. (2004) Nigeria: National Economic Empowerment and Development Strategy. Accessed July, 20 2012 from http://www.cenbank.org/out/publications/guidelines/rd/2004/needs.pdf

Chiemeka, U. (2002) Female Prisoners: A Case Study of Kiri-kiri Women's Prison Lagos. An unpublished PhD Thesis submitted to the Department of Sociology, University of Ibadan.

Dees, J. G. (2001) *The Meaning of Social Entrepreneurship*. Working paper, Fuqua School of Business, Duke University.

De Viggiani, N. (2007). Unhealthy prisons: exploring structural determinants of prison health. *Sociology of Health & Illness*, 29(1), 115-135.

Durham, A. (1994) *Crisis and Reform: Current Issues in American Punishment*. Boston: Little, Brown.

Enuku, U. E. (2001) Humanizing the Nigerian Prison through Literacy Education: Echoes from Afar. *Journal of Correctional Education,* 52, 1:18-22. Retrieved October 22, 2006, from http://www.nwlincs.org/correctional_education/articles/nigerian-prison-enuku.pdf.

Foucault, Michel. (1977) *Discipline and Punish: The Birth of the Prison.* Transl. Alan Sheridan. New York: Vintage.

Howe, A. (1994) *Punish and Critique: Towards a Feminist Analysis of Penalty.* London: Routledge.

Ikuteyijo, O. L., and O. M. Agunbiade. (2009) Social Dynamics of Prison Philosophies in Nigeria. In Jaishankar, K. (ed.), *International Perspectives on Crime and Justice.* Oxford: UK Cambridge Scholars Press, pp.690-710.

Jefferson, A. M. (2007) Prison officer training and practice in Nigeria: contention, contradiction and re-imagining reform strategies. *Punishment and Society* 9(3): 253–269.

Johnson, S. (2000) Literature Review on Social Entrepreneurship. Canadian Centre for Social Entrepreneurship.

Martin, Roger L., and Sally Osberg. (2007) Social Entrepreneurship: The Case for Definition. *Stanford Social InnovationReview* 5: 29–39.

Marsh, I. (2006)*Theories of Crime.* Abingdon: Routledge.

McLean, A. (2012) What makes a social entrepreneur? An Introductory article. http://www.africanprisons.org/images/uploads/banners/What_Makes_a_Social_Entrepreneur.pdf

Murphy, J. (1995) *Punishment and Rehabilitation,* 3d ed. Belmont, CA: Wadsworth.

Rotimi, A. (1982) Prison administration in Modern Nigeria. *International Journal of Comparative and Applied Criminal Justice* 9, 1:73-83.

Sarkin, J. (2008) Prisons in Africa: An evaluation from a human rights perspective. *International Journal of Human Rights.* http://www.surjournal.org/eng/conteudos/getArtigo9.php?artigo=9,artigo_sarkin.htm.

Smith, R. (2009) Entrepreneurship: A divergent Pathway out of Crime. In Jaishankar, K. (ed.) *International Perspectives on Crime and Justice.* Oxford: UK Cambridge Scholars Press, pp. 162-184.

Stevenson, H. H. (1999) A Perspective on Entrepreneurship. In Sahlman, William A., Howard H. Stevenson, Michael J. Roberts, and A. Amar Bhide (eds.), *The Entrepreneurial Venture* (2nd ed.). Boston: Harvard Business School Press, pp.7-22.

ThisDay (2012) Nigerian Prisons: Death Traps or Reform Centres? Retrieved July 22, 2012, from http://www.thisdaylive.com/articles/nigerian-prisons-death-traps-or-reform-centres-/115669/.

The Nigerian Tribune. (2011) Behold! First Church in Northern Nigeria. Retrieved July 30, 2012, from http://tribune.com.ng/sun/church-features/3194-behold-first-church-in-northern-nigeria-established-in-1929.

Chapter 29

REDUCING YOUTH UNEMPLOYMENT IN NIGERIA THROUGH ENTRPRENEURSHIP: A POLITICAL SCIENCE APPROACH

Adedoyin, J. O.

Introduction

The issue of unemployment and the concomitant efforts at reducing its impact on Nigerian youths has become a recurring decimal in the history of Nigeria's political economy. The wastefulness and recklessness in which the nation's resources were utilized by successive administrations (both military and civilian) between 1966 and the 1980s witnessed a drastic plunge of the economy of an oil-boom rich country into an oil-doomed one. During the oil-boom era of the 1970s, graduates of the nation's universities did not need to throng the streets in search of jobs. Instead, employers of labour besieged the campuses and offered potential graduates employment. Job opportunities abounded and parents hinged their hopes and aspirations on their children (graduates) to provide for them in their old age. This was indeed paradise.

In the 1980s, this situation began to change steadily. The military regimes of General Obasanjo (1976–1979), the Shagari civilian administration of (1979–1983), the Buhari-Idiagbon regime (1983–1985), and the Babangida administration (1985–1995) took the country to another level. These governments embarked on wasteful spending with careless abandon. There were discontinuities and inconsistencies in government policies. Evidences of gigantic (white-elephant) projects dotted the country's landscape, and few resources were devoted to education, while the required basic and social infrastructure witnessed rapid decline.

The massive unemployment in the country reached its peak during the reign of General Ibrahim Badamosi Babangida. The Babangida administration introduced the Structural Adjustment Programme (SAP) as part of its policy programme to enhance the nation's economy. Rather than generate employment, SAP further worsened the level of existing employment, while all the sectors of the economy also experienced systemic decline in their capacity to generate employment (Usman 2008:183). The liberalization of the economy through the twin policies of privatization and commercialization of government-owned enterprises also resulted in job losses, thereby swelling the country's unemployment figure. To add to these problems, companies found it difficult to meet up their production costs, and prices of goods and services spiraled upwards and uncontrollable inflation became the order of the day.

This situation created a downward trend in the condition of lives and the standard of living of the people; consequently, unprecedented poverty became predominant among the people. With these grim conditions on ground, unemployment and poverty became pervasive. Those youths who were lucky to have jobs became under-employed. Parents had to continue fending for their graduate children. The youths had no hope. They became a large part of a lost generation. Paradise was unbelievably turning into hell.

To reduce unemployment in the country, successive governments have come up with various strategies, notably the National Poverty Eradication Programme (NAPEP) and the National Economic Empowerment and Development Strategy programme (NEEDS). These strategies, one must say, have not been able to maximally, achieve their stated objectives. The problems of policy inconsistencies, discontinuities, and incoherencies further complicated the situation in which the political will and commitment to achieve stated objectives were often lacking. Above all, the focus on "book-based," "four wall" certificate accumulation and a blue collar-oriented educational approach also act as worsening factors.

In contemporary times, however, albeit in conforming to international best practices, emphasis is now placed on education based on entrepreneurship. It is on this premise that the study proceeds to examine and analyze the contributions and impact of political science and the role of government in reducing unemployment through entrepreneurship in Nigeria. To achieve this aim, an analysis of the conceptual framework for the study, literature review and the various strategies to be employed by the successive governments will be examined. At the end of the work, recommendations shall be made on how to effectively tackle youth employment through entrepreneurship in Nigeria.

The Role and Function of Government

Political science as a field of study deals with the study of politics and the organization as well as the responsibilities of government and the duties and obligations of the citizens within the state. Politics is about who gets what, when and how. Politics deals with the authoritative allocation of values and the distribution of public goods in an equitable manner. Since resources are scarce and cannot go round to everybody in the polity, the government is endowed with the power and authority to share the nation's resources in such a manner that they are equitably distributed. It is the duty of the government to provide the necessary framework in which the ideals of a good life, employment, orderliness, peace, and security can be realized. Government exists at any level to maintain order, that is, protecting life and property and ensuring security.

A logical derivation of this fact is that after government has established basic order, it must then provide public goods such as water, housing, health, education, employment, parks, etc., for its citizenry. In addition, government must also provide equal opportunities (economic, social and political) for the people. To this end, the government must ensure that the youths are well guided and the psyche re-oriented from certificate accumulation for white collar jobs into proper all-round holistic education, involving book learning, skill acquisition, creativity and the willingness to work in any environment.

It is indeed disheartening to state that in Nigeria, which is our focus of study, the government has reneged on this basic responsibility. The continued complexity of state governance, the uncontrollable astronomical population explosion, massive unemployment, and unavailability of basic needs as well as government insensitivity and unresponsiveness to the yearnings of the electorate have produced a situation of "revolution of rising frustration" among the masses. These frustrations are manifested through a high and increasing incidence of restiveness, especially among the youth; a high rate of delinquent behaviour, such as drug abuse; general decay in moral values;

prostitution and child abuse; poor health and malnutrition; and, above all, ignorance (Adelodun 2007); as well as rural–urban drift; infrastructural decay; and a general state of insecurity.

The conceptual framework behind the role and functions of government in providing meaningful employment for the youth can be found in the Utilitarian philosophy of Bentham (1789) and Mill (1937) and exemplified by the maxim of government providing "the greatest happiness for the greatest number of people" (Hampsher-Monk 2007:319).

Bentham's basic thesis of the principle of utility is instructive. Bentham showed that an understanding of utility informed us that the state ought to pursue the collective principle, which is the sum of the interests of the individuals within the state. Consequently, to ensure the happiness of the people, government needs to moderate economic inequalities within the framework of democracy (Rodee 19:230). Inequality diminishes the sum of happiness, while a few people having more money creates unhappiness for the poor. The government must ensure the delivery of public goods and services, such as the provision of employment, health, and good roads, and provide material goods by giving people the greatest incentive to work while ensuring that each person gets the maximum amount of the product of his or her labour.

It is within the framework of the utilitarian analysis that one can understand the various attempts by government to provide the youth with employment and implement policies to reduce the harsh (painful) effects of unemployment and poverty while ensuring security. Policies such as the establishment of the National Directorate of Employment (NDE) and the National Economic Empowerment and Development Strategy (NEEDS) are cases of note. The NDE was established in order to reduce inequality and generate employment opportunities for the unemployed, uplift the dignity of labour, and upgrade the social status of the Nigerian youth (NDE 1989). To achieve the stated objectives, the NDE is further empowered with a unique assignment to "create employment with emphasis on self reliance and entrepreneurship" (NDE 1987). The National Economic Empowerment and Development Strategy (NEEDS) is another policy embarked upon by government to ensure the prosperity of the citizens. NEEDS focuses on four (4) key areas, namely, reorienting values, reducing poverty, creating wealth, and generating employment. NEEDS is the government's way of letting the people know how it plans to overcome the deep and pervasive obstacles to progress and redirect efforts aimed at improving the lives of the Nigerian people (NEEDS 2004).

Undoubtedly, the pursuit of the NDE and NEEDS policies by the government is an indication that at the core of political science is the pursuit by government of the provision of the greatest happiness for the greatest number of people within its territory.

Public Policy, the Policy-Making Process and Development Administration

Public policy is a crucial field of political science, which impacts on the way and manner governments implement programmes through the creation and establishment of institutions and the adoption of processes and structures as well as appoint public officials endorsed with considerable responsibility and authority for controlling significant parts of people's lives (Eminue 2005:72). Policy, therefore, is simply a statement of the goals and objectives of an organization in relation to a particular subject and the description of the strategies by which the goals and objectives are to be achieved. The policy-making process, an adjunct of public policy, looks at how public policies are made and implemented. It describes the role of formal institutions and procedures as well as the informal aspect of decision-making (Kesselman 2007:32). The process also enables public officials in ministries, government agencies, and planning commissions, like the NDE, to play a critical role in identifying problems, synthesizing data, and presenting to political leaders alternative solutions and their implications. The impact of policy is felt more in the area of attempts by government to generate employment for the teeming youths and to eradicate poverty through organizations such as NDE and the NEEDS policy.

Emanating from public policy is the concept of development administration. Development administration involves the administration of development programmes, notably by government, to implement policies and plans designed to meet developmental objectives. The term *development administration* was first coined by Goswami (1955) and later popularized by scholars such as Riggs (1960), LaPalombara (1963), and Weidner (1964).

A summary of the objectives of development administration relating to government attempts at reducing unemployment through entrepreneurship involves:

1)   designing action / goal-oriented change;
2)   formulating plans and policies and implementing projects directed toward nation-building and development;
3)   adopting welfare-oriented programmes geared toward uplifting the masses.

The focus on development administration enables us to better understand the driving force behind a government's resolve (particularly in a country like Nigeria) to tackle headlong the issue of youth unemployment. To provide employment through entrepreneurship, the government has to come up with a viable plan, consistent policies, and sustainable programmes and objectives which could assist the country in eliminating poverty by improving the quality of life of its populace. From this perspective, the task of development administration has become that of setting developmental goals, which are planned, directed, and controlled by public agencies. In this wise, one cannot but agree with Hazary (2006) that, in contemporary times, development administration is about:

> the fight (of the state) against hunger, malnutrition, deprivation . . .
> and the decentralization of economic and political power. Through
> this process, developing economies attempt to transform a semi-

feudal extractive agricultural economy into a comparatively more rational economy of agriculture, industry and trade.

Our understanding of the core areas of development administration relating to employment generation through entrepreneurship can be summarized as follows:

1) There is emphasis on economic growth and capacity building, that is, the cultivation of skills, with further focus on wealth creation, and improving and equitably distributing the material conditions of life;
2) empowerment of the people, which involves the creation of an enabling environment for expanded opportunities for individuals and collectives to participate in economic and political transaction;
3) eliminating poverty and providing employment and the basic needs of life to every citizen;
4) ensuring good governance—ensuring a political system in which leaders are honest and transparent.

A cursory look at the activities of the Nigerian government since 1986, when the National Directorate of Employment (NDE) was established, will attest to the crucial impact of development administration as a backdrop of multiple developmental roles in the economy. At inception, the NDE was mandated, among others things, to:

1) design and implement programmes to combat mass unemployment,
2) articulate policies aimed at developing programmes with labour-intensive potentials, and
3) tackle employment problems in both the short- and long-term perspective by formulating and administering job creation as well as employment-related training (NDE Act 1989; NDE Annual Report2000).

An important aspect of development, which emphasizes human capacity-building and technological development, can be found in the works of Rodney (1972) and Ake (1981). These two scholarly works are classical examples of how political science has made immense contributions to employment generation strategies through entrepreneurship.

Rodney's analysis hinges on the premise that the individual must first of all have an increased skill and capacity, greater freedom, creativity, self-discipline, responsibility and material well-being. The point, according to Rodney (1972), is that the "achievement of any of those aspects of personal development is very much tied in with the state of the society as a whole". For a state to resolve the problem of unemployment and develop through entrepreneurship, Rodney (1972:10) suggested that:

a. A society develops economically as its members increase jointly their capacity for dealing with the environment. This capacity is dependent on the extent to which they understand the laws of nature (science) and devise tools (technology) and on the manner in which work is organized.

b.   The countries of Africa and (some parts) of Asia rely on agriculture and have little or no industry. Their agriculture is unscientific, and the yields are far less than those in developed countries.

c.   It takes a large number of skilled people to make an industrial economy function. Middle-level skills in fields such as welding are lacking.

d.   Development means a capacity for self-sustaining growth. It means than an economy must register advances, which in turn will promote further progress.

e.   One of the features associated with technological advance is a spirit of scientific inquiry closely related to the process of production. This leads to inventiveness and innovation.

The concern with inventiveness and technology in reducing unemployment is closely related to the analysis of Ake (1981) with respect to colonialism and local technology. Ake expounded that the history of African economies reveals their heavy reliance on foreign technology, which is limited and complex in nature. During the colonial period, local skills and technologies were de-emphasized. Accordingly, colonial trade tended to destroy the traditional crafts and artisanship in Africa (Ake 1981:38). The situation was worsened by the deliberate flooding of African markets with . . .

> substitutes, which were cheaply produced but considered exotic, more desirable or more functional . . . than the traditional wares. Colonial trade merely encouraged primary production with its emphasis on unskilled labour. Thus, colonial trade was in effect bringing a regress in the development of production forces. . . The little technology made available to the people then was not integrated into the local culture and system of production; hence, its ability to stimulate further technological development was severely limited (Ake 1981:88–109).

The regression in the development of African economies led to a state of haphazard development, in which the economies became predominantly agrarian and the majority of youths and graduates of higher institutions relied heavily on white-collar jobs requiring no specialized entrepreneurial skill. To get out of this logjam and cushion the effects of unemployment, suggestions have been made on how to acquire technology both locally and through technological transfer and borrowing. In his contribution, Rodney (1972:105) expounded that "when a society, for whatever reason, finds itself technologically trailing behind others, it catches up not so much by the independent inventions but by borrowing. Once a principle or a tool is known, it spreads or diffuses to other people".

It is important to restate here that at this point in Nigeria's quest for economic development, policy planners should endeavour to pursue the skills required for entrepreneurship found in the first two stages of Rostow's economic growth (Rostow 1960). Although Rostow's work has been criticized for being too Eurocentric, the reality is that the Nigerian economy lacks credible industry, with no forward and backward linkages. The focus therefore, is on developing the individual capacity to generate employment through the acquisition of basic skills that will guarantee/sustain his life chances and generate income to boost his standard of living. To this end, Harrison'sstudy

(1974:300) posits that the technology required for employment generation through entrepreneurship in Nigeria should focus on:

a. craft-technology, in which the level of mechanization is low and much of the work is done by hand;

b. machine-tended technology, in which workers who tend machines carry out the bulk of the productive process.

All-automated technology will surely take the country back to the period of technological dependence,in which obsolete and out-dated technology were imported into the country. Truly, the concentration of skills within the craft and machine-tended skills level is likely to give rise to four primary system outputs that will assist in reducing unemployment in the country, viz. (Harrison 1974:329):

a. Production: which is a measure of organizational accomplishment relative to the resources committed to it;

b. Innovation: which is technological change involving new products or new uses for existing products;

c. Satisfaction: which is a measure of fulfillment of human needs; and

d. Development: a measure of the organization/polity as a more viable entity or the individual as a more accomplished performer.

Strategies for Reducing Unemployment in Nigeria Through Entrepreneurship: The Polical Science Approach

This section examines specific strategies to reduce youth unemployment through entrepreneurship. These strategies, one must say, are derived from the concepts of political science analyzed under the conceptual framework section. Some of the methods are listed hereunder:

The government should come up with a deliberate plan, that is, the promulgation of government policy in the national development plan. The Vision 2020, for instance, is a step in the right direction. The government should ensure that the goals and stated objectives be backed by the requisite political will and commitment. The commitment should be backed up with adequate budgetary and financial provisions for youth employment and education and the provision of social infrastructure.

It is important that government also come up with a realistic investment policy as well as create an enabling environment for trading activities, which will encourage foreign investment in the country. The adoption of concessionary methods, such as tax holidays and exemptions, an adequate supply of water and electricity, construction of good roads, and security, are areas that also need re-focusing.

The government needs to encourage infant industries whose area of concentration involves the use of artisans, technicians, engineers. To this end, there is the need for indigenous capacity-building in engineering, science and technology. These locally developed skills should be applicable to all the sectors of the economy. Consequently, the government should encourage capacity-building in human skills, institutional and organizational structures and institutional procedures. Most importantly, emphasis should be on (Eminue 2005:223 and 498):

a) Developing human capital and inculcating in the citizenry specific (trade) skills.
b) Removing sources of systemic failure, which result in the poor use of available resources.
c) Addressing factors which contribute to an inadequate or inconducive procedural and institutional environment.
d) Ensuring adequate provision for retraining; job research and relocation assistance for employed workers through the use of yellow pages or labour magazines, for instance, will be a useful means of improving the operation of the labour market. They will also serve as useful guides for unemployed workers to find and take up job vacancies.
e) Assisting small-scale industries through the provision of credit facilities, granting of tax holidays, and relaxation of legislation inhibiting the creation of new enterprises. "Promotion of resource-based industries will generate a multiplier effect, which could be captured within the economy".
f) Emphasizing the use of labour-intensive technology, especially within the manufacturing industry and the agriculture sector, will contribute significantly in absorbing labour. Applied technology villages or centres to nurture technology-based but employment-generating industries should also be established.

It is pertinent to state that the government should focus more on commercial farming and re-direct its attention on the training of youths in modern-farming techniques as well as establish communal farming settlements with effective funding and monitoring.

Government should also rehabilitate and upgrade the moribund production facilities of River Basin Development Authorities (RBDA) through partnership with the private sector and reawaken its agricultural development programmes in the areas of extension services, sensitization awareness, capacity building and institution strengthening. Efforts should also be geared toward the reopening of the farm settlement scheme by creating farm institutes and farm centres to encourage young school leavers to pursue careers in farming andthe renewal of school agricultural gardens, where each student is encouraged to cultivate, tend and harvest his/her garden.

Finally, and speaking from a political science perspective, it is important to emphasize civic education as a means of reducing unemployment through entrepreneurship. To disabuse the minds of Nigerians away from white-collar jobs, it is important to enlighten and sensitize the populace to the advantages of skills-based personal employment. To achieve this objective, the present educational curricula at the primary, secondary and tertiary levels should expand their course content to embrace the values of patriotism, skilled labour, self-fulfillment, self-worth, dignity of labour, and self-confidence.

Conclusion

This study examined and analyzed the contributions and impact of political science and the role of government at reducing unemployment through entrepreneurship in Nigeria. Our analysis emphasized that government exists at any level to maintain order, that is, to protect life and property and ensure security. To ensure the happiness of the people, government needs to moderate economic inequalities within the framework of democracy. To understand the dynamics of ensuring equal opportunities to all Nigerians, we analyzed the discontinuities and inconsistencies in government policies since the 1970s, especially during the Babangida administration, which worsened the level of employment in the country. The privatization and commercialization of government-owned enterprises also resulted in job losses, thereby swelling the country's unemployment figure. To reduce unemployment in the country, successive governments have come up with various strategies, notably the National Poverty Eradication Programme (NAPEP) and the National Economic Empowerment and Development Strategy programme (NEEDS). The problems of policy inconsistencies, discontinuities, and incoherencies as well as the political will and commitment to achieve stated objectives were attributed to factors hindering the effective provision of employment opportunities to the teeming youths in the country.

To achieve sustainable development and economic growth, the government has to reduce inequality and generate employment opportunities for the unemployed, uplift the dignity of labour, and upgrade the social status of the Nigerian youth. The government also has to "create employment with emphasis on self-reliance and entrepreneurship". The study has been able to show that the pursuit of the NDE and NEEDS policies by the government is an indication that at the core of political science is the pursuit by government of the provision of the greatest happiness to the greatest number of people within its territory.

The study also focused on the contribution of political science in reducing unemployment in Nigeria through its sub-field of the public policy-making process and development administration. The impact of policy are felt more in the area of attempts by government to generate employment for the teeming youths and eradicate poverty through organizations as NDE and the NEEDS policy.

The area of development administration enables government to implement policies and plans designed to meet developmental objectives, such as reducing youth unemployment, eliminating poverty, and providing employment and the basic needs of life to every citizen. An important aspect of development, touched upon in this study, is that which focused on human capacity building and technological development as a capacity for self-sustaining growth.

In conclusion, this study is of the view that Nigerian youth must be empowered with the requisite skills that would enable them to fit properly into the job market, both locally and internationally. In the present globalized economy, youths with soaring imagination, creativity, and technical skills and imbued with competitive spirit are needed to help the nation achieve its developmental objective. To achieve this feat, however, the government must effectively carry out its role as the provider of the greatest happiness to the greatest number of people. Government must ensure it by providing the youths with the social and economic opportunities that will enable them to realize their life potentials. Availability of employment, good roads, qualitative health care facilities and schools; maintenance of law and order; and the provision of security, which are the basic responsibilities of government, are necessary in this regard.

Above all, there is the need to embark on a general review of the nation's school curriculum system. In addition, the government must provide adequate funding for the educational sector, while emphasis should be placed upon the acquisition of skills both during and after the formative school years.

References

Ake, C. (1981) *A Political Economy of Africa*. London: Longman Publishers.

Eminue, O. (2005) *Public Policy Analysis and Decision Making*. Lagos: Concept Publications Ltd.

Hampsher-Monk, I. (1992) *A History of Modern Political Thought*. Malden, MA: Blackwell Publishers.

Harrison, E. F. (1978) *Management and Organizations*. Boston: Houghton Mifflin Company.

Hazary, N. (2006) *Development Administration*. Delhi, India: APH Publishing Company.

Janda, K., J. M. Berry, and J. Goldman. (2008) *The Challenge of Democracy*, 9th Edition. Boston: Houghton Mifflin Company.

LaPalombara, J. (1963) *Bureaucracy and Political Development*. Princeton, NJ: Princeton University Press.

Kesselman, M., J. Krieger, and W. A. Joseph. (2007) *Introduction to Comparative Politics*, Fifth Edition. Stamford, CT: Cengage Learning.

Mill, James. (1937) *An Essay on Government*. Cambridge: Cambridge University Press.

National Directorate of Employment (NDE). (1987) Creating more jobs opportunities. Abuja: Federal Government Press.

———. (1989) Entrepreneurship development programme for youth corps members. Abuja: Federal Government Press

———. (2002) Annual Report. Abuja: Federal Government Press.

———. (2007) NDE Employment Generation as the grassroots through capacity building and rural/infrastructural development. A paper presented at a Workshop for Local Government Chairmen and Secretaries, Kaduna, Nigeria, April 2–3.

———. (2011) Annual Report. Abuja: Federal Government Press.

National Planning Commission. (2004) NEEDS: Meeting Everyone's Needs. Abuja: Federal Government Press.

Riggs, F. W. (1960) *Ecology of Public Administration*. New York: Asia Publishing House.

Rodee, C. C., T. J. Anderson, C. Q. Christol, and T. H. Green. (1983) *Introduction to Political Science*. New York: McGraw-Hill Publishing Company.

Rodman, N. P. (1968) Development Administration: Obstacles, Theories and Implications for Planning. International Institute of Educational Planning (IIEP) Occasional Papers No. 2. Paris, France: UNESCO.

Rodney, W. (1982) *How Europe Underdeveloped Africa*. Nigeria: Ikenga Publishers.

Rostow, W. W. (1960) *The Stages of Economic Growth*. Cambridge: Cambridge University Press.

Singhal, A. (2006) *Evolution of Development and Development Administration Theory*. New Delhi, India: Indian Institute of Public Administration.

Stone, D. (1965) Government Machinery Necessary for Development. In Driesberg, Martin (ed.), *Public Administration in Developing Countries*. Washington, DC: Brookings Institution.

Trivedi, K. D. (1987) *Perspectives in Development Administration*. New Delhi: Mittal Publications.

Usman, A. (2008) Trends and Structure of Employment and Wages. In Saliu, H., A. Aderinto, I. H. Jimoh, and G. T. Arosanyin (eds.), *Nigeria's Economic Policies in the Fourth Republic*. Lagos: Concept Publications Ltd.

Chapter 30

THE CONSTRAINT OF ENTREPRENEURIAL GROWTH IN NIGERIA

Ayeni, O. O.

Introduction

"As Nigeria goes, so goes Africa" (Rotberg 2007) was a prominent statement in the 1960s when the Nigerian State emerged as an independent country and assumed the leadership role in the continent, owing to its natural resources, human resources and the population. According to the UNDP (2009), Nigeria is naturally endowed with millions of acres of arable land, 38.5 billion barrels of stated oil reserves, a variety of unexploited minerals, and a wealth of human capital by virtue of its estimated population of 150 million. Nigeria is also rated as the world's eighth largest exporter of oil, and Africa's second largest economy. Despite these resources, insecurity, unemployment, youth restiveness and poverty remain prominent features of Nigeria as a result of inadequate entrepreneurial growth that would have created an alternative to insufficient white collar jobs and mitigated against unemployment, which is the catalyst for various un-developmental indices in the polity.

Entrepreneurship, as a cradle of jobs and wealth, appears not to be given top priority and seriousness both in the national policy and in implementation strategy, given the above problems. This paper therefore examines the constraints on entrepreneurial growth in Nigeria, the potentials for its development, and ways to remove those constraints for sustainable development in a developing nation state like Nigeria.

Conceptual Clarification

Entrepreneurship, as a concept, is derived from the French word 'entreprendre', meaning 'to undertake'. Entrepreneurship is the activity of venturing into new enterprises. It is different from management. It is the creation of new enterprises to meet new challenges and opportunities presented by a given situation. It is also a process of bearing a non-insurable risk so as to achieve business objectives (Awe and Ayeni 2008). In the same vein, Zimmerer and Scarborough (2006) opine that, although the creation of business is certainly an important facet of entrepreneurship, it is not the complete picture. The characteristics of seeking opportunities, taking risks beyond security, and having the tenacity to push an idea through to reality combine into special perspectives that permeate entrepreneurs. To Agboola and Kenneth (2012), entrepreneurship or enterprise is regarded in economics as a factor for productive use. It simply means the organization of production of land, labour and capital. In line with Agboola and Kenneth's position, Meredith (1992) sees entrepreneurs as people who have the ability to see and evaluate business opportunities, to gather the necessary resources to take advantage of them and to initiate appropriate action to ensure success.

Schumpeter described the entrepreneur as an innovator. In another work, Schumpeter, cited in Swayne and Tucker (1973), described the entrepreneur's roles as 'creative destruction'. In his view 'creative destruction' occurs when innovation renders old ideas and technology obsolete. An entrepreneur is an innovator, developing new things and making them accessible to the customers. To Schumpeter, entrepreneurs are motivated by aspiration for both economic and political power. Letchford (1975) opines that the main task of the entrepreneur is to organize production by bringing together and setting to work the (other) three factors of production. He further observed that one of his particular functions is that of decision making, which involves making estimates. Strauss (1944) claims that 'the firm is the entrepreneur', and the entrepreneur holds two fundamental responsibilities: 'the assumption of risk' and 'the assumption of management'. For further emphasis on the characterization of the entrepreneur in respect to other factors that operate in the firm, Baumol (1968) avows that the entrepreneur's position is 'the apex of the hierarchy that determined the behaviour of the firm'. He further distinguishes between entrepreneurial and managerial functions. To him, a manager is an individual 'who oversees the ongoing efficiency of continuing process'. He supervises the allocation of inputs; ensures that schedules, controls and contracts are respected; and makes decisions about pricing and advertising. In other words, the manager is in charge of routine activity, while the entrepreneur's function concerns the development and the implementation of new ideas; he is 'the Schumpeterian innovator'.

However, Hisrich and Peters (2002) opine that the entrepreneur is a person who searches for change, responds to the change, and exploits the change as an opportunity. They further describe an entrepreneur as someone who is proactive, unassuming and ready to move at the slightest opportunity, who pursues the opportunity, and who brings together all factors of production to make profits. To Udu and Agu (1989), an entrepreneur organizes human and material resources for the production of goods and services. According to them, an entrepreneur is the driving force behind the production and movement of goods and services. In the same vein, Beyene (2002) gives a comprehensive condition for entrepreneurial development in any country. According to him, a potential entrepreneur needs to search for (business) opportunities and must posses technical and commercial skills and entrepreneurial spirit. He requires finance, infrastructure and a conducive or favorable macro-economic environment. In all entrepreneurial activities the role of government is central. Unfortunately, many developing countries often pay lip service to these, which is a major challenge to the growth of entrepreneurship in a country like Nigeria.

An Overview of Entrepreneurship Development in Nigeria

Views are divergent in attempts to put entrepreneurship in Nigeria in a historical perspective. According to Osalor (2008), people of the Ibo community in Nigeria are considered to be one of the oldest entrepreneurs in history, their experience stretching back to times before modern currency and trade models had developed elsewhere on the planet. This may not be peculiar to the Ibos alone, as many other ethnic groups that constitute Nigeria engaged in various activities even in the pre-modern government, at least, to provide basic needs for the citizens and for commercial purposes. Some basic entrepreneurial activities characterize different ethnic groups which have been their normal practice in history. Occupations such as dying, blacksmithing, bricklaying, crafting, hunting, farming were notable entrepreneurial activities that are not only peculiar to the Ibos but also the Yorubas, who engaged in them for both personal use and commercial purposes. The Hausa-Fulani also engaged in farming, rearing of animals and other businesses. The implication of this is that nobody can lay claim in the real sense of it to the originality of entrepreneurial activities in Nigeria.

However, the entrepreneurial activities in Nigeria were on the rightful path before the discovery of oil in the '50s. The billions of dollars generated from oil took the attention of government away from creating a necessary environmental condition for the growth of entrepreneurship in Nigeria. Unfortunately, the entrepreneurial activities are going down, while the government is concentrating on oil exploration and exploitation, in which 80% of its reserve benefits just 1% of the population. Owing to over-dependence on oil, of Nigeria's youth population of 80 million, representing 60% of the total population of the country, 64 million are unemployed, while 1.6 million are underemployed (Awogbenle and Iwuamadi 2010).

In line with the above predicaments, various attempts have been made to reposition entrepreneurship towards job creation in Nigeria. In 1977, the National Policy on Education was promulgated and inculcated vocational skills' acquisition into the educational curriculum. As a result of government's lackadaisical attitude at all levels towards this, the program was rendered ineffective and the purpose for its creation became moribund as a result of political corruption, which has become the bane of governance in Nigeria. On March 26, 1986, another giant step was taken by the government of General Ibrahim Babangida by setting up the Chukwuma Committee to look into the problem of unemployment in Nigeria (Omoniyi and Osunde 2004). At that time, it became conspicuous that government efforts at creating jobs might not yield fruits after all. Emphasis was, therefore, laid on government to create an enabling environment for the growth of entrepreneurship, which is the major source of job creation, even in developed economies. The report of this committee necessitated the establishment of the National Directorate of Employment (NDE) in the same year. Since 1986, efforts towards entrepreneurship development have been profound, with the establishment of the Better Life Programme (BLP), the Family Support Programme (FSP), the National Poverty Eradication Programme (NAPEP), and the Community Bank.

Considering the mineral resources and human capital of a nation like Nigeria, it is not an aberration to say that Nigeria has the potential for steady development. This has been impeded by the inability of the government to put the country on the path of entrepreneurship growth and to end the frustration of the youths, who target the very government that alienated them.

The Potentials for Entrepreneurship Growth in Nigeria

The potentials for entrepreneurship development vary in different nations. While some nation-states are yearning for these potentials, some cannot articulate theirs for sustainable development, most especially when nations are compared. It is germane to say here that nations cannot experience equal and tremendous entrepreneurship growth owing to variations in potentials that can be put up for reengineering of such a venture. In understanding the constraints, there is a need to first examine the potentials.

(a) *Democracy*

Democracy, as a particular type of government regime in which the political process facilitates and regulates the strategic interaction of social actors to realize collective benefits, has almost become a general practice, as about 121 countries, including Nigeria, practice it. Governance, therefore, can be classified as good only when it gives room for gainful employment, innovations, and breaking of new ground and when it gives necessary freedom to do this. Obviously, this was lacking before the emergence of democratic rule on May 29, 1999. Prior to this time, Nigeria's former military rulers failed to diversify the economy away from its overdependence on the capital-intensive oil sector, which provides 95% of foreign exchange earnings and about 80% of budgetary revenues (Index Mundi 2011). The enthronement of democracy in Nigeria was followed by the IMF Stand-By Agreement in August 2000, through which Nigeria received a debt restructuring deal from the Paris Club and a $1billion credit from the IMF. The debt relief of 2005 and many other external assistance deals that followed were made possible as a result of Nigeria's transition from military rule to democracy. This obviously created a fertile ground for entrepreneurial growth in Nigeria, as either Small Scale Enterprises (SMES) or Large Scale Enterprises (LSE). No business can grow in the atmosphere of fear which characterizes military government. The freedom to determine who govern and the freedom to challenge any misrule (democracy) have led to the resuscitation of some entrepreneurial policies (National Directorate of Employment Scheme, The Bank of Industry, Small and Medium Enterprise Development Agency of Nigeria and Small and Medium Industries Equity Investment Scheme) and the initiation of new ones.

(b) *Oil*

Nigeria is strongly positioned for entrepreneurial development as a result of huge oil deposits in the country and as a strong member of the Organization of Petroleum Exporting Countries (OPEC) as well as one of the largest producers of crude oil in the world. This potential is enormous, as many nations that are not so blessed are striving to create an enabling environment for their entrepreneurs. Apart from providing the necessary capital, oil itself can create a lot of entrepreneurial business and employment for the teeming population of Nigeria

(c) *Telecommunication*

Since 2000, the Nigerian telecommunications sector of the economy has become a great potential for the take-off and development of many enterprises. Apart from creating an infrastrucral base, it has been a source of income to many small- and large-scale businessmen and -women. Nigeria could only boast of about 25,000 analogue cellular mobiles (ACM) in 2000, but the country now has about 92.1 million active subscribers in 2011 (Ndukwe 2011). It is assumed that a reasonable percentage of these subscribers are using their lines for entrepreneurial purposes. As part of the infrastructure needed for the growth of entrepreneurship, it has also been a potential for the development of entrepreneurship in Nigeria.

(d) *Human Resources and Market*

Human resources and markets are pre-conditions for entrepreneurial growth in any country. Considering the available human resources and the population of Nigeria, Nigeria is a fertile ground for any business. As of July 2012, theNigerian population is 170,123,740, with youth representing 60% of the total population of the country (Index

Mundi, 2012). Many of these youths are well trained but unengaged because the potentials for entrepreneurship in the country are not utilized. Countries like China and India are densely populated, and this has been the major strength towards their economic advancement. Entrepreneurship cannot grow without domestic and external markets for the entrepreneurial products. China, with a population of more than 1.3 billion, has the largest market for any product (ibid.). In the same vein, the population of Nigeria, with about 170 million, is a great asset for entrepreneurial development if the necessary infrastructure and enabling environment are created.

Entrepreneurial Qualities

It is not every entrepreneur who succeeds, but every intending entrepreneur or businessman or -woman must possess the following qualities to enable him or her to drive the business profitably:

(a)   the readiness to face challenges;

(b)   the readiness to break new ground;

(c)   an appreciation of humble beginnings;.

(d)   dependability, energy and health;

(e)   understanding of his/her economic and political environment;

(f)   the ability to take risks;

(g)   the ability to make the right choices; and

(h)   possession of purposive leadership traits.

In the same vein, Awe (2006) highlighted the characteristics which an entrepreneur needs to achieve the objectives set for himself. These include:

> Self confidence, assertiveness, boldness, courage, optimism, and willingness to take control risks, a capacity for hard work, discipline, diligence, and perfectionism, ambition, persistence, determination and commitment to a goal, leadership ability, decisiveness, efficiency and the ability to delegate authority, team spirit, concern for others, and ability to solve problems, resourcefulness, incentiveness, organizational attitude, flexibility and adaptability. He must be a man of integrity and honesty, who must be committed to high standard of quality. He must be intelligent and possess the ability to give good judgment.

These are personal traits that an intending businessman or entrepreneur must possess to succeed in his/her business. Despite the practice of all these traits, many entrepreneurs still fail in achieving their target, most especially in a developing country like Nigeria, owing to a lot of constrains that inhibit growth of entrepreneurship on a daily basis.

The Constraints on Entrepreneurship in Nigeria

An attempt to single out the constraints on entrepreneurship alone in Nigeria may be an odious task, as the country itself is facing a lot of challenges which have necessitated government to set up various Special Purpose Vehicles (SPVS), intervention funds, agencies and institutions to tackle the challenges in a way that will have a significant impact on the economy. According Okereke (2001), the programs and activities of such agencies and SPVS as Asset Management Corporation of Nigeria (AMCON), Debt Management Office (DMO), Power and Aviations Interventions Funds (PAIF), Commercial Agriculture Credit Scheme (CACS), Textile Support Fund (TSF), Small and Medium Enterprise Credit Guarantee (SMECGS), among others, impacted on the economy all through 2010. Despite these improvements and the establishment of SMECGS, entrepreneurial growth in Nigeria is being constrained by a lot of factors.

According to Olusegun Obasanjo (2011), when he was examining the disposition of African leaders towards job creation, he opined:

> I want to underline this as a situation that must signal red alert for us in Africa; I am worried; I am apprehensive about unemployment in our continent. It is not being taken as seriously as it should be. I give my own example of my country Nigeria: we have 120 universities. When I was growing up and I had to go to university, there was only one university with polytechnics and other tertiary institution; now we have more than 200. We have over 600,000 graduates every year and we are not creating 100,000 jobs for the graduates. The youth can be ignited anytime and now we have about 165 million population. We must be talking about jobs, jobs and jobs.

The above, no doubt, has shown the African dilemma. Unemployment has created many other avoidable problems, not only in Nigeria but on the continent of Africa. Entrepreneurship as a 'creative destruction', which is a major source of job creation in the developed countries, is facing the following challenges in Nigeria.

(a) *Corruption*

The capacity of Nigeria to experience tremendous entrepreneurial development has been limited by a lack of accountability, efficiency and effectiveness in the public domain. Sharp practices have been the major factor militating against businesses in Nigeria. According to Ajayi (2007), between 1960 and 2006, Nigerian leaders stole a total sum of $500 billion or 80 trillion naira. General Sani Abacha alone allegedly stole more than $3 billion between 1993 and 1998. For the past 50 years African leaders had stolen about $613 billion. This has been the major reason for financial constraint which has been responsible for the impediment against the growth of entrepreneurship not only in Nigeria but in Africa.

(b) *Insecurity*

Insecurity is also another constraint on entrepreneurial growth in Nigeria. From 1999 till date, security in Nigeria has been threatened by the activities of armed militants such as Boko Harram, Bakasi Boys, O'odua Peoples Congress (OPC) and Egbesu Boys. To develop a nation and any business, an atmosphere of peace is a major precondition. Crisis, either political or religious, has destroyed a lot of businesses and discouraged youths from venturing into such. Any enterprise that is serious about doing business must ensure its own security outfit, and the financial involvement in doing this has made entrepreneurial business in Nigeria a major challenge.

(c) *Infrastructure*

Good roads, constant power supply, access to information and communication, technology and good transportation system are central to the development of entrepreneurship in any country. Unfortunately, the inadequate provision of these infrastructures has frustrated many businesses and intending business men. The cost of providing alternatives to this has increased the cost of production and reduced the profits. Attempts by the businessmen and -women in Nigeria to keep themselves in business despite this hike in the cost of production have made the price of locally produced goods higher than that of imported ones, thereby making buyers prefer the imported to the locally produced goods.

(d) *Education*

Since entrepreneurship is all about inventions, innovations, modifications and copying existing ideas, it means an entrepreneur must be familiar and in tune with happenings around him. To achieve these, education has become very crucial. Nigeria is not developing today because lip service has been paid to education and to entrepreneurship education. For example, until recently entrepreneurship as a course,was not included in our educational curriculum. When entrepreneurship is not taught, how can one develop new ways of doing it? To be a successful entrepreneur, one needs to move from 'raw idea to valid idea', i.e., to clarify ideas, clarify what needs they meet, see them work in operating conditions, ensure practicability, satisfactory quality, customer identification, check for business barriers, and identify competition and learn from it (Awe 2003). To achieve these requires adequate education, which unfortunately is not adequate in Nigeria today.

Conclusion

There is no doubt that entrepreneurship has become an acceptable practice in almost all economies. It has a veritable way of addressing unemployment and other social vices that emanate from it. To promote economic growth and development, there is a need to annex the human resources and capital resources towards entrepreneurial growth in Nigeria. Discussion has shown that certain constraints have inhibited entrepreneurial growth in Nigeria, namely, corruption, insecurity, lack of adequate infrastructures, and lack of education. These constraints have made entrepreneurship a difficult task in Nigeria. The resultant effects of these anomalies are poverty and an increase in the crime rate. For Nigeria to get out of the identified problems arising from constraints on entrepreneurial growth, government needs to focus on the constraints, as they are not insurmountable.

To achieve this, there is a need to shun corruption (informal and formal) at all levels of government and therefore use the available resources to provide a conducive atmosphere for the growth of entrepreneurship in Nigeria. However, constraints can inhibit growth and development. The basic infrastructures such as good roads, telecommunications, water, transportation, and electricity are therefore necessary to drive entrepreneurship and economic development. More importantly, the public and private sectors of the economy need to partner towards entrepreneurship growth by formulating and implementing favourable tax policies and provide necessary funds for the growth of both small and medium enterprises in Nigeria.

It is also important that government should encourage the Nigerian youth to learn trades by establishing more entrepreneurship centres and also by providing adequate funds to the existing ones. This will not only reduce people's agitation for white collar jobs but create more employment opportunities for Nigeria's teeming population.

References

Agboola, O. F., and O. Kenneth. (2012) *Effectiveness and Constraints of Promoting Entrepreneurship for the Growth and Development of African Economy.* Benin City: Benson Idahosa University.

Ajayi, K. (2007) Is this Democracy? The Leadership Crises in Africa. *Journal of Political Behaviour,* Vol. 2, No. 1, pp. 63–72.

Awe, A. A and Ayeni, R. K. (2008) The Entrepreneur and Economic Development. In Omotosoetal (ed.), *Entrepreneurship Development in Nigeria.* Ado-Ekiti: University of Ado-Ekiti Press.

Awe, O. I. W. (2005) *Strategic Entrepreneurship Development.* Ado-Ekiti: University of Ado-Ekiti Press.

Awogbenle, A. C., and K. S. Iwuamadi. (2010) Youth Unemployment: Entrepreneurship Development Programme as an Intervention Mechanism. *African Journal of Business Management,* Vol. 4 (6), pp. 831–835.

Baumol, W. J. (1968) Entrepreneurship in Economic Theory..*American Economic Review,* 58(2), 64-71.

Beyene, A. (2002) Enhancing the Competitiveness and Productivity of Small and Medium Scale Enterprises (SMEs) in Africa: an Analysis of Differential Roles of National Governments Through Improved Support Services. *Africa Development,* Vol. XXVII, No. 3, pp. 130–156.

Hirsich, R. D., and M. P. Peters. (2002). *Entrepreneurship.* Boston: Mcgraw Hill / Irwin.

Index Mundi. (2011) *Nigeria GDP-Real Growth Rate.* Bolivia: Index Mundi.

Letchford, S. (1975) *The Economic System.* Johannesburg: Donnington Press.

Meredith, C. G. (1992) *The Practice of Entrepreneurship.* Geneva: ILO.

Ndukwe, E. C. (2011) A Decade of Telecom Revolution in Nigeria. *Online Business Day.* Retrieved December 1, 2012.

Obasanjo, O. (2011) Task United Nations, ILO, Government on Job Creation on June 17, 2011. http:/www.vanguardngr.com. Retrieved February 2, 2012.

Okereke, M. (2011) Economy: Dealing with Reform Shocks. In: Nigeria: Fiscal Governance Challenges and Solutions in 2011, *Zenith Economic Quarterly,* Vol. 6, No. 1.

Omoruyi, F. E. O., and A. U. Osunde. (2004) Evaluating the Effectiveness of the National Youth Employment and Vocational Skill Acquisition Programme in Midwestern Nigeria. www.iiz-dvv.de/index.

Osalor, Peter O. http://EzineArticles.com/?expert=Peter_O_Osalor. Retrieved January, 2012.

Rotberg, R. (2007) Nigeria Neglect Carries Cost. In: *Belfer Center Programs or Projects: Intrastate Conflict Program.* Cambridge, MA: Harvard University's John F. Kennedy School of Government.

Swayne, C., and W. Tucker. (1973) *The Effective Entrepreneur.* Morristown, NJ: General Learning Press.

Stauss, J. H. (1944) The Entrepreneur: The Firm. *Journal of Political Economy,* 52(2), 112–127.

Udu, E., and G. A. Agu. (1989) *New System Economics.* Onitsha, Nigeria: Africana Publishers Ltd.

Zimmerer, T. W., and R. Scarborough. (2006) *Essentials Entrepreneurship and Small Business Management.* New Delhi: Prentice-Hall of India.

Index

373

About the Author

Professor Ogunbameru Olakunle Abiona, the current head of the Department of Sociology and Anthropology, Obafemi Awolowo University, Ile-Ife, Osun State, Nigeria, is a specialist in the following fields: industrial sociology, gerontology, human resource management, and sociological theory. He has to his credit twelve published books, both in Nigeria and abroad. His latest edited book is titled: *Human Resource Management: Basic and Contemporay Issues* (2013).

CPSIA information can be obtained at www.ICGtesting.com
Printed in the USA
LVOW09s0518291113

363157LV00003B/52/P

9 780989 481441